£7.50

1670

D1336639

# ANNOTATED BIBLIOGRAPHY
# OF THE
# LITERATURE ON
# AMERICAN INDIANS
# PUBLISHED IN
# STATE HISTORICAL
# SOCIETY PUBLICATIONS

---

NEW ENGLAND and MIDDLE ATLANTIC STATES

---

Algonquian Indian Village  *Courtesy of the American Museum of Natural History*
An idealized depiction of a village of Eastern Indians (before any contact with whites) painted by Arthur A. Jansson

# ANNOTATED BIBLIOGRAPHY OF THE LITERATURE ON AMERICAN INDIANS PUBLISHED IN STATE HISTORICAL SOCIETY PUBLICATIONS

---

## NEW ENGLAND and MIDDLE ATLANTIC STATES

---

By

## ARLENE B. HIRSCHFELDER

KRAUS INTERNATIONAL PUBLICATIONS

Millwood, New York      London, England      Nendeln, Liechtenstein
A Division of the Kraus-Thomson Organization Limited

Copyright © 1982 Arlene B. Hirschfelder

All rights reserved.
No part of this work covered by the copyright hereon
may be reproduced or used in any form or by any means—
graphic, electronic, or mechanical, including photocopying,
recording or taping, information storage and retrieval systems—
without written permission of the publisher.

First Printing

Printed in the United States of America

Library of Congress Cataloging in Publication Data

Hirschfelder, Arlene B.
  Annotated bibliography of the literature on American
Indians published in state historical society publications,
New England and Middle Atlantic states.

  Includes indexes.
  1. Indians of North America—Periodicals—Indexes.
I. Title.
Z1209.2.U5H57   1982   [E75]   974'.00497        82-17213
ISBN 0-527-40889-1

To Dennis, Brooke, and Adam—an exceptional family

# CONTENTS

# ILLUSTRATIONS

# INTRODUCTION

This annotated bibliography contains those materials by and about American Indians that have appeared in publications of thirteen state-level historical societies in eleven New England and Middle Atlantic states. Coverage extends from the publication of the first volume in each series until the last volume published in 1979. The symbol "+" indicates the series continues to be published. Following is a list of the titles which were systematically examined for the bibliography.


Connecticut Historical Society
> *Bulletin of the Connecticut Historical Society*   +
>> vol. 1, no. 1 (November 1934) — vol. 44, no. 4 (October 1979)
> *Collections of the Connecticut Historical Society*
>> vol. 1 (1860) — vol. 24 (1979)

Historical Society of Delaware
> *Delaware History*   +
>> vol. 1, no. 1 (January 1946) — vol. 18, no. 4 (Fall–Winter 1979)
> *Historical and Biographical Papers of the Delaware Historical Society*
>> no. 1 (1879) — no. 67 (1922) and New Series, vols. 1+2
>> (1927–1930)

Historical Society of Pennsylvania
> *Memoirs of the Historical Society of Pennsylvania*
>> vol. 1 (1826) — vol. 14 (1895)
> *Pennsylvania Magazine of History and Biography*   +
>> vol. 1, no. 1 (1877) — vol. 103, no. 4 (October 1979)
> *Proceedings of the Historical Society of Pennsylvania*
>> vol. 1 (1845–1847)

Maine Historical Society
> *Collections of the Maine Historical Society*
>> Series 1, vol. 1 (1831) — vol. 9 (1887)
>> Series 2, vol. 1 (1890) — vol. 10 (1899)
>> Series 3, vol. 1 (1904) — vol. 2 (1906)
> *Maine Historical Society Newsletter*
>> vol. 1, no. 1 (June 1961) — vol. 12, no. 4 (Spring 1973)
>> Continued by *Maine Historical Society Quarterly*

*Maine Historical Society Quarterly*   +
    vol. 13, no. 1 (Summer 1973) — vol. 19, no. 2 (Fall 1979)
    Continues *Maine Historical Society Newsletter*

Maryland Historical Society
    *Fund Publications of the Maryland Historical Society*
        no. 1 (1867) — no. 37 (1901)
    *Maryland Historical Magazine*   +
        vol. 1 no. 1 (March 1906) — vol. 74, no. 4 (December 1979)
    *Publications of the Maryland Historical Society*
        no. 1 (1844) — no. 40 (1867)

Massachusetts Historical Society
    *Collections of the Massachusetts Historical Society*   +
        Series 1, vol. 1 (1792) — vol. 10 (1809)
        Sereis 2, vol. 1 (1814) — vol. 10 (1823)
        Series 3, vol. 1 (1825) — vol. 10 (1849)
        Series 4, vol. 1 (1852) — vol. 10 (1871)
        Series 5, vol. 1 (1871) — vol. 10 (1888)
        Series 6, vol. 1 (1886) — vol. 10 (1899)
        Series 7, vol. 1 (1900) — vol. 10 (1915)
        vol. 71 (1914) — vol. 82 (1978)
    *Proceedings of the Massachusetts Historical Society*   +
        Series 1, vol. 1 (January 1791) — vol. 20 (December 1883)
        Series 2, vol. 1 (January 1884) — vol. 20 (March 1907)
        vol. 41 (April 1907) — vol. 91 (1979)

New Hampshire Historical Society
    *Collections of the New Hampshire Historical Society*
        vol. 1 (1824) — vol. 15 (1939)
    *Historical New Hampshire*   +
        vol. 1, no. 1 (November 1944) — vol. 34, nos. 3+4 (Fall/Winter
            1979)
    *Proceedings of the New Hampshire Historical Society*
        vol. 1 (1872–1888) — vol. 5 (1905–1912)

New Jersey Historical Society
    *Collections of the New Jersey Historical Society*   +
        vol. 1 (1875) — vol. 15 (1979)
    *New Jersey History*   +
        vol. 85, no. 1 (Spring 1967) — vol. 97, no. 4 (Winter 1979)
        Continues *Proceedings of the New Jersey Historical Society*
    *Proceedings of the New Jersey Historical Society*
        Series 1, vol. 1 (1845) — vol. 10 (1866)
        Series 2, vol. 1 (1867) — vol. 13 (1895)
        Series 3, vol. 1 (1896) — vol. 9 (1914)
        New Series, vol. 1 (1916) — vol. 16 (1931)
        vol. 50, no. 1 (January 1932) — vol. 84, no. 4 (October 1966)
        Continued by *New Jersey History*

New York Historical Society
    *Collections of the New York Historical Society*
        vol. 1 (1868) — vol. 85 (1975)

*Quarterly Bulletin of the New York Historical Society* +
> vol. 1, no. 1 (April 1917) — vol. 63, no. 4 (October 1979)

New York State Historical Association
> *New York History, Quarterly Journal of the New York State Historical Association* +
>> vol. 13, no. 1 (January 1932) — vol. 60, no. 4 (October 1979)
>> Continues *Quarterly Journal of the New York State Historical Association*
> *Proceedings of the New York State Historical Association*
>> vol. 1, Second Annual Meeting (1901) — vol. 17, Nineteenth Annual Meeting (1919)
>> Continued by *Quarterly Journal of the New York State Historical Association*
> *Quarterly Journal of the New York State Historical Association*
>> vol. 1, no. 1 (October 1919) — vol. 12, no. 4 (October 1931)
>> Continues *Proceedings of the New York State Historical Association*
>> Continued by *New York History, Quarterly Journal of the New York State Historical Association*

Pennsylvania Historical Association
> *Pennsylvania History* +
>> vol. 1, no. 1 (January 1934) — vol. 46, no. 4 (October 1979)

Rhode Island Historical Society
> *Collections of the Rhode Island Historical Society*
>> vol. 1 (1827) — vol. 34, no. 4 (October 1941)
>> Continued by *Rhode Island History*
> *Proceedings of the Rhode Island Historical Society*
>> 1871–1914
> *Publications of the Rhode Island Historical Society*
>> New Series, vol. 1 (1893) — vol. 8 (1900)
> *Rhode Island History* +
>> vol. 1, no. 1 (January 1942) — vol. 38, no. 4 (November 1979)
>> Continues *Collections of the Rhode Island Historical Society*

Vermont Historical Society
> *Collections of the Vermont Historical Society*
>> vols. 1–2 (1870–1871)
> *Proceedings of the Vermont Historical Society*
>> Series 1, 1860–1928
>> New Series, vol. 1, no. 1 (1930) — vol. 11, no. 1 (March 1943)
> *Vermont History* +
>> vol. 22, no. 1 (January 1954) — vol. 47, no. 4 (Fall 1979)
>> Continues *Vermont Quarterly, the Proceedings of the Vermont Historical Society*
> *Vermont History News* +
>> vol. 27, no. 4 (July/August 1976) — vol. 30, no. 6 (November/December 1979)
>> Continues *VHS News and Notes*
> *Vermont Quarterly, the Proceedings of the Vermont Historical Society*
>> New Series, vol. 11, no. 2 (June 1943) — vol. 21, no. 4 (October 1953)
>> Continued by *Vermont History*

*VHS News and Notes*
vol. 1, no. 1 (September 1949) — vol. 27, no. 3 (May/June 1976)
Continued by *Vermont History News*

This bibliography will be a vital research tool for American Indian communities and individuals, secondary and college-level students, scholars, teachers, librarians, historians, anthropologists, geographers, legal researchers, and others interested in Indian studies. No guide presently exists that lists American Indian materials buried in the hundreds of volumes each of these historical societies has published. Indices to historical society publications, when they exist, list documents by author and title or by broad subject terms. Author-title indices are of little value because thorough searching or guesswork is required to determine which materials concern Indians. Subject indices, while often containing "Indian" entries, almost never convey information about the contents of the documents.

Historical societies publish both primary and secondary articles in their series. Within each group, a wealth of valuable material about Indians can be recovered through a meticulous search. In the primary sources, particularly collections of letters, transcribed speeches, and diary entries, Indians are sometimes the focus of lengthy discussions or the subjects of brief comments. Papers given at historical society meetings and articles written for historical society publications are rich secondary sources of information about Indians. These documents treat topics such as religion, Indian alliances, land concepts, languages, place names, trade, treaties, British-French rivalry for Indian allies, Indian-white conflicts, and descriptions of native cultures both in the past and in the present. This bibliography lists every paper and article about Indians and those letters and journal entries or other primary materials that are discrete units dealing in their entirety with Indians. Primary materials that only briefly mention Indians have been excluded.

These primary and secondary documents reflect the beliefs and prejudices of historians, clerics, colonial administrators, army officers, settlers, and others who recorded their observations, theories, and feelings about American Indians and their cultures, languages, place names, trade relations, alliances, and conflicts with whites. Glancing through the entries, one can see that the history of Indian-white relations has constantly been rewritten as succeeding generations have viewed Indians from different perspectives. One also gets glimpses, in the deeds, speeches, depositions, and other statements made by Indians, of Indian attitudes towards Europeans and Euro-Americans during the formative stages of the American nation. Taken together, the materials in this bibliography constitute a report of the varieties of historical writings about Indians and Indian-white relations during the colonial and revolutionary periods.

In most cases, Indian deeds are listed either under the name of the individual Indian grantor, the first of a number of Indian grantors, or the tribe which granted the lands. These Indians and tribes were important participants in early American history and deserve the recognition accorded Samuel Groton, Roger Smith, Cadwallader Colden and others. Petitions, agreements, speeches, memorials, wills, and depositions are alphabetized under the names of the persons or tribes petitioning, testifying, etc.

Journals and diaries which have been edited by others are listed under the name of the person who kept the record. Meetings of different colonial governments and commissioners are listed under the name of the issuing colonial body: New York Council, Connecticut Council, Massachusetts Commissioners, etc.

Over the centuries, spellings of the names of American Indians, colonial leaders, missionaries, tribal nations, and others have varied considerably. Tribal spelling such as *Abenakis, Algonquians,* and *Caughnawagas* have been used in preference to other spellings and *Sebastien Rasles, Lapowinsa,* and *Ninigret* illustrate spellings that are preferred over other forms. Spellings of people or tribes within journal titles have not been changed; however, contemporary, preferred spellings are used within the annotations.

Brackets around titles indicate the documents are untitled in the journals; quotation marks around titles indicate the actual titles appearing within the journals. In the Index, tribal affiliations are bracketed after Indian personal names.

The Index of Subjects concerns topics such as religion, wars, treaties, land matters and trade. The Index of Persons, Places and Titles treats those persons who are subjects of the various journal articles, including missionaries, government officials, authors, editors, military officers, captives, etc. Also listed here are relevant place names (Indian and non-Indian) and book titles. The Index of Indian Nations lists tribes, sub-tribes and village names as well as Indians identified by broad geographic designations, such as Northwest Coast, Western and Vermont Indians.

A special thank you to Joseph Gambino and the entire staff of the New York Public Library Stack Maintenance and Delivery Division. They made my job infinitely easier with their courteous, speedy delivery of hundreds of historical society volumes.

*Arlene B. Hirschfelder*

# BIBLIOGRAPHY

**Massacre by the "Paxton Boys"**   *Courtesy of the Library of Congress*
This early nineteenth century print depicts the 1763 incident at Lancaster, Pennsylvania, in which some Scots-Irish Presbyterians murdered a group of peaceful, Christianized Conestogas

1. Aaron. "Examination of Aaron, Mohawk, Before the Commissioners of Indian Affairs." *New York Historical Society Collections for the Year 1919, Cadwallader Colden Papers,* vol. 3 (New York, 1920): 233–236.

   Aaron and a party from the Six Nations who went to Canada report on July 19, 1746 that the group informed French Indians that they were allies and supposed to be at peace, that the war was between England and France, and that Indians were to remain neutral. He tells how his group warned French Indians that if the Six Nations engaged in war with them they would continue to do so even if the European powers made peace. Aaron tells of the French Indians' reply that despite the alliance they had chosen to die with the governor of Canada. Aaron also reports that the governor of Canada insists British encroachments in his country must stop or the British will be killed. Aaron informs the commissioners that an expedition of French Indians is planning to march against Albany.

2. Abraham. "Speech of Abraham, a Mohawk Chief, to Sir William Johnson." *New York Historical Society Collections for the Year 1922, Cadwallader Colden Papers,* vol. 6 (New York, 1923): 347–349.

   In an interview dated September 20, 1764, Abraham, representing six Mohawk chiefs and warriors, reminds Sir William Johnson how they assisted the British in reducing Canada and punishing the western Indian nations for attacking the British. He tells Johnson they are concerned because they have learned the British intend to deprive them of their chief tract of hunting land, called Kayaderosseras. He urges Johnson to write the governor of New York asking him not to deprive them of their lands, or else "it must alarm all the Nations of Indians, and shew them what a bad Return we have for our Services to the English." Abraham informs Johnson that some Mohawks have found several settlements of English on the tract of hunting land and demands that these people be moved.

3. "Abenakis and English Dialogues." *Vermont History,* vol. 23, no. 1 (January 1955): 75–76.

   These pages contain a brief note about a book entitled *Abenaki and English Dialogue* by Joseph Laurent, an Abenaki, published in 1884 in

3 (*continued*)
Quebec. A number of words in Abenaki are listed with their English equivalents.

4. Adams, Charles Francis. "Thompson's Island and Squantum." *Massachusetts Historical Society Proceedings*, vol. 41 (1907–1908): 532–540.
Adams gives an account of Captain Miles Standish and two of his trips, one an exploratory visit to Thompson's Island in 1621 and one to Wessagusset in 1623, where Indians were killed in "a measure of self-preservation." A long paper published in 1894 by Elizabeth Taylor Horton is reprinted. It discusses the settling of Thompson's Island and Squantum, which is one-half mile away.

5. Adams, John. [Letter to James Warren] *Massachusetts Historical Society Collections*, vol. 72 (Boston, 1917): 53.
Writing on June 7, 1775. Adams discusses whether or not the Americans should march into Canada to "overawe" the Indians and Governor Carlton. He describes the Indians along the frontiers as warlike but neutral, not yet having taken up the hatchet against the Americans. He writes that there is no evidence that Carlton or Johnson has attempted to persuade them to make war. He concludes with his opinion that Indians are without humanity.

6. Adams, Paul K. "Colonel Henry Bonquet's Ohio Expedition in 1764." *Pennsylvania History*, vol. 40, no. 2 (April 1973): 139–147. Illustrated.
The writer discusses the work of Colonel Bouquet in curbing Indian forces previously allied with the French in October of 1764. He tells how the Indians were determined to halt white incursions upon their lands in Ohio country and how Bouquet met with them, persuaded them to agree to aid the British, and obtained the release of white captives. The article is illustrated with an engraving of Indian depredations on the frontier, done in 1876.

7. Adams, Percy G. "Crevecoeur and Franklin." *Pennsylvania History*, vol. 14, no. 4 (October 1947): 273–279.
Adams tells how Crevecoeur fabricated a conversation with Benjamin Franklin in which Franklin aired his views on three subjects: the origins of North American Indians, the possibility of Indians being native to the Western Hemisphere, and the newly discovered remains of ancient Indian fortifications and tombs. Adams lists prominent American writers used by Crevecoeur who provided materials that appear in a speech said to be Franklin's.

8. Adlum, John. "John Adlum on the Allegheny: Memoirs for the Year 1794. Part 1." Edited by Donald H. Kent and Merle H. Deardorff. *Pennsylvania Magazine of History and Biography*, vol. 84, no. 3 (July 1960): 265–324. Illustrated.
Adlum's memoir covers his surveying expeditions in northwestern Pennsylvania and his dealings with the Senecas, whom he persuaded

not to obstruct him in his work and to delay going to war against the United States. He gives details of British posts on American soil, recounts his negotiations with Cornplanter, the Seneca chief, reports on speeches exchanged with Cornplanter and other Indians, and describes Indian customs, council procedures, social organization, ceremonies, and dances which give a picture of Seneca life on the upper Allegheny River in 1794. Adlum's map of 1790 of north-western Pennsylvania and western New York is included. [*Continued* in *Pennsylvania Magazine of History and Biography*, vol. 84, no. 4 (October 1960): 435–479. Illustrated. There are brief notes by the editors in both parts of the memoir.]

**9.** Aghsarigowa, Tuscarora, and Teheaniyoghiwat, (*Oneida* Indians). "Address to General Sullivan." *New Hampshire Historical Society Collections*, vol. 15 (Concord, 1939): 138–140.

Aghsarigowa and Teheaniyoghiwat address General John Sullivan on October 1, 1779. They discuss the general's treatment of Cayugas and tell him they hope to bring in some of them so they will be spared and well treated. They give intelligence about a deserted Indian village.

**10.** Agnaurasa, (French Indian). "French Indian to Indian Commissioners." *Connecticut Historical Society Collections*, vol. 11 (Hartford, 1907): 182–183.

On June 14, 1744, Agnaurasa, a French Indian sent by the sachems at Caughnawaga, reports that these Indians are not inclined to meddle in the war between the French and the British; they intend to keep the peace and not assist the French even if the English attack the French in Canada. *See:* "Indian Commissioners to French Indian," pages 194–195. Replying on June 20, 1744, the Commissioners promise to observe neutrality but demand that all the Indians in Canada reciprocate by not molesting any British subjects.

**11.** Aiello, Lucy L. "Burlington Island." *New Jersey History*, vol. 91, no. 1 (Spring 1973): 24–34.

Aiello discusses artifacts unearthed by Charles C. Abbott on Burlington Island, called Mattinneconk in the Algonquian language. The findings provide information on contact and struggle between the original Indian inhabitants and Dutch settlers. The article also recounts the names by which Burlington Island has been known over the centuries. She discusses the murders on Burlington Island and the conflict in 1670 between the Dutch and Indians for domination over the small island. There are footnotes.

**12.** Albany Council. "Opinion of the Council of Albany Regarding Indians Joining in an Attack on Canada." *New York Historical Society Collections for the Year 1919, Cadwallader Colden Papers*, vol. 3 (New York, 1920): 262–265.

The Albany Council, in an opinion dated August 25, 1746, feels that the Six Nations should be entered into action against France and allied Indians; otherwise they will learn that they have been deceived re-

**12** (*continued*)

garding the design of attacking Canada by sea and by land. The Council advises that the French fort at Crown Point be destroyed and French settlements everywhere be harassed by the Indians. The Council feels that if the Crown Point fort is reduced Montreal may be attempted with ease.

13. Albany Register of Indian Affairs. "Extracts from the Register of Indian Affairs in Albany." *New York Historical Society Collections for the Year 1920, Cadwallader Colden Papers*, vol. 4 (New York, 1921): 292–294.

The extracts from the Albany Register include a speech of the Five Nations on August 16, 1694 to Governor Fletcher in which the Indians state to the governor of Canada that they will not admit any settlement at "Cataracqui" followed by a statement of the governor of New York that if the Five Nations allow France to build forts on New York territory, this will enslave them. He tells the Five Nations that if the French attempt to build forts he expects the Indians to assist him in preventing this infringement on the King's territories. There is an extract from a speech of the Five Nations to Lieutenant Governor Nanfan on July 19, 1701 in which the Indians complain that the French in Canada are encroaching on their territories and building forts on their lands without consent. They ask the King to prevent the French from building a fort at Detroit because the French are taking over their beaver hunting lands. There is a note that tells Robert Livingston carried the Five Nations' message to the King; but Queen Anne's War prevented him from doing anything other than negotiating with France. The note adds that no redress was ever obtained in any of the French encroachments, including one at Niagara which would exclude the Five Nations from their beaver country and prevent communication between the English and the Indians in Canada.

14. Alden, Timothy. "An Account of the Captivity of H. Gibson." *Massachusetts Historical Society Collections*, ser. 3, vol. 6 (Boston, 1837): 141–153.

Alden recounts Gibson's trials and sufferings among the Delaware Indians from the latter part of July, 1756 to the beginning of April, 1759. Gibson tells Alden of his capture, his adoption by a Delaware family headed by Bisquittam to replace a member of the family that was killed. He tells of barbarities he was forced to see, the places he lived with the Indians, his kindly treatment by the family that adopted him, and his escape.

15. Alden, Timothy. "Indian Names of the White Hills and Piscataqua River." *Massachusetts Historical Society Collections*, ser. 2, vol. 2 (Boston, 1814, 1846): 266–267.

Writing in 1806, Alden discusses the names given to the White Hills and Piscataqua River by the eastern tribes.

16. Alexander, James. [On New Jersey Regulations for Registering Indians] *New York Historical Society Collections for the Year 1921, Cadwallader Colden Papers*, vol. 5 (New York, 1923): 48–51.

Alexander briefly discusses how New Jersey plans to defend its frontiers. This is followed by the reasons for an order that all Indians in
New Jersey register, obtain a certificate with their vital statistics and
wear a red ribbon on their heads. (The Cranberry Christian Indians
and others had petitioned for help because they feared both English-
allied Indians, who might fire on them as enemies, and Delaware
Indians because they had refused to join the Delaware in destroying
the English.) Alexander suggests to Cadwallader Colden that he regulate those Indians who visit his house. This piece is dated December
11, 1755.

17. Alexander, James. "Notes on the Governor of Canada's Letter of August
10, 1751." *New York Historical Society Collections for the Year 1920, Cadwallader
Colden Papers*, vol. 4 (New York, 1921): 288–291.
    Writing on August 27, 1751, Alexander attacks the Governor of
    Canada's claims made in a letter of August 10, 1751 and argues that
    the French treat the British and the treaties of Utrecht and Aix La
    Chapelle with contempt. He suggests that a copy of the governor's
    letter be sent to the governor of Pennsylvania, because four English
    traders were taken prisoner on the Ohio River in the Pennsylvania
    grant by the French, who forbid the English to trade there. Alexander
    comments on other parts of the letter, arguing that it is "unparalleled
    Effrontery" for the French to deny that the Five Nations were ever
    subjects of the King of Great Britain and rejecting the French claim
    that they were the first white people on lands of the Five Nations. He
    gives the reasons why the English insisted at the Treaty of Utrecht on
    acknowledgement of the dominion of Great Britain over the Five
    Nations. He charges that the French fortification at Niagara is being
    built in defiance of the Five Nations and the Utrecht Treaty and is
    designed to stop communication between the English and the Five
    Nations.

18. Allan, John. "Letter to the Massachusetts Council. From Archives, vol. 153,
page 362." *Maine Historical Society Collections*, ser. 2, vol. 7 (Portland, 1896):
435–436.
    Writing on May 28, 1790, Allan tells of British intrigues aimed at
    confusing the Indians, mentions the low supply of provisions, and
    remarks on the fairer, more honorable terms of British traders com-
    pared to American traders.

19. Allen, Zachariah. "The Conditions of Life, Habits, and Customs of the
Native Indians of America, and Their Treatment by the First Settlers." *Rhode
Island Historical Society Proceedings, 1877–1878*. (Providence, 1880): 97–151.
    In the first part of this essay, Allen demonstrates that "Christian
    virtues and beneficence" have not kept pace with the progress of
    technology in the age of steel, gunpowder, and steam. He argues that
    the principal motives that induced most early settlers to come to New
    England were profits of the sea coast fisheries and the availability of
    land under royal license; the immediate motives of wealthy settlers

**19** (*continued*)

were personal ambition and the desire to be independent rulers. Allen
tells of the Narragansett alliance with Rhode Island, which angered
adjacent colonies that coveted Narragansett lands; he also explains
Puritan pretenses and plans for appropriating Indian lands, recounts
their efforts to destroy both Narragansetts and Mohegans, and notes
that leading Puritans of New England took part in the profits realized
by seized Indian lands. Allen explains the wrongs done by the Four
United Colonies of New England (Connecticut, New Haven, Massachusetts, and Plymouth) to the Indians. The second part of the essay
contains a discussion of Indian agriculture, housing, clothing, marriage and domestic life, hospitality, religion, language, trade and
manufactures, travel, wampum, cookery, government, medicine,
fishing and hunting, and mourning customs.

**20.** Allison, Samuel. "A Fragmentary History of the New Jersey Indians." *New
Jersey Historical Society Proceedings,* ser. 2, vol. 4, no. 1 (1875): 31–50.

Allison argues that the New Jersey history of Indian-white relations
illustrates that hostility between the two people is not necessary. He
lists the members of the New Jersey Society formed to help Indians in
April 1757, gives the preamble of the group's charter and recounts its
plan (which never was realized) to promote Indian welfare. Allison
discusses the treaty conference of 1758, at which Indian claims to New
Jersey lands were extinguished, except for the right to hunt and fish
and to use a tract of land purchased for the Delaware Indians south of
the Raritan. He also describes the Easton Conference in 1758, at
which Indian claims to land north of the Raritan were extinguished.
Allison discussses the role of Teedyuscung, an important Delaware
chief, in the Easton proceedings. He tells of the Brotherton Indians,
who lived on the state's first Indian reservation until 1801, when they
accepted an invitation to live with a kindred tribe in New York. He
goes on to discuss the disposal of the Brotherton tract to twenty-two
purchasers, and describes the last official dealings between New Jersey and the Delaware Indians in 1832, during which the latter asked
the legislature for compensation for certain abandoned rights. The
article is footnoted with historical material.

**21.** Allumchoyce. "Examination of Allumchoyce." *Connecticut Historical Society
Collections,* vol. 21 (Hartford, 1924): 277–281.

Dated June 6, 1682, the examination of Allumchoyce by the special
Connecticut Court of Assistants concerns his part in killing a deer and
selling part of it for rum, and his knifing of a woman while drunk.
Allumchoyce maintains he was too drunk at the time of the stabbing to
know what he was doing. The examination is followed by a certificate
of a coroner's jury, dated June 7, 1682, which finds the cause of the
woman's death to have been a knife stab in the back. This is followed
by testimony of four people at the trial of Allumchoyce, on June 8,
1682, regarding his attack on the woman.

**22.** Allummapees, or Sassoonan. "Allummapees, or Sassoonan, a Delaware." *Pennsylvania Magazine of History and Biography,* vol. 33, no. 2 (1909): 249.

This is a brief discussion of Allummapees, or Sassoonan, a Delaware whose name appears frequently in colonial records as early as 1718, and who died in 1747. The discussion treats Allummapees' excessive drinking and tells of Lapappiton, who declined to be his successor as an important chief of the Delawares.

**23.** Alsop, George. "A Relation of the Customs, Absurdities, and Religion of the Susquehannock Indians In and Near Maryland." In *A Character of the Province of Maryland. Maryland Historical Society Fund Publication,* no. 15 (Baltimore, 1880): 71–81.

Writing in 1666, Alsop describes the Susquehannocks as warlike, devoid of clothing, and without a distinct government. He describes their treatment of prisoners and their religion, burial customs, work, status, and the condition of their men and women. Included are notes by an editor on Maryland Indians, pages 117–124.

**24.** Amherst, Jeffrey. [Letter to Cadwallader Colden] *New York Historical Society Collections for the Year 1922, Cadwallader Colden Papers,* vol. 6 (New York, 1923): 241–242.

Writing on October 27, 1763, General Jeffrey Amherst tells Colden that it is impractical to pursue offensives against enemy Indians during the winter, but that it is necessary to arm the militia and to send out scouts to protect frontier settlements. He informs Colden that the militia is not sufficiently supplied and cannot perform its defensive duties properly.

**25.** Amherst, Jeffrey. "Talk to the Several Indian Tribes and Nations of Indians. Enclosed in His Letter to General Stanwix." *Massachusetts Historical Society Collections,* ser. 4, vol. 9 (Boston, 1871): 240–242.

Writing on April 28, 1760, General Amherst warns the Indians to remain good and faithful or they will be punished. He orders them to build forts or trading houses in parts of their country, and promises that they will be rewarded for their friendship.

**26.** Amory, Thomas C. "General Sullivan's Expedition in 1779." *Massachusetts Historical Society Proceedings,* ser. 1, vol. 20 (1882–1883): 88–94.

Amory discusses the 1779 expedition into Indian country in western New York under General John Sullivan. He explains that the operations were intended not only to punish the Iroquois and protect white settlements, but also to do reconnaissance and pave the way for future operations against the English in Canada. Amory tells of Sullivan's instructions, given to him by Washington, to destroy Indian dwellings and crops, but argues that only towns of Six Nations tribes were harmed. He reports that scalping and other inhumanities were rare and not sanctioned by officers.

27. Amsterdam, W. Max Reid. "The Coming of William Johnson. Afterward Baronet." *New York State Historical Association Proceedings, Thirteenth Annual Meeting*, vol. 11 (Lake George, 1912): 56–61.

Amsterdam discusses the man honored by the Iroquois, William Johnson, an Irishman who came to the Mohawk Valley in 1738. He explains that due to an unfortunate love affair, Johnson was induced by his uncle to emigrate to America. There follows a discussion of Johnson's marriages and his children by Native women.

28. Anderson, Robert. [Letter to Benjamin Drake] *Pennsylvania Magazine of History and Biography*, vol. 4, no. 2 (1917): 251–252.

Writing on November 8, 1839, Anderson discusses an Indian informant named Chamblee, a chief of the Potawatomi Indians, who tells of Tecumseh's death by pistol shot, which Chamblee witnessed when he was young. Tecumseh, a Shawnee chief, attempted to forge a tribal alliance against white encroachment on Indian lands. Anderson goes on to give his opinion of Indians as treacherous, ungrateful, and consistently hostile to whites.

29. Anderson, William de la Roache. "The Indian Legend of Watchung." *New Jersey Historical Society Proceedings*, n.s., vol. 11, no. 1 (January 1926): 45–48.

Anderson recounts a legend that the people of Watchung portray in an annual community pageant. The legend concerns the conflict between a band of white settlers from Perth Amboy and a tribe of Indians from the Watchung Hills. The Indians captured the band of settlers and were about to torture Captain Michelson, leader of the group, when the Captain's foster child, an Indian "princess" named Wetumpka, recognized the Watchung Chief One Feather. By reminding One Feather that she had years ago saved his life, she in turn saved her foster father from death. Peace is restored, the land is divided between Indians and whites, and Wetumpka and One Feather wed.

30. "Articles of Peace with the Indians Inhabiting New Hampshire and Maine." *New Hampshire Historical Society Collections*, vol. 8 (Concord, 1866): 257–258.

These articles of peace, dated September 8, 1685, provide for punishment of any Englishman or Indian who breaks the peace. The Indians of New Hampshire and Maine are required to assist the English in fighting other Indians, in return for English protection against the Mohawks. The articles also require the Indians to inform the English if they plan to move their families.

31. Ashley, Edward. "Edward Ashley, Trader at Penobscot." *Massachusetts Historical Society Proceedings*, vol. 45, (1911–1912): 493–498.

This set of documents, dated July, 1631, deals with an inquiry regarding the conduct of Edward Ashley, who was charged with selling guns and ammunition to the Indians. Texts of the examination of seven witnesses concerning Ashley's unlawful trading are included.

**32.** Atkins, T. Astley. "Relations of the Dutch and the Indians Prior to the Massacre of 1655." *New York State Historical Association Proceedings, Eleventh Annual Meeting,* vol. 9 (Lake George, 1910): 237–255.

> This article consists of quotations, taken chiefly from the official records, dealing with relations between the Dutch and Indians prior to 1655. Information is included on place name changes from Indian to Dutch, and of "purchases" from Indians that show the fraudulent sales methods of the Dutch. A selection of quotes tells of the conflicts between the Dutch and Indians in the 1640s and lasting to the massacre of 1655, in which many Dutch were killed in revenge for their deceptions.

**33.** Auger, Leonard A. "St. Francis Through Two Hundred Years." *Vermont History,* vol. 27, no. 4 (October 1959): 287–304.

> Auger tells of the St. Francis Indians, a branch of the Abenakis, from 1759 to 1959. He describes the raid against their village by 142 colonial rangers, led by Major Robert Rogers, and discusses some of the stories based on this event. He describes the group's destitution, its Catholic religious life, factionalism during the American Revolution, counterespionage and scouting activities for both English and patriots after 1776, and its life during the nineteenth and twentieth centuries. Extensive explanatory footnotes are included.

**34.** Aupaumut, Hendrick. "A Narrative of an Embassy to the Western Indians." *Historical Society of Pennsylvania Memoirs,* vol. 2 (Philadelphia, 1827): 61–131.

> This narrative deals with the history of an Indian negotiation as recorded by an Indian. In prefatory remarks, Dr. B. H. Coates discusses the authenticity of the narrative, speculates on when it was written, and explains that Hendrick Aupaumut is a Mohegan. The narrative tells of Aupaumut's 1791 mission to the western tribes to restrain them from warring against frontier settlements of the United States in the Northwest Territory. He tells of the longstanding Delaware friendship with America, of divisions within the tribes, and of the activities of British agents. The narrative also affords a glimpse into Indian manners and Delaware history. The narrator records speeches by members of the Five Nations, Shawnees, Delawares and others. He records Indian complaints of white duplicity and his own arguments that the United States is not like the British government. Aupaumut assures his listeners that he has not come to count their warriors nor to report this intelligence to the U.S. government.

**35.** Auringer, O. C. "Aboriginal Stone Implements of Queensbury." *New York State Historical Association Proceedings, Ninth Annual Meeting,* vol. 8 (Lake George, 1909): 103–118.

> Auringer discusses the Indian antiquities of Queensbury and focuses on two or three stone implements in his collection that indicate that paleolithic people may have occupied this region. He outlines places

**35** (*continued*)
of residence and speculates on the character and subsistence of the early people of New York. The article deals with the relationship of Eskimos to the inhabitants of Canada and the upper half of New York state, where Eskimo-like tools have been found. Auringer discusses traces of Mohawks after the arrival of Europeans in the Queensbury tract, tells of local materials used by aborigines, and classifies implements into Earliest, Agricultural, Eskimo, Intermediate, and Mohawk periods.

**36.** Awasunckes (sachem of *Saconnet*). "Articles of Agreement Between the Court of New Plymouth and Awasuncks, the Squaw Sachem of Saconnet." *Massachusetts Historical Society Collections*, ser. 1, vol. 5 (Boston, 1798): 193–194.
On July 24, 1671, Awasuncks voluntarily submits her people and their weapons to the Court of New Plymouth. In return, the English promise to protect the group's territory from white settlement.

**37.** Awasuncks (sachem of *Saconnet*). [Letter to Governor Prince] *Massachusetts Historical Society Collections*, ser. 1, vol. 5 (1798): 195–196.
Writing on August 11, 1671, Awasuncks promises to submit to English authority despite the protests of other Indians. She notes that she is enclosing a list of Indians obedient to her (not included in this letter), and discusses problems involved in delivering her people's guns to Governor Prince. [*See:* Letter of Governor Prince to Goodman Cooke. *Massachusetts Historical Society Collections*, ser. 1, vol. 5 (Boston, 1798): pages 196–197. On August 24, 1671, Governor Prince writes that the Saconnet Indians can have their arms back and asks Cooke to arrange this. *See also:* Letter of Governor Prince to Awasuncks. *Massachusetts Historical Society Collections*, ser. 1, vol. 5 (Boston, 1798): page 197. On October 20, 1671, Prince tells Awasuncks of his disappointment that members of her family disregard British interests, and indicates that the list of names Awasuncks has submitted falls short of his expectations.]

**38.** Ayamanugh. "The Indian Deed of 1710." *New Jersey Historical Society Proceedings*, n.s., vol. 9, no. 3 (July 1924): 300–305.
This document, dated May 9, 1710 and signed by an Indian woman named Ayamanugh and the sachems of several Indian nations, conveys a large tract of land in the northern and northwestern portions of Bergen and Passaic counties to Elias Boudinet and two others. The boundaries of the tract are specified, and a clause is included explaining that the Indians were "all entirely sober" when they signed the deed. The deed is followed by a "Memorial to the Indian Chieftan Oratam," a Hackensack tribal leader who died over forty years before the deed was signed.

**39.** Ayscough, John. [Letter to Cadwallader Colden] *New York Historical Society Collections for the Year 1920, Cadwallader Colden Papers*, vol. 4 (New York, 1921): 167.
Writing on December 2, 1749, Ayscough tells Colden that the traders

at Oswego are making a practice of taking Indian children in exchange for rum and sugar. He tells how one trader refused to return a boy to his parents when they paid their debt because his father had not come at the appointed time to redeem him. Ayscough tells Colden of another Indian child who was a victim of "downright Kidnapping" and argues that his practice must be prevented, since it aids French efforts to recruit Indians against the English.

**40.** Ayscough, John. [Letter to Cadwallader Colden] *New York Historical Society Collections for the year 1920, Cadwallader Colden Paper,* vol. 4 (New York, 1924): 241–242.

Writing on December 11, 1750, Ayscough urges Colden to write to all governors of colonies with Indian allies or dependents and invite them to sign a treaty with the Six Nations in June 1751. The proposed pact, Ayscough claims, would frustrate French plans to divide the Indians and break up their alliance with the English.

**41.** "The History of Bacon's and Ingram's Rebellion: The Indian Proceedings." *Massachusetts Historical Society Proceedings,* ser. 1, vol. 9 (1866–1867): 299–325.

This history of Bacon's 1676 rebellion, by an unknown author, is according to an editor "contemporaneous with the events described, or written not long after their occurence." The history tells of the failure of the government to provide adequate protection from Indians and describes Indian hostilities. The history is also reprinted in *Massachusetts Historical Society Collections,* ser. 2, vol. 1 (Boston, 1814): 33–59.

**42.** Badger, Stephen. "Historical and Characteristic Traits of the American Indians in General and Those of Natick in Particular." *Massachusetts Historical Society Collections,* ser. 1, vol. 5 (1798): 32–45.

Writing in February 1797, Badger answers seven questions put to him about Indian longevity and the effects of civilization and Christianity on Indians. He assesses the reasons for the decline of the Indian population, which he attributes to pressure on Indians to change their old way of life and substitute another in its place. He notes that Christian missionaries among Indians have had little success. Badger also discusses the "vagrant" state of Indians, their habits of "indolence and excess," and physical differences between Indians and the English.

**43.** Bailey, Jacob. "Observations and Conjectures on the Antiquities of America." *Massachusetts Historical Society Collections,* ser. 1, vol. 4 (1795): 100–105.

**43** (*continued*)

Writing on April 10, 1795, Bailey speculates on what caused the decline of Indian nations north of Mexico before white contact. He argues that "civilized" Native nations once existed in America but views contemporary Indians as "savages." [*See:* "Remarks on Mr. Bailey's Letter, By Rev. John Thorton Kirkland," pages 105–107. The remarks are dated May 1, 1795.]

**44.** Bailey, John H. "A Stratified Rock Shelter in Vermont." *Vermont Historical Society Proceedings*, n.s., vol. 8, no. 1 (March 1940): 3–30. Illustrated.

Bailey discusses the excavation of a rock shelter on the Vermont shore of Lake Champlain and describes the skeletal material and various implements and artifacts that were found. He concludes that the first inhabitants were a non-ceramic hunting people and that the last inhabitants brought with them a good grade of pottery. The article is illustrated with a map, photographs of the site and materials found in the shelter, and two diagrams of the rock shelter.

**45.** Baker, Charles E. "The Story of Two Silhouettes." *New York Historical Society Quarterly Bulletin*, vol. 31, no. 4 (October 1947): 218–228. Illustrated. Bibliography.

Baker tells the story of Kish-Kau-Kou, a Chippewa chief from Saginaw, Michigan, who lived between 1774 and 1825. In his travels to promote the commerce of his tribe, Kish-Kau-Kou met and fell in love with Catherine Sanders, who refused to marry him. The woman's father offered, in lieu of his daughter, her silhouette portrait, and the chief had his own portrait cut as well. After the rejection, Kish-Kau-Kou supported the British during the War of 1812, helped negotiate a treaty with the U.S. government establishing reservations for the Chippewas and other Indians, and struggled constantly to keep back the tide of settlers inundating his homeland. Baker recounts how Kish-Kau-Kou bartered his silhouettes for whiskey at a trading post, and how the portraits later were reclaimed by Catherine Sander's brother. The chief, indicted for murdering another Indian, committed suicide rather than face hanging. Photographs of the two silhouettes are included.

**46.** Baker, Virginia. "Glimpses of Ancient Sowams: Reminiscences of the Aborigines—Their Sayings and Doings." *Rhode Island Historical Society Publications*, n.s., vol. 2 (Providence, 1894): 196–202.

Baker discusses the reminiscences of Frank Loring, or Big Thunder, a Penobscot who tells her of the sites of Indian villages and relics, none of which can be located. She also retells some of the traditions preserved by the Penobscots regarding the Wampanoags and King Philip's War.

**47.** Ballard, Edward. "Character of the Penacooks." *New Hampshire Historical Society Collections*, vol. 8 (Concord, 1866): 428–445.

Ballard discusses the Penacooks, who lived peacefully along the Merrimack River, and tells of Passaconaway and his son, Wonnelanset and their fidelity to the English through most of the seventeenth century. The article also mentions Kancamagus, eldest son of Passaconaway, who led an attack on present-day Dover in 1689. Ballard tells of the eventual scattering and resettlement of Penacooks in Canada among the St. Francis Indians.

**48.** Ballard, Edward. "Indian Mode of Applying Names." *New Hamshire Historical Society Collections,* vol. 8 (Concord, 1866): 446–452.

Ballard gives evidence to support his contention that aboriginal New Hampshire names are confined to simple locality. He explains that the Indians of New Hampshire never gave a name to the whole length of a river but only to places that were important for hunting and fishing. He illustrates his point with the Merrimack river, citing the many Indian names that were descriptive of particular spots along the waterway. A list entitled "Indian Names Connected with the Valley of the Merrimack" follows the article.

**49.** Bandel, Betty. "The Battle of the Book." *Vermont History,* vol. 22, no. 3 (July 1954): 159–171.

Bandel discusses Reverend Daniel Clarke Sanders' much-criticized book, *History of the Indian Wars with the First Settlers of the United States, Particularly in New England,* published in 1812. This was a relatively favorable account of Indians by New England standards, and thus was unacceptable to orthodox Puritans. Bandel also reviews images of Indians in earlier New England histories, which were strongly biased against the natives. The article is footnoted with sources.

**50.** Bandel, Betty. "Daniel Clarke Sanders and the Indians: A Belated Footnote to a Controversial Book." *Vermont History,* vol. 36, no. 2 (Spring 1968): 91–93.

Bandel discusses a story in Sanders' book, *History of the Indian Wars with the First Settlers of the United States, Particularly in New England,* that demonstrates the "civilized" nature of many Indians. She tracks down the original source of the story to show that Sanders did not fabricate it. Bandel explains how Sanders' attitude towards Indians was humane and liberal for his time, not always viewing them as aggressors in their wars with Puritan settlers. Bandel notes that Sanders was severely censured by a conservative magazine published in Middlebury.

**51.** Barclay, Henry. [Letter] *New York Historical Society Collections for the Year 1934, Cadwallader Colden Papers,* vol. 8 (New York; 1937): 279–285.

Writing on December 7, 1741, Barclay, a missionary of the Society for the Propagation of the Gospel, remarks on the customs and character of the Mohawk Indians. He notes that the Mohawks have already begun to assimilate white ways and lose ancient customs. He describes their method of making war, customs of hospitality, marriage, and

51 (*continued*)

burial, and comments on their religious morals and language. He talks of Mohawk intemperance and his efforts to reform them, and he describes the Indian school he established.

52. Barnes, Harry Lee. "The Wallum Pond Estates." *Rhode Island Historical Society Collections,* vol. 15, no. 2 (April 1922): 33–48. Illustrated.

Barnes discusses Wallum Pond, located in the southern part of what was called Nipmuck country, in the vicinity of present-day Douglas, Massachusetts, and Burrillville, Rhode Island. He reviews various opinions on the meaning of "Allum," the name for the pond more frequently used before 1850. Included are details about the life of Allumps, whose name resembles that of the pond. Barnes discusses Indian traditions regarding Wallum Pond and describes Indian relics that have been found in the area. He tells of Black James, or Walomachin, a Nipmuck, and others who deeded part of Nipmuck country, including lands at the north end of Wallum Pond, to Massachusetts Colony in 1682. There is brief mention of Patty Pease, the last of the Nipmucks, and her son and grandsons. A photograph of a Wallum Pond relic and a map of the Pond and vicinity are included. [*See* the Appendix in *Rhode Island Historical Society Collections,* vol. 16, no. 1 (January 1923): 28–31. Here is found a discussion of Allumps, a renegade Narragansett who lived among Nipmucks and other groups. The material includes a verbatim text of an investigation of Allumps in 1704.]

53. Barton, Benjamin Smith. "Historical Notes." *Pennsylvania Magazine of History and Biography,* vol. 9, no. 3 (1885): 334–338.

Barton's notes, made in 1789, deal with the eloquence of American Indians, particularly of Beaver Chief, a Delaware of New Jersey. Barton tells of the Indians' criticism of General Braddock's army, and comments that Indians are troubled with scrofula. He repeats John Pemberton's criticisms of Benjamin West's "Picture of the Treaty of the Indians," and agrees that accuracy should not be sacrificed in historical painting. The article includes some information on William Penn and his treaties with the Indians.

54. Barton, Thomas. "Journal of an Expedition to the Ohio, Commanded by His Excellency Brigadier-General Forbes, in the Year of our Lord 1758." *Pennsylvania Magazine of History and Biography,* vol. 95, no. 4 (October 1971): 431–483.

The journal, dated July 12–September 28, 1758, tells of military action against Indians in the Ohio Valley. Explanatory footnotes and introductory notes are provided by the editor, William A. Hunter.

55. Barton, William. "Journal of Lieutenant William Barton Kept During General Sullivan's Expedition Against the Six Nations of Indians in 1779." *New Jersey Historical Society Proceedings,* vol. 2, no. 1 (1846): 22–42.

George Washington planned a punitive expedition against the Six

Nations, who occupied the western parts of Pennsylvania and New York, for siding with the British during the American Revolution. The principle American force consisted of three thousand men under General John Sullivan, who was ordered to destroy Seneca settlements. Barton was in a brigade from New Jersey under General Maxwell. During the expedition he kept a journal whose entries begin on June 8, 1779 and end on October 9, 1779.

**56.** Bassett, T. D. Seymour. "A Ballad of Rogers' Retreat, 1759." *Vermont History*, vol. 46, no. 1 (Winter 1978): 21–23.

Bassett discusses an incident of the French and Indian War: Major Robert Rogers' destruction of St. Francis, an Indian village allied to the French, whose warriors had frequently raided the New England frontier. The extract from the ballad deals with the raid and retreat of Rogers from St. Fancis, and the starvation which threatened the rangers. Explanatory notes are included.

**57.** Baxter, James P. "The Abnakis and Their Ethnic Relations." *Maine Historical Society Collections,* ser. 2, vol. 3 (Portland, 1892): 13–40.

Baxter outlines the theory then accepted regarding the origin of American Indian tribes. After discussing the resemblance between Indian tribes of America and Asiatic peoples, he briefly describes the Algonquian peoples along the Atlantic seaboard, and examines the cultural traits of one of their branches: The Abenakis of New England. Baxter examines the religious beliefs of the Abenakis and describes their pottery, implements, arrow heads, and other remains.

**58.** Baxter, James P. "Campaign Against the Pequakets." *Maine Historical Society Collections,* ser. 2, vol. 1 (Portland, 1890): 353–371.

Baxter discusses the causes and effects of the protracted wars waged between Indians and colonists during the close of the seventeenth and the first half of the eighteenth century. He argues that French machinations, particularly the influence of Jesuit missionaries on the eastern Indians, were responsible for the wars. He discusses Lovewell's expedition against the Pequakets in 1725, which convinced the Indians that the English were dangerous enemies and temporarily ended the Indian-settler conflict.

**59.** Beane, Samuel Collins. "General Enoch Poor." *New Hampshire Historical Society Proceedings,* vol. 3 (Concord, 1895–1899): 452–460.

This biographical sketch discusses the military career of Enoch Poor, whose brigade was part of General John Sullivan's 1779 expedition against the Six Nations. Beane describes Poor's brigade at the battle of Newtown on August 29, and comments on the character of the expedition "with its ruthless destructiveness and its disrespect of age or sex. . . ."

60. Beauchamp, William M. "Indian Raids in the Mohawk Valley." *New York State Historical Association Proceedings, Sixteenth Annual Meetings,* vol. 14 (Lake George, 1915): 195–206. Illustrated.

This article is a brief history of Indian raids in the Mohawk Valley beginning in the early seventeenth century. Beauchamp describes warfare among Indians in 1669 and Indian attacks on white settlements through 1781. His information includes the size and destructiveness of various raids. A drawing of Fort Stanwix illustrates the text.

61. Beauchamp, William M. "The Principal Founders of the Iroquois League and Its Probable Date." *New York State Historical Association Quaterly Journal,* vol. 7, no. 1 (January 1926): 27–36. Illustrated.

Beauchamp discusses three leading founders of the Iroquois League: Deganawidah, Hiawatha, and Atotarho. He tells of the legends and history associated with the three, and examines tradition and town sites to determine when and how the Iroquois League was formed. Beauchamp sets the League's origin at about 1600.

62. Beavin, Daniel. "A New Look at the Vermont Indians." *Vermont History,* vol. 31, no. 4 (October 1963): 272–276.

Beavin discusses the discovery of agricultural implements and other archaeological finds that point to the existence of permanent settlements of Indians in pre-white Vermont. He points out that historians and archaeologists now surmise that Vermont's Indians lived in villages and grew a portion of their food, rather than traveling great distances in search of hunting lands, as formerly supposed. Footnotes and a bibliography are included.

63. Belcher, Jonathan, Jr. [Message to Penobscot Indians] *Massachusetts Historical Society Collections,* ser. 6, vol. 6 (Boston, 1893): 344.

Writing on July 28, 1733, Belcher, the son of the governor of Massachusetts Bay, discusses how he will suitably lodge Penobscots when they come to trade, tells them that rum will be given sparingly, and says they must make restitution for cattle killed by young men of the tribe.

64. Belknap, Jeremy. "Journal of Dr. Belknap of His Tour to Oneida." *Massachusetts Historical Society Proceedings,* ser. 1, vol. 19 (1881–1882): 393–422.

Jeremy Belknap visited the Oneida Indians in the early summer of 1796, while serving on a committee assigned to report on the condition of missions there. In correspondence dated June 9 to July 6, 1796, he describes Oneida country, notes the slow progress of white civilization and Christianity among the Oneida people, tells of meetings with Indians and describes their daily life.

65. Benedict, Thomas E. "The Valley of the Rondout and Neversink and Its Unsettled Colonial Questions" *New York State Historical Association Proceedings, Thirteenth Annual Meeting,* vol. 11 (Lake George, 1912): 71–87. Illustrated.

Benedict describes some of the physical and historic memorials of the Rondout-Neversink Valley. These include the site of an old Indian fort and village, destroyed in 1663 by Captain Martin Krieger in the course of an expedition to punish the Esopus Indians and to rescue a number of white captives. Benedict discusses the location of lands relinquished by Indians to the government of New York. He also describes Indian-white conflicts in the valley from 1659, when Indians massacred settlers at Wiltwyck, to 1780. A map of the valley is provided. [*See:* Augustus H. Van Buren. "Wiltwyck Under the Dutch." *New York State Historical Association Proceedings, Thirteenth Annual Meeting*, vol. 11 (Lake George, 1912): 128–131. Van Buren discusses the events preceding the 1659 massacre, gives an account of the attack on Wiltwyck, and briefly describes the Second Esopus War of 1663, in which Krieger participated.]

**66.** Benedict, William H. "The Nine Roads of New Brunswick." *New Jersey Historical Society Proceedings*, n.s., vol. 14, no. 2 (April 1929): 163–180.
   Benedict discusses six major roads in the New Brunswick area that follow former Indian trails. These include the road to Trenton, to Burlington, to Piscataway and on to Amboy and Elizabeth; the road to Middletown and Shrewsbury; the road up the northeast bank of the Raritan; and the road to Amwell, Middlebush and Old York.

**67.** Bennett, C. E. "Burning of Schenectady." *New York Historical Society*, vol. 13, no. 4 (October 1932): 413–419.
   Bennett discusses the 1690 burning of Schenectady by the French and allied Indians, arguing that the reasons for it were: trade with the Ottawas, instability among the "praying" Indians (Christianized Iroquois under influence of French priests), animosity between the French and the Iroquois since 1615, religious differences, the expulsion of Indians from New England and, the immediate cause—the burning of Montreal by the Iroquois. The French had invaded the Seneca region in 1687 and the Iroquois retaliated with an attack on Montreal in 1689.

**68.** Bernard, Francis. Letter to Cadwallader Colden. *New York Historical Society Collections for the Year 1922, Cadwallader Colden Papers*, vol. 6 (New York, 1923): 157–158.
   Governor Bernard of Massachusetts reports that Hunkamug, a Stockbridge Indian who murdered another Indian named Chineagun, has been jailed in Massachusetts. He explains that the relatives of the slain Indian want justice done according to English law rather than by the customary method of vengeance. Bernard asks that the prisoner be transferred to a New York jail, since the murder was committed in the county of Albany.

**69.** Bickford, Christopher P. "The Abraham Panther Broadside." *Connecticut Historical Society Bulletin*, vol. 42, no. 3 (July 1977): 72–74. Illustrated.
   Bickford discusses the Indian captivity narrative, written by Abraham

**69** *(continued)*

Panther, a name generally accepted as a pseudonym. His account tells of a young woman captured by Indians in 1777 and returned to her father nine years later. Bickford argues that evidence points to Woodward and Green in Middletown as the printer of the broadside, acquired by the Connecticut Historical Society. Bickford also notes that the writer of the broadside is unknown. A photograph of the Society's copy of the broadside is included.

**70.** "Bill of Sale of an Indian." *Massachusetts Historical Society Proceedings*, vol. 44 (1910–1911): 656–657.

In a document dated December 17, 1728, Henry Limbrey of Boston sells his Indian man, twenty years old, to John Dolbear for £ 80. This bill of sale is followed by another dated March 27, 1729, in which Dolbear sells the Indian again to Arthur Savage, also for £ 80.

**71.** "Some Old Bills Relating to the Entertainment of Indians." *Pennsylvania Magazine of History and Biography*, vol. 32, no. 1 (1908): 122–124.

One bill, dated June 26, 1737, deals with the cost of a canoe, borrowed by Indians for a trip to Philadelphia and subsequently lost. The few other bills included deal with the expenses of Teedyuscung and other Indians attending a treaty conference for the month of June 1762.

**72.** Billington, Ray. "The Fort Stanwix Treaty of 1768." *New York History*, vol. 25, no. 2 (April 1944): 182–194. Illustrated.

Billington discusses the Fort Stanwix Treaty of 1768, intended to replace the Proclamation Line of 1763 with a satisfactory border between white settlements and Indian lands. He criticizes it as one of the "worst" treaties in the history of Anglo-Indian relation, a result of speculative pressure on the white side and tribal generosity on the Indian side. He tells how the treaty left Indians angry, the frontier turbulent, and created a great gap in the demaraction line between Tennessee and the Great Kanawha Rivers. Colonial Indian superintendents were also left open to increased pressure from land speculators, who sought to move boundaries westward with political backing. Included is a section of Guy Johnson's map of 1768.

**73.** Bingham, Abel. "Journal of Abel Bingham, 1822–1828." *New York History*, vol. 60, no. 2 (April 79): 157–193.

In journal entries dated April 4, 1822, to July 20, 1827, Bingham tells of his missionary work among Seneca Indians, discusses in some detail the conflict between Christian and pagan parties, and provides insights into attitudes of well-meaning Christians who lacked the ability to understand Indian ways. A painting of Red Jacket (leader of the pagan faction among the Senecas) and a sketch of a woman's dance illustrate the text.

**74.** Birdsey, Nathan, "An Account of the Indians in and about Stratford, Connecticut." *Massachusetts Historical Society Collections*, ser. 1, vol. 10 (Boston, 1809): 111–112.

In correspondence dated September 3, 1761, Birdsey writes to Ezra
Stiles about the number of Indian families in and around Stratford,
Connecticut, forty to ninety years earlier.

**75.** Black, William. "Journal of William Black." *Pennsylvania Magazine of History
and Biography*, vol. 1, no. 2 (1877): 117–132; vol. 1, no. 3 (1877): 233–249; vol 1,
no. 4 (1877): 405–419; and vol. 2, no. 1 (1878): 40–49.

Black was secretary of the commissioners appointed by Governor
Gooch of Virginia to meet with Iroquois Indians in an effort to obtain
Iroquois lands west of the Allegheny Mountains. Commissioners
from the colonies of Maryland and Pennsylvania also attended the
conference. Black's journal is dated May 17 to June 15, 1744, and
contains the texts of letters written to Governor Gooch by the commissioners. The correspondence includes details regarding the Indians
traveling to the treaty conference and the expenses involved in signing a treaty with the Iroquois.

**76.** Blackie, William R. "Indians of New York City and Vicinity." *New York State
Historical Association Quarterly Journal*, vol. 4, no. 1 (January 1923): 41–48.

Blackie discusses the Algonquian inhabitants of the New York City
area, and the coming of the Iroquois into the northern part of this
territory. Evidence is also presented regarding the pre-Algonquian
occupants of the area. Blackie lists several tribes of Algonquians and
the territories they controlled, including the Canarsies, Reck-
gawawancs, Siwanoys, Weckwaesgaeks, Sinsinks, and Kitchawancs.
He describes winter subsistence technques of New York Indians,
explains types of tools and dishes used by the Algonquians and describes their land tenure, burial rites and customs associated with
wampum.

**77.** Board of Trade. [Message to Sir William Johnson] *New York Historical
Society Collections for the Year 1922, Cadwallader Colden Papers*, vol. 6 (New York,
1923): 324–328.

In a letter dated July 10, 1764, the Board of Trade asks Johnson for
his opinion on the Board's plan to regulate Indian affairs throughout
North America by dividing the Continent into two districts, each
having one agent or superintendent, and each including designated
tribes. The Board suggests that trade with Indians be fixed at certain
posts and tribal towns in the southern district, and at fortified posts
and tribal towns in the southern district, and at fortified posts in the
northern district. Johnson is asked to report on the annual quantity
and value of goods sold to Indians, on peltry received from them in
return, on duties that could realistically be levied and points where
they could be collected, and on estimated expenses of the posts and
presents given to Indians.

**78.** Bolling, John. "A Private Report of General Braddock's Defeat." Edited by
John A. Schutz. *Pennsylvania Magazine of History and Biography*, vol. 78, no. 3
(July 1955): 374–377.

78 *(continued)*
In a letter dated August 13, 1755 a Virginia burgess (Bolling) tells his seventeen-year-old son in England of the great disaster that befell General Edward Braddock on July 9, 1755 in the Ohio country at the hands of French and their allied Indians. The editor provides background information.

79. Bonney, Orrin E. "The Battle at Nichols Pond: Champlain and His Force of French and Hurons Against the Oneida Indians." *New York History,* vol. 19, no. 2 (April 1938): 140–143.
Bonney recounts an unprovoked, surprise attack on Oneidas in October 1615 by Samuel de Champlain, explorer, and of Hurons. He describes the stockaded Oneida village, based on Champlain's narrative, and tells of the three-day battle, Champlain's defeat and retreat to Canada. The invasion embittered the Iroquois against the French and strengthened their resistance to future encroachments. Bonney concludes that this development prevented the northeastern portion of the United States from being settled by the French. [*See* Harold O. Whitnall. "The Future of Nichols Pond." *New York History,* vol. 19, no. 2 (April 1938): 144–147. Whitnall focuses on the construction of the Oneida stockade recorded in Champlain's papers. He argues that the stockade should be restored, and states that the fight at Nichols Pond was "one of the decisive battles of the world."]

80. Bostock, Allen K. "Searching for Indian Relics in Vermont: Part 1." *Vermont History,* vol. 23, no. 3 (July 1955): 233–240. "Searching for Indian Relics in Vermont: Part 2." *Vermont History,* vol. 23, no. 4 (October 1955): 327–332.
Bostock describes his travels around Vermont as an amateur archaeologist seeking evidence of Indian settlements.

81. "Arguments, c. 1765, About the Boundaries of Evans' and Other Patents, in Orange and Ulster Counties, New York." *New York Historical Society Collections for the Year 1935, Cadwallader Colden Papers,* vol. 9 (New York, 1937): 193–198.
This piece contains arguments regarding Captain John Evan's first and second purchases of land from Esopus and Murders Creek Indians. Evans tries to prove that the area in question falls within the bounds of lands granted to him and does not belong to the patent of Minisink.

82. "Bounty of Indian Scalps." *Maryland Historical Magazine,* vol. 4, no. 4 (December 1909): 391.
This page contains a note, dated March 19, 1764, in which James Davis of Virginia acknowledges receiving a bounty of £50 from Maryland for killing and scalping an Indian.

83. Bouquet, Henry; Gage, Thomas; and Bradstreet, John. "Colonel Bradstreet's Treaty of Peace Made at Ance Aux Feuilles, Near Presque Isle." *New*

*York State Historical Society Collections for the Year 1881*, vol. 14 (New York, 1882): 526–531.

These pages contain correspondence between Colonel Bouquet, General Gage and Colonel Bradstreet on the subject of Bouquet's plan to invade Indian territories in the Ohio Valley. In a letter to Gage dated May 2, 1764, Bouquet gives his views on the prospective Indian Treaty. This is followed by Gage's reply of May 14 and a discussion (dated October 16) of Bradstreet's treaty of peace with the Shawnees and Delawares, negotiated at Ance Aux Feuilles by Captain Montresor. In further correspondence, both Gage and Bouquet condemn the Bradstreet treaty. Also included is a letter from Colonel Bradstreet to Colonel Bouquet, dated October 17, 1764, in which Bradstreet writes that it was impossible to execute General Gage's orders which limited him to offering peace, not concluding articles of peace.

**84.** Bouquet, Henry. [Letters to Henry Monckton] *Massachusetts Historical Society Collections,* ser. 4; vol. 9 (Boston, 1871): 411–414.

Writing on May 4 and May 15, 1761, Colonel Bouquet tells Monckton that Shawnee Indians are stealing horses and boats, and that Shawnee chiefs declare they have lost all influence over the young men committing the crimes. He also writes that the Delawares are stealing horses from traders going to Detroit.

**85.** Bouquet, Henry. [Orders from Colonel Henry Bouquet] *New York Historical Society Collections for the Year 1921, Cadwallader Colden Papers,* vol. 5 (New York, 1922): 247–249.

In correspondence dated July 13, 1758, Colonel Bouquet orders a subordinate to go to Fort Cumberland and consult with Colonel Washington on presents to be given to the Catawbas, Nottoways, and Cherokees for their services during an expedition. The orders are followed by a memorandum entitled "Calculation of Expenses of Indian Warriors for their Service during the Campaign" dated July 23, 1758, which lists the value of each present given to an Indian who participated in the expedition. The list contains such items as stroud mantles, stockings, knives, shirts and wampum. This is followed by a similar note from Bouquet, "List of Goods for the Use of the Cherokee Indians with Colonel Byrd at Fort Cumberland," dated July 24, 1758. Bouquet's list includes knives, arm bands, ribbon, black and white wampum, ruffled shirts, stroud mantles, gorgets, breast plates, and shells.

**86.** Bouquet, Henry. [Orders of Colonel Henry Bouquet to Captain Bosomworth] *New York Historical Society Collections for the Year 1921, Cadwallader Colden Papers,* vol. 5 (New York, 1923): 257–258.

On September 3, 1758, Colonel Bouquet orders Bosomworth and his troops, including Indians, to reconnoitre French positions. Bosomworth is to see the Indians under his command do not disturb the

**86** *(continued)*
Delawares and other Indians on the west side of the Ohio River who
seem disposed to concluding peace with the British. Bouquet orders
Bosomworth to be sure that his Indians wear identifying badges when
they leave the camp.

**87.** Bouquet, Henry. "Selections from the Military Correspondence of Colonel
Henry Bouquet." *Pennsylvania Magazine of History and Biography,* vol. 32, no. 4
(1908): 433–458; vol. 33, no. 1 (1909): 102–117; and vol. 33, no. 2 (1909):
216–227.
> Colonel Bouquet's letters relate to military matters connected with the
> expedition against Fort Duquesne, led by General John Forbes in
> November, 1758, and with subsequent events. The expeditionary
> force included Indian allies, and Bouquet's letters, written in 1758
> and 1759, tell of their military role and the actions of enemy Indians.

**88.** Braddock, Edward. "Braddock on July 9, 1755." *Maryland Historical
Magazine,* vol. 60, no. 4 (December 1965); 421–427.
> This letter, whose writer and date are unknown, describes General
> Braddock's defeat at the hands of the French and allied Indians. The
> writer conveys his enmity for Braddock and questions his compe-
> tence. The first and last page of the letter are missing.

**89.** Bradford, William. [Letter to John Winthrop] *Massachusetts Historical Society Collections,* ser. 4, vol. 2 (Boston, 1854): 119.
> Writing on October 11, 1645, Bradford appeals on behalf of some
> Indians of Yarmouth. They are owed trading cloth and a pair of
> britches for services they rendered to a white man, who pressured
> them to leave their hunting grounds.

**90.** Bradley, Samuel. "Bradley Monument." *New Hampshire Historical Society
Collections,* vol. 6 (Concord, 1850): 110–123.
> This article describes the dedication of a monument on August 22,
> 1837, honoring Jonathan Bradley and four others slain by Indians at
> Concord, N.H. on August 11, 1746. The article reviews the
> background of the English-French wars, tells of New Hampshire
> settlements attacked by Indians around 1746, recounts the situation at
> Concord in 1746 as the town tried to ward off attacks, outlines events
> leading to the massacre, and describes the aftermath. The text of an
> ode by George Kent and an historical ballad by Mary Clark are also
> included.

**91.** Bradner, Leicester. "Ninigret's Naval Campaign Against the Montauks."
*Rhode Island Historical Society Collections,* vol. 18 no. 1 (January 1925): 14–19.
> Bradner discusses the unfortunate situation of the Montauks, at-
> tributing their suffering to rule by the Pequots Connecticut demands
> for tribute, and Ninigret's rule. He describes the enmity between the
> Pequot-Mohegan group of Connecticut and the Narragansett-Niantic
> group of Rhode Island, and explains how the Montauks of Long

Island were subject to the Pequots until the latter were destroyed by Captain Mason in 1637. Bradner tells how Ninigret, a Niantic chief, subsequently attacked the Montauks in 1638 and 1660. The quarrel between the two tribes was complicated by interference from the colony of Connecticut, which demanded from the Montauks the same tribute it had formerly received from the Pequots. The Niantic-Montauk feud resulted in the near-extermination of the Montauks.

**92.** Brett, Catharyna. [Letter to Sir William Johnson] *New York Historical Society Collections for the Year 1922, Cadwallader Colden Papers*, vol. 6 (New York, 1923): 190–192.

Writing on August 26, 1762, Mrs. Brett tells of her troubles with Indians and whites in a land dispute some years before. She explains that a few Indians have remained her friends throughout the ordeal.

**93.** Brewster, Jonathan. [Letter to John Winthrop] *Massachusetts Historical Society Collections*, vol. 7, ser. 4 (Boston, 1865): 67–68.

Writing on June 18, 1636, Brewster tells of a Pequot plan to attack an English ship, and warns that the Pequots are threatening war against the English and allied Indians.

**94.** Bridenbaugh, Carl. "The Old and New Societies of the Delaware Valley in the Seventeenth Century." *Pennsylvania Magazine of History and Biography*, vol. 100, no. 2 (April 1976): 143–172. Illustrated.

Bridenbaugh examines Lenni Lenape society in the Delaware Valley between 1610 and 1700, as well as the tribe's relations with the Dutch, English, Finnish and Swedes who settled the area. Bridenbaugh describes the period of 1675 to 1700 when the Indian population began to decline and ceased to be a determining factor in the lives of the valley people. The article is illustrated by a map of Virginia and Maryland in 1673 and a map of the Delaware Valley settlements at about 1700.

**95.** Brinley, Francis. "A Brief Narrative of That Part of New England Called the Narragansett Country." *Rhode Island Historical Society Publications*, n.s., vol. 8 (Providence, 1900): 72–96.

Brinley recounts the sales by Indians of tracts of land to the English, beginning with the first transaction in 1634 between Roger William and Canonicus, and describes the disputes over land purchases in Narragansett country. [This document is also published in *Massachusetts Historical Society Collections*, ser. 3, vol. 1 (Boston, 1825, 1866): 209–288.]

**96.** Brinton, Daniel G. "American Languages, and Why We Should Study Them." *Pennsylvania Magazine of History and Biography*, vol. 9, no. 1 (1885): 15–35.

Brinton argues that language is a clue to the structure of Indian social units, and a means of tracing ancient connections and migrations of

**96** *(continued)*
Indian nations in America. He views the study of American Indian languages as essential to the science of linguistics, and discusses some of the characteristics of the vocabularies and structures of Indian languages.

**97.** "British Newspaper Accounts of Braddock's Defeat." *Pennsylvania Magazine of History and Biography,* vol. 23, no. 3 (1899): 310–328.
These fifteen newspaper accounts, dated from August 27 to November 10, 1755, describe the disastrous expedition of General Edward Braddock against Fort Duquesne in Pennsylvania. The accounts report on the reaction to the catastrophe in the colonies, tell of the Indians' role in the fighting, and consider Braddock's questionable tactics.

**98.** Brooke, John. "Anthony Wayne: His Campaign Against the Indians of the Northwest." *Pennsylvania Magazine of History and Biography,* vol. 19, no. 3 (1895): 387–396.
Brooke recounts the history of hostile Indian-white relations in the Northwest Territory and the failure of the U.S. Army to subdue the Shawnees, Delawares and other members of the Miami Confederacy. He describes how a reorganized army under General Anthony Wayne finally marched into the heart of Indian country and, from 1792 to 1794, made the area safe for settlement. The resulting Treaty of Greenville wrested an immense territory along the Ohio and Mississippi Rivers from the Indians.

**99.** Brown, Alan S. "The Role of the Army in Western Settlement: Josiah Harmar's Command, 1785–1790." *Pennsylvania Magazine of History and Biography,* vol. 93, no. 2 (April 1969): 161–178.
Brown discusses the years in which Harmar organized and trained the only defense force in the U.S., negotiated Indian treaties, and aided the settlement of the Ohio country. He describes the worsening relations between settlers and Indians during this period, and recounts the failure of Harmar's 1790 expedition against the Wabash Indians.

**100.** Brown, Dewi. "Address of Dewi Brown, a Cherokee Indian." *Massachusetts Historical Society Proceedings,* ser. 1, vol. 12 (1871–1873): 30–38.
Speaking around 1830, Brown expresses indignation over the suffering Europeans have caused Indians, discusses the place of religion in Indian life and points out the importance of missionary work among Indians.

**101.** Brown, W. McCulloh. "Fort Frederick." *Maryland Historical Magazine,* vol. 18, no. 2 (June 1923): 101–108.
Brown provides a history of Fort Frederick, completed around 1756, one of the most formidable fortresses along the frontier of English settlement before the American Revolution. The fort served as a supply base, a place of refuge for settlers attacked by Indians and a center for negotiations between friendly Indian leaders and English

officers. Fort Frederick was also important as a base for operations against the French at Fort Duquesne in 1758 and protected hundreds of people during Pontiac's War. The last part of the article deals with the fort's preservation.

102. Brunhouse, Robert L. "The Founding of Carlisle Indian School." *Pennsylvania History*, vol. 6, no. 2 (April 1939): 72–85.

Brunhouse discusses the founding of Carlisle Indian School in 1879, the first government-supported, non-reservation Indian school in the country and a model for other non-reservation schools. He explains that the aim of Richard Henry Pratt, the founder of Carlisle, was to take Indians away from their reservations and teach them the rudiments of modern life in a "civilized community." The government, for its part, hoped that educating the children of tribal chiefs would provide a means of holding restless tribes in check. The article includes footnotes.

103. Bryce, Peter H. "Sir John Johnson Baronet; Superintendent-General of Indian Affairs, 1743–1830." *New York State Historical Association Quarterly Journal*, vol. 9, no. 3 (July 1928): 233–271.

Bryce discusses the life of Sir John Johnson, a colonel during the American Revolution, who as Superintendent-General was responsible for relations with the Six Nations and with Indians in Canada between 1782 and 1830.

104. Bryce, Peter H. "Sir William Johnson, Baronet. The Great Diplomat of the British-French Frontier." *New York State Historical Association Quarterly Journal*, vol. 8, no. 4 (October 1927): 352–373. Illustrated.

Bryce discusses the period 1740–1766, when Johnson played a prominent role in the Indian diplomacy of the British-French frontier. He stresses Johnson's knowledge of Indian psychology, which kept the Six Nations loyal to the British despite French victories during the early part of the French and Indian War. Bryce describes Johnson's success in leading Iroquois warriors against the French and in keeping the Six Nations (except for the Senecas) from participating in Pontiac's War. The article concludes with an account of the conference of 1766 between Sir William and Pontiac.

105. Buck, William J. "Lapowinsa and Tishcohan, Chiefs of the Lenni Lenape." *Pennsylvania Magazine of History and Biography*, vol. 7, no. 2 (1883): 215–218.

Buck states the few facts known concerning these two sachems, whose portraits were presented to the Pennsylvania Historical Society by Granville Penn in 1834. He describes Lapowinsa and his role in the Walking Purchase of August 1737, along with other events in which he had a part. Buck also tells of Tishcohan's role in the Walking Purchase, lists the variant spellings of his name and describes his appearance.

**106.** Bulkley, John. "Inquiry into the Right of the Aboriginal Natives to the Lands in America, and the Titles Derived From Them." *Massachusetts Historical Society Collections,* ser. 1, vol. 4 (1795): 159–181.

> In a theoretical discussion of Indian land rights, Bulkey maintains that the right of Indians to own property depends on whether they live in a state of nature (which he defines at length) or whether they have formed communities with laws regulating property in land. Bulkley argues that Indians only have rights or titles to lands they have improved, that chiefs have more right to property than their subjects, and that English have rights to lands that are not improved by the Indians. He also argues that the principle, held by many, that native right is the only valid title to lands in America, is a foolish and "vulgar error."

**107.** Bull, William. [Letter to Cadwallader Colden] *New York Historical Society Collections for the Year 1922, Cadwallader Colden Papers,* vol. 6 (New York, 1923): 54–56.

> Writing on July 15, 1761, Governor Bull of South Carolina reports on a successful military expedition against the Cherokees headed by Lieutenant Colonel James Grant. He praises the support given to the colonial forces by the Chickasaw Indians.

**108.** Bump, Charles Weathers. "Indian Place-Names in Maryland." *Maryland Historical Magazine,* vol. 2, no. 4 (December 1907): 287–293.

> Bump discusses the origin and interpretation of Patapsco and other geographic names in Maryland, commenting on the methods used by William Wallace Tooker to interpret Indian names.

**109.** Burns, Brian. "Massacre or Muster? Burgoyne's Indians and the Militia at Bennington." *Vermont History,* vol. 45, no. 3 (Summer 1977): 133–144. Illustrated.

> Burns investigates the traditional connection made between the murder of Jane McCrea by Indian allies of the British (July 27, 1777) and Lieutenant General John Burgogyne's defeat by American militia at the Battle of Bennington (August 16, 1777). He concludes that no connection existed between Jane McCrea's death and the gathering of the militia at Bennington during the Saratoga campaign. Explanatory notes, two illustrations of Jane McCrea and a view of British prisoners taken at the Battle of Bennington are included.

**110.** Cabeen, Francis Von A. "The Society of the Sons of Saint Tammany of Philadelphia." *Pennsylvania Magazine of History and Biography,* vol. 25, no 4 (1901): 433–438.

Cabeen discusses the Delaware chief Tamanend, for whom the Society was named. He gives extracts from two deeds, dated June 23, 1683 and July 5, 1697, in which Tamanend granted land to William Penn and others. He cites Heekewelder, who presents a high estimate of Tamanend's character. Cabeen notes the belief that Tamanend made a treaty with the founders of the Society, and discusses the controversy over the chief's burial spot.

111. Cabot, William B. "The Meaning of Indian Place Names." *Rhode Island Historical Society Collections*, vol. 22, no. 2 (April 1929): 33–38. Illustrated.
Cabot discusses a number of descriptive Indian place names in Rhode Island. The article includes a map of Indian camp sites near Point Judith Pond. [*See* William B. Cabot. "Cocumcussoc." *Rhode Island Historical Society Collections*, vol. 28, no. 1 (January 1935): 25. This article includes a brief note explaining the meaning of the Indian word "Cocumcussoc."]

112. Cammerhoff, J.C.F. "Bishop J.C.F. Cammerhoff's Narrative of a Journey to Shamokin, Pennsylvania, in the Winter of 1748." *Pennsylvania Magazine of History and Biography*, vol. 29, no. 2 (1905): 160–179.
Bishop Cammerhoff narrates his two-week trip to Shamokin, an important Indian town in Pennsylvania where a Moravian mission had been established. He tells of encounters with Indians along the way, considers the reputations of Indian traders, and notes the prevalence of disease among the Indians. Cammerhoff reports on a speech which he delivered before Shikellamy, Indian "viceroy" of the town and the town's Indian Council, asking for deerskins and additional land for the Moravian missionaries. He records the presents he gave to the Indians and the thirteen resolutions made by the missionaries regarding their treatment of the Indians. A brief biography of Cammerhoff preceded the narrative. Footnotes with historical and geographical information are included.

113. Cammerhoff, J.C.F. "List of Goods for Presents to Indians at Onondago." *Pennsylvania Magazine of History and Biography*. vol. 39, no. 2 (1915): 244.
In May 1750, when Bishop J.C.F. Cammerhoff visited representatives of the Six Nations at Onondago, he took with him a number of goods as presents to the Council. His list of jewelry, foods, tobacco, implements, and wampum totals over £49.

114. Campbell, B. U. "Early Christian Missions Among the Indians of Maryland." *Maryland Historical Magazine*, vol. 1, no. 4 (December 1906): 293–316.
Campbell discusses the efforts of Jesuit priests between 1633 and 1655 to convert Indians of Maryland to Christianity. He focuses on Father Andrew White's work among the Piscataways and provides extracts from the letters of missionaries illustrating their successes, failures and hardships.

115. Campbell, Donald. [Letters to Colonel Henry Bouquet] *Massachusetts Historical Society Collections,* ser. 4, vol. 9 (Boston, 1871): 423–429.

Writing on June 16 and June 21, 1761, Campbell tells of Iroquois efforts to enlist the Delawares and Shawnees in a war in the Illinois country against the English. He describes an Iroquois plan to cut lines of communication at Niagara, Fort Pitt, and Detroit, and to seize the goods of traders at Sandusky.

116. Campbell, Paul R. and LaFantasie, Glenn W. "Scattered to the Winds of Heaven—Narragansett Indians, 1676–1880." *Rhode Island History,* vol. 37, no. 3 (August 1978): 67–83. Illustrated.

The authors trace the decline of the Narragansett Indians, (including the group known as "Niantics") beginning with King Philip's War and ending with the successful effort of Rhode Island to "detribalize" the Narragansetts in 1880–83. They discuss the effects of King Philip's War, which decimated the Narragansetts except for remnant groups living in Charlestown and Westerly, Rhode Island. They explain how the surviving Indian population in what was called Narragansett country was actually an aggregate of peoples who became known as Narragansetts, with the Niantic designation disappearing after 1700. The authors explain how Narragansetts became disunified and plagued with internal divisions and political factionalism. They also describe Rhode Island's attempts to detribalize the Narragansetts, subsequently accomplished by 1883. The article is heavily documented and includes a map and other illustrations.

117. Campbell, Thomas J. "The First Missionaries on Lake Champlain." *New York State Historical Association Proceedings, Twelfth Annual Meeting,* vol. 10 (Lake George, 1911): 127–138.

Campbell recounts a canoe expedition to Huron Indian territory undertaken in August 1642 by several Catholic missionaries and Christian Hurons. The party was ultimately destroyed by Iroquois attacks. The story of the captures and eventual killing of Father Joques as well as the Iroquois captures of the Hurons Theresa and her Uncle Teondechoren are also told.

118. Campfield, Jabez. "Diary of Jabez Campfield. Surgeon in Spencer's Regiment, While Attached to Sullivan's Expedition Against the Indians. From May 23rd to October 2, 1779." *New Jersey Historical Society Proceedings,* vol. 3, no. 3 (1873): 117–136.

Campfield describes an expedition of New Jersey troops from Morristown "against the Indians and Tories who had cruelly destroyed our frontiers." He recounts his reluctance at the destruction of Indian towns and crops and concludes with remarks on the expedition's organization and leadership.

119. Canajoharie Sachems. [Message from Three Indians to Mr. Goolding] *New York Society Historical Society Collections for the Year 1920, Cadwallader Colden Papers,* vol. 4 (New York, 1921): 411.

Writing on October 25, 1753, three sachems of the Canajoharie Indians insist that Goodling come immediately to survey lands that they wish to give as a gift to David Schuyler, his son, and Nicholas Pickert.

120. Canasatego. "Speech of Canasatego." *Historical Society of Pennsylvania Memoirs*, vol. 11 (Philadelphia, 1876): 49–52.

Canasatego recounts, in a speech made June 26, 1744, to the commissioners of Pennsylvania, Virginia, Maryland at a treaty conference in Lancaster, that various Europeans wanted his lands, and in return gave him and other Indians such items as knives, guns, and hatchets, which the English and Dutch insisted were necessary for supporting life. Canasatego explains that the Indians are better off with their own tools and weapons and are now "in want of deer . . ." since the Europeans came.

121. Canonicus and Miantonomo. "Deed for Providence." *Rhode Island Historical Society Collections*, vol. 5 (Providence, 1843): 26–27.

In a communication dated March, 1639, two Narragansett sachems, Canonicus and Miantonomo, enlarge and then confirm the bounds of a land grant made to Roger Williams. The marks of the two Indians are reproduced. The ambiguities and vagueness of this deed, the first purchase of Providence, are discussed in the same volume in a chapter entitled "Purchases of the Natives, and Divisions of the Town" in *Annals of the Town of Providence* by William R. Staples, pages 563–565.

122. "List of Captives Taken by the Indians and Delivered to Colonel Bouquet by the Mingoes, Delawares, Shawanese, Wyondots, and Mohickons at Tuscarawas and Muskingam, in November, 1764." *Pennsylvania Magazine of History and Biography*, vol. 20, no. 4 (1896): 570–571.

This list, taken from the *Pennsylvania Gazette* of January 17, 1765, contains the names of 91 Virginians and 116 Pennsylvanians captured by Indians.

123. Carlson, Richard G. "George P. Peters' Version of the Battle of Tippecanoe (November 7, 1811)." *Vermont History*, vol. 45, no. 1 (Winter 1977): 38–43.

Peters was present at the battle of Tippecanoe, where William Henry Harrison defeated Tecumseh, a Shawnee chief who was attempting to forge a tribal alliance against further white encroachments on Indian lands. Peters' eyewitness account, taken from a letter dated January 17, 1812, provides details not found elsewhere but does not contradict accepted versions of the battle. Explanatory notes are included.

124. Carr, Arthur A. "Indian Harvest Festival at Ticonderoga." *New York History*, vol. 29, no. 2 (April 1948): 151–156.

Carr discusses the story behind the Indian Harvest Festival sponsored by the Society for the Preservation of Indian Lore. He also decribes the contents of the drama.

**125.** Carrington, Edward. [Letter to James Madison] *Massachusetts Historical Society Proceedings*, ser. 2, vol. 17 (1903): 469–470.

Writing on July 25, 1781, Carrington discusses Indian Affairs in the Northeast, explaining Indian grievances over land surveys in Ohio country. He suggests that money would be better spent in making treaties with the Indians than in warring with them.

**126.** Casco Bay Indians. "Deed from Indian Sagamores to George Munjoy." *Maine Historical Society Collections*, ser. 1, vol. 1 (Portland, 1865): 553.

This is the text of a deed, dated June 4, 1666, by which two Indians of Casco Bay give a tract of land to George Munjoy.

**127.** Cassasinament. [Petition to the General Assembly] *Connecticut Historical Society Collections*, vol. 21 (Hartford, 1924): 162.

Cassasinament, appointed governor of the Pequots by Connecticut authorities, petitions the General Assembly of Connecticut on May 10, 1666, to specify the boundary lines of a tract of land given to the Pequots. He also asks that an Englishman be appointed to oversee the Pequots and reinforce his authority.

**128.** Caughnawaga Indians. "An Extract from a Speech Designed to be Made by Caughnawaga Indians to Governor Jonathan Belcher, Massachusetts Bay." *New York Historical Society Collections for the Year 1920, Cadwallader Colden Papers*, vol. 4 (New York, 1921): 202–203.

In a communication dated August 18, 1732, the Caughnawagas indicate they desire one Mr. Lydius to dwell at Otter Creek so they can "discharge their debts" to him. They ask why the governor does not build a fort at Otter Creek as the French have done at Crown Point.

**129.** Chamberlain, John. "John Chamberlain, the Indian Fighter at Pigwacket." *Maine Historical Society Collections*, ser. 2, vol. 9 (Portland, 1898): 2–14.

The author discusses the life of John Chamberlain, a scout who fought the Pequaket Indians and is sometimes credited with killing the Pequaket chief, Paugus, in 1725. The writer suggests that Chamberlain should be given this honor.

**130.** Chapin, Howard M. "Indian Implements Found in Rhode Island." *Rhode Island Historical Society Collections*, vol. 17, no. 4 (October 1924): 105–124. Illustrated.

Chapin describes the principal types of Indian implements found in Rhode Island—arrowheads, spearheads, and knife blades—and the general design groups into which they fall. Other tools such as axe heads, adzes, chisels, pestles, hammers, ceremonial stones, soapstone utensils and pipes, as well as stone ornamentation, are also discussed. Photographs show implements found in Rhode Island [Chapin continues his discussion in *Rhode Island Historical Society Collections*, vol. 18, no. 1 (January 1925): 22–32. This part of the study deals with bone implements, basketry, wampum and pottery of Rhode Island Indians.]

**131.** Chapin, Howard M. "Queen's Fort." *Rhode Island Historical Society Collections,* vol. 24, no. 4 (October 1931): 141–156. Illustrated.

Chapin discusses a fort and village of Narragansett Indians, once located at the highest point of North Kingston, Rhode Island. He draws on contemporary documents to discuss the location of the village of the "old queen" Matantuck, a Niantic, probably located near Queen's fort. He tells the stories and traditions connected with the fort, apparently part of a long series of Indian forts in the area. A photograph of a cave near the site of the fort illustrates the text. [*See* Elisha Potter's article on this fort in *Rhode Island Historical Society Collections,* vol. 3 (1835): 84.]

**132.** Chapin, Howard M. "Quetenis Island or Dutch Island." *Rhode Island Historical Society Collections,* vol. 19, no. 3 (July 1926): 88–91.

Chapin briefly discusses Dutch activity in Narragansett Bay, beginning with the voyage of Adrian Block in 1614, and describes Dutch trade with the Wampanoags and other Indians in the area.

**133.** Chapin, Howard M. "A Survey of the Indian Graves the Have Been Discovered in Rhode Island." *Rhode Island Historical Society Collections,* vol. 20, no. 1 (January 1927): 14–32. Illustrated.

Chapin discusses the Indian graves discovered in many parts of the state and deplores the frequency of the grave robberies that began in 1653. He explains the kinds of objects found in the graves, and speculates on the tribes to which the skeletons belonged. Photographs of funerary objects illustrate the text.

**134.** Chapin, Howard M. "Unusual Indian Implements Found in Rhode Island." *Rhode Island Historical Society Collections,* vol. 19, no. 4 (October 1926): 117–128. Illustrated.

Chapin discusses unusual types of Indian implements and objects found in Rhode Island, including stone effigies, stone mortars, and pierced stones. Photographs of some of these objects are included.

**135.** Charlton, Mary Fletcher. "The Crown Point Road." *Vermont Historical Society Proceedings,* n.s., vol. 2, no. 4 (1931): 163–193. Illustrated.

This history of the road from Crown Point to Charlestown, New Hampshire, long known as the "Indian Road," includes many references to the pre-Revolution use of the road by Indians. Charlton draws on diaries and journals to document the road's location and use. She stresses that its military value was instrumental in deciding the outcome of the French and Indian wars, and tells of highway captures, raids, and relics found along the route. A map showing the "Old Military Road" built in 1759 is imposed on a modern map of the state of Vermont.

**136.** Chidsey, A. D., Jr. "Easton Before the French and Indian War." *Pennsylvania History,* vol. 2, no. 3 (July 1935): 156–171.

Chidsey describes the spread of white settlement to the area of present-day Northampton and Lehigh Counties, resulting in the founding of Easton by 1750. He also discusses the area's Indians, the Delawares and the Shawnees, who resisted subservience to the Six Nations and joined the French in attacking the frontiers of western Pennsylvania. Chidsey describes the first Indian conference held at Easton in 1756, at which Governor Morris of Pennsylvania read the King of England's declaration of war against France. [*See* A.D. Chidsey, Jr. "William Parsons, Easton's First Citizen." *Pennsylvania History,* vol. 7, no. 2 (April 1940): 89–102. In this short biography, Chidsey discusses Parson's life from 1754 to 1757, the period when the Delawares and Shawnees, allied with the French, attacked the Pennsylvania frontier and when the first Indian conference at Easton was held in 1756.]

**137.** Christian. "Indian Deed, 1679." *Pennsylvania Magazine of History and Biography,* vol. 32, no. 1 (1908): 104.

An Indian, whose English name was Christian, deeds 400 acres of land to Richard Leuick on December 10, 1679. The Indian received matchcoats, bottles of liquor, and handfuls of shot and powder in return.

**138.** Clark, James T. "Sir William Johnson and Pontiac." *New York State Historical Association Proceedings, Fifteenth Annual Meeting,* vol. 13 (Lake George, 1914): 85–107. Illustrated.

Clark first discusses how the French were more advanced than the English in conciliating the Indians and using them as allies in war and as agents in extending their political and commercial province. He tells how the Algonquians and their allies were tied to the French and the Iroquois were tied to the English. He discusses Johnson's responsibilities as superintendent of Indian affairs of New York and later of the area from Nova Scotia to the Mississippi River, gives his opinion of Indians, and describes Pontiac, chief of the Ottawas and western tribes. He also describes the French-English struggle for the continent, ending in English supremacy as Detroit, the most important of the western posts, surrendered to the English in 1760. Clark tells of Johnson's trip to Detroit in 1761 to make a peace treaty with the western tribes, explains Pontiac's plan to attack all English posts and reinstate the French in the West, describes the failure of his plan, and the meeting of Sir William Johnson and the Iroquois with Pontiac at Oswego, to conclude a peace treaty in July 1766. Clark tells of Johnson's later years and Pontiac's assassination in 1769. Photographs of Fort Ontario are included.

**139.** Clinton, Amy Chency. "Historic Fort Washington." *Maryland Historical Magazine,* vol. 32, no. 3 (September 1937): 228–233.

In a portion of this article, Clinton discusses how, when Maryland was first settled in 1634, an Indian village known as Piscataway was situated on the fort site. She tells how the Piscataways played an important part in the life of early Maryland colonists, describes the attacks of the Susquehannocks on the Piscataways, and discusses their emigration to Pennsylvania around 1697.

**140.** Clinton, George. [Letter to Cadwallader Colden] *New Jersey Historical Society Collections,* vol. 4 (Newark, 1852): 261–267.

Writing on August 24, 1745, New York's Governor Clinton warns of French efforts to incite the Indians to revolt against the English. He explains that he had designated October 4 as the day for a conference with the Indians. Enclosed with Clinton's letter are letters from the Albany Commissioners of Indian Affairs dated August 9 and August 12, 1745, telling of attacks by Canadian Indians on English settlements, and of the governor of Canada telling Indians that the English plan to attack him as well as their nations. Governor Morris writes Governor Clinton on September 2, 1745, page 269, that he is not apprehensive about the Indians attacking the English.

**141.** Clinton, George. [Letter to Cadwallader Colden] *New York Historical Society Collections for the Year 1919, Cadwallader Colden Papers,* vol. 3 (New York, 1920): 403–406.

Writing on July 8, 1747, Governor Clinton reports that leaders of the Six Nations have complained to him about lack of British military support against the French and their Indian allies. He tells how Hendrick complained in front of the Indians that the British had betrayed them, and Clinton reports he promised his assistance.

**142.** Clinton, George. [Letter to Cadwallader Colden] *New York Historical Society Collections for the Year 1920, Cadwallader Colden Papers,* vol. 4 (New York, 1921): 187–188.

Writing on February 9, 1749, Governor Clinton's letter contains two extracts from Sir William Johnson, dated January 6 and January 22, 1749. Johnson warns of increased French activity among the Five Nations, particularly encouraging the Mohawks to go to war against the Catawbas. Clinton tells Colden that Johnson has indicated he can no longer maintain the expenses of Indian affairs and would be glad to withdraw from this work unless he is repaid.

**143.** Clinton, George. [Meeting with the Mohawk Indians] *New York Historical Society Collections for the Year 1919, Cadwallader Colden Papers,* vol. 3 (New York, 1920): 406–408.

Meeting with Governor Clinton on July 16, 1747, Mohawk leaders announce their intention of raiding Canada to avenge the killing of several important Mohawk warriors by the French. The Mohawks request British support for their raids and British protection for the Canajoharie Indians, who are exposed to French attack. Clinton

143 *(continued)*
agrees to both requests, assures them of his good intentions, and promises to exchange intelligence with the Mohawks.

144. Clinton, George. [Speech to the Six Nations of Indians] *New York Historical Society Collections for the Year 1919, Cadwallader Colden Papers,* vol. 3 (New York, 1920): 247–253.

Speaking to the Six Nations on August 19, 1746, Governor Clinton reminds them that they have not kept their promise to attack the French and allied Indians for hostilities they have committed at Saratoga and along the frontiers of New England. Clinton informs the Indians that the King of England has ordered the governors of Virginia, Maryland, Pennsylvania, and New York to join forces and attack Canada by land and that the colonies of Massachusetts Bay, Connecticut, Rhode Island, and New Hampshire will join the British ships of war and attack Canada by sea. Clinton also informs the Six Nations that the King expects them to join the enterprise, reminding them of what the French have done to them. He concludes by promising the Six Nations goods and ammunition if they will join the British.

145. Clinton, George. [Speech to the Six Nations of Indians] *New York Historical Society Collections for the Year 1920, Cadwallader Colden Papers,* vol. 4(New York, 1921): 69–72.

Speaking to the Six Nations in July 1748, Clinton tells them that he suspects the French may try to draw a number of them to Canada on some pretense in order to win them over and encourage them to break with the British. He tells the Indians that although a cessation of arms is agreed to between the kings of France and England, peace remains uncertain and the Indians should refrain from taking up arms. Clinton says he has sent a number of French prisoners to Canada in order to redeem captive Six Nations warriors.

146. Clinton, George. "Proclamation of Governor George Clinton Against all Indians in League with the French." *New York Historical Society Collections for the Year 1919, Cadwallader Colden Papers,* vol. 3 (New York, 1920) 149–151.

In this proclamation, dated September 5, 1745, Governor Clinton prohibits all traffic and correspondence between the inhabitants of New York province and Indian allies of the French, including those in Canada. Clinton explains that because the Indians of Canada have a treaty of neutrality with Indian nations allied with the British, they have frequent contact with the English of Albany, where they are supplied with goods and spy on the English. He points out that the Indians allied to the British are not permitted to travel into Canada, and that the French Indians have committed hostilities in New England in violation of the treaty, that stipulated that Indians of neither allied nation would meddle in the war between the two rival crowns.

147. Clinton, George. "Propositions Made by Governor George Clinton to Five of the Six Nations." *New York Historical Society Collections for the Year 1919, Cadwallader Colden Papers,* vol. 3 (New York, 1920): 166–173.

In correspondence dated October 10, 1745, Governor Clinton reveals to the Mohawks, Oneidas, Onondagas, Cayugas and Tuscaroras (excluding the Senecas) that he knows of their meeting with the governor of Canada, that he knows the Canadian government has prevailed on the Six Nations to attack the English; and that he knows the French Indians have violated the treaty of neutrality by attacking the British. Clinton explains about the war between England and France, explains that the Indians' honor has been compromised because they have refused to attack the French Indians, and finally informs them that he expects them to join with England in an impending fight against France.

148. Clinton, George. "Propositions Made by Governor Clinton to River Indians." *New York Historical Society Collections for the Year 1919, Cadwallader Colden Papers*, vol. 3 (New York, 1920): 253–254.
In a communication dated August 21, 1746, Governor Clinton asks the River Indians to join forces with the British and the Six Nations against the French and their Indian allies. He promises arms, ammunition, clothing, and provisions in return for the assistance of the River Indians.

149. Clinton, James. "James Clinton's Expedition." *New York History*, vol. 13, no. 4 (October 1932): 433–438. Illustrated.
Included here is a collection of documents regarding the 1779 expedition of General James Clinton from Canajoharies to Tioga Point to join General John Sullivan in a campaign against the Indians living in western New York. A letter, a plan of the line of march down the Susquehanna, orders for the light infantry, and a list of Tories found in Indian country are included as well as a copy of the sketch of the line of march dated July 1779.

150. Clough, Abner. "Abner Clough's Journal." *New Hampshire Historical Society Collections*, vol. 4 (Concord, 1834): 201–214.
These journal entries, dated July 14 to September 28, 1746, provide an account of the march of Captain Daniel Ladd and his men who were sent by the Governor and Council of New Hampshire to protect the inhabitants of Rumford and adjacent towns from Indian raids.

151. Coates, B. H. "Origin of the Indian Population of the Americas." *Historical Society of Pennsylvania Memoirs*, vol. 3, part 2 (Philadelphia, 1836): 3–63.
Coates argues that the Indians are of Mongolian descent and originally colonized America from Asia by one of two northwest routes— the Bering Strait or by Alaska and the Aleutian Islands. He explains his rejection of the theory that Indians were a separate race. He also examines arguments favoring South Sea islanders as the principal source of the American Indian population as well as other theories that argue that Jews, Celts, Normans or other groups were the source.

**152.** Coffin, Paul. "Remarks Upon the Fight at Piggwacket." In "Journal of a Tour to Piggwacket." *Maine Historical Society Collections,* ser. 1, vol. 4 (Portland, 1856): 290–292.

Reverend Coffin recounts the battle between the Pequaket Indians and Captain John Lovewell in May 1725 at present-day Fryeburg, Maine, in which Lovewell and most of his troops were killed. Coffin discusses the number of casualties on both sides.

**153.** Colden, Alexander. [Letter to Cadwallader Colden, His Father] *New York Historical Society Collections for the Year 1935, Cadwallader Colden Papers,* vol. 9 (New York, 1937): 129–134.

Writing on November 7, 1753, Colden tells his father about the refusal of the Mohawks to allow him to survey land for a license. The Indians have claimed that they were cheated by white settlers, but agreed at the request of Sir William Johnson to let Colden carry out his task, except for some property purchased by "Teady McGin" about whom the Indians have complaints. Colden also reports Indian complaints about a man claiming to act as the senior Colden's deputy.

**154.** Colden, Alexander. Letter to Cadwallader Colden, his Father. *New York Historical Society Collections for the Year 1921, Cadwallader Colden Papers,* vol. 5 (New York, 1923): 168–169.

Writing on July 15, 1757, Colden reports the French capture of Fort William Henry (on Lake George) due to lack of cannons and ammunition. He describes the massacre of British troops at the fort and the murder of women and children by Indian allies of the French.

**155.** Colden, Alexander. [Letters to Cadwallader Colden, His Father] *New York Historical Society Collections for the Year 1921, Cadwallader Colden Papers,* vol. 5 (New York, 1923): 171–173.

Writing on August 18 and August 21, 1757, Colden gives further details on the capitulation of Fort William Henry (see above). He also speculates whether the fort could have been saved if certain actions had been taken. He tells how the French are removing everything from the fort and are planning to demolish it. He explains how Colonel George Munro has asked the French for a better escort and for protection from the Indians, and reports that Montcalm has given the garrison of Fort William Henry a double escort to prevent the Indians from massacring them.

**156.** Colden, Cadwallader. "Colden's Account of the Conference Between Governor Burnet and the Five Nations, 1721." *New York Historical Society Collections for the Year 1917, Cadwallader Colden Papers,* vol. 1 (New York, 1918): 128–134.

Colden explains how Consora, a Seneca sachem who was usually chosen as a spokesperson for the Five Nations of Indians at conferences, was unacceptable to Governor Burnet, who insisted on another conference speaker. Colden describes Consora's policy of neutrality vis-a-vis France and England, and points out how Consora had tried to dissuade the Indians from going to war with the English against the French. Colden relates a speech given by New York's Governor William Burnet to seventy or eighty sachems of the Five Nations. Burnet requests (1) that the Indians resist the French at Niagara, (2) that the Five Nations allow other Indians to pass freely through their territory to trade at Albany, (3) that the Indians refrain from killing cattle in New York, (4) that the Five Nations observe Virginia's boundaries, and (5) that the Indians help the governor of Virginia recover runaway "negro slaves," for which they will be rewarded. Colden reports that the Indian leaders agree to all of Burnet's demands. Colden describes how sachems maintain their authority, explains the Five Nations practice of taking prisoners, and tells how he bases his information on eyewitness reports he has received.

**157.** Colden, Cadwallader. "Colden's Conference with the Five Nations at Onondaga, April 24–26, 1748 to Retain Their Friendship." *New York Historical Society Collections for the Year 1920, Cadwallader Colden Papers*, vol. 4 (New York, 1921): 50–60.
This meeting between Colden and sachems of the Five Nations centers on a dispute over efforts to rescue Indians held captive by the French in Canada. Ganughsadeagah, an Onondaga sachem, explains how annoyed the Five Nations are that the British have asked them not to go to Canada to try to release their imprisoned relatives, and that they blame the British Army for having done nothing to help their release. They also complain that trade goods are too expensive, and that they are hungry. In response, Colden argues that the Indians should renounce their intentions to raid Canada and he insists that the matter of the imprisoned relatives be left to negotiations between the British and the French. The Indians finally promise to cooperate with Colden, but disclaim responsibility for the actions of other tribes allied to the British.

**158.** Colden, Cadwallader. "Continuation of Colden's *History of the Five Indian Nations, for the Years 1707 Through 1726.*" *New York Historical Society Collections for the Year 1935, Cadwallader Colden Papers*, vol. 9 (New York, 1937): 359–434.
This document is part of Colden's continuing history beginning with *The History of the Five Indian Nations Depending on the Province of New York*, which ended in 1697. No manuscript has been found for the years 1697 to 1707. Colden discusses such topics as Indian customs and the French-British competition over Indian allies, focusing on the role of the Five Nations in New York history. This portion of the *History* contains a number of Indian speeches.

**159.** Colden, Cadwallader. "Cure of Wounds." *New York Historical Society Collections for the Year 1919, Cadwallader Colden Papers*, vol. 3 (New York, 1920): 89–90.
In a letter dated December 1744, Colden discusses the use by

**159** *(continued)*
Mohawks of hamamelis, or witch hazel, to cure blindness and inflammation of the eyes. Colden also briefly describes herbal remedies for other kinds of wounds.

**160.** Colden, Cadwallader. "Colden's Orders to Colonel Thomas Ellison in Reference to Indian Attacks," *New York Historical Society Collections for the Year 1922, Cadwallader Colden Papers,* vol. 6 (New York, 1923): 70–71.

Responding to Indian threats against settlements in Ulster and Orange counties, Colden orders out the militia on August 31, 1761 to protect the settlers from violence. He orders the militia to avoid using force against the Indians until every other method is tried.

**161.** Colden, Cadwallader. "Colden's Petition to Lieutenant Governor Delancey." *New York Historical Society Collections for the Year 1921, Cadwallader Colden Papers,* vol. 5 (New York, 1923): 107–109.

Writing to Lieutenant Governor James Delancey in 1757, Colden requests that the colonial government again provide protection for the frontier in northern and western New York; when the previous guard was withdrawn, the Indians murdered, scalped, and kidnapped a number of residents. He tells Delancey that the few farmers remaining cannot guard the area and at the same time provide adequately for their families.

**162.** Colden, Cadwallader. [Letter to Archibald Kennedy] *New York Historical Society Collections for the Year 1935, Cadwallader Colden Papers,* vol. 9 (New York, 1937): 165–167.

Writing on November 17, 1756, Colden describes the hardships of the frontier: for the inhabitants, as victims of Indian depredations, and for the militia, as possessing very little authority.

**163.** Colden, Cadwallader. [Letter to Cadwallader Colden, Junior] *New York Historical Society Collections for the Year 1876, Cadwallader Colden Letter Books,* vol. 1 (New York, 1877): 223.

Writing on August 3, 1763, Colden in discussing recent troubles with Indians on the frontiers of New York, suggests that if the people are vigilant and do not desert the frontier this will create fear in the minds of Indians, and the latters' hostilities will cease. Colden's letters to Sir William Johnson and Colonel Hardenbergh, both dated July 28, 1763, deal with the same subject.

**164.** Colden, Cadwallader. [Letter to Dr. John Mitchell] *New York Historical Society Collections for the Year 1935, Cadwallader Colden Papers,* vol. 9 (New York, 1937): 18–34.

Writing on July 6, 1749, Colden discusses at length the state of affairs in New York, focusing on Indian affairs. He tells of the failure of the British plan to attack the French fort at Crown Point, of Governor Clinton's follow-up plan to secure the frontiers and harass the French, and of the refusal of the New York General Assembly to provide provisions for the expedition. An extended description of the struggle for power between Clinton and the General Assembly follows. Colden concludes that defects in colonial government are responsible for the loss of British influence over the Indians.

**165.** Colden, Cadwallader. [Letter to Dr. John Mitchell] *New York Historical Society Collections for the Year 1935, Cadwallader Colden Papers,* vol. 9 (New York, 1937): 98–100.

Writing on July 18, 1751, Colden answers several questions put to him by Dr. Mitchell in an earlier letter (q.v., April 5, 1751, pages 87–90). These concern the territorial claims of the Five Nations and French behavior towards the British and Indians in North America. Colden argues that French influence could be destroyed if the British effectively supported the Five Nations as allies.

**166.** Colden, Cadwallader. [Letter to Dr. John Mitchell] *New York Historical Society Collections for the Year 1935, Cadwallader Colden Papers,* vol. 9 (New York, 1937): 103–107.

Writing on August 17, 1751, Colden condemns the treatment of Indians by many so-called Christian white people citing several examples: a man at Oswego supplied Indians with kegs of water, presumed to be rum, but escaped prosecution when he was elected to the Assembly; a person feigning kindness cheated Indians of their land; a young Indian boy was stolen from his family.

**167.** Colden, Cadwallader. [Letter to General Jeffrey Amherst] *New York Historical Society Collections for the Year 1876, Cadwallader Colden Letter Books.* vol. 1 (New York, 1877): 94–95.

Writing on June 29, 1761, Colden reviews British land policy in North America and stresses that no person may take land from Indians either by purchase or otherwise without first obtaining a license. He also states the facts of a land dispute involving the gift of a large tract to Sir William Johnson from the Six Nations Indians. Prior to the gift, Colonel Delancey and others had already obtained licenses to purchase this same tract. Colden hopes to settle this by a compromise between the parties. Colden also informs Sir William that he cannot stop the purchases of land in an area along the Hudson River because a great number of people who wish to settle there would become very resentful. [*See* Cadwallader Colden. Letter to Sir William Johnson. *New York Historical Society Collections for the Year 1876, Cadwallader Colden Letter Books.* vol. 1 (New York, 1877): 96–97. This letter, dated July 2, 1761, contains further discussions of the land dispute.]

**168.** Colden, Cadwallader. [Letter to General Thomas Gage] *New York Historical Society Collections for the Year 1876, Cadwallader Colden Letter Books,* vol. 1 (New York, 1877): 255.

Writing on November 28, 1763, Colden reports on efforts by Sir Jeffrey Amherst commander-in-chief of the army of America, to raise

**168** *(continued)*
a militia force to suppress a "dangerous insurrection of the Indians" and to keep open lines of communication between Albany and Oswego. Colden informs Gage that the New York General Assembly, unwilling to raise the entire force itself, has called for assistance first from New England governments. The Assembly agrees to raise the 300 men demanded by Amherst.

**169.** Colden, Cadwallader. [Letter to General Thomas Gage] *New York Historical Society Collections for the Year 1876, Cadwallader Colden Letter Books*, vol. 1 (New York, 1877): 419.
Writing on December 8, 1764, Colden reviews new regulations governing trade with the Indians, requiring each trader to be bonded and licensed by the royal governor. Traders must promise not to sell to any Indians beyond the Christian settlements and to restrict trade to garrisons.

**170.** Colden, Cadwallader. [Letter to Governor Charles Hardy] *New York Historical Society Collections for the Year 1921, Cadwallader Colden Papers*, vol. 5 (New York, 1923): 105–107.
In a letter of uncertain date (possibly the summer of 1756), Colden relates a murder-scalping incident on the road between Minisink and Rochester and discusses the desirability of providing a stong, publicly-financed frontier guard. He notes that this is especially necessary during harvest time, when settlers are preoccupied with their own crops and cannot afford to keep scouts on the frontier. Colden also recommends the construction of blockhouses as part of a frontier defense system. Colden and Hardy exchange letters on this topic May 11 and May 16, 1756, pages 74–78 and Colden writes Hardy on the same subject in 1756 or 1757, pages 110–111.

**171.** Colden, Cadwallader. [Letter to Governor George Clark] *New York Historical Society Collections for the Year 1918, Cadwallader Colden Papers*, vol. 2 (New York, 1919): 158–160.
Writing on November 3, 1736, Colden cites cases of deception in the purchase of land from Mohawk Indians, the Indians having been persuaded to sign deeds without fully understanding the language and measures mentioned in the documents. "Quieting the Indians' mind by doing them Justice" he claims, is the best way to preserve peace in New York. Colden urges that, in the future, all lands to be purchased from Indians be surveyed in their presence and the terms of the deal fully explained before any deed is signed.

**172.** Colden, Cadwallader [Letter to Governor George Clinton] *New York Historical Society Collections for the Year 1920, Cadwallader Colden Papers*, vol. 4 (New York, 1921): 101–102.
Writing on February 19, 1748, Colden discusses French efforts to win the allegiance of the Six Nations by promising the release of Indians held captive in Canada. Colden suggests ways to defeat this French

plan. [*See* "Colden's Conference with the Five Nations at Onondaga, April 24–26, 1748," entry no. 157 above, which deals with the same problem.]

**173.** Colden, Cadwallader. [Letter to Governor George Clinton] *New York Historical Society Collections for the Year 1920, Cadwallader Colden Papers,* vol. 4 (New York, 1921): 271–287.

Writing on August 8, 1751, Colden discusses the current state of Indian affairs and the British-French rivalry for Indian allies as well as the problems of Sir William Johnson. Noting Johnson's great influence with the Indians, Colden reports that Johnson has resigned as Indian agent for New York due to the province's failure to reimburse him for the large sums which he spent in the conduct of Indian affairs. Colden discusses French efforts to subvert the loyalty of England's Indian allies and recommends several steps to frustrate these designs, including Johnson's continuation in office. Colden concludes by proposing that a special tax be levied on all the British colonies to help prevent incursions by Indians allied to the French.

**174.** Colden, Cadwallader. [Letter to Governor George Clinton] *New York Historical Society Collections for the Year 1920, Cadwallader Colden Papers,* vol. 4 (New York, 1921): 297–299.

Writing on September 10, 1751, Colden notes the capture of English traders on the Ohio River by the French, and warns that the French are resolved to destroy British trade with the Indians.

**175.** Colden, Cadwallader. [Letter to Governor William Shirley] *New York Historical Society Collections for the Year 1920, Cadwallader Colden Papers,* vol. 4 (New York, 1921): 125–128.

Writing on July 25, 1749, Colden criticizes British neglect of Indian affairs and comments on continuing French efforts to win the allegiance of the Six Nations by offering the release of Indian prisoners held in Canada. [*See also* "Colden's Conference with the Five Nations at Onondaga, April 24–26, 1748," entry no. 157 above, which deals with the same problem.] Colden explains that the New York General Assembly has refused to grant funds necessary to send British representatives to Canada to negotiate the release of the Indian prisoners.

**176.** Colden, Cadwallader. [Letter to Governor William Shirley] *New York Historical Society Collections for the Year 1935. Cadwallader Colden Papers,* vol. 9 (New York, 1937): 52–56.

Writing in late 1749 or early 1750, Colden discusses evidence he has found to support the British and Indian claims to lands where the French fort at Crown Point is situated. He tells of a grant of land by the Mohawks to Dellius, a pastor to the Indians. He also notes a French proposal for a line of demarcation between French and English territories in North America.

**177.** Colden, Cadwallader. [Letter to Guy Johnson] *New York Historical Society Collections for the Year 1877, Cadwallader Colden Letter Books,* vol. 2 (New York, 1878): 354.

Writing on August 22, 1774, Colden congratulates Johnson on conclusion of a treaty with the Indians begun by his father, Sir William Johnson. He also suggests punishment for George Klock, a settler who has defrauded and mistreated the Indians.

**178.** Colden, Cadwallader. [Letter to Guy Johnson] *New York Historical Society Collections for the Year 1877, Cadwallader Colden Letter Books,* vol. 2 (New York, 1878): 379–380.

Writing on January 13, 1775, Colden discusses complaints against George Klock, a merchant accused of defrauding and mistreating some Mohawks. Colden urges Johnson to present evidence against Klock at the next meeting of the General Assembly.

**179.** Colden, Cadwallader. [Letter to His Excellency Benjamin Franklin] *New York Historical Society Collections for the Year 1876, Cadwallader Colden Letter Books,* vol. 1 (New York, 1877): 248–249.

Writing on October 18, 1763, Colden discusses the orders he has given to the colonels of the militia for the defense of western New York. He notes that he has directed the colonels in the part of the colony adjoining Pennsylvania to assist the Pennsylvania militia whenever it is required. He asks Franklin to issue reciprocal orders to his officers. Colden also informs Franklin that the British military commander, Sir Jeffrey Amherst, intends to use the Five Nations against other Indian tribes harrassing the frontiers.

**180.** Colden, Cadwallader. [Letter to Lord Loudoun] *New York Historical Society Collections for the Year 1921, Cadwallader Colden Papers,* vol. 5 (New York, 1923): 205–206.

Writing on October 21, 1757, Colden proposes construction of five blockhouses to defend the frontier against Indian attack. The fortifications, to be garrisoned by 20 men each, would be built by the militia along a line 20 miles long from the foot of the Shawangunk Mountains to the northern end of an impassable morass. In a letter to Governor Delancey dated about November 1757, Colden elaborates on his blockhouse plan (pages 209–211).

**181.** Colden Cadwallader. [Letter to Peter Collinson] *New York Historical Society Collections for the Year 1921, Cadwallader Colden Papers,* vol. 5 (New York, 1923): 211–214.

Writing on December 31, 1757, Colden explains that he has been forced to move his family to Flushing, Long Island due to Indian raids along the frontier. He reports that a large group of French and allied Indians destroyed a German village on the Mohawk River despite the settlers' belief that they were included in a private trading neutrality agreement with the Mohawks and Indian allies of the French. Colden suspects that French spies are trying to persuade British settlers along the frontiers that they would be more secure under the French government.

**182.** Colden, Cadwallader. [Letter to Right Honorable Earl of Halifax] *New York Historical Society Collections for the Year 1876, Cadwallader Colden Letter Books*, vol. 1 (New York, 1877): 259–261.

Writing on December 8, 1763, Colden tells of British efforts to raise a militia force to fight Indians along the northern frontier. He complains that demands for men have been made in Pennsylvania, New Jersey, New York and Virginia, but not in New England. The New York General Assembly, he reports, is unhappy over New England's exemption but does agree to raise 300 men in order to defend settlements on the Mohawk River and keep communications open between Albany and Oswego. Colden also discusses the treachery of the Senecas and asserts that they should be chastised as an example to the other Indian nations.

**183.** Colden, Cadwallader. [Letter to Right Honorable Earl of Halifax] *New York Historical Society Collections for the Year 1876, Cadwallader Colden Letter Books*, vol. 1 (New York, 1877): 272–275.

Writing on December 22, 1763, Colden discusses the background of the British alliance with the Six Nations and the breaking off of the Senecas from this alliance following the Peace of Utrecht. He tells how the French bent on fermenting conspiracy have been furnishing some Iroquois Indians with arms and ammunition. Colden advises that peace be made with the Indians at Detroit, Indian trade with Canada be prohibited, steps be taken so that the Indians become dependent on the British rather than the French for subsistence on the Mississippi, trade at Detroit posts be continued, and the Senecas be punished as an example to other Indians.

**184.** Colden, Cadwallader. [Letter to Right Honorable Earl of Halifax] *New York Historical Society Collections for the Year 1876, Cadwallader Colden Letter Books*, vol. 1 (New York, 1877): 306–308.

In a letter dated February 13, 1764, Colden advises the Earl of Halifax that the "Chenessioes" (Senecas) are the least trustworthy of the Five Nations and should be punished as an example to the other Indian nations. He dismisses the suggested policy of stirring up trouble between Indian nations.

**185.** Colden, Cadwallader. [Letter to Right Honorable Earl of Halifax] *New York Historical Society Collections for the Year 1876, Cadwallader Colden Letter Books*, vol. 1 (New York, 1877): 314.

In a letter dated March 10, 1764, Colden discusses the great influence of Sir William Johnson among the Six Nations, comments on the hostile relationship between the Delawares and the Five Nations, and argues that kindness without punishment is not a practical Indian

185 *(continued)*
policy. He suggests that it is "difficult to make one Indian Native attack another, when the quarrel was not their own. . . ."

186. Colden, Cadwallader. [Letter to Right Honorable Earl of Halifax] *New York Historical Society Collections for the Year 1876, Cadwallader Colden Letter Books,* vol. 1 (New York, 1877): 335–337.

In a letter dated July 9, 1764, Colden reports that Sir William Johnson in an effort at peace-making, has gone to Niagara to hold a conference with western Indians. Colden also informs him that the Indians who were attacking the frontiers of Virginia and Pennsylvania had been furnished ammunition from the French governor at Fort Chartres and that the French in Illinois are reaping great profits in their trade with Indians.

187. Colden, Cadwallader. [Letter to Right Honorable Earl of Halifax] *New York Historical Society Collections for the Year 1876, Cadwallader Colden Letter Books,* vol. 1 (New York, 1877): 463–464.

Colden's letter, dated January 28, 1765, explains how the British administered Indian affairs at the local levels. In addition, he refers to the death of a man who was both secretary for Indian Affairs and clerk of the city of Albany, recommending that the positions be filled with two people. He argues that it is impractical for one person to hold both positions since the handling of Indian affairs has become so extensive a job.

188. Colden, Cadwallader. [Letter to Right Honorable Earl of Hillsborough] *New York Historical Society Collections for the Year 1877, Cadwallader Colden Letter Books,* vol. 2 (New York, 1878): 5–8.

In his letter of May 31, 1765, Colden observes that although the British constitution does not allow any person to hold lands solely on an Indian title, the Indians still regard that as one of their rights. When a king's grant for a land parcel is given, the Indians contend that their sale of a land parcel supersedes a later king's grant to another purchaser for the same parcel. They "would not suffer such Grantee to settle without the consent of the Purchaser from them."

189. Colden, Cadwallader. [Letter to Right Honorable, The Lords Commissioners for Trade and Plantations] *New York Historical Society Collections for the Year 1876, Cadwallader Colden Letter Books,* vol. 1 (New York, 1877): 176–183.

In a letter dated March 1, 1762, Colden first responds to a charge that he is interested in purchasing land from Indians, interested in a license to purchase, or wants a grant of land. He gives an account of the proclamation he issued in 1760 inviting people to settle and cultivate uncleared country on the frontiers. He explains how the New York Council refused to confirm a deed of land conveyed to Sir William Johnson by the Mohawks because it was an invasion of established rules. He informs the Lords of the policy followed in New

York since 1736 designed to prevent fraud in purchasing land from
the Indians.

**190.** Colden, Cadwallader. [Letter to Right Honorable, The Lords Commissioners for Trade and Plantations] *New York Historical Society Collections for the
Year 1876, Cadwallader Colden Letter Books,* vol. 1 (New York, 1877): 268−271.
   In a letter dated December 19, 1763, Colden writes the Lords that the
   French-allied Indians at Detroit have sued for peace because they
   need ammunition and they need to go hunting. According to Colden,
   the Indians have confirmed that the French incited them to hostilities
   and supplied them with ammunition from Canada. He believes that
   the Indians of the Five Nations, who have assured Sir William
   Johnson of their devotion to the English, know what happened to the
   Indians at Detroit. His opinion is that England can never be secure
   from Indians and he assures the Lords that the Indians have not been
   cheated of their lands by the English.

**191.** Colden, Cadwallader. [Letter to Right Honorable, The Lords Commissioners for Trade and Plantations] *New York Historical Society Collections for the
Year 1876, Cadwallader Colden Letter Books,* vol. 1 (New York, 1877): 321−323.
   In a letter dated April 14, 1764, Colden reports on the success of two
   parties of the Five Nations sent against the Delawares who, with
   others, were harassing settlements on the frontiers of Pennsylvania.
   He also reports that the Five Nations, including the Senecas who have
   assisted the French in a revolt, desire peace with the English.

**192.** Colden, Cadwallader. [Letter to Right Honorable, The Lords Commissioners for Trade and Plantations] *New York Historical Society Collections for the
Year 1876, Cadwallader Colden Letter Books,* vol. 1 (New York, 1877): 380−386.
   In a letter dated October 12, 1764, Colden discusses the plan for
   regulating trade with the Indians. He explains how important it is to
   establish an easy method of obtaining justice in every dispute involving Indians, pointing out that "any delay of Justice is in effect a denyal
   of Justice to them," therefore, appeals should be ruled out in controversies between traders and Indians or in disputes among Indians
   themselves but not in cases involving disputes between traders. He
   says it is absolutely necessary to allow Indian evidence. Colden feels
   that trade should be confined to certain posts and that peace can be
   preserved if traders are not allowed to go among the Indians, with
   the exception of the Mohawks whose dwellings are intermixed with
   Christians. He suggests that land be purchased from Indians to establish a few farms for raising crops in order to save the expense of
   carrying provisions to distant posts. He is at a loss to make a judgment
   on the prohibition of rum and liquor to be sold to Indians because
   they are "a valuable branch of trade & the Indians have every where
   gained so strong an Appetite to it, that the Prohibition may give them
   great disgust." Colden suggests methods of putting duties on Indian

**192** *(continued)*
trade and comments that the regulations governing the purchase of
Indian lands for the past twenty years or so are effective. He argues
that, despite the expense, it would be wise to extend posts into Indian
country as far as possible to prevent and counteract French influence.

**193.** Colden, Cadwallader. [Letter to Right Honorable, The Lords Commissioners for Trade and Plantations] *New York Historical Society Collections for the
Year 1876, Cadwallader Colden Letter Books,* vol. 1 (New York, 1877): 392–394.
    In a letter dated November 6, 1764, Colden argues for the annulment
of the Kayaderosseras Patent. He discusses Indian property concepts;
their lands are "all in common and are only distinguished as to private
property by occupancy." He describes how the Indian deed for the
lands in the Kayaderosseras Patent was made by three Indians of
unknown affiliation, that the Indians were ignorant of English measures of length, that boundaries in the patent were uncertain, and that
the patentees have neither established settlements nor made improvements on the land. [*See* Colden's letters to Sir William Johnson
of October 15, pages 378–379, and October 22, 1764, page 379, in
which he tells Johnson to round up evidence proving that the Indians
have continually said the purchase of the Kayaderosseras tract was not
fairly made and that few or no improvements have been made by the
proprietors.]

**194.** Colden, Cadwallader. [Letter to Right Honorable, The Lords Commissioners for Trade and Plantations] *New York Historical Society Collections for the
Year 1876, Cadwallader Colden Letter Books,* vol. 1 (New York, 1877): 399–400.
    In a letter dated November 10, 1764, Colden tells the Lords that it will
be expensive to purchase Indian lands at this time because they are
demanding high prices and because the costs involved in the deliberations are expensive for a land purchaser.

**195.** Colden, Cadwallader. [Letter to Right Honorable, The Lords Commissioners for Trade and Plantations] *New York Historical Society Collections for the
Year 1876, Cadwallader Colden Letter Books,* vol. 1 (New York, 1877): 477–479.
    In a letter dated April 13, 1765, Colden informs the Lords that the
unavoidable delays in settling the Kayaderosseras Patent are making
the Indians uneasy, and, to quiet the Indians, he has directed the
attorney general to bring a legal proceeding against the patent.

**196.** Colden, Cadwallader. [Letter to Right Honorable, The Lords Commissioners for Trade and Plantations] *New York Historical Society Collections for the
Year 1877, Cadwallader Colden Letter Books,* vol. 2 (New York, 1878): 8–12.
    In a letter dated May 31, 1765, Colden explains to the Lords the
practice of present-giving by Indians at the beginning and conclusion
of conferences. According to Colden, the Canajoharie tribe of
Mohawks gave Sir William Johnson the present of a considerably
large tract of land in gratitude for his services, and Johnson informed
Colden of the present soon after is was made. The Council felt that the

gift was too large a tract to be granted to one person and was inconsistent with the king's requirement of a license. Colden tells the Lords that he has advised Sir William to apply to the king for a license. He also discusses the contests over other tracts of land in New York.

**197.** Colden, Cadwallader. [Letter to Right Honorable, The Lords Commissioners for Trade and Plantations] *New York Historical Society Collections for the Year 1877, Cadwallader Colden Letter Books*, vol. 2 (New York, 1878): 13–14.

In a letter dated June 7, 1765, Colden tells the Lords that he was able to prevent two Mohawks from being shipped to Germany for exhibition in a scheme to make money, and that the "vile" practice had offended the Mohawk Nation. He informs the Lords that he had granted licenses to fifty traders to trade with Indians at fixed garrisons only.

**198.** Colden, Cadwallader. [Letter to Right Honorable, The Lords Commissioners for Trade and Plantations] *New York Historical Society Collections for the Year 1877, Cadwallader Colden Letter Books*, vol. 2 (New York, 1878): 17–19.

In a letter dated June 8, 1765, Colden explains how the Mohawks gave Sir William Johnson a present of a considerably large tract of land in gratitude for services rendered but that the New York Council refused his application for a grant to this land because he had not obtained a license for it. Colden explains that no purchases of land have been made in a certain part of the country although licenses have been issued to several persons. He asks the Lords to consider granting the land to Sir William on the same terms that lands are granted to officers of the British army who have served in America, telling the Lords that although the land is a gift to Sir William, according to Indian custom, Johnson has made a suitable return of "1200 Pieces of Eight." Colden directs the Surveyor General to make a map of all the lands that the Indians have given to Sir William.

**199.** Colden, Cadwallader. [Letter to Sir Jeffrey Amherst] *New York Historical Society Collections for the Year 1876, Cadwallader Colden Letter Books*, vol. 1 (New York, 1877): 284–285.

In a letter dated January 25, 1764, Colden informs Sir Jeffrey Amherst that New York and Pennsylvania are complying with his request for men to fight Indians, that Massachusetts refuses to obey the order and that neither Connecticut nor Rhode Island have replied. Colden also tells Amherst that he believes the Iroquois are willing to attack the Shawnees and Delawares in exchange for arms and ammunition.

**200.** Colden, Cadwallader. [Letter to Sir Jeffrey Amherst] *New York Historical Society Collections for the Year 1876, Cadwallader Colden Letter Books*, vol. 1 (New York, 1877): 319.

In a letter dated April 13, 1764, Colden describes the successes of parties of the Five Nations sent out against enemy Delawares on the

**200** *(continued)*
branches of the Susquehanna and Ohio Rivers. He reports that fourteen Delawares have been jailed in New York, including the leader
Captain Bull, and that the prisoners contend they were not at war.

**201.** Colden, Cadwallader. [Letter to Sir William Johnson] *New York Historical
Society Collections for the Year 1876, Cadwallader Colden Letter Books*, vol. 1 (New
York, 1877): 70–71.
In a letter dated March 7, 1761, Colden tells Johnson to assure the
Indians that they will not be defrauded in any land purchases. He
describes two tracts of land purchased from the Indians on the south
side of the Mohawk River. George Klock is mentioned. [*See* Colden's
letters of November 22, 1761, pages 130–132.]

**202.** Colden, Cadwallader. [Letter to Sir William Johnson] *New York Historical
Society Collections for the Year 1876, Cadwallader Colden Letter Books*, vol. 1 (New
York, 1877): 130–132.
In a letter dated November 22, 1761, Colden states that the Council is
preventing Johnson from possessing the lands the Indians gave him.
He tells Johnson to write a letter to the Council about George Klock's
attempt to defraud Indians of their land. [*See* Colden's letter to
Johnson, dated December 27, 1761, pages 143–144, in which Colden
writes that the Council seems satisfied that Klock had defrauded the
Indians but the incident needs further affidavits. He asks Johnson to
get the Indians to write out a formal complaint explaining all the
particulars and the persons involved. *See also* Colden's letter to
Johnson, dated April 5, 1762, pages 185–186, in which Colden tells
Johnson that George Klock has appeared before the Council and that
he will do everything in his power to satisfy the Indians.]

**203.** Colden, Cadwallader. [Letter to Sir William Johnson ] *New York Historical
Society Collections for the Year 1876, Cadwallader Colden Letter Books*, vol. 1 (New
York, 1877): 247–248.
In a letter dated October 8, 1763, Colden informs Johnson that an
Indian named Hendrick Wamash claims that he is owed payment for
certain pieces of land at Fishkill. Colden says that he told the Indian of
a similar complaint made forty years before that was settled to the
satisfaction of the same man's grandfather, and that he has told the
Indian to contact Johnson to see if there was any need for a hearing.

**204.** Colden, Cadwallader. [Letter to Sir William Johnson] *New York Historical
Society Collections for the Year 1876, Cadwallader Colden Letter Books*, vol. 1 (New
York, 1877): 267–268.
Reporting in December 19, 1763, Colden writes that though the
Indians at Detroit have sued for peace saying they need ammunition
for hunting, he suggests that only a small amount of ammunition be
supplied to the Iroquois to prevent Indian independence and dis-
tribution of ammunition to hostile Indians. He argues that the
Genesee Village of Senecas should be punished for the unprovocated

murders they have committed. [*See also* Colden's letter to Johnson, dated December 28, 1763, on similar topics.] Colden also informs Johnson that he has been requested to send out volunteers to chastise the Indians living on the Susquehanna near the New York frontiers.

205.  Colden, Cadwallader. [Letter to Sir William Johnson] *New York Historical Society Collections for the Year 1876, Cadwallader Colden Letter Books,* vol. 1 (New York, 1877): 324–325.

On April 14, 1764, Colden informs Johnson that, as required by the king, he will visit him in the coming summer to witness his purchase of land from the Indians. In preparation, Johnson is told to have the land surveyed in the presence of a number of Indians. He states that if the Council refuses to allow Johnson to obtain the grant of land from the Indians, he will personally attempt to secure the king's order for a land grant. [*See* Colden's letters to Johnson, November 19, 1764, pages 405–407, and January 6, 1765, pages 442–444, dealing further with Johnson's holdings of former Indian lands.]

206.  Colden, Cadwallader. [Letter to Sir William Johnson] *New York Historical Society Collections for the Year 1876, Cadwallader Colden Letter Books,* vol. 1 (New York, 1877): 356–357.

In a letter dated September 3, 1764, Colden commends Johnson on the latter's success in negotiating with the Indians at Niagara. Colden asks Johnson's advice regarding the terms on which licenses to trade with Indians should be granted, although he knows of Johnson's view that trade should be confined to garrisoned posts and that traders should not be allowed to go among Indians. Colden suggests that to secure the Indian's friendship, a method to obtain swift justice needs to be established.

207.  Colden, Cadwallader. [Letter to Sir William Johnson] *New York Historical Society Collections for the Year 1876, Cadwallader Colden Letter Books,* vol. 1 (New York, 1877): 369–370.

In a letter, dated October 1, 1764, Colden informs Johnson that he must review the plan of the Lords of Trade to regulate trade with the Indians. He writes that his greatest difficulty is how to regulate trade with the Mohawks and other Indians who live near the frontiers and daily go to "Christian houses." He mentions that he is trying to devise a way for those engaged in trade to contribute to the public expense, and to prohibit trade in rum and other liquors.

208.  Colden, Cadwallader. [Letter to Sir William Johnson] *New York Historical Society Collections for the Year 1876, Cadwallader Colden Letter Books,* vol. 1 (New York, 1877): 473–474.

In a letter dated March 15, 1765, Colden tells Johnson that he must inform the Indians that the two of them have done everything in their power to do them justice regarding the Kayaderosseras Patent, but that justice cannot be speeded up, since the legal proceedings are slow

**208** *(continued)*
and require patience. He also tells Johnson that he has recommended passing an Act of Parliament by which the Mohawks may obtain summary justice outside the common law courts.

**209.** Colden, Cadwallader. [Letter to Sir William Johnson] *New York Historical Society Collections for the Year 1877, Cadwallader Colden Letter Books*, vol. 2 (New York, 1878): 19–21.

In a letter dated June 13, 1765, Colden urges Johnson to investigate the leadership and influence of the Six Nations over other Indian nations and to encourage the western Indians around Detroit as well as the Shawnees and the Delawares to become independent of the Six Nations. He indicates that he has sent a letter to the Commissioners for Trade and Plantations asking them to grant Johnson the land the Indians gave him as a present. Colden reveals that he is trying to vacate the Kayaderosseras Patent, and he offers his belief that "not one of the great tracts were fairly purchased." He also suggests that where Indians claim rights to unsettled land tracts, just decisions should be made.

**210.** Colden, Cadwallader. [Letter to Sir William Johnson] *New York Historical Society Collections for the Year 1877, Cadwallader Colden Letter Books*, vol. 2 (New York, 1878): 183–185.

In a letter dated January 11, 1769 concerning Indian trade, Colden tells Johnson that the Assembly's recent decision to permit Albany to draw up trade regulations amounts to allowing the traders to regulate themselves even though they have been committing fraud and abusing the Indians.

**211.** Colden, Cadwallader. "On Colden's History of the Five Indian Nations." *New York Historical Society Collections for the Year 1918, Cadwallader Colden Papers*, vol. 2 (New York, 1919): 207–208, 210, 250–251, 258.

These pages contain passages of correspondence between Colden and Peter Collinson regarding Colden's work on his *History of the Indian Nations* and his instructions to Collinson regarding the editing and publishing of the manuscript. The letters were written on March 5, 1740 and on April 9 and in May of 1742.

**212.** Colden, Cadwallader. "On Mismanagement of Indian Affairs Related by Colden." *New York Historical Society Collections for the Year 1918, Cadwallader Colden Papers*, vol. 2 (New York, 1919): 259–261.

In a letter dated May, 1742, Colden explains that he preferred to leave out the details of the mismanagement of Indian affairs from his *History* because "it must throw severe reflections upon particular persons or families now in this Province." He relates facts about the first Dutch settlers, whom he condemns as avaricious, telling how some Dutchmen coerced Indians into going to bed with their wives, how some supplied Indians with ammunition which killed their own people, how one Dutchman sold Indians kegs of water presumed to be rum and escaped prosecution by being elected to the Assembly. Colden explains that these practices prevent Indians from truly trusting the English or in fact anyone from Albany at all. He also comments that the richest traders are not ashamed when their illicit trading practices are discovered.

**213.** Colden, Cadwallader. "On the Mismanagement of Indian Affairs." *New York Historical Society Collections for the Year 1919, Cadwallader Colden Papers,* vol. 3 (New York, 1920): 137–139.

In a letter dated August 7, 1745, Colden discusses how the French in Canada are trying to incite the Indians of the Six Nations against the English. He discusses the diffidence of the Indians in dealing with the Commissioners of Indian Affairs, suggesting one or two men should manage Indians rather than a commission of twenty. He writes that Indians are not reticent in dealing with those who have not abused their confidence and argues that the management of Indian affairs must be put in the proper hands.

**214.** Colden, Cadwallader. "Remarks on the Subject Matter of the Papers Sent Me by His Excellency." *New York Historical Society Collections for the Year 1920, Cadwallader Colden Papers,* vol. 4 (New York, 1921): 34–42.

In a letter dated April 5, 1748, Colden comments on how important it is to British colonial interests to preserve the friendship of the Six Nations. He observes that the policy of neutrality can be of little or no benefit unless the Indians allied with the French also become neutral. Colden explains why he expects the French to obstruct a general neutrality, enumerates the reasons why some people in New York desire neutrality and indicates why the Six Nations could be involved in the war against France. He points out that the Six Nations must be constantly employed in order to negate the rumor spread by the French that the English want the Indians destroyed so they may take their lands. He considers the advantages to be gained by having the Six Nations engaged in war and concludes by suggesting that the disunity among the colonies is partly responsible for the constant harassment on the frontiers by the French and allied Indians.

**215.** Coleman, John M. "The Treason of Morden and Land." *Pennsylvania Magazine of History and Biography,* vol. 78, no. 4 (October 1955): 439–451.

Coleman discusses the story behind the 1780 execution of Ralph Morden for helping a Tory named Robert Land jump bail and escape to Canada. He gives background on both men, discusses their relationship with Indians, and details the charges against Morden for being a British spy attempting to incite Indians to attack the settlers.

**216.** Colman, Benjamin. "Some Memoirs of the Continuation of the History of the Troubles of the New England Colonies, from the Barbarous and Perfidious

**216** *(continued)*
Indians, Instigated by the More Savage and Inhuman French of Canada and
Nova-Scotia." *Massachusetts Historical Society Collections,* ser. 1, vol. 6 (Boston,
1800): 108–118.

> Colman's memoirs, begun in November of 1726, deal with the peace
> made between the governors of Massachusetts Bay, New Hampshire,
> and Nova Scotia with Wenemovet, chief sachem of the Penobscots. He
> discusses outrages committed by the French and allied Indians against
> English settlements, French attempts to incite the St. Francis Indians
> to attack the English, and the sincere wish of some tribes, for example
> Norridgewock and Wewenoc, to keep the peace.

**217.** "Commission of Review." *Connecticut Historical Society Collections,* vol. 5
(Hartford, 1896): 18–23.

> On June 3, 1737, the Crown issues a patent creating a commission to
> review the struggle between the colony of Connecticut and the Mohe-
> gan tribe over land titles.

**218.** Commissioners of Indian Affairs. "Meeting of the Commissioners of
Indian Affairs." *New Jersey Historical Society Collections,* vol. 4 (Newark, 1852):
305–308.

> On January 22 and February 25, 1746, the Commissioners instruct
> the Six Nations to join the English in a war against the French and
> allied Indians. The Commissioners inform the Indians of the re-
> wards, depending on age, for the scalps of enemies. The Six Nations
> respond that it is not easy for them to go to war against Indians who
> are related to them by marriage and alliance; therefore they will
> remain neutral in England's war with the French.

**219.** Commissioners of Indian Affairs. "Proceedings of the Commissioners of
Indian Affairs." *Connecticut Historical Society Collections,* vol. 13 (Hartford,
1911): 9–12.

> In communications dated August 9 and August 12, 1745, the
> Mohawks and Tuscaroras report to the Commissioners on their meet-
> ing with the governor of Canada. They explain that the Onondagas
> have renewed their alliance with Canada, that France has learned of
> English designs on Canada, and that French presents have declined
> because of the English blockade. They report that Indians allied to the
> French will defend the governor of Canada, that the governor says the
> English are planning to destroy the Six Nations and has invited them
> to come live in Canada and take up arms against the English, and that
> the Indians are considering the offer at their Council at Onondaga.

**220.** Commissioners of the United Colonies. "Instructions to Governor Josiah
Winslow in Philip's War." *Massachusetts Historical Society Collections,* ser. 3, vol. 1
(Boston, 1825, 1866): 66–68.

> On November of 1675, the Commissioners instruct Governor
> Winslow to march to Narragansett country to surprise the enemy,
> punish him, and offer to make a treaty.

**221.** Commissioners of the United Colonies. "Intrusion of the Rhode Island People Upon the Indian Lands." *Massachusetts Historical Society Collections*, ser. 3, vol. 3 (Boston, 1833): 209–210.

On September 13, 1669, the Commissioners declare that the intrusion of Rhode Islanders into Narragansett lands is unjust and recommend a hearing on the question.

**222.** Commissioners of the Twelve United Colonies. "Journal of the Treaty Held at Albany, in August 1775 With the Six Nations By the Commissioners of the Twelve United Colonies." *Massachusetts Historical Society Collections*, ser. 3, vol. 5 (Boston, 1836): 75–100.

This journal, dated August 15 to August 31, 1775, records the proceedings of the Commissioners for the Northern Department of Indian Affairs, which includes the Six Nations and all tribes north of them. The Commissioners dwell on the need to secure the alliance of the Six Nations, or at least their neutrality, during the impending conflict with the English. The journal contains the texts of speeches by the Commissioners, Abraham, a Mohawk, and Tiahogwando, an Oneida. Abraham tells of the determination of the Six Nations not to take part in the "family affair."

**223.** Connecticut Commissioners. "Conference with the Six Nations of Indians." *Connecticut Historical Society Collections*, vol. 11 (Hartford, 1902): 183–185.

In June 1744, the Connecticut Commissioners commend the Six Nations for their loyalty to England despite French attempts to break up the alliance. The Commissioners warn the Six Nations to keep the covenant and continue to resist the French.

**224.** Connecticut Committee of the General Assembly. "Report of the Committee of the General Assembly on Indian Claims at Sharon." *Connecticut Historical Society Collections*, vol. 11 (Hartford, 1907): 61–64.

In a report, dated October 1742, on its investigation of Indian land claims in the towns of Sharon and Salisbury, the committee concludes that the Indians will be peaceful Christian neighbors and should be favored in their claims.

**225.** Connecticut Committee of the General Assembly. "Report of the Committee of the General Assembly on Samuel Mason's Petition." *Connecticut Historical Society Collections*, vol. 5 (Hartford, 1896): 180–185.

In a report dated October 1739, the committee argues that Mason's petition contains many false representatives of fact and that it reflects badly on the Connecticut government. The committee responds to the complaints in the petition and says it is preparing a defense.

**226.** Connecticut Council. "Council of Connecticut to the Commissioners of the United Colonies." *Connecticut Historical Society Collections*, vol. 21 (Hartford, 1924): 227–228.

**226** *(continued)*
In a communication dated October 7, 1675, the Council of Connecticut explains the necessity for all the New England colonies to wage the Indian war as vigorously as possible, and vows to continue assisting neighboring colonies in defending their towns until it is forced to recall its troops to protect its own borders. The Council says that it is sending both Mohegans and Pequots to join the English army and that Uncas, a Mohegan, recommends a surprise expedition against the hostile Indians. [*See* the order of the Commissioners of the United Colonies to Connecticut, dated October 25, 1675, pages 229–230, requesting that new forces be raised in each colony, and commenting on the war's conduct.]

**227.** Connecticut Council. "Council of Connecticut to Governor Edmund Andros." *Connecticut Historical Society Collections,* vol. 21 (Hartford, 1924): 226–227.
In its communication dated October 6, 1675, the Council reports on the destructive Indian expeditions against the towns of Quabaug, Suckquakeheag, Pocumtuck, and Springfield, Massachusetts. Suggesting that either the French or the Mohawks are supplying the Indians with arms and ammunition, the Council asks Governor Andros to prohibit any further supplies to the hostile Indians.

**228.** Connecticut Council. "Council of Connecticut to Governor Edmund Andros." *Connecticut Historical Society Collections,* vol. 21 (Hartford, 1924): 267–269.
In a communication dated September 24, 1677, the Council blames part of the disaster at Hatfield, where residents were killed or taken captive by Indians, on Governor Andros for allowing the Mohawks to harbor hostile Indians. The Council accuses New York of "hatching creatures that devour British subjects" in New England.

**229.** Conodahto. "Petition from Conodahto, King of the Susquehanna or Conestoga Indians, and of Mecallona, King of the Shawnees, Against Sylvester Garland, Jonas Askin, and James Reed." *Historical Society of Pennsylvania Memoirs,* vol. 9 (Philadelphia, 1870): 1–3.
In March of 1700, Conodahto and Mecallona petition the government for relief and protection, explaining how Askin, Reed, and Garland had forced them to give up four Indians whom the men claimed as their servants.

**230.** "On Cooks of Dozens." *New Jersey Historical Society Proceedings,* vol. 7, no. 1 (1853): 4–6.
In a deed that lists presents given to Indians in exchange for a grant of land to Captain William Sandford in 1668, the words "2 cooks of dozens" appear. A correspondent of the New Jersey Historical Society suggests that the proper rendering is "coats of duffels."

**231.** Coolidge, Guy Omeron. "The French Occupation of the Champlain Valley from 1609–1759." *Vermont Historical Society Proceedings*, n.s., vol. 6, no. 3 (September 1938): 143–308. Illustrated.

Coolidge discusses the indeterminate sovereignty of the Iroquois over the valley of Lake Champlain from the arrival of Samuel de Champlain in Iroquois country in 1609 to the conquest by the English in 1759. He explains why neither Iroquois nor Algonquians wished to remain in Vermont after 1650, when the Algonquians were driven out of New England and had to look for a new home. Coolidge details French plans to develop the southern end of Champlain Valley and the determination of the English to expand into the same territory. The resulting struggle between the two rival crowns and the role of the Algonquians and Iroquois in this conflict until the French defeat in 1759 are also discussed. Maps and plans are included.

**232.** Cooper, Thomas. "Fabulous Traditions and Customs of the Indians of Martha's Vineyard." *Massachusetts Historical Society Collections*, ser. 1, vol. 1 (Boston, 1792): 139–140.

Cooper, an Indian of Gay Head, narrates to Benjamin Basset the traditions and customs of Indians of Martha's Vineyard as told to him by his grandmother. His stories of the first Indians who came to the Vineyard describe, among other things, Indian methods of treating illnesses.

**233.** Corning, Charles R. "An Exploit in King William's War, 1697: Hannah Dustan." *New Hampshire Historical Society Proceedings*, vol. 2, part 2 (Concord, 1891): 122–151.

Corning discusses French plans in North America, their rivalry with the English, and the Iroquois who held the balance of power between the two rivals. He relates how Saco, Wells, York, Haverhill, Andover, Dunstable, and Groton were scenes of warfare waged by Christian Indians of Canada and Abenakis of the East, focusing on the Indian attack at Haverhill in 1697. This was part of the long series of hostilities between English settlers and Canadians and Indians known as King William's War. Corning describes Indian warfare of the time, supplies text of Cotton Mather's 1697 account of the Dustan affair and evaluates the information in this account that is based on other sources. Although Corning basically accepts Mather's story about Mrs. Dunstan, her capture by and escape from Indians, he finds that portions of the story require criticism.

**234.** Cornplanter (*Seneca*). "Letter of Cornplanter." *Pennsylvania Magazine of History and Biography*, vol. 14, no. 3 (1890): 320.

On December 3, 1795, Cornplanter, a chief of the Senecas, explains how he has tried to eradicate intemperance from his nation, discussing some of the evil effects of liquor. He also praises the U.S. government for its friendship with his people.

235. Cornu, Donald. "Captain Lewis Ourry, Royal American Regiment of Foot." *Pennsylvania History*, vol. 19, no. 3 (July 1952): 249–261.

Cornu discusses Ourry's command of Fort Bedford from 1760 to 1764 and the part he played in the defense of Pennsylvania during Pontiac's uprising in 1763. He relates how Ourry witnessed the capitulation of hostile border tribes in the Ohio country and the return of some 200 white captives to Colonel Henry Bouquet. Included in the journal is a contemporary artist's rendering of Ourry listing the white captives as they are delivered to Colonel Bouquet. Cornu also quotes from Ourry's letters on military administration.

236. Cotton, Josiah. "Cotton's Vocabulary of the Massachusetts (Or Natick) Indian Language." *Massachusetts Historical Society Collections*, ser. 3, vol. 2 (Boston, 1830): 147–257.

A brief biography of Cotton precedes remarks on his orthography and pronunciation of the Massachusetts language. Originally published in 1707–1708, the vocabulary is followed by an appendix with examples from the *Indian Primer*, the Lord's Prayer in the Indian language, Eliot's Bible, the Ten Commandments in Indian language and English, and sermons in both languages preached by Cotton to the Massachusetts Indians in 1710.

237. Court of St. James. "Additional Instructions for Governor Robert Monckton Concerning Indian Land Deeds." *New York Historical Society Collections for the Year 1922, Cadwallader Colden Papers*, vol. 6 (New York, 1923): 101–104.

In a communication dated December 9, 1761, the Court of St. James prohibits Monckton, the governor of New York, from granting to any persons lands occupied and claimed by Indians of New York and bordering colonies. The Court orders that people relinquish any lands claimed by Indians, and that the governor prosecute people claiming Indian lands without the proper license and transmit all details of any application for a license to purchase lands from Indians. These instructions are to be made public to British subjects so they may obey the royal orders and to Indian tribes so they may know the royal desire to support their rights.

238. Craft, David. "Journals of the Sullivan Expedition, 1779." *Pennsylvania Magazine of History and Biography*, vol. 3, no. 3 (1879): 348–349.

Craft lists the journals kept by officers connected with the Sullivan Expedition against the Six Nations in 1779 and known to him as of 1879. Twenty-one journals are listed, the places where they have been published, and the location of each original manuscript. He also lists five persons who wrote narratives and where the narratives were published.

239. Craig, Isaac. "Letter of Major Isaac Craig to General William Irvine." *Pennsylvania Magazine of History and Biography*, vol. 36, no. 4 (1912): 507.

In a letter dated April 5, 1783, Major Craig tells of Indian depredations along the frontiers of Pennsylvania, explains that ammunition is
needed as well as a sufficient force to go after the Indians, and
maintains that England is not controlling its allies.

**240.** Crevecoeur, St. Jean de. "Letter to St. Jean de Crevecoeur." *Massachusetts Historical Society Proceedings,* vol. 55 (1921–1922): 42–46.

In a letter dated June 6, 1788, Crevecoeur discusses the account given
to him by a member of Congress from Kentucky of a discovery of
Indian mounds near present-day Nashville. He describes the mounds
that the colonists might have seen.

**241.** Crochet, Monique. "An Addendum to Maine Indians' Concept of Land
Tenure." *Maine Historical Society Quarterly,* vol. 13, no. 3 (Winter 1974): 178–184.

Crochet translates two letters written by Eastern Indians that appeared in French in the *Massachusetts Historical Society Collections,* ser. 2,
vol. 8 (Boston, 1819): 259–263. The first letter, dated July 27, 1721,
addressed to Governor Samuel Shute, explains the Maine Indians'
concept of land, that since it was received "from God alone," it could
not be conveyed to anyone by conquest, grant, or purchase. The
Abenakis ask the people who they claim have misused their lands to
withdraw from them. In the second letter, dated July 28, 1721, the
Abenakis and their allies claim all the land agreements that have been
made with the English are now voided because they were not accepted
by the whole nation and they were the result of trickery. The signatures of eleven Abenakis and allied Indian nations (Iroquois, Algonquians, Hurons, Micmacs) have been reproduced.

**242.** Croghan, George. "Captain Croghan's Journal to Presque Isle and Intelligence Received Lately." *Massachusetts Historical Society Collections,* ser. 4, vol. 9
(Boston, 1871): 283–289.

In his letter dated July 7 to July 31, 1760, Croghan describes the
march to Presque Isle, and records the text of a speech he made to the
Indians there on the necessity of establishing a post at Presque Isle.
[*See:* "Croghan's Journal," dated October 2, 1760 to January 7, 1761,
on pages 362–379. Croghan set off for Fort Pitt to join Major Roberts
at Presque Isle in order to proceed with troops to take possession of
Fort Detroit. He records the speech by Indians in which they declare
their friendship for the English and their abandonment of the
French, Croghan also reports on his speech to Wyandots, Potawatomis, and Ottawas in which he tells them to adhere to the British
interest and to return their prisoners.]

**243.** Croghan, George. "George Croghan's Journal, 1759–1763." Edited by
Nicholas B. Wainwright. *Pennsylvania Magazine of History and Biography,* vol. 71,
no. 4 (October 1947): 305–444. Illustrated.

In an introduction to the journal, the editor gives a sketch of

243 *(continued)*
Croghan's role in frontier diplomacy which was an attempt to ally
Indians to the British cause and undermine the French influence in
the Ohio country. In 1756, Croghan was appointed Deputy Superintendent for Indian Affairs under Sir William Johnson who was
Superintendent of Indian Affairs in the Northern Department. The
journal covers Croghan's activities and those of his agents with Indian
agents from April of 1759 to April of 1763. One can trace in this
journal the development of British Indian policy in terms of money,
vast sums being spent on the Indian interest during Croghan's term of
office. Later the flow of Indian presents and other expenses were
curtailed when Canada was secured and Croghan's influence over the
Indians dwindled. The journal includes speeches delivered at conferences by Indians of different nations. A map of Fort Pitt-Presque Isle
in 1760 is included.

**244.** Croghan, George. "Letters of Colonel George Croghan." *Pennsylvania
Magazine of History and Biography*, vol. 15, no. 4 (1891): 429–439.
Dated April 17, 1768 to August 12, 1774, Croghan's letters discuss the
attitudes of Indians in the area of Fort Pitt, and illustrate his work in
pacifying the Indians and conciliating them to the British interests
during the pre-Revolutionary period.

**245.** Croghan, George. [Letters of George Croghan] *Massachusetts Historical
Society Collections*, ser. 4, vol. 9 (Boston, 1871): 246–253.
In his letters dated May of 1760, Croghan discusses how he has
negotiated with the western Indians to go to war against the
Cherokees who threaten the southern British colonies, how he has
very few goods left with which to transact business, and how he has
sent Indian spies to Fort Detroit to learn what Indians would do in the
event that an expedition is sent against Detroit. He relates how the Six
Nations did not send deputies to console with those Indians who lost
people at Niagara. He also explains how he uses Mohawk spies to keep
track of the actions of French and allied Indians.

**246.** Croghan, George. "The Opinions of George Croghan on the American
Indian." *Pennsylvania Magazine of History and Biography*, vol. 71, no. 2 (April
1947): 152–159.
These pages contain the answers of George Croghan to a number of
questions put to him by Dr. William Robertson of Edinburgh who was
writing a history of America. Croghan, who had intimate knowledge
of nearly forty northern and western tribes, answered questions dealing with physical characteristics, sexual customs, the position of
women within Indian society, disease, food preferences, warfare and
prisoners, religion, intemperance, life expectancy, songs, dances, and
speeches.

**247.** Cross, Dorothy. "The Indians of New Jersey." *New Jersey Historical Society
Proceedings*, vol. 70, no. 1 (January 1952): 1–16. Bibliography.
Cross discusses the Lenni Lenapes who were divided into three geo-

graphically distributed groups: the Munsee of the north, the Unami in the central portion, and the Unalachtigo in the southern part of the state. She reconstructs the life of the Delawares (Lenni Lenapes) while they were living in New Jersey, describing food, shelter, clothing, transportation, trade and barter, trails, religion, and social and political institutions, and briefly traces the history of Indian-white contacts until 1801 when the remaining Delawares left the state. She discusses several Delaware chiefs, contributions, Indian place names, and agricultural products, and includes a list of six recommended readings.

**248.** Crouse, Nellis M. "Forts and Block Houses in the Mohawk Valley." *New York State Historical Association Proceedings*, Sixteenth Annual Meeting, vol. 14 (Lake George, 1915): 75–90. Illustrated.

Crouse discusses the forts erected in the Mohawk Valley to defend the settlers from French and allied Indians. She describes Fort Orange, the "Old Fort," Fort Ball, Craven, Newport, Bull, Clyde, Plain, Plank, Willett, Fort Stanwix, and others built between the years 1624 and 1780.

**249.** Crowley, James E. "The Paxton Disturbance and Ideas of Order in Pennsylvania Politics." *Pennsylvania History*, vol. 37, no. 4 (October 1971): 317–339.

Crowley discusses the ideas and motives of the Paxtonians, members of the Scots-Irish Presbyterian community in Lancaster County, who murdered a group of innocent Indians and marched on Philadelphia to kill other Indians whom the government was protecting in 1763. He explains how the Paxtons believed Pennsylvania government cared more for the safety of Indians than for that of white settlers and that Quaker policy designed to maintain friendly relations with Indians was part of a plot against their liberties. The frontier people were unhappy with the inadequate border defenses and the government's neglect of their interests. He describes the tendency of these people to determine for themselves the applicability of laws to particular situations. He argues that the Paxton affair showed that political concepts established in Pennsylvania could not justify extra-legal actions undertaken on the basis of personal necessity and in defiance of authority. [*See* James Kirby Martin. "The Return of the Paxton Boys and the Historical State of the Pennsylvania Frontier, 1764–74." *Pennsylvania History*, vol. 38, no. 2 (April 1971): 117–133. Martin discusses the Paxton Boys and their grievances, focusing on Frederick Stump who murdered Indians and was aided in his escape from Pennsylvania. According to Martin, the incident proves that these people understood force better than democracy, and when established government did not recognize their basic desires, they turned to violence.]

**250.** Cummings, E. C. "Capuchin and Jesuit Fathers at Pentagoet." *Maine Historical Society Collections*, ser. 2, vol. 5 (Portland, 1894): 161–188.

Cummings uses extracts from the *Jesuit Relations* that show how

250 *(continued)*
"French humanity and keen practical judgment" governed the conduct of Jesuit missionaries in dealing with Indians, and that illustrate the French method of teaching Indian children. Cummings describes the Capuchin friars in New France and their hospice at Pentagoet, tells of subsequent missionaries who worked with the Abenakis at Pentagoet, and argues that the Pentagoet Mission retreated to Old Town.

251. Cummings, E. C. "The Rasles Dictionary." *Maine Historical Society Collections,* ser. 2, vol. 6 (Portland, 1895): 144–152. Illustrated.
Cummings discusses the missionaries and their work with Indian languages, focusing on the Abenaki dictionary of Father Sebastien Rasles. He describes the book's physical characteristics and outlines the contents in detail. A facsimile of a page from Father Rasles' dictionary is included.

252. Cummings, Hubertis. "The Frontier Posts of Provincial Pennsylvania." *Pennsylvania History,* vol. 14, no. 1 (January 1947): 41–43.
Cummings describes the chain of forts extending along the Kittochtinny Hills from Delaware to the Susquehanna from 1756 to 1757 whose purpose was to provide protection to frontier people from Delawares and Shawnees. He tells of the men, such as Conrad Weiser, who developed the chain and the names and locations of these forts.

253. Dalton, Captain. "Estimates of the Indian Nations, Employed by the British in the Revolutionary War, with the Number of Warriors Annexed to Each Nation." *Massachusetts Historical Society Collections,* ser. 1, vol. 10 (Boston, 1809): 123.
In his communication dated August 5, 1783, Captain Dalton estimates that the twenty-seven tribes had a total of 12,690 warriors and that the Delaware and four other tribes in 1794 had a total of 1,550 warriors.

254. Danforth, Samuel. "Chronological Table of Samuel Danforth." *Massachusetts Historical Society Proceedings,* ser. 1, vol. 10 (1867–1869): 327–329.
A "Chronological Table of some few Memorable Occurences" was appended to the Almanac of Samuel Danforth for the year 1649. Many of the events, recorded from 1630 to 1645, tell of disease among the Indians, a treaty and peace, massacres by the Pequots, the conspiracy of Indians against the English, and conflicts between Indian tribes.

255. Darlington, William M. "The Montours." *Pennsylvania Magazine of History and Biography,* vol. 4, no. 2 (1880): 218–224.

Darlington discusses the life of "Madame Montour" who was born in Canada about 1684, brought up by Iroquois Indians who captured her when she was ten years old, and who married an Oneida war chief. He examines Madame Montour's influence among the Indians and her role as interpreter at conferences between colonial governments and the Five Nations, and mentions her children. Darlington gives some contemporary observations about Madame Montour and considers some erroneous information that exists about her.

**256.** Dartmouth Indians. "Dartmouth Indians' Engagement." *Massachusetts Historical Society Collections,* ser. 1, vol. 5 (Boston, 1798): 194–195.

On September 4, 1671, the Dartmouth Indians pledge themselves loyal subjects to England and promise to warn and assist the English in wars against enemies.

**257.** Davis, Andrew McFarland. "Journals of the Sullivan Expedition of 1779." *Massachusetts Historical Society Proceedings,* ser. 2, vol. 2 (1885–1886): 436–44.

Davis accounts for all existing journals of the Sullivan expedition in 1779, as of 1886. He lists twenty-four published diaries, journals, or narratives of the expedition including names of the writers and the periods covered by the journals, together with the titles of the publications which contain them. He also lists eight other unpublished manuscripts that he has examined and where they may be located, and mentions other magazines that contain lists of published and unpublished diaries and journals of the Sullivan campaign.

**258.** Davis, George T. "The St. Regis Bell," or "Destruction of Deerfield by Indians." *Massachusetts Historical Society Proceedings,* ser. 1, vol. 11 (1869–1870): 311–321.

On February 29, 1704, the town of Deerfield, Massachusetts, was sacked and burned by a force of French and allied Indians, and 112 men, women, and children were captured. Davis discusses the authenticity of the account of the raid given by Hoyt in his book on *Indian Wars* published in 1824, focusing on the story that when Deerfield was destroyed, the Indians took a small bell which is now hanging in an Indian church in St. Regis. Davis draws on historical records to argue that the story of the Deerfield or St. Regis bell was invented and is not sustained by the evidence.

**259.** Davis, Sylvanus. "Declaration of Sylvanus Davis about his Captivity." *Massachusetts Historical Society Collections,* ser. 3, vol. 1 (Boston, 1825, 1866): 101–112.

Davis, who lived in Falmouth, Maine, gives an account of his capture in 1690 by the French and allied Indians who took him to Canada where he was held at Quebec for four months and then released. He conveys the information he gathered while in captivity about French designs on the English.

**260.** Day, Gordon M. "The Indian Occupation of Vermont." *Vermont History,* vol. 33, no. 3 (July 1965): 365–374.

Day considers the village sites of Vermont Indians that are known to have existed between 1660 and 1780 and the nature of the Indian occupancy in Vermont, both agricultural and the system of family hunting territories which varied from region to region. He discusses the four most commonly mentioned Indians in Vermont: the Missisquois, the Mahican occupation in southwestern Vermont, the Coos settlement at Newbury, and the Squakheags whom he identifies with the Sokokis. The article contains references to historical sources.

**261.** Day, Gordon M. "Rogers' Raid in Indian Tradition." *Historical New Hampshire,* vol. 17 (June 1962): 3–17.

Day selects one brief episode for comparison of existing accounts of the raid by Rogers's Rangers on the St. Francis Indians on October 4, 1759. He outlines the story, based on Rogers's own account of the attack itself, and considers the contribution of the St. Francis Indian tradition to knowledge of the event. He recounts some of the oral testimony of Indians, giving dimension to the New England picture of Rogers' Raid. References are given.

**262.** Dayton, Captain. "Journal of Captain Dayton: On an Expedition to Detroit in 1764." *New Jersey Historical Society Proceedings,* vol. 9, no. 4 (1863–1864): 174–179.

In his journal dated April 30 to September 15, 1764, Captain Dayton describes events on the route to Detroit, difficulties encountered with tribes of Indians and peacemaking activities with Indians following the defeat of Pontiac's plan.

**263.** Deane, Charles. "Indians Kidnapped from Maine." *Massachusetts Historical Society Proceedings,* ser. 2, vol. 2 (1885–1886): 35–38.

Deane discusses five Maine Indians, kidnapped by Captain George Weymouth in 1605 and carried off to England. Three were seized by Sir Ferdinando Gorges, two were subsequently lost, and one was eventually returned in 1614 to the American coast.

**264.** Deane, Charles. "Notes on Hubbard's Map of New England." *Massachusetts Historical Society Proceedings,* ser. 2, vol. 4 (1887–1889): 13–21.

Deane discusses two editions of William Hubbard's map made for his *Narrative of the Troubles with the Indians in New England* which was published in 1677. [*See* Samuel A. Green, "Remarks on Hubbard's Map of New England," pages 199–206, which is illustrated with a facsimile of the map, a woodcut 12″ by 15″ in size.]

**265.** Deane, James. "Letter from James Deane, Interpreter, to Major General Schuyler." *New York Historical Society Collections for the Year 1879, Revolutionary Papers,* vol. 2 (New York, 1880): 118–119.

In his letter dated June 25, 1777, Deane informs Schuyler that he has dispatched Thomas and a group of Caughnawaga Indians to obtain intelligence on the enemy. He reports that the Oneidas inform him that it is useless to send messages to Brant as he is not interested in anything that the Americans have to say to him. Deane explains that the Oneidas will try to prevent their people from joining Joseph Brant's party. He also provides information to Schuyler on the movements and plans of British troops and allied Indians in Canada.

**266.** DeJong, Gerald Francis. "Dominie Johannes Megapolensis: Minister to New Netherland." *New York Historical Society Quarterly Bulletin,* vol. 52, no. 1 (January 1968): 22, 27–29.

DeJong discusses Reverend Johannes Megapolensis who figured prominently in the religious history of colonial America and who served seven years in Rensselaerswyck (1642–1649). Detailing Megapolensis' relations and missionary work with the Mohawks, De-Jong quotes a letter written by Megapolensis explaining the problems he encountered in trying to converse with the Indians in their own language. DeJong discusses how Megapolensis aided a French Jesuit missionary in escaping from Mohawk captors and also reports on the reverend's limited success in converting the Indians to Christianity.

**267.** Delabarre, Edmund B. "Chief Big Thunder: A Problematic Figure in Rhode Island Annals." *Rhode Island Historical Society Collections,* vol. 28, no. 4 (October 1935): 116–128.

Delabarre discusses the "picturesque" personality of Big Thunder, or Francis Loring, a Penobscot who was a "show-man." In particular, he describes the hoax Loring created with an ancient book made of skins containing a pictographic record of Wampanoag history.

**268.** Delabarre, Edmund B. "The Inscribed Rocks of Narragansett Bay." *Rhode Island Historical Society Collections,* vol. 13, no. 1 (January 1920): 1–28. Illustrated. Bibliography.

The author argues that the characters of the inscription on the Mount Hope Rock are Cherokee. He describes the location and appearance of the rock, reproduces the previous drawings of the inscription, supplies new photographs of it, assembles all previous descriptions of it, adds new ones, relates all that is known of its history, and tries to solve its origin and meaning. A bibliography is included. (Continued in *Rhode Island Historical Society Collections,* vol. 13, no. 3 (July 1920): 73–93. Delabarre corrects some errors in his previous article on the Mount Hope Rock. In this piece, he deals with inscribed rocks in the town of Portsmouth; these are now gone but were thoroughly studied and drawn before their disappearance. He argues that the inscriptions were made by Indians, not Norsepeople or Phoenicians. He includes a number of drawings of the Portsmouth inscriptions.)

**269.** Delabarre, Edmund B. "The Inscribed Rocks of Narragansett Bay: The Arnold Point Cup Stone and the Fogland Ferry Rock in Portsmouth." *Rhode*

**269** *(continued)*
*Island Historical Society Collections,* vol. 14, no. 1 (January 1921): 10–22. Illustrated.

Delabarre offers hypotheses concerning the inscribed rocks at Portsmouth which he cannot absolutely verify as Indian. He illustrates this article with views of rocks and charts of Narragansett Bay.

**270.** Delabarre, Edmund B. "The Inscribed Rocks of Narragansett Bay: Contributions of Newport and Middletown." *Rhode Island Historical Society Collections,* vol. 15, no. 1 (January 1922): 1–15.

In this article, Delabarre discusses examples of markings that are natural, and accidents that may have led people to misinterpret them as inscriptions made by human beings.

**271.** Delabarre, Edmund B. "The Inscribed Rocks of Narragansett Bay: The Written Rocks at Tiverton." *Rhode Island Historical Society Collections,* vol. 15, no. 3 (July 1922): 65–76. Illustrated.

Delabarre argues that the considerable number of rocks at Tiverton, only one of which was exposed to view in 1922, were inscribed by Indians. He includes a photograph of a Tiverton inscription and drawings of the inscriptions made in 1768 and 1835.

**272.** Delabarre, Edmund B. "Inscribed Rocks of Narragansett Bay: The 'Mark Rock' in Warwick." *Rhode Island Historical Society Collections,* vol. 16, no. 2 (April 1923): 46–64. Illustrated.

Delabarre describes the location, history, characteristics, and important features of the rock carvings and goes into some detail regarding the close correspondence between the rock carvings and documentary signatures. He argues that the Mark Rock proves the mixed Indian and white origin of the markings. He includes photographs of the Mark Rock glyphs, a map of the vicinity of the rock in 1917, a rough plan of the Mark Rock Ledge, and reproductions of the Indian marks or signatures.

**273.** Delabarre, Edmund B. "The Inscribed Rocks of Narragansett Bay: Dighton Rock; Miscellaneous Inscribed Rocks and Stones." *Rhode Island Historical Society Collections,* vol. 18, no. 2 (April 1925): 51–79. Illustrated.

Delabarre discusses the Dighton Rock, first mentioned in 1680, which has received a great deal of attention, aroused much controversy, and resulted in a bibliography of over 600 titles. As of 1925 these titles cover a range of 250 years, include more than twenty attempts to depict its inscriptions in drawings and a dozen attempts to photograph it, and more than twenty theories devised and disputed concerning its origin and meaning. Delabarre argues his own theory regarding the Dighton Rock inscriptions; adds supplementary notes about the Mount Hope Rock, the Portsmouth Rocks, and the Mark Rock; summarizes all the material arguing that the great majority of inscriptions were made by Indians in colonial times, that rock inscriptions were not Native American practice but were imitative of European examples; and argues that in New England, Indian carvings were ornamental and pictorial designs without symbolic significance, until perhaps toward the end of the seventeenth century when a few stones were inscribed with truly symbolic writings. He includes photographs of the Dighton Rock, the Hammond Tablet, the Portsmouth Rocks, and the Mark Rock glyphs. A map shows the locations of the inscribed rocks and stones of the Narragansett Basin.

**274.** Delabarre, Edmund B. "Miguel Cortereal: The First European to Enter Narragansett Bay." *Rhode Island Historical Society Collections,* vol. 29, no. 4 (October 1936): 97–119.

Delabarre argues that Miguel Cortereal was the first European to enter Narragansett Bay and examine the coast of Rhode Island around 1502. His reasons for believing this are based on Verrazano's observation that metal plates found among Indians in 1524 were proof that some other explorer had been there before him. He explains how Cortereal made himself sachem of the Wampanoags in place of one who was killed during a conflict with Cortereal's group. He speculates about the degree to which certain Indian names or titles can be taken as indicative of Cortereal's former leadership and the probability that Wampanoags had an infusion of white blood derived from members of the 1502 expedition.

**275.** Delabarre, Edmund B. "A Unique Indian Implement from Warren: Inscribed, Perforated, Double-Edged." *Rhode Island Historical Society Collections,* vol. 12, no. 3 (July 1919): 96–100. Illustrated.

Delabarre describes in detail the unique stone, probably ceremonial, with its combination of axe-like shape, double blade, perforation for hafting, and inscribed characters suggesting a possible alphabetic significance. He also discusses the place where it was found in Warren near the Kickamuit River. Two photographs are included.

**276.** Delancey, James. "Governor Delancey's Instructions to Mr. William Johnson: Expedition Against Crown Point." *Maryland Historical Magazine,* vol. 9, no. 3 (September 1914): 249–252.

In his communication dated April 16, 1755, Governor Delancey of New York appoints William Johnson to command forces of several colonies in an expedition against the French encroachments at Crown Point. He instructs Johnson to engage as many of the Six Nations Indians as possible to join the expedition and to use Indians to gather intelligence about the French, and to inform the Indians that the British intend to recover their lands at Niagara.

**277.** Delancey, James. "Journal of the Proceedings of the Congress Held at Albany, 1754." *Massachusetts Historical Society Collections,* ser. 3, vol. 5 (Boston, 1836): 1–74.

The journal kept by Governor James Delancey of New York, dated June 19 to July 10, 1754, records the proceedings of the commission-

**277** *(continued)*

ers who met in Albany for the purpose of dealing with the Six Nations and uniting the British colonies. The journal is prefaced by instructions to the commissioners of Massachusetts, Connecticut, Rhode Island, and Pennsylvania maintaining the need to ally the Six Nations with the British against the French and discussing the matter of presents to the Indians.

**278.** Denny, Ebenezer. "Military Journal of Major Ebenezer Denny." *Historical Society of Pennsylvania Memoirs*, vol. 7 (Philadelphia, 1860): 237–409. Illustrated.

In his journal dated May 1, 1781 to May 31, 1795, Denny records treaty-making with Indians, particularly Shawnees and Delawares, and reports how the United States exhorts Indians to be peaceful and threatens those that are hostile. He recounts the struggle of Indians to hold onto their lands and to maintain their boundary lines against the power of the United States, and also tells of expeditions against Indians who raided the frontier settlements. A description of his assignment in 1794 to command an expedition to Presque Isle, a post established to cut off communication between the Six Nations and the Miamis, is included. There is an appendix of letters, pages 413–477, many of which contain brief references to Indians during the period 1784 to 1799, and there is a view of "Maumee" towns destroyed by General Harmar, 1790.

**279.** Denny, Ebenezer. "Vocabulary of Words in Use with the Delaware and Shawnee Indians." *Historical Society of Pennsylvania Memoirs*, vol. 7 (Philadelphia, 1860): 478–485.

Denny's glossary was the result both of a Delaware treaty conference in January 1785 at Fort McIntosh and a Shawnee woman's help at Fort Finney in January 1786.

**280.** Denny, William. "Memoir of His Excellency William Denny, Lieutenant Governor of Pennsylvania." *Pennsylvania Magazine of History and Biography*, vol. 44, no. 2 (1920): 97–121.

Letters written by or to Governor Denny in November of 1756 discuss the expedition led by Colonel Armstrong against Delaware Indians in which Captain Jacobs was killed and the Delaware Indian town of Kittanning was burned. Denny discusses the appointment of Sir William Johnson to manage Indian affairs in "these parts." In a lengthy letter dated April 8, 1757, Denny discusses the charges of Delaware Indians against whites in Pennsylvania, the Indian conference at Easton, and Teedyuscung's role in it. He describes the state of the frontiers with their Indian hostilities and the difficulties of recruitment and expenses of the provincial forces. In a letter dated November 26, 1758, General John Forbes informs Denny that the French were expelled from Fort Duquesne and the various tribes of Indians living near it were reconciled to British interests.

281. "Dighton Rock." *Rhode Island Historical Society Proceedings, 1872-1873.*
(Providence, 1872): 71-76.
> Extracts from the correspondence of Thomas H. Webb, Reverend
> Frank E. Kittredge, and John R. Bartlett are concerned with the
> inscriptions on Dighton Rock.

282. Dolan, John W. "Father Jogues." *New York State Historical Association
Proceedings, Fifth Annual Meeting,* vol. 4 (Lake George, 1904): 30-53.
> Dolan analyzes the life and motives of Isaac Jogues who was born in
> 1607 and who became a Jesuit missionary to the Hurons, whose
> language he learned. He tells of Jogues's travels among other Indians
> to spread Christianity. Dolan describes Huron-Iroquois hostility, and
> regarding the capture of Jogues by Iroquois in 1642, he relies on the
> priest's narrative of his tortures in captivity and his apparent willing-
> ness to remain with his captors because it benefited his fellow prison-
> ers. Finally he used Dutch assistance to escape in 1643. Dolan recounts
> Jogues's return to Europe, his trip back to Canada in 1644, and his
> missions to the Mohawks in 1646 by whom he was killed. Jogues's
> death is reported by a Huron.

283. Dondore, Dorothy. "White Captives Among the Indians." *New York History,* vol. 13, no. 3 (July 1932): 292-300.
> In this discussion of the popularity of captivity literature, how it has
> been branded as fictitious, included on lists of religious publishing
> houses, and used in advertising Indian territories to prospective
> settlers, Dondore examines the historic value of captivity literature
> and counters the harsh statements about the Indians' treatment of
> whites by considering the number of whites who elected to stay among
> the Indians.

284. Donehoo, George P. "The Indians of the Past and of the Present."
*Pennsylvania Magazine of History and Biography,* vol. 46, no. 3 (1922): 177-198.
> Donehoo offers a general discussion on the diversity of Indian lan-
> guages, estimates the Indian population at the time of "discovery" of
> the continent, and that of Pennsylvania in particular, and looks at the
> 1920 census. He outlines the history of the difficult tribes of Indians
> and their conflicts with whites starting with John Smith's voyage of
> discovery up the Susquehanna River around 1608. He studies the
> Indians of Pennsylvania in three geographical divisions: Delaware,
> Susquehanna, and Allegheny. Donehoo concludes by recounting the
> injustices done to Indians and argues that citizenship should be given
> to them.

285. Dorr, Henry C. "The Narragansetts." *Rhode Island Historical Society Collections,* vol. 7 (Providence, 1885): 137-237.
> Dorr discusses the relationship between the settlers of Rhode Island
> and the Narragansetts. He reports some of the observations of the

285 *(continued)*

Massachusetts settlers, particularly Roger Williams, regarding Narragansett character, beliefs, and political institutions. He describes Massachusetts and its despotic dealings with the tribe, tells of Canonicus, Narragansett sachem, and his counsels of self-restraint and peace, and of his nephew Miantonomo. Dorr describes Williams's unsuccessful attempts to civilize and Christianize the Narragansetts, and he discusses the tribe's enemies including Massachusetts, the Dutch, and lawless white elements. He disputes the assertion that founders of Rhode Island were protected by Narragansetts, and maintains that Narragansetts were threatened by Massachusetts, were anxious to secure themselves by seeking a protectorate from the English crown, and that the only protector of Rhode Island is the English government. Dorr examines the period between 1647, Canonicus's death, and 1675, King Philip's War, the hopeless uprising of Narragansett Indians against numerous English, the decline of their power, and the "debasement" of the Indians in Rhode Island in the eighteenth and nineteenth centuries.

**286.** Dorr, Henry C. "The Peculiar Title to the Lands." In "The Proprietors of Providence and their Controversies with the Freeholders." *Rhode Island Historical Society Collections,* vol. 9 (Providence, 1897): 1–12.

In a study of the controversies between the proprietors and the freeholders of Rhode Island, Dorr tells how Roger Williams secured a promise of land sufficient for a town from Canonicus and Miantonomo, how two memorandums were prepared in 1639—the texts of which are given—verifying the promise. Dorr explains how the memos, the first of which was vague and inconsistent in its description of the property conveyed and the second which was legally invalid, were the way Williams procured title exclusively in himself. There are scattered references to Narragansetts throughout the study.

**287.** Doty, Lockwood R. "The Massacre at Groveland." *New York Historical Association Quarterly Journal,* vol. 11, no. 2 (April 1930): 132–140. Illustrated.

Doty discusses the battle of Newtown in August of 1779 and the ambush in September of 1779 of a small group under Lieutenant Boyd and Sergeant Parker on Groveland Hill by Butler's rangers and allied Indians, which upset Colonel Butler's plan to resist the Sullivan advance. There is an extract from Mary Jemison's narrative which describes the Indians' consternation at the approach of Sullivan. Included are a map of the route of Sullivan's army and the Groveland ambush and two photographs of monuments.

**288.** Douglas, Ephraim. "Letter of Ephraim Douglas to General William Irvine, 1783." *Pennsylvania Magazine of History and Biography,* vol. 37, no. 1 (1913): 126–127.

In a letter dated July 6, 1783, Douglas reports that the Indians will cease hostilities against the people of the United States provided the whites refrain from hostilities and confine themselves to one side of the river.

**289.** Douglas, Ephraim. "Indian Troubles in Western Pennsylvania: Letters from Ephraim Douglas to General James Irvine." *Pennsylvania Magazine of History and Biography,* vol. 1, no. 1 (1877): 44–49.

Two letters dated July 26 and August 4, 1782, discuss the vicious conflicts between Indians and whites in western Pennsylvania, detailing murders by Indians, captives taken, tortures, and the escape of an Indian from his white captor.

**290.** Downes, Randolph C. "George Morgan, Indian Agent Extraordinary, 1776–1779." *Pennsylvania History,* vol. 1, no. 4 (October 1934): 202–216.

Downes discusses George Morgan who arrived in Pittsburgh in 1776 to succeed Butler, the first American Indian agent, relating his theories on peaceful trade relations, belief in Indian promises of neutrality and concern for fair treatment. He then recounts how Morgan's policy of general pacification and neutrality was ruined, describes Morgan's growing contempt for the Indian policy which he argued would terminate in a general war, and discusses Morgan's final resignation in 1779 from public office.

**291.** Drake, Thomas E. "William Penn's Experiment in Race Relations." *Pennsylvania Magazine of History and Biography,* vol. 68, no. 4 (October 1944): 372–387.

Drake discusses the known facts of Penn's friendly relations with the Indians, compares his policy with that of his contemporaries, and examines its implications for the twentieth century world. He explains why Penn's Quaker policy failed to build a more enduring peace between the English and the Indians, noting, in conclusion, that Pennsylvania's Indian relations were peaceful as long as Penn and the Quakers were in command but deteriorated rapidly thereafter.

**292.** Druillettes, Gabriel. "Letter of Jesuit Missionary, Father Gabriel Druillettes, to John Winthrop, Governor of Connecticut." *Massachusetts Historical Society Proceedings,* ser. 1, vol. 11 (1869–1870): 152–154.

In a letter dated January 1651, Father Druillettes asks, on behalf of the governor of Quebec, that the Connecticut colony undertake a war against the Mohawks who have been attacking Christian Indians in Canada near Quebec and who intend to destroy Christian Indians allied to Canadian Indians living on the Kennebeck River.

**293.** Duane, William. [Letter of William Duane to Jefferson] *Massachusetts Historical Society Proceedings,* ser. 2, vol. 20 (1906–1907): 273–274.

In his letter dated January 7, 1802, Duane argues one way to deprive European nations of influence over Indians would be to allow each of the Indian nations a representative in Congress. He adds that a Canadian Englishman deprecates the idea.

**294.** Dubois, Cornelius. "Cornelius Dubois' Affidavit about Indian Captives." *New York Historical Society Collections for the Year 1935, Cadwallader Colden Papers,* vol. 9 (New York, 1937): 200–201.

**294** *(continued)*

In this communication dated August 27, 1765, Dubois recounts how some of his relatives were taken captive by Indians and how he heard his uncle, one of the captured, and father discuss the boundary between Esopus and the Highland Indians.

**295.** Dubois, Cornelius. "Cornelius Dubois' Deposition." *New York Historical Society Collections for the Year 1923, Cadwallader Colden Papers,* vol. 7 (New York, 1923): 52.

In this communication dated August 27, 1765, Dubois describes how several Dubois were taken captive by Esopus Indians, two Dubois children living with the Indians for so long that they only spoke "Indian" when they returned.

**296.** Dubois, Hendricus. "Hendricus Dubois' Deposition." *New York Historical Society Collections for the Year 1923, Cadwallader Colden Papers,* vol. 7 (New York, 1923): 54–55.

Dubois explains, on August 27, 1765, that when an Indian named Monhan came to his father's house fourteen or fifteen years ago, he overheard a conversation regarding the boundaries between the Minisink and Esopus Indians. He further describes the mutual boundary between the two nations and how the agreement was made concerning rights to a pond for beaver hunting.

**297.** Dudley, Paul. "A Short Account of the Names, Situation, Numbers, and Distances of the Five Indian Nations or Tribes in Alliance with the Government of New York and Under the Protection of the Crown of Great Britain." *Massachusetts Historical Society Collections,* ser. 2, vol. 8 (Boston, 1826): 243–245.

In this 1721 report, Dudley reports locations of the Five Nations and gives the numbers of their fighting men. He tells how the French are trying to seduce the Five Nations, particularly the Senecas, because they are the closest to those Indian tribes in alliance with the French.

**298.** Dudley, Thomas. "Indian Tribes on the Bays and Rivers." *New Hampshire Historical Society Collections,* vol. 4 (Concord, 1834): 225–226.

Governor Thomas Dudley cites the names of different Indian leaders, their locations on rivers or bays and the number of their followers.

**299.** Dunlap, A. R. "Early Delaware Land Records." *Delaware History,* vol. 6, no. 1 (March 1954): 27–30.

Dunlap gives the translated texts of three land records: the first, dated June 1, 1629, is the record of a purchase of land by Gillis Hossit from the Indians; the second, dated July 13, 1651, is a confirmation of a sale of land made on March 29, 1638, by Indians to a group of Swedish; and the third, dated July 16, 1651, is a confirmation by the Swedish that land has been sold to them at New Castle by Indians (land on which the Dutch were building).

**300.** Dunlap, A. R., and Weslager, C. A. "More Missing Evidence: Two Depositions by Early Swedish Settlers." *Pennsylvania Magazine of History and Biography*, vol. 91, no. 1 (January 1967): 35–45.

The writers discuss how two depositions, one dated January 11, 1683, and the other March 25, 1684, contain statements regarding Lord Baltimore and information about Swedish land purchases from the Indians. They test the accuracy of the depositions, whose texts are given, by comparing them with established historical records. They discuss how the depositions provide new information about the Lenape Indian names of places and persons.

**301.** Dunlap, A. R., and Weslager, C. A. "Names and Places in an Unrecorded Delaware Indian Deed." *Delaware History,* vol. 9, no. 3 (April 1961): 282–292. Illustrated.

The two writers give the text of an original, unrecorded document dated May 5, 1681, for the sale of land near Wilmington by Indian owners to Hans Petersen. The authors discuss other land purchases by Hans Petersen in the vicinity of Shellpot Creek, giving extracts from two documents, dated 1680, which tell of his purchase of land for a mill. They explain how the deed exhausted the Indians' right to land between Brandywine and Shellpot but tell how the mill was never built on the Brandywine because the proprietors of Pennsylvania protested. They discuss both Indian and non-Indian geographical and personal names in the deed. There are sketches of Petersen's purchase superimposed on a recent map, a copy of the sketched map on the deed, and the mill land purchase.

**302.** Dunlap, William. "Diary of William Dunlap" in "Letters of William Dunlap to his Wife, January 1–March 6, 1806." *New York Historical Society Collections for the Year 1930. Publication Fund* vol. 63 (New York, 1930): 388–393.

In an entry, dated February 25, 1806, Dunlap describes his visit with a chief of the "Rickeraw" Indians who has come from a distant part of Louisiana Territory as a deputy for his and other nations, accompanied by a French trader who acted as an interpreter. Dunlap describes the dress, face, and behavior of the Chief while he sat on a mattress scraping and cutting guinea-hen feathers. He tells how the Indian traced his entire route on a map, and how by sign language he described his country and his trip to Washington. Dunlap describes some of the signs the Indian used to communicate information, and theorizes about the intelligence of the "Rickeraws."

**303.** DuPonceau, Peter S., and Fisher, J. Francis. "A Memoir on the History of the Celebrated Treaty Made by William Penn with the Indians Under the Elm Tree at Shackamaxon, in the Year, 1682." *Historical Society of Pennsylvania Memoirs,* vol. 3, part 2 (Philadelphia, 1836): 141–203.

Drawing on all the evidence and testimonies they could find, the two authors discuss the details of Penn's treaty. They describe the Indians'

303 *(continued)*
veneration of Penn and of his full intention to be just with them. They review what historians have written about the subject of the treaty, beginning in 1708, and examine the speech of an Indian printed in a 1759 pamphlet that connects the treaty with the purchase of lands. They review all the land purchases in Pennsylvania and argue there is none which can be connected with the treaty under the elm tree. The appendix contains the text of a council held at the Indian town of Conestoga on May 26, 1728, in which Governor Gordon tells the Indians of the nine original covenants made between Penn and the Indians in the treaty of 1682.

**304.** Dwight, Joseph. "Two Letters from Colonel Joseph Dwight and Colonel Patridge to Governor Shirley." *Massachusetts Historical Society Collections,* ser. 1, vol. 5 (Boston, 1798): 119–122.
Dated February 1754, the letters discuss the necessity for a system of forts in the Six Nations Indian country, if these tribes are to be retained by the English. Forts would also benefit the fur trade, make the Indians dependent on the English, and be a line of communication from the English settlements to the Mississippi River, preventing the French from encircling all the English provinces in North America. The letters tell how the French are building forts in Indian country thereby gaining ascendancy over the Indians.

**305.** Eavenson, Howard N. "Who Made the 'Trader's Map'?" *Pennsylvania Magazine of History and Biography,* vol. 65, no. 4 (1941): 420–438. Illustrated.
Eavenson discusses a map that is untitled, undated, and without a maker's name; he speculates that John Pattin, an Indian trader who was seized by the French in 1750, is the map-maker. He includes texts of "A Journal or Account of the Capture of John Pattin," and "John Pattin's Account of Distances Computed by Indian Traders From Log's Town to Pipe Creek (or Pipe Hill)." By examining records, Eavenson argues that Pattin made the map because he was the only man who had traveled the routes, that he had made a record of his journeys, and a table of distances that agree exceedingly well with the map. An orthography of Indian place names and a reproduction of the map are included.

**306.** Easton, John. "Letter from John Easton to Governor Josiah Winslow of Plymouth Colony." *Massachusetts Historical Society Collections,* ser. 1, vol. 6 (Boston, 1806): 36.
In a letter dated March 14, 1675, Easton reports that Ninigret, sachem of the Niantics, wants the goods of twelve drowned Indians restored, according to Indian custom, to the appropriate sachems.

**307.** Echeverria, Durand. "The Iroquois Visit Rochambeau at Newport in 1780: Excerpts from the Unpublished Journal of the Comte de Charlus." *Rhode Island History*, vol. 11, no. 3 (July 1952): 73–81. Illustrated.

Echeverria describes how a delegation of Iroquois Indians came to pay a visit to the French forces under the command of General Rochambeau who was encamped at Newport in 1780. Extracts of the account of the visit by the Comte de Charlus, dated August–September 1780, tell how the French were trying to win back Indian allegiance by means of presents, describe how the Indians were dressed and how they danced, and how the French entertained the Indians. An illustration of the landing of the French army at Newport in 1780 is included.

**308.** "The Eckerlin Captivity and its Sangmeister Version." *Pennsylvania Magazine of History and Biography*, vol. 68, no. 3 (July 1944): 306–308.

The Eckerlin Captivity, described in *Chronicon Ephratense* in 1889, states how the Mohawks under the French command captured Eckerlin and his brother. The Sangmeister version is twice the length and richer in details regarding the Indians' treatment of their captives.

**309.** Edson, Walter H. "The Eries, the Nation of the Cat." *New York History*, vol. 16, no. 1 (January 1935): 36–44.

Edson discusses the Erie Nation and the use of the term "Nation of the Cat" applied by the French to these Indians. He discusses the meager record of the Eries—a tribe which ceased to exist as a nation around 1656—contained in *Jesuit Relations* from which he quotes.

**310.** Edwards, Daniel. "Report of the Committee of the General Assembly respecting Indian Affairs." *Connecticut Historical Society Collections*, vol. 10 (Hartford, 1907): 89–92.

In his communication dated May 22, 1743, Edwards reports on the status of land claims of certain Indians in Salisbury and Sharon and the desire of the Indians to be instructed both in schooling and preaching.

**311.** Edwards, Jonathan. "Doctor Edwards' Observations on the Mohegan Language." *Massachusetts Historical Society Collections*, ser. 2, vol. 10 (Boston, 1823, 1843): 81–98.

In his observations originally printed in 1788, the author first describes general analogies among the dialects of the language spoken by all Indians throughout New England, and then discusses specifically Mahican (Mohegan) grammar and its similarities to the Hebrew language. This is followed by "Notes by the Editor," pages 98–134, containing a comparison of Native vocabularies, as to numerals, labials, gender, case, number, relative pronouns, adjectives, degrees of comparison, the verb to be, verbs formed from nouns, tense, and abstract terms. This is followed in the same volume by a "Comparative Vocabulary of Various Dialects of the Lenape (or Delaware) Stock of

311 *(continued)*
North American Languages Together with a Specimen of the Winnebago (or Nipegon) Language," pages 135–154, and an "Index of Mohegan and Other Indian Words, Explained in Edwards' Observations," pages 155–160.

312. Edwards, Jonathan. "Letter Relating to the Indian School at Stockbridge." *Massachusetts Historical Society Collections,* ser. 1, vol. 10 (Boston, 1809): 142–154.

In his letter, dated August 31, 1751, Reverend Edwards discusses the Mohawks who accepted a proposal to have their children instructed at Stockbridge. He argues that the best way to secure the Indians as British allies, and alienate them from the French, is to instruct them in the Protestant religion. He explains that the major difficulty in teaching the Indian children is to help them learn English, so he suggests that English children be brought to the school or Indian children sent to live in English homes. A note explains that although Edwards' proposal to educate Mohawk children was not fully carried out, the Indian school did serve the Stockbridge Indians.

313. Egremont, Earl of. "Earl of Egremont to Thomas Fitch." *Connecticut Historical Society Collections,* vol. 18 (Hartford, 1920): 224–225.

In his communication, dated January 27, 1763, the Earl of Egremont explains that the king is displeased that some Connecticut whites, under pretense of purchase, insist on settling near the Susquehanna River contrary to the wishes of the Indians; this may provoke an Indian war. The Earl asks Governor Fitch to prevent the settlement.

314. Eliot, John. "Account of Indian Churches in New England." *Massachusetts Historical Society Collections,* ser. 1, vol. 10 (Boston, 1809): 124–129.

In his account, dated June 22, 1673, Eliot describes the present state of gospel work among the Indians, detailing the number of churches involved, church officers, pastors who administer the sacraments, the discipline in churches, the manner of admission of new converts, church care for children, schools that exist, and the converted Indians' opinion of the English.

315. Eliot, John. "Historical Account of John Eliot, the First Minister of the Church in Roxbury." *Massachusetts Historical Society Collections,* ser. 1, vol. 8 (Boston, 1802): 5–35.

In this biography of Eliot, who began preaching to Indians in October 1646, there are remarks on how he learned the Indians' language, on his belief in "civilizing" Indians before converting them, on the "praying" towns he set up, and on the laws the sachems agreed to follow. There is information about the opposition Eliot met from certain Indians, on his work at the Indian town of Natick which was built in 1651, and on his defense of "praying" Indians during King Philip's War in 1675–1676. The biography is followed by a list of Eliot's publications. [*See* "Memoir Towards a Character of Reverend John

Eliot." *Massachusetts Historical Society Collections*, ser. 2, vol. 1 (Boston, 1883): 211–248.]

**316.** Eliot, John. "The Indian Grammar Begun: or, An Essay to Bring the Indian Language into Rules." *Massachusetts Historical Society Collections*, ser. 2, vol. 9 (Boston, 1832): 243–312.

In his grammar, published in 1666, Eliot deals with the English rules for making words and ordering them in speech. He considers pronouns, nouns, "adnouns," verbs, adverbs, interjections, rules for and examples of constructing words, and he notes the differences between English and Indian grammars. Eliot's work is followed by Peter S. DuPonceau's "Notes and Observations on Eliot's Indian Grammar," on pages i–xxix. DuPonceau offers insight into the nature, forms, and construction of the Massachusetts language. He remarks on the contents of Eliot's grammar under the following topic headings: Alphabet, Noun Substantive, the Article, Adjectives, Pronouns, and Verbs. This is followed by "Supplementary Observations," on pages xxx–xlvii, by an editor who focuses on the verb "to be" and numerals. There is an index of Indian words in Eliot's grammar including select words from his translation of the Bible, on pages xlviii–liv.

**317.** Eliot, John. "Instructions from the Church at Natick to William Anthony." *Massachusetts Historical Society Collections*, ser. 1, vol. 6 (Boston, 1800): 201–203.

In August 1671, Eliot states he is sending two brethren with a message for the Missogkonnog (Nipmuck) Indians, presently quarreling with the people of Plymouth, the emissaries urging that the whole matter should be referred to the judgment of the Massachusetts government. Eliot beseeches both the Massachusetts Indians and the governor of Massachusetts to make peace, not war.

**318.** Eliot, John. "Letters of John Eliot." *Massachusetts Historical Society Proceedings*, ser. 1, vol. 17 (1879–1880): 245–253.

In letters, dated August 8, 1657 to April 17, 1681, Eliot writes the London officers of the Society for Propagating the Gospel Among Indians in America about the state of the "praying" Indians on Martha's Vineyard, Nantucket, Elizabeth Islands, Plymouth, Mashpee, Natick, Nipmuck, etc. He explains that the Indians are suffering, are in danger from other Indians, and that they need Bibles.

**319.** Eliot, John. "Letters of Reverend John Eliot." *Massachusetts Historical Society Collections*, ser 1, vol. 3 (Boston, 1794): 177–188.

Dated September 30, 1670 to April 22, 1684, Eliot's letters discuss "praying" Indians, the attacks of other Indians on them, the need for Bibles in the Indian language, and describes the religious ways of the "praying" Indians.

**320.** Eliot, Samuel A. "From Scalping Knife to Can Opener: A Sketch of the Origins and Work of an Old Massachusetts Society." *Massachusetts Historical Society Proceedings*, vol. 66 (1936–1941): 107–125.

The author discusses the work of the Society for Propagating the Gospel Among the Indians and Others in North America, focusing on the place and the people who organized it in 1787. He gives brief biographies of some of the twenty-one original incorporators of the Society, historical background of other missions to Indians, beginning with John Eliot in 1649, and theorizes about the beginning of the Society at its first meeting on December 7, 1787. Eliot concludes with mention of the accomplishment since 1911 of the Society which has been wholly devoted to Indian work.

**321.** Ellis, Mary W. "John Strong: A Pioneer of Addison, Vermont." *Vermont Quarterly*, n.s., vol. 14, no. 2 (April 1946): 62–69.

This essay tells of the trials of a Vermont pioneer family in establishing a home at Addison, focusing in particular on the "savagery" of Indians by relating a few alarming encounters between the John Strong family and the Indians from 1766 to 1776.

**322.** Elmer, Ebenezer. "Extracts from a Journal Kept by Doctor Ebenezer Elmer During General Sullivan's Expedition." *New Jersey Historical Society Proceedings*, vol. 2, no. 1 (1846): 43–50.

The extracts from Elmer's journal, dated June 18 to August 12, 1779, are important because they either contain additional incidents or matters or confirm the material in the journal of Lieutenant Barton.

**323.** Elmer, Ebenezer. "Journal Kept During an Expedition to Canada in 1776." *New Jersey Historical Society Proceedings*, vol. 2, no. 3 (1847): 95–146.

Elmer recounts events of New Jersey troops in their struggle against the English from March until July of 1776. Extracts from a journal kept by Captain Bloomfield, the commander of Elmer's company, are included. The entries dated May 20 to May 22, 1776, discuss relations with the Iroquois tribes; the culture and behavior of Iroquois allied with the Americans or the English and battles with the Indians. [Continued in *New Jersey Historical Society Proceedings*, vol. 2, no. 4 (1847): 150–194, for the dates July 17 to September 7, 1776. On July 23, 1776, there is a lengthy entry about the customs and manners of the Six Nations Indians attending a treaty conference at German Flats (pages 157–161). Continued in *New Jersey Historical Society Proceedings*, vol. 3, no. 1 (1848): 21–56, dated September 8, 1776, to January 23, 1777, and *New Jersey Historical Society Proceedings*, vol. 3, no. 2 (1848): 90–102, dated January 24 to November 3, 1777.]

**324.** Ely, William D. "Report on Indian Names in Rhode Island." *Rhode Island Historical Society Proceedings, 1890–1891.* (Providence, 1891): 71–79.

Ely reports that the difficulties which have prevented uniformity in spelling and pronunciation of Indian languages are phonetic and have a polysynthetic nature. He lists the principal rules to guide one in fixing the proper form and mode of spelling of Indian names.

**325.** Ely, William D. "Roger Williams' *Key:* Beanes vs Barnes." *Rhode Island Historical Society Publications,* n.s., vol. 2 (Providence, 1894): 189–196.

Ely discusses why beans, a great vegetable product of Indians, have been omitted from Williams' list of vegetables in his *Key.* Part of the discussion centers on the hypothesis that there was a misprint in the *Key,* i.e., "Barnes" for "Beanes," and considers the objections to this hypothesis. There is also a lengthy philological discussion.

**326.** "Eskimo Influence in Vermont." *Vermont Quarterly,* n.s., vol. 21, no. 3 (July 1953): 257.

This brief note tells how a "semilunar knife" found near Vergennes, Vermont, indicated an Eskimo influence on the area. An 1881 article is cited as explainng the pattern of semilunar knives derived from Eskimos with whom the northern Algonquians were frequently in contact.

**327.** Ettwein, John. "Letter of Bishop Ettwein." *Pennsylvania Magazine of History and Biography,* vol. 39, no. 2 (1915): 219.

In an undated letter to the Honorable Arthur Lee, Bishop Ettwein discusses the Delawares' knowledge of whales. Their forefathers, he claims, lived far eastwards where they saw these animals and had a word for them which meant "water spout."

**328.** Ettwein, John. "Reverend John Ettwein's Notes of Travel from the North Branch of the Susquehanna to the Beaver River, Pennsylvania, 1772." *Pennsylvania Magazine of History and Biography,* vol. 25, no. 2 (1901): 208–219.

In entries, dated June 11 to August 1, 1772, Reverend Ettwein recounts the overland travels of the Indian converts from the abandoned Moravian Indian town, Wyalusing, who moved to Friedenstadt on the Beaver River. The notes describe the physical characteristics of Pennsylvania and the day-to-day life of Indian converts along the route. The notes are footnoted with geographical place-name information.

**329.** Evans, Griffith. "Journal of Griffith Evans, Clerk to the Pennsylvania Commissioners at Fort Stanwix and Fort McIntosh, 1784–1785." *Pennsylvania Magazine of History and Biography,* vol. 65, no. 2 (April 1941): 204–233.

The writer of this journal was in the position to observe the consummation of treaties with the Six Nations and the western nations in 1784, which marked the beginnings of a federal Indian policy in the United States. In his entries, dated September 22, 1784, to January 27, 1785, Evans describes councils with Indians and their oratories, comments on Indian ways of conveying ideas, playing games, and dressing, and discusses ways in which goods were distributed to tribes.

**330.** Evans, Samuel. "Letter from Reverend Thomas Barton regarding the Farm of the Conestoga Indians." *Pennsylvania Magazine of History and Biography,* vol. 4, no. 1 (1880): 119–120.

Evans supplies the text of a letter dated December 18, 1770, in which Reverend Barton describes the events surrounding the history of a 500-acre farm originally settled as a town by the Conestogas, who were cruelly dispossessed by the Paxton people. After some of their group were murdered, and the town burned, the remaining Conestogas were removed to Lancaster for safety.

**331.** Ewers, John C. "An Anthropologist Looks at Early Pictures of North American Indians." *New York Historical Society Quarterly,* vol. 33, no. 4 (October 1949): 223–234. Illustrated.

Ewers briefly discusses the most common differences in facial appearance between Indians and whites and then, from an anthropologist's viewpoint, evaluates the early pictures, created by those artists who had historically proven, firsthand knowledge of Indians (Jacques Le Moyne de Morgues, John White, and A. De Batz). Ewers explains how early artists concentrated on the material culture of Indians rather than on their facial characteristics, a technique which has benefited ethnologists, but not physical anthropologists. He discusses several early nineteenth century American artists who drew portraits of Indians, including Charles Bird King, George Catlin, Karl Bodmer, Paul Kane, and John Mix Stanley, and he provides seven illustrations.

**332.** Ewers, John C. "Three Ornaments Worn by Upper Missouri Indians A Century and a Quarter Ago." *New York Historical Society Quarterly Bulletin,* vol. 51, no. 1 (January 1957): 25–33. Illustrated.

Ewers discusses three types of ornaments worn by Indian men of the upper Missouri River that are ingenious examples of Indians combining trade articles with materials obtained in their own country. These ornaments are recorded in the portraits of Indian men by George Catlin and Carl Bodmer (1831–1834). Ewers describes manufacture and tribal distribution of hair pipes, two-banded beaded neck chokers and beaded hair bows and he discusses trade beads furnished in considerable quantities to upper Mississippi tribes by American traders in the 1830s. There are portraits by Catlin and Bodmer and pictures of the trade articles: dentalium shells, hair pipes fashioned from West Indian conch shells by New Jersey wampum makers, brass tubes, and glass beads from Venice, Italy.

**333.** Fadden, Ray (Aren Akwaks). "The Visions of Handsome Lake." *Pennsylvania History,* vol. 22, no. 4 (October 1955): 341–358. Illustrated.

Handsome Lake, a Seneca, restored self-respect to the Iroquois by way of visions he received in 1799 and 1800 when he was on the

Cornplanter Tract, located on the Allegheny. During the visions, messengers from the Creator presented him with the Good Word which he in turn was to convey to his fellow Senecans. Mr. Fadden, a Mohawk, has told the story of Handsome Lake in symbolic patterns of ancient Indian pictographs through the medium of colored beads like the wampum made of shell beads by his ancestors. He translates his wampum, symbol by symbol, for readers of this story. The version presented is an abridgement of a larger narrative. There are photographs of Fadden's Bead Record of Handsome Lake and wampum belts and drawings that illustrate the story.

334. Farmer, John. "Note on the Penacook Indians." *New Hampshire Historical Society Collections,* vol. 1 (Concord, 1824): 218–227.

Farmer discusses the Penacooks who belong to the Pawtucket Nation and who lived in present-day Concord and the surrounding country. He describes Passaconaway, as well as other sachems of the Penacooks, and their relationships with the English colonists. He includes the text of two letters from 1689 in which the writers discuss the Penacook plot against the inhabitants of Dover. Farmer explains that the Penacooks were not heard of as a separate tribe after August of 1703.

335. Farmington Indians. "Farmington Indians to the General Assembly." *Connecticut Historical Society Collections,* vol. 21 (Hartford, 1924): 204–205. Illustrated.

In a petition to the Connecticut General Assembly, dated May 9, 1672, the Farmington Indians present their grievance that as certain meadowlands of Farmington still belong to them, they should not be forced from the lands. The Indians say that the English occupying the lands should prove they have title. There is a sketch of the meadowlands that illustrates the Indians' claim against the English.

336. Fenton, William N. "The Hyde de Neuville Portraits of New York Savages in 1807–1808." *New York Historical Society Quarterly Bulletin,* vol. 38, no. 2 (April 1954): 119–137. Illustrated.

Fenton briefly reviews the history of the Six Nations after the American Revolution and during the first decade of the new federal government. He examines the events leading to the Pickering Treaty of 1794 with the Six Nations, discusses the state of the Oneidas who were divided into factions around 1808, and tells of the disorganized Iroquois culture in general. He gives estimates of the Six Nations population and other background information to explain why the French refugees found "the noble savage of [their] expectations had become by 1807 rather disenchanting." Fenton discusses the Baron Hyde de Neuville who, with his artist wife, spent nearly two years in upstate New York among the Six Nations, and describes the water colors and pencil sketches of Madame De Neuville and comments on their correspondence regarding the Indians. Fenton details the Hyde de Neuville collection at the New York Historical Society, comments

336 *(continued)*
on the traits of Indian culture and the white influence, and considers the value of these Indian portraits as a record of the Indian scene early in the nineteenth century. There are nine portraits by the Baroness and one painting of Red Jacket by Robert W. Weir painted in 1828.

337. Ferguson, Alice L. L. "The Susquehannock Fort on the Piscataway Creek." *Maryland Historical Magazine*, vol. 36, no. 1 (March 1941): 1–9. Illustrated.

Over the objection of Maryland officials, a refugee band of Susquehannocks settled near Piscataway Fort in 1674. In September 1675, the fort was attacked and the Indians escaped to Virginia, killed Bacon's overseer and, the author argues, caused Bacon's Rebellion. The rest of the article deals with the excavation of the Piscataway Fort. There are drawings of the area surrounding the fort and a map of the fort of Piscataway Creek.

338. Fessenden, Thomas. "Letter from Reverend Thomas Fessenden of Walpole to Reverend Jeremy Belknap of Boston." *New Hampshire Historical Society Collections*, vol. 4 (Concord, 1834): 290–292.

In a letter, dated January 22, 1790, Fessenden describes the 1755 murders of Twitchell and Flint by Indians, the fight between Colonel Bellows and a group of Indians, and the Indians' unsuccessful assault on the garrisoned house of Mr. John Kilburn. [*See:* "Attack of the Indians at Walpole in 1755." *New Hampshire Historical Society Collections*, vol. 2 (Concord, 1827): 49–58.]

339. Fisher, John S. "Colonel John Armstrong's Expedition Against Kittanning." *Pennsylvania Magazine of History and Biography*, vol. 51, no. 1 (1927): 1–14.

Fisher surveys the English-French rivalry in North America, briefly outlines the helpless state of the Pennsylvania government and its lack of defenses, looks at the bloody struggles between Indians and whites on the frontier, describes Indian tortures, and considers Governor Morris's proclamation of April 14, 1756, offering rewards for Indian prisoners and Indian scalps. He explains why the town of Kittanning was the principal point from which the Indian war parties left, and describes how Colonel Armstrong had a successful expedition against Kittanning in September of 1756 and killed Captain Jacobs, a Delaware chieftain.

340. Fiske, Nathan. "An Historical Account of the Settlement of Brookfield in the County of Worcester, and its Distresses During the Indian War." *Massachusetts Historical Society Collections*, ser. 1, vol. Í (Boston, 1792): 257–264.

In this account, written in 1775, Fiske discusses the Quabaugs, the original Indian inhabitants of Brookfield; the English settlements of the town; the 1675 burning of the town by Indians; Indian raids in Brookfield during Queen Anne's War; and the last Indian raid on Brookfield in 1710. [*See* the appendix, pages 269–270, for a deed, dated November 10, 1665, for the purchase of lands at Quabaug, now called Brookfield, from an Indian named "Shattoockquis."]

**341.** Fitch, James. "Reverend James Fitch's Suggestions Regarding Uncas." *Connecticut Historical Society Collections,* vol. 21 (Hartford, 1924): 257–259.

Fitch discusses the untrustworthiness of Uncas, citing his collusion with Philip, even though Uncas was helpful to the English. He claims that Uncas took many Indians into his town during the war contrary to English order, that he schemes to prevent his own removal so he can be settled under the English, that he allowed some of his people to escape, and that he attempts to dissuade his people from becoming Christians.

**342.** Fitch, Thomas. "The Fitch Papers: Correspondence and Documents During Thomas Fitch's Governorship of the Colony of Connecticut, 1745–1766." Vol. 1: *Connecticut Historical Society Collections,* vol. 17 (Hartford, 1918); Vol. 2: *Connecticut Historical Society Collections,* vol. 18 (Hartford, 1920).

Indians are mentioned briefly throughout both volumes. The first volume covers May 1754 to December 1758 and the second volume covers January 1759 to May 1766.

**343.** Five Nations. "The Five Nations Answer Propositions of Governor George Clinton." *New York Historical Society Collections for the Year 1919, Cadwallader Colden Papers,* vol. 3 (New York, 1920): 173–177.

The Five Nations reaffirm their alliance to the British on October 12, 1754, informing Clinton that they will "take up the hatchet" against the French and allied Indians. The Five Nations insist, however, that they need two months to inform their allies, the French Indians, that they demand satisfaction for wrongs done to the British, and if the French Indians refuse to give satisfaction, then the Five Nations are ready to go to war. The Five Nations also agree to go to war immediately if the French commit further hostilities, and they conclude by requesting that prices be lowered for trade goods and ammunition. The Governor answers that the price of goods depends on scarcity and plenty and that war goods are scarce and consequently expensive.

**344.** Flick, A. C. "New Sources on the Sullivan-Clinton Campaign in 1779." *New York State Historical Association Quarterly Journal,* vol. 10, no. 3 (July 1929): 185–224. Illustrated.

Flick resurveys the Sullivan Expedition and argues that it should be renamed the "Sullivan-Clinton Campaign." He discusses the contemporary criticisms leveled at the campaign, repeats the old interpretation of the campaign as an act of revenge against the Indians for their "outrages" committed against border settlements, and argues that denouncing the expedition as a punishment to misguided Iroquois is a narrow view. He summarizes the contents of new sources of information that enable historians to reinterpret the causes, characters, purposes, and results of the campaign. He argues that the campaign

**344** (*continued*)

had a double purpose: to force the Six Nations away from the American frontiers and to weaken the commissary departments of England. The Six Nations country was an important source of food for the British army as well as for the Loyalists. Flick also points out that the campaign was aimed at seizing Canada and was intended to stake claims that would secure western Pennsylvania, New York, and territories south of the Great Lakes for the United States. He looks at Washington's preliminary plans, summarizes information given to Washington by four military officers, and supplies the texts of letters which demonstrate the Indian-Tory side of the campaign. There is a photograph of one of the thirty-five markers placed along the routes of the march of the armies and pictures of Sullivan, Clinton, and Washington. [*See* "New Sources on the Sullivan-Clinton Campaign in 1779." *New York State Historical Association Quarterly Journal*, vol. 10, no. 4 (October 1929): 265–317. Illustrated. This section includes the texts of letters of the Indian-Tory side of the question, some new source materials on the American side, and a few letters and reports printed since the 1887 publication of *"General John Sullivan's Indian Expedition"* of 1779 by the state of New York. Flick concludes by giving numbers of the military forces on each side, the units in the main army under Generals Sullivan and Clinton, and both the immediate and remote results of the Sullivan-Clinton Campaign. There is a map of the route of the armies of Sullivan, Clinton, and Brodhead.]

**345.** Follette, Clara E. "The Iroquoian Claim on Vermont." *Vermont History*, vol. 23, no. 1 (January 1955): 54–55.

Follette lists three reasons given by the Vermont legislature for refusing Iroquois claims to Vermont lands made between 1798 and 1953. She also gives four opinions of the Vermont legislature as to why they refused the Iroquois petition of 1953.

**346.** Folsom, Joseph Filford. "The Going of Indian John." *New Jersey Historical Society Proceedings*, ser. 3, vol. 10, no. 2 (April 1915): 47–48.

Folsom's poem about Indian John was prompted by a statement he found in Reverend Charles T. Berry's sketch of Caldwell that the last Indians left the boundaries of Horse Neck (Caldwell) in 1761.

**347.** Folsom, Nathaniel. "Fight at Lake George." *Massachusetts Historical Society Proceedings*, ser. 2, vol. 18 (1903–1904): 317–325.

In a letter dated March 27, 1756, Captain Folsom narrates from memory a skirmish near Lake George with French and allied Indians on September 8, 1755. There is additional commentary regarding the fighting at Lake George.

**348.** Forbes, John. "Letters of General John Forbes, 1758." *Pennsylvania Magazine of History and Biography*, vol. 33, no. 1 (1909): 86–98.

General John Forbes led the army that captured Fort Duquesne in

1758. His letters include information on Indians allied to the British
and describe movements of the enemy Indians. [*See:* "Selections from
the Military Correspondence of Colonel Henry Bouquet." *Pennsylvania Magazine of History and Biography*, vol. 32, no. 4 (1908): 433–458.]

**349.** "Fort Dummer and the Conference with the Scatacook Indians." *Massachusetts Historical Society Proceedings*, ser. 2, vol. 6 (1890–1891): 359–381.

These pages include a number of original papers relating to the
construction and first occupancy of Fort Dummer. There are letters
and a muster roll, which shows efforts made to secure recruits from
the Mohawks and other western Indians, and documents regarding
the [June?] 6, 1728 conference held at Fort Dummer, focused on
Indians procuring large quantities of rum, on the murder of English
people by Indians, and on questions of peace and war between Indians and whites.

**350.** Foulke, William Parker. "Notes Respecting the Indians of Lancaster
County, Pennsylvania." *Historical Society of Pennsylvania Memoirs*, vol. 4, part 2
(Philadelphia, 1850): 188–219.

Foulke discusses the history of Indians within Lancaster County beginning with the first account of three villages located on Captain
Smith's map in 1608. He explains how for a period between 1608 and
1680, the portion of Lancaster County lying on the Susquehanna was
inhabited by Susquehannocks who were eventually overthrown and
absorbed by the Five Nations. He recounts how, by the mid-
eighteenth century, the Shawnees who had settled near the Conestogas in 1698 were removed from Lancaster County. Foulke also
discusses other Indians such as the Conoys and Nanticokes who
moved to Lancaster County.

**351.** Franklin, Benjamin. [Letter] *New York Historical Society Collections for the
Year 1920, Cadwallader Colden Papers*, vol. 4 (New York, 1921): 430–431.

In his letter, dated December 6, 1753, Franklin expresses hopes that
Indian trade will be regulated by the government so that goods can be
furnished to the Indians at a cheap rate without profit, as is done in
Massachusetts, and so that France can be vastly undersold and the
Indians allied to the English interest.

**352.** Freeman, John. [Letter to Thomas Hinckley, Governor of New
Plymouth] *Massachusetts Historical Society Collections*, ser. 4, vol. 5 (Boston, 1861):
131–132.

In his letter, dated March 20, 1685, Freeman describes which Indians
frequent meetings on Sabbath days. He complains that the English
ministers are paid too much for the meager service they provide
Indians and discusses the inequity of wages between Indians and
English ministers.

**353.** Freeman, Nathaniel. "Indian Places Within or Near the County of Barnstable." *Massachusetts Historical Society Collections,* ser. 1, vol. 1 (Boston, 1792): 230–232.

In a letter, dated September 23, 1792, Freeman discusses the meanings of Indian place names around Barnstable County.

**354.** Frost, Charles, and Hooke, Francis. [Letter to the Governor and Council of Massachusetts] *Massachusetts Historical Society Collections,* vol. 80 (Boston, 1972): 195–198.

In their account, dated March 25, 1690, Frost and Hooke describe a French and Indian attack on Salmon Falls in which people were killed or captured, property destroyed, and other losses incurred in fighting off the Indians. There is a list of persons captured and slain at Salmon Falls.

**355.** Frothingham, O. B. "Memoir of Francis Parkman, LL.D." *Massachusetts Historical Society Proceedings,* ser. 2, vol. 8 (1892–1894): 520–562.

In this memoir, the writer considers Francis Parkman's character, religious and political views, and his opinions about the character of American Indians. He also comments on Parkman's historical methods.

**356.** Gage, Thomas. [Letter to Cadwallader Colden] *New York Historical Society Collections for the Year 1922, Cadwallader Colden Papers,* vol. 6 (New York, 1923): 394–395.

On December 7, 1764, General Thomas Gage reports to Colden that the Shawnees, Delawares, and other tribes on the Ohio have been defeated by Colonel Bouquet and that a general peace has been made with these nations. He reports that Bouquet's troops have forced the Indians to give up all their prisoners, including the children born of white women, and that the troops have taken over 200 Indian prisoners including a number of chiefs.

**357.** Gage, Thomas. [Letter to Cadwallader Colden] *New York Historical Society Collections for the Year 1923, Cadwallader Colden Papers,* vol. 7 (New York, 1923): 34.

In his letter, dated May 26, 1765, General Gage tells Colden that the Shawnees and other tribes have brought forty or more prisoners to Fort Pitt; some of these no longer speak English because they have lived with Indians for a long time. Gage also explains that the Delawares are internally divided and that some insist that they will only deal with Quakers.

**358.** Gage, Thomas. [Letter to Sir William Johnson] *Pennsylvania Magazine of History and Biography*, vol. 35, no. 4 (1911): 373–375.

In his letter, dated October 14, 1764, Gage writes about the need for a general system of managing Indian affairs and suggests that trade needs to be regulated as well as the treatment of Indians at posts and the quantity and nature of presents to be furnished to them.

**359.** Garden, Alexander. [Letter to Cadwallader Colden] *New York Historical Society Collections for the Year 1921, Cadwallader Colden Papers*, vol. 5 (New York, 1923): 361–363.

In his letter, dated October 26, 1760, Garden tells Colden about the troubles with Cherokee Indians in South Carolina, the success of Colonel Montgomery in destroying their towns and defeating them, and Colonel Bird's success in threatening the Cherokees into making peace with South Carolina. Garden also discusses how the garrison of Fort London was starved out and eventually surrendered to the Indians who put about forty people to death and enslaved the others.

**360.** Gardiner, John Lyon. "Sketch of the Montock Tribe of Indians in *Gardiner's East Hampton; Notes and Observations on the Town of East Hampton at the East End of Long Island,* Written by John Lyon Gardiner of the Isle of Wight in April, 1798. . . ." *New York Historical Society Collections for the Year 1869. Publication Fund* vol. 2 (New York, 1870): 257–259.

Gardiner briefly discusses the Montauk Tribe, its sachems, language, and war against the Block Island Indians who were allied with the Narragansetts. On pages 261–264, Gardiner discusses an epidemic which killed a large number of Indians on the east end of Long Island. He also discusses the Indians of Long Island who sold the island.

**361.** Gardiner, Lion. "His Relation of the Pequot Warres." *Massachusetts Historical Society Collections*, ser. 3, vol. 3 (Boston, 1833): 131–160.

Gardiner, an engineer who erected a fort at Saybrook, Connecticut, and commanded it when Captain John Mason conquered the Pequots, gives his account, which was originally published in 1660, of the Pequot wars. [*See* Alexander Gardiner, "Lion Gardiner." *Massachusetts Historical Society Collections*, ser. 3, vol. 10 (Boston, 1849): 173–185. Gardiner corrects some misinformation about Lion Gardiner that is published in the biographical sketch of him that accompanies the "Relation."]

**362.** Gifford, Archer. "The Aborigines of New Jersey." *New Jersey Historical Society Proceedings*, vol. 4, no. 4 (1850): 163–198.

From a mid-nineteenth century point of view, Gifford discusses theories about the origins of Indian tribes and how Indians became inhabitants of North America. He describes characteristics of tribes that are located in New Jersey and, relying on early accounts of the Delawares, he describes their culture and land transactions. He tells

**362** *(continued)*

how Indian titles to all lands were conveyed and how most Indians left New Jersey by 1758 except for the Brotherton Indians who left later in 1801 to live with the Oneidas. He concludes by offering suggestions to remedy the generations of injustice done to Indians by forcible relocation. In his opinion the Indians should be allowed a government of their own so they can "improve" and become "civilized."

**363.** Gillingham, Harrold E. "Indian and Military Medals from Colonial Times to Date." *Pennsylvania Magazine of History and Biography,* vol. 51, no. 2 (1927): 97–110. Illustrated.

The author describes personal medals and decorations. He discusses the colonial medals given to Indians, including the Patomeck Medal that was the earliest Indian medal of the thirteen colonies of which there is record and that was given in Virginia around 1661. He discusses the medals given to the Six Nations by New York and Pennsylvania, the medal given to Colonel John Armstrong and his officers for their successful 1756 expedition against the Delawares, the medal struck for the Friendly Association for Preserving Peace with the Indians in 1757, and medals presented to chiefs for faithful service to King George III. He discusses French medals given to friendly Indians of Canada and the western territory of America, medals issued after the Declaration of Independence, the Washington Indian Peace Medals, and those Indian peace medals of other presidents from Jefferson to Garfield. The Kittanning and Washington Peace Medals are illustrated.

**364.** Gillingham, Harrold E. "Indian Silver Ornaments." *Pennsylvania Magazine of History and Biography,* vol. 58, no. 2 (1934): 97–126. Illustrated.

Gillingham cites the earliest records from the 1750s to document the silver ornaments given to Indians, mentioning the fact that few bear the mark of the maker. He discusses the presentation of silver medals and ornaments to Indians by government authorities and others such as the Friendly Association, cites the bills of silversmiths who made Indian ornaments before the Revolution, and gives extracts from account books of stores in Pennsylvania with entries on silver articles from 1761 to the Revolution. He discusses oval silver medals given during the presidency of Washington. There are illustrations of oval medals, medals of the Friendly Association, and a certificate that was presented by Sir William Johnson in 1770.

**365.** Gillingham, Harrold E. "Indian Trade Silver Ornaments Made by Joseph Richardson, Jr." *Pennsylvania Magazine of History and Biography,* vol. 67, no. 4 (October 1943): 83–91. Illustrated.

Gillingham discusses Joseph Richardson, a Philadelphia silversmith who made over 4,400 separate pieces of trade silver ornaments between 1796 and 1798 for the U.S. trading stations in Indian Territory, describing the only surviving piece of such trade silver. A summary of Richardson's biography, quotes from entries in his daybook, and the text of a bill for the largest order he recorded (1,926 pieces of silver) are included. There are photographs of silver medals.

**366.** Glover, Waldo F. "Ancient Indian Camp Site in Groton." *Vermont Historical Society News and Notes,* vol. 9, no. 4 (December 1957): 33–34.

Glover offers new information on the location of an Indian campsite in Groton and describes where relics have been found nearby.

**367.** Glover, Waldo F. "Squaw-Mang: A Green Mountain River." *Vermont Quarterly,* n.s., vol. 18, no. 2 (April 1950): 51–63. Illustrated.

Glover identifies the Indian "Squaw-mang River" and traces the route of what was probably the first company of English captives to be taken over the Vermont trails to Canada. He begins with the first mention of the Squaw-mang in the captivity narrative of Quinten Stockwell of Deerfield in 1677 and quotes from the narrative for clues as to the approximate course of the trail over which Stockwell was led from Squaw-mang to Lake Champlain. He compares the information in Stockwell's story with stories of other journeys over the same course and concludes that the Squaw-mang is the Wells River. There are some notes about Stockwell's life and a map of Stockwell's and Captain Benjamin Wright's routes.

**368.** Godfrey, John E. "Ancient Penobscot." *Maine Historical Society Collections,* ser. 1, vol. 7 (Portland, 1876): 3–22.

Godfrey discusses the variant spellings of Penobscot and suggests that the name in its several forms was either applied to different camping grounds or may have been applied to the whole territory. He discusses the locations of villages of Abenakis based on historical sources such as the journal of Daniel Little, a missionary, and other documents regarding an Indian conference in 1786. Godfrey discusses two settlements of land by the Indians in 1796 and 1818 in exchange for such items as cloth, ammunition, corn, hats, rum, salt, ribbons, pipes, and kettles, etc., which released the Indians' interest in the territory except for four towns and islands. He tells how after separating from Massachusetts in 1820, Maine assumed obligations for the Indians. [*See* the note on pages 103–105 for a brief discussion of the Penobscots on Oldtown Island around 1876 and the state of their education.]

**369.** Godfrey, John E. "Bashaba and the Tarratines." *Maine Historical Society Collections,* ser. 1, vol. 7 (Portland, 1876): 93–105.

Godfrey quotes from a number of seventeenth century sources and argues that the word "Bashaba" was the name of a powerful person in the Penobscot rather than the title of a chief.

**370.** Godfrey, John E. "Jean Vincent, Baron de Saint Castin." *Maine Historical Society Collections,* ser. 1, vol. 7 (Portland, 1876): 39–72.

Godfrey discusses the life of St. Castin who lived among the Tarratine Tribe, his marriage to the daughter of Madokawando around 1667,

**370** *(continued)*

his trade and influence with the Indians, and his role in the English-French rivalry in New England. There is a brief discussion of his life after 1687. [*See* Godfrey's article entitled "Castine the Younger," pages 75–92, about Anselm, one of the sons of St. Castin who is confused with his father by some historians. He tells of Anselm's role at the 1707 siege of Port Royal where he had direct command of a detachment of Indians.]

**371.** Goffe, Captain. "Captain Goffe's Letter to Governor Benning Wentworth." *New Hampshire Historical Society Collections,* vol. 4 (Concord, 1834): 215–216.

Dated May 5, 1746, Goffe's letter tells of Indian depredations on the frontier and of the needs of the soldiers.

**372.** Goldthwart, Joseph. Letter. *Massachusetts Historical Society Collections,* ser. 1, vol. 10 (Boston, 1809): 121–122.

In a letter, dated July of 1764, Goldthwart lists the different Indian nations that met with Sir William Johnson at Niagara to make peace; he estimates their number at 1,942.

**373.** Gomez, Isabel. "Rogers' Rangers at St. Francis." *Vermont History,* vol. 27, no. 4 (October 1959): 313–318. Bibliography.

Gomez discusses the conflict between the Abenakis and Five Nations and the battles between French-Canadian and English-American settlers, each with their Indian allies. She explains how Vermont was a buffer between the two factions and a battleground and pathway for raids by the French and Abenakis on Massachusetts and New York. She discusses Robert Rogers and his rangers who, in October 1759, destroyed the village of the St. Francis Indians, who had been attacking English settlers. There are notes and a bibliography.

**374.** Goodwin, William B. "Notes Regarding the Origin of Fort Ninigret in the Narragansett Country at Charlestown." *Rhode Island Historical Society Collections,* vol. 25, no. 1 (January 1932): 1–16. Illustrated.

Goodwin argues that the fort on Charlestown Pond called Ninigret's Fort was built by the Dutch prior to the time they acquired Dutch Island as a trading post rather than by Ninigret, the Eastern Niantic chieftain. He cites seventeenth century documents as well as finds from excavations at the fort and concludes that there is a real possibility that the Dutch built Fort Ninigret sometime after 1627 and before 1630, abandoning it when their trade was destroyed by years of war between the Pequots and Narragansetts. [*See* Bradner Leicester, "Ninigret's Fort: A Refutation of the Dutch Theory." *Rhode Island Historical Society Collections,* vol. 14, no. 1 (January 1921): 1–5. Leicester argues that the fort was not Dutch.]

**375.** Gookin, Daniel. "Historical Collections of the Indians in New England, Of Their Several Nations, Numbers, Customs, Manners, Religion, and Government Before the English Planted There." *Massachusetts Historical Society Collections,* ser. 1, vol. 1 (Boston, 1972): 141–227.

Gookin's narrative, written around 1675, discusses the origins of Indians, the principal nations of Indians in New England, their language, customs, manners, and religion. He discusses the state and condition of the "praying Indians," how they were converted, the number, names, and situation of Indian "praying" towns of Massachusetts, and the progress of gospel work among the Indians at New Plymouth Colony, Martha's Vineyard, Nantucket, Connecticut, and Rhode Island. There are proposals for civilizing and christianizing Indians by the Corporation for Propagating the Gospel Among Them located in London. A short biographical account of Gookin, who was a magistrate of Massachusetts Colony, is on pages 228–229.

**376.** Gookin, Daniel. "Letter to the Constables of Sherborn, Natick, and Elsewhere." *Massachusetts Historical Society Collections,* vol. 80 (Boston, 1972): 165–167.

In a letter, dated May 26, 1683, Gookin, an Indian Commissioner with jurisdiction over Indian affairs, tells of the complaint of Richard Parkes who claimed his wife was raped by an Indian. In a piece dated September 2, 1682, Gookin informs the constables of Natick that they should appoint six English-speaking Indian men to a jury for the trial of John Nepauett, the accused Indian.

**377.** Goold, Nathan. "Stephen Manchester, the Slayer of the Indian Polin, at New Marblehead, Now Windham, Maine, in 1756. . . ." *Maine Historical Society Collections,* ser. 2, vol. 8 (Portland, 1897): 313–327.

Goold discusses the life of Manchester, one of the earliest settlers at New Marblehead. He cites Polin's opposition to this settlement, as well as his other grievances toward English settlers, and describes the events of May 14, 1756, when Manchester killed Polin.

**378.** Goold, William. "Fort Halifax: Its Projectors, Builders, and Garrison." *Maine Historical Society Collections,* ser. 1, vol. 7 (Portland, 1876): 197–289. Illustrated.

Goold gives a history of Fort Halifax which was completed in 1755 on the Sebasticook River and explains how and why the Plymouth Colony possessed the property on which Fort Halifax was built. Goold tells of forty years of settlements protected from Indian raids and wars, Massachusetts governor Shirley's plans for building a fort with approval of the Norridgewock and Penobscot Indians, the site of the fort, hardships endured during the building, and the resentment of Indians. Included is a group of official documents relating to Fort Halifax, two etchings, and ground plans of the fort.

**379.** Gorrell, Lieutenant. "Lieutenant Gorrell's Journal." *Maryland Historical Magazine,* vol. 4, no. 2 (June 1909): 183–187.

In his journal dated August 17, 1763 to January 1764, Gorrell, a

379 *(continued)*
commander of a post on Lake Michigan from 1761 to 1763, describes
an expedition to Montreal, the attack by Indians on Lake Erie, and
explains how a white man among the attacking Indians scalped one of
the wounded soldiers.

380. Gorton, Samuel. "About Narragansetts." In "Simplicity's Defense Against
the Seven-Headed Policy." Edited by William R. Staples. *Rhode Island Historical
Society Collections,* vol. 2 (Providence, 1835): 153–172.

In Gorton's narrative published in 1646, concerning the persecution
he suffered for his religious opinions, he discusses the submission of
the Narragansetts to the English government and gives the text of
"The Act and Deed of the Voluntary and Free Submission of the
Chief Sachem, and the Rest of the Princes, With the Whole People of
the Narragansetts, unto the Government and Protection of that Honorable State of Old-England . . . ," dated April 19, 1644, with the
marks of Pessicus, Nanicus, Mixan, and two others reproduced. The
text of a letter written by Pessicus and Canonicus to the Massachusetts,
dated May 24, 1644, concerns the relations between the two tribes in
light of the Narragansetts submitting to the laws of England. Gorton
discusses how the Narragansetts wish to revenge the death of Miantonomo who was murdered by Uncas, a Mohegan, with the assent of
the Puritan authorities. In Appendix seven, on pages 213–224, there
are extracts from the proceedings of the United Colonies, which refer
to the injuries received by the English from the Indians and jurisdic-
tional questions between Massachusetts and Plymouth over a tract of
land that had belonged to Pomham and Saccononoco.

381. Graeff, Arthur D. "Transplants of Pennsylvania Indian Nations in Ontario." *Pennsylvania History,* vol. 15, no. 3 (July 1948): 180–193.

Graeff discusses the story of the trek of Pennsylvania Indian nations
to Canada beginning with the incidents leading to the 1764 march of
the Paxton Boys against Philadelphia where a group of Indian converts known as Moravian Indians were sheltered. He tells how the
Moravian leaders moved the converts to Ohio, Indiana, and Detroit,
Michigan, ending in Canada.

382. Grant, Francis. "Journal from New York to Canada, 1767." *New York
History,* vol. 13, no. 2 (April 1932): 181–196.

Dated April 27 to June 9, 1767, Grant's journal tells of a tour from
New York to Canada and a meeting with the Six Nations. Their dress
and ornaments are described. [*Continued* in *New York History,* vol. 13,
no. 3 (July 1932): 305–322. Dated June 10 to July 21, 1767, Grant tells
of seeing Indian villages.]

383. Graymont, Barbara. "New York State Indian Policy After the Revolution." *New York History,* vol. 57, no. 4 (October 1976): 438–474. Illustrated.

Graymont examines and analyzes the process by which the Iroquois
gave up almost all their lands in central and western New York. She

divides New York State Indian policy after the Revolution into three headings: extinguishing any claims of the U.S. Congress to sovereignty over New York Indian affairs; extinguishing title of the Indians to the soil; and extinguishing sovereignty of the Six Nations. There is a map of the territory of the Six Nations and paintings of Good Peter, chief of the Six Nations, Philip Schuyler, and George Clinton.

384. Graymont, Barbara. "Tuscarora New Year Festival." *New York History*, vol. 50, no. 2 (April 1969): 143–163. Illustrated.

Graymont describes the Tuscarora Nu Yah ceremony and traces its evolution from ancient traditional origins to the present. She discusses the similarities between the Tuscarora festival and the Longhouse Midwinter Festival. There are photographs of contemporary Tuscaroras and sketches of Samuel Kirkland, Handsome Lake, and a bark communal house.

385. Green, Samuel A. "Remarks on an Anonymous Indian Tract." *Massachusetts Historical Society Proceedings*, ser. 2, vol. 6 (1890–1891): 392–395.

Green discusses the authorship of an anonymous tract entitled "The Day-Breaking, if not the Sun Rising of the Gospell With the Indians in New England" published in 1647. The tract relates the attempt to convert the Indians of New England to Christianity by the Corporation for Propagating the Gospel Among the Indians."

386. Green, Samuel A. "Some Indian Names." *Massachusetts Historical Society Proceedings*, ser. 2, vol. 4 (1887–1889): 373–374.

Green produces an extract from a deed dated December 3, 1660, which mentions three Indian names, two of which are still in use, Pennichuck and Souhegan. He argues that fragmentary facts about Indian names of places are worth saving for historical and philological value.

387. Greene, John, and Others. [Petition] *Connecticut Historical Society Collections*, vol. 21 (Hartford, 1924): 252.

On October 2, 1676, Greene and other men petition for the return of their "squaws" who had been stolen.

388. Grube, Bernhard Adam. "Biographical Sketch of Reverend Bernhard Adam Grube." *Pennsylvania Magazine of History and Biography*, vol. 25, no. 1 (1901): 14–19. Illustrated.

These pages contain a sketch of the life of Reverend Grube who entered the ministry of the Moravian Church in 1740 and then entered the Indian mission service in January of 1752. Outlined are Grube's different appointments among Indians and his various translations into Delaware language of German hymns and gospels. These works were printed between 1762 and 1763 and were widely used in Indian missions in Pennsylvania and Ohio. Mentioned is the seques-

**388** *(continued)*
tering of some Indian converts in Philadelphia and their later removal
to Wyalusing in 1765, to protect them from murder attempts by the
Paxton Boys. Grube died in 1808. His picture is included.

**389.** Grube, Bernhard Adam. "A Missionary's Tour to Shamokin and the West
Branch of the Susquehanna, 1753." *Pennsylvania Magazine of History and Biography*, vol. 39, no. 4 (1915): 440–444.
    A brief introduction includes a description of the Indian town of
Shamokin and the Viceroy Shikellmy who ruled on behalf of the Six
Nations, the tributory tribes that lived along the Susquehanna. From
1728 to 1748 he played an important role in peacefully resolving the
questions between Indians and Whites. In addition the journal contains information on the Indian towns along the west branch in 1753.
The journal is dated August 21 to August 31, 1753.

**390.** Guzzardo, John C. "The Superintendent and the Ministers: The Battle
for Oneida Alliances, 1761–1775." *New York History*, vol. 57, no. 3 (July 1976):
255–283. Illustrated.
    Guzzardo discusses the struggle between Sir William Johnson and two
Presbyterian ministers, Eleazar Wheelock and Samuel Kirkland, for
the alliance of the Oneida Indians. He tells how factions of Oneidas
lent allegiance to whichever nation or program best suited their purpose, thus abetting the polarizing process which shattered the tribe.
He explains how traditional splits within Iroquois society intensified
because of activities of Kirkland and Johnson and explains that when
Sir William Johnson died, Kirkland was able to deliver the allegiance
of the Oneidas to the patriots. Paintings of the three principals are
included.

**391.** Gyles, John. "John Gyles' Statement of the Number of Indians." *Maine
Historical Society Collections*, ser. 1, vol. 3 (Portland, 1853): 356–358.
    In his statement, dated November 24, 1726, Gyles estimates there are
389 Indians over age sixteen in the following tribes: St. John's River,
Passamaquoddy, Penobscot, Norridgewock, Androscoggin, and Pigwacket.

**392.** Hale, Horatio. "Horatio Hale." *Massachusetts Historical Society Proceedings*,
ser. 1, vol. 19 (1881–1882): 241–243.
    These pages contain a brief discussion of a pamphlet by Horatio Hale
on the origin of the Iroquois Confederacy and Hale's *Book of
Rites.* Included is an extract from Hale's letter in which he names the
several chiefs who instructed him in the grammatical analysis of

nearly every word in the Mohawk portion of the *Book of Rites,* and he answers other inquiries regarding how he wrote the book.

393. Hale, Horatio. "The Origin and Nature of Wampum." *Pennsylvania Magazine of History and Biography,* vol. 8, no. 3 (1884): 349–350.

Hale describes the monetary currency in common use among Indians of the United States and Canada, discussing the shape, color, material, uses, shell arrangements, and value. He reports on the existence of other media of commercial exchange among the Asian peoples and suggests these may have a relationship to wampum.

394. Halifax, Earl of. [Orders of the Earl of Halifax] *New York Historical Society Collections for the Year 1922, Cadwallader Colden Papers,* vol. 6 (New York, 1923): 238–239.

In his communication dated October 9, 1763, the Earl of Halifax orders the colonies to raise troops for an offensive against the Indians. [*See* the Halifax letter of May 12, 1764, pages 309–310, in which he acknowledges New York's difficulties in raising money for the troops and running the government.]

395. Hamilton, James. [Letter to General Monckton] *Massachusetts Historical Society Collections,* vol. 9, ser. 4 (Boston, 1871): 278–281.

In a letter dated July 24, 1760, Governor James Hamilton reports that the Delawares on the Ohio request a council to consider measures to be taken regarding New England and the Six Nations. Hamilton reports that the Senecas refuse to allow the English messengers from Amherst through their territory. Hamilton expresses the hope that Teedyuscung will enter into a peace treaty with England and release his prisoners.

396. Hamilton, Kenneth G. "Cultural Contributions of Moravian Missions Among the Indians." *Pennsylvania History,* vol. 18, no. 1 (January 1951): 1–15.

Hamilton outlines and appraises civilizing influences of the early Moravian missions upon Indians in the eighteenth century. He briefly discusses their cultural contributions such as knowledge of the scriptures, schools, cultivation of music, living standards, and social relations. He concludes by discussing the price paid by the Christian Indians for these "Cultural advances." Hamilton draws on contemporary accounts to illustrate the text.

397. Hamilton, Milton W. "Guy Johnson's Opinions on the American Indian." *Pennsylvania Magazine of History and Biography,* vol. 77, no. 3 (July 1953): 311–327.

This piece contains Guy Johnson's answers to a set of questions written by Dr. William Robertson concerning the nature and culture of the American Indians. Johnson's answers provide a comparison or verification of opinions previously expressed by George Croghan to

397 *(continued)*
the same set of queries. [*See Pennsylvania Magazine of History and Biography*, vol. 71, no. 2 (April 1947): 152–159. An editor analyzes the differences and similarities between the two sets of answers.]

398. Hamilton, Milton W. "Joseph Brant—The Most Painted Indian." *New York History*, vol. 39, no. 2 (April 1958): 119–132.
Hamilton discusses several locations where paintings of Joseph Brant, a Mohawk Indian, were done: London, Albany, Philadelphia. He details Brant's expression and dress in each painting and discusses his work among the Indians. Included are reproductions of Romney's, Stuart's, and Ames's paintings of Brant, and lengthy footnotes. [*See* Milton W. Hamilton, "Joseph Brant Painted by Rigaud." *New York History*, vol. 40, no. 3 (July 1959): 247–254. Illustrated. Hamilton discusses the work of an artist who painted Brant on his second visit to London in 1786. Rigaud's nineteenth century portrait is reproduced.]

399. Hamilton, Milton W. "The Library of Sir William Johnson." *New York Historical Society Quarterly Bulletin*, vol. 40, no. 3 (July 1956): 209–252.
Hamilton describes the contents of Johnson's library, the growth of the library, and Johnson's interests and great knowledge of American Indians. He explains how Sir William's knowledge of American Indians was reflected in subsequently published works which he aided in one way or another, such as Peter Wraxall's *An Abridgement of the Records of Indian Affairs. . . Transacted in the Colony of New York from the Year 1678 to the Year 1751*. Hamilton enumerates the people who sought information on Iroquois Indians from Johnson. There is a partial checklist of fifty-nine books in Sir William Johnson's library.

400. Hamilton, Milton W. "Sir William Johnson and Pennsylvania." *Pennsylvania History*, vol. 19, no. 1 (January 1952): 52–74. Illustrated.
Hamilton discusses the life of Sir William Johnson, appointed Superintendent of Indian Affairs for the Northern Department in 1756 by the crown, a post which he held until his death in 1774. He describes Johnson's Indian diplomacy, and how, through his deputy, George Croghan, he directed Indian relations in Pennsylvania, which prior to 1755 had been in the hands of governors and agents like Conrad Weiser. Hamilton focuses on Johnson's diplomacy at the Treaty of Fort Stanwix in 1768 at which the Indians agreed to a line demarking their eastern boundaries. Included is a copy of an engraving of Sir William.

401. Hancock, James E. "The Indians of the Chesapeake Bay Section." *Maryland Historical Magazine*, vol. 22, no. 1 (March 1927): 23–40.
Citing Father White, who came into contact with Indians of the Chesapeake and its tributaries, and other reports of early explorers, Hancock gives an account of the habits, customs, and beliefs of Maryland Indians in colonial times. He lists the Indians who occupied different sections of Maryland when it was first colonized; discusses

Powhatan, to whom major tribes on the western shore were closely related; and explains that Maryland Indians had practically disappeared from that area by 1800.

**402.** Harnden, Samuel. [Petition of Samuel Harnden] *Massachusetts Historical Society Collections,* vol. 74 (Boston, 1918): 120–122.

In his communication, dated May 25, 1763, Harnden describes how he recovered two out of three of those known to be living from the Preble family, most of whom were captured and killed by Indians in 1758. He explains that a third child is in France, and petitions the Massachusetts General Court to have her released and returned.

**403.** Harris, William. [On King Philip's War] *Rhode Island Historical Society Collections,* vol. 10 (Providence, 1902): 162–179.

In his long, contemporary account, dated August 12, 1676, Harris discusses King Philip's War. Explanatory footnotes help to illustrate the conduct of the war in Rhode Island and the murder of King Philip.

**404.** Hasbrouck, G. D. B. "History from Lake Mohonk." *New York State Historical Association Quarterly Journal,* vol. 4, no. 3 (July 1923): 127–147.

In the first part of this article, Hasbrouck names and locates six clans of the Esopus, or Munsee, one of the three Delaware subtribes who lived in the river valleys around Lake Mohonk: the Waoranecks, Warranawonkongs, Warwarsinks, Mamekoting, Catskills, and Minisinks. He gives an account of the coming of the Dutch and describes the first Esopus war of 1660 and the second Esopus war of 1663.

**405.** Hastings, Hugh. "Sir William Johnson." *New York State Historical Association Proceedings,* Second Annual Meeting, vol. 1 (Lake George, 1901): 35–41.

Hastings describes how Johnson established an intimate relationship with the Iroquois and how he neutralized the influence of the French over the Iroquois and created a feeling of confidence in the English. Hastings discusses distinctions between the English and the French treatment of Indian allies, recounts Johnson's mediation between Indians and whites and Johnson's expedition and victory against Crown Point in 1755 in which Hendrick and Williams were killed. [*See* "Colonel Ephraim Williams" by James Austin Holden, pages 42–53, for the biography and discussion about Colonel E. Williams who with a force of 1000 white men and 200 Mohawks under King Hendrick was detailed to go to the assistance of Fort Lyman.]

**406.** Haswell, Robert; Hoskin, John; and Boit, John. "Voyages of the *Columbia* to the Northwest Coast, 1787–1790 and 1790–1793." Edited by F. W. Howay. *Massachusetts Historical Society Collections,* vol. 79 (Boston, 1941): 518 pp.

Four journals, two by Haswell and one each by Hoskin and Boit, give firsthand ethnographic information about Haidas, Kwakiutls, Nootkas, and Indians of California, Oregon, and Washington. The explor-

**406** *(continued)*

ers describe food, dress, ornaments, housing and villages, physical appearances, domestic life, music, medicine, religion, amusements, canoes, language, vocabulary, government, the role of women, weapons, manners, and trade. They also relate attempted attacks on the *Columbia.* The journals include explanatory footnotes.

**407.** Hauptman, Laurence M. "The Iroquois School of Art: Arthur C. Parker and the Seneca Arts Project, 1935–1941." *New York History,* vol. 60, no. 3 (July 1979): 283–312. Illustrated.

Hauptman gives an account of Seneca Parker's experiment in combining the work relief program with artistic renewal during the economic traumas of the 1930s. He describes the Seneca plan to manufacture articles and records the activities and ceremonies of New York Indians, and describes the Indians who were involved, focusing in particular on Parker's leadership role. Hauptman discusses the success of the project, which was reflected in the quality and quantity of art produced and in the Seneca response which contributed to the tribe's economic and cultural survival, and the project's later demise. There are photographs taken at Tonowanda of Senecas who were involved with the project.

**408.** Hawley, Gideon. "A Letter from Reverend Gideon Hawley of Marshpee, Containing an Account of His Services Among the Indians of Massachusetts and New York and a Narrative of His Journey to Onohoghgwage." *Massachusetts Historical Society Collections,* ser. 1, vol. 4 (Boston, 1795): 50–74.

In a letter, dated July 31, 1794, Gideon describes his missionary work among Indians, describes the customs, manners, and intemperance of Indians, and his journey to Onohoghgwage. He reports some success in converting Indians at Martha's Vineyard, Nantucket, Barnstable, and Plymouth. Gideon answers nine questions about Indian population figures, the number of warriors, morals, and disposition to the civilization of whites.

**409.** Hawley, Gideon, and Rasles, Sebastien. "Numbers in Mohawk and Norridgewock Languages." *Massachusetts Historical Society Collections,* ser. 1, vol. 10 (Boston, 1809): 137–138.

Reverend Hawley records the number of Indians who speak the Mohawk language, and Father Rasles records the number speaking the Norridgewock language.

**410.** Haynes, Henry W. "On Indian Hemp and Tomahawks." *Massachusetts Historical Society Proceedings,* ser. 2, vol. 6 (1890–1891): 34–38.

Haynes draws on more than ten primary sources dating from 1620 for notes about Indian hemp. He considers discrepancies in the earlier historical accounts of the manner in which the Indian tomahawk was used.

**411.** Haynes, John. [Letter to John Winthrop] *Massachusetts Historical Society Collections,* ser. 4, vol. 6 (Boston, 1863): 358–359.

In a letter, dated July of 1648, Haynes reports that Nincunnet requests leave to hunt in Pequot country but feels it is improper because the Indian is under suspicion for hiring Mohawks and other Indians to attack Uncas, an activity which offends the English. Haynes's letter to John Winthrop, dated October 1, 1643, on pages 356–357, deals with this topic.

412. Hazard, Ebenezer. [Letter to Jeremy Belknap] *Massachusetts Historical Society Collections,* ser. 5, vol. 2 (Boston, 1877): 22–24.

In a letter, dated December 15, 1779, Hazard comments on Sullivan's Expedition, particularly the destruction done and "good consequences" arising from destroying Indian towns and crops. These acts, he claims, will intimidate the Indians and "make them cautious how they fight against us in the future." He also states that the country can acquire the Indian territory since Indians never attempt a resettlement of a place from which they have been driven.

413. Heckewelder, John. *"History, Manners, and Customs of the Indian Nations Who Once Inhabited Pennsylvania and the Neighboring States."* Edited by Reverend William C. Reichel. *Historical Society of Pennsylvania Memoirs,* vol. 12 (Philadelphia, 1876): 1–518.

Published in 1819, the first part of Heckewelder's book deals with historical traditions of the Indians, their account of the first arrival of the Dutch at New York Island, Indian reports of European conduct towards them, the fate of the Lenapes and kindred tribes, and the Iroquois. He then gives an account of Indian government, education, languages, signs, oratory, metaphorical expressions, names, intertribal communication, political maneuvres, marriage, the aged, wars, treaties, observations of whites, food and cookery, dress and ornaments, dance, scalping, health and disease, remedies, physicians and surgeons, superstitions, initiation of boys into manhood, Indian mythology, suicide, intemperance, friendship, funerals, preachers, and computation of time. He gives brief biographies of Tamanend and Teedyuscung and compares Indians and whites. The last part contains correspondence pertaining to Indian languages, lists of words and phrases, and short dialogues.

414. Heckewelder, John. "Names and Significations which the 'Lenni Lenape,' Otherwise Called 'the Delawares,' Had Given to Rivers, Streams, Places, etc. Within the States of Pennsylvania, New Jersey, Maryland and Virginia, Together With the Names of Some Chieftains and Eminent Men of This Nation." *Historical Society of Pennsylvania Proceedings,* vol. 1, no. 11 (August 1847): 121–135.

Heckewelder gives the names of rivers, streams, and other noted places in the Pennsylvania counties of Philadelphia, Delaware, Chester, Montgomery, Bucks, Northampton, Lehigh, Wayne, Pike, Berks, Schuylkill, Luzerne, Susquehanna, Ontario, Tioga, Lycoming, Northumberland Centre, Clearfield, Potter, McKean, Warren, Erie, Crawford, Mercer, Venango, Jefferson, Armstrong, Butler, Beaver,

**414** *(continued)*

Allegheny, Westmoreland, Fayette, Green, Indiana, Somerset, Cambria, Huntingdon, Bedford, Franklin, Cumberland, Mifflin, Dauphin, Adams, York, and Lancaster. He also records the names of rivers and other landmarks in New Jersey. [*Continued* in *Historical Society of Pennsylvania Proceedings*, vol. 1, no. 12 (September 1847): 139–154. In this portion, Heckewelder gives the Indian names of rivers, creeks, etc. in Maryland, and the Indian names of rivers and persons in Virginia that evidence Delaware possession of that country. He also lists the names of chiefs and other important people in the Delaware Nation from the arrival of William Penn until 1810 together with the significance of some of the names and a few short biographical sketches.]

**415.** Heckewelder, John. "Narrative of John Heckewelder's Journey to the Wabash in 1792." *Pennsylvania Magazine of History and Biography*, vol. 11, no. 4 (1887): 466–475.

Heckewelder accompanied a commission authorized to conclude a treaty of peace with Indians on the northwest bank of the Ohio. Dated May 26 to June 27, 1792, his narrative of the journey comments on the numerous hostile Indian raids against settlers that are reported to him and the settlers' fear of the Indians. [*Continued* in *Pennsylvania Magazine of History and Biography*, vol. 12, no. 1 (1888): 34–54, dated June 26 to August 26, 1792. Heckewelder discusses prisoners held by Indians and a burial, and he quotes the explanation given to the Indians of the U.S. coat of arms by Judge Symmes. *Continued* in *Pennsylvania Magazine of History and Biography*, vol. 12, no. 2 (1888): 165–184, dated August 27, 1792 to January, 1793. Heckewelder describes the embitterment and troubles between Indians and whites around Post Vincennes. He discusses the peace conference with several Indian nations.]

**416.** Heckewelder, John. "Notes of Travel of William Henry, John Heckewelder, John Rothrock, and Christian Clewell, to Gnadenhuetten on the Muskingum, in the Early Summer of 1797." *Pennsylvania Magazine of History and Biography*, vol. 10, no. 2 (1886): 125–157.

Heckewelder's journal, dated April 17 to July 20, 1797, records descriptions of Indians who accompanied the travelers en route to survey lands given to the Society for Propagating the Gospel. He describes the Indian life observed along the way. Historical and geographical notes are included.

**417.** Heisey, John W., trans. and ed. "Extracts from the Diary of the Moravian Pastors of the Hebrew Church, Lebanon, 1755–1814." *Pennsylvania History*, vol. 34, no. 1 (January 1967): 44–63.

Extracts from the Hebron Diary, dated June 19, 1755 to April 1814, describe the founding of the Hebron Congregation, Indian hostility, raids, and murders, and the French and allied Indian attacks on the village of Gnadenhuetten in 1755.

**418.** Hendrick, David, and Abraham. [Indian Deed] *New York Historical Society Collections for the Year 1920. Cadwallader Colden Papers,* vol. 4 (New York, 1921): 409–411.

Hendrick, David, and Abraham, three Mohawks, grant a tract of land in the county of Albany to King George on October 19, 1753. Hendrick Frey, a justice of the peace, certifies the purchase, for the sum of six shillings and presents, and certifies that he has surveyed the tract of land.

**419.** Henry, Jane. "The Choptank Indians of Maryland Under the Proprietary Government." *Maryland Historical Magazine,* vol. 65, no. 2 (Summer 1970): 171–180. Illustrated.

The Choptank tribe, on the eastern shore of Maryland, are related to the Nanticoke Indians of Algonquian stock. Henry discusses the growing pressure on the Choptanks from white settlers by 1669 and the unsuccessful efforts of the Maryland government to protect the tribe, which included establishing a Choptank Indian reserve in 1669. She gives examples of Indian complaints between 1676 and 1756. Eventually the Indians were overcome by white settlements, and the tribe ceased to exist when the last Choptanks sold their reservation lands. There are footnotes and pictures of two Calverts.

**420.** Henry, Matthew S. "Indian Names in New Jersey." *New Jersey Historical Society Proceedings,* vol. 8, no. 2 (1856): 52–53.

Henry discusses how the Indians, who, unlike the Europeans, had no names for rivers, streams and creeks, distinguished these bodies of water. He explains how certain writers translate Indian words inaccurately and even invent words in Native languages or put their own meanings on Indian words. [See *New Jersey Historical Society Proceedings,* vol. 9, no. 1 (1860): 9–10, in which Henry supports his argument that Indians had no names for rivers or creeks prior to the arrival of European settlers.]

**421.** Henry, Stephen Chambers. "Letter of Surgeon Stephen Chambers Henry, Detroit, 1813, Addressed to His Mother." *Pennsylvania Magazine of History and Biography,* vol. 21, no. 1 (1897): 123–124.

In a letter, dated October 3, 1813, Henry, a surgeon, states that the British are trying to incite Potawatomis to burn settlements around Detroit, discusses those Potawatomis and other Indians who desire peace, describes the actions of General Harrison against hostile Indians, and cites Indian depredations against Americans.

**422.** Hepburn, William. [Letter to Mr. John Painter] *Pennsylvania Magazine of History and Biography,* vol. 55, no. 218 (April 1931): 192.

In his letter, dated January 8, 1819, Hepburn recounts how Painter fought British and allied Indians on the frontier during the Revolutionary War.

**423.** Herchheimer, Hans Joost, and Frank, Conrad. "On an Oneida Murdering a Man." *New York Historical Society Collections for the Year 1922, Cadwallader Colden Papers,* vol. 6 (New York, 1923): 42.

In an account, dated June 17, 1761, the authors report on a group of Oneidas who came to Burnetsfield to have children christened and how one of them killed a white man during an argument. According to the report, the argument was a result of the Indian's having killed the white man's hog. [*See* General Amherst's letter to Colden dated June 25, 1761, pages 47–48, in which he writes that the Oneida must be brought to justice. There is also another Amherst letter dated July 2, 1761, page 50, on the same topic.]

**424.** Hesselius, Andreas. "Journal of Andreas Hesselius, 1711–1724." *Delaware History,* vol. 2, no. 2 (September 1947): 61–118.

A Swedish cleric, who was appointed missionary to Swedish churches on the Delaware and who did conversion work among Indians, describes habits, and other aspects of Indian society, including burials, medical remedies, British-Indian relations, clothing, food, religion, and various ceremonies. The journal is preceded by introductory notes and a biography of Hesselius.

**425.** Higginson, Francis. "Description of Indians" in *New-England's Plantations. Massachusetts Historical Society Proceedings,* vol. 62 (1928–1929): 315–317.

Higginson describes Indians in his *New-England Plantation* published in London in 1630. He discusses their government, the incidence of disease among them, their physical characteristics, weaponry, homes, religion, and the Indians' positive attitude toward the settlers.

**426.** Higginson, John. "Testimony of John Higginson, Senior, Concerning Indian Lands." *Massachusetts Historical Society Collections,* ser. 5, vol. 9 (Boston, 1885): 118–120.

In his testimony, dated September 12, 1683, Higginson tells what he remembers about the land transactions between English people in Connecticut and the Indians along the coast from Quilipole to Manatoes, beginning in the year 1638.

**427.** Hight, Horatio. "Mogg Heigon—His Life, His Death, and Its Sequel." *Maine Historical Society Collections,* ser. 2, vol. 5 (Portland, 1894): 345–360. Illustrated.

Hight discusses Mog Hegon, *alias* Mogg, *alias* General Mog, of unknown tribal origin, who was alternately friend or foe of the English settlers along the coast of Maine. Hight argues that Mogg was a Saco, describes the hunting grounds he deeded to Major Phillips, the campaign he waged against the English at Black Point in 1676, his trip to Boston and the peace treaty he was induced to sign there (November 13, 1676), on behalf of Madokawando, chief sachem of the Abenaki tribes. There is a drawing of Mogg's hunting grounds deeded May 31, 1664 to Major William Phillips. [*Continued* in *Maine Historical Society*

*Collections,* ser. 2, vol. 6 (Portland, 1895): 256–280. Hight tells how Mogg was killed by Lieutenant Tippin at Black Point while he was leading a force against the garrison, May 16, 1677. Hight tells of the circumstances of the Battle of Black Point on June 29, 1677 in which the Indians avenge Mogg's death.]

**428.** Hilborn, John. "Captivity Narrative of John Hilborn" in "Extracts From the Journal of Samuel Preston, Surveyor, 1787." *Pennsylvania Magazine of History and Biography,* vol. 22, no. 3 (1898): 354–359.

John Hilborn, who accompanied the surveyor, tells of his two-year captivity, his treatment by Delaware Indians, his friendship with a Mohawk, and his eventual release by the Indians with the assistance of Captain Brant, a Mohawk commander allied with the British.

**429.** Hill, Esther V. "The Iroquois Indians and Their Lands Since 1783." *New York State Historical Association Quarterly Journal,* vol. 11, no. 4 (October 1930): 335–353.

Hill considers the post-Revolution relationship between the Six Nations and the U.S. discussing those Mohawks who left the U.S. for Canada, the attempt of New York State to expel the Six Nations from all unceded territory in the state, the 1784 treaty in which the Iroquois were treated as a conquered people, and the 1794 treaty, some stipulations of which still hold today and which was the last council held between the U.S. and the Six Nations. She describes the dispute between Massachusetts and New York over conflicting claims to the western portion of New York, discusses those people anxious to buy Indian title in New York State, land speculation companies, and the way Six Nations title to lands was transferred to Whites in western New York. Hill briefly traces the history of the Seneca, Tuscarora, Cayuga, Onondaga, and Oneida reservations.

**430.** Himmelwright, A.L.A. "French-and-Indian War Fort in Sussex County." *New Jersey Historical Society Proceedings,* n.s., vol. 13, no. 2 (April 1928): 261–262.

In a letter, Himmelwright discusses an old fort from the French and Indian war of 1754 to 1763 located on property near Stockholm in Sussex Country; included is a description of how the fort was used to protect colonists of the region from raids and depredations of the Six Nations.

**431.** Hinckley, Thomas. [Letter to William Stoughton and Joseph Dudley] *Massachusetts Historical Society Collections,* ser. 4, vol. 5 (Boston, 1861): 132–134.

In a letter dated April 2, 1685, Governor Hinckley of New Plymouth gives information concerning Indian teachers to the Company for Propagating the Gospel Among the Indians in New England. The number, location, and names of teachers of Indians in New Plymouth are listed and Hinckley also discusses Indian intemperance and Indians' serious execution of religious exercises as compared to the English.

**432.** Hinsdale, Ebenezer. "Letter of Colonel Ebenezer Hinsdale to Governor Benning Wentworth, 1755." *New Hampshire Historical Society Collections,* vol. 5 (Concord, 1837): 254–256.

In a letter dated July 22, 1755, Hinsdale reports to the Governor of New Hampshire that a party of Indians attacked seven men near Hinsdale's fort and five of these are missing. He asks the governor for protection, particularly from Connecticut. An extract from a letter by Mrs. Hinsdale, describing the Indian attack, is appended.

**433.** Hoberg, Walter R. "Early History of Colonel Alexander McKee." *Pennsylvania Magazine of History and Biography,* vol. 58, no. 1 (1934): 26–36.

Hoberg discusses Colonel McKee, a British Indian agent who took charge of Indian affairs at Fort Pitt after 1772, and his diplomacy in keeping reprisals of Indians from spreading throughout western Pennsylvania. In discussing Lord Dunmore's War, an Indian uprising, Hoberg assesses McKee's reputation for remaining loyal to the British government. Footnotes are included.

**434.** Hoberg, Walter R. "A Tory in the Northwest." *Pennsylvania Magazine of History and Biography,* vol. 59, no. 1 (January 1935): 32–41.

Hoberg discusses loyalist Colonel McKee's activities in Ohio country during the Revolutionary War period. McKee led British-allied Indians in raids against the Americans, and after the war agitated those Indians who did not wish peace with the Americans. He tells of United States efforts to arrange peace with the Indians in 1793, General Wayne's victory at Fallen Timbers in 1794 when he also destroyed McKee's property, and the subsequent treaties in which the Indians were humiliated by the U.S., forced to surrender the "Old Northwest" and submit to American rule. Hoberg concludes by telling of McKee's work in locating those tribes in Canada who did not want to live under American rule.

**435.** Hodge, F. W. "On Indian Inferiority." *New Jersey Historical Society Proceedings,* ser. 3, vol. 9, no. 3 (July and October 1914): 161–162.

These extracts from letters debate the issue of Indian inferiority. Hodge argues that Indians are inferior when compared to whites but that some tribes have reached a "high stage of development." There is some discussion about the fact that Binet tests were not administered to students at the U.S. Indian school at Carlisle, Pennsylvania.

**436.** Hogan, William W. [Letter to Colden] *New York Historical Society Collections for the Year 1922, Cadwallader Colden Papers,* vol. 6 (New York, 1923): 340–341.

In his letter, dated August 15, 1764, Hogan gives an account of the peace made by Colonel Bradstreet with Delaware and other Indians. The following terms were agreed upon: Indians are to give grants of lands, to allow the British government to erect forts on their land, and to turn over to the British any Indian who commits hostilities, the offender to be tried by a court composed of Indians and English.

**437.** Hogkins, John. "Four Letters or Petitions from John Hogkins, Commonly Called Hawkins, One of the Sachems of the Pennacook Indians." *New Hampshire Historical Society Collections,* vol. 8 (Concord, 1866): 253-255.

Hogkins's letters, dated May 15-May 16, 1685, tell of his fear of the Mohawks, his friendship for the English, and his promise to punish any of his Indians who do wrong.

**438.** Holcomb, Captain Richmond C. "The Early Dutch Maps of Upper Delaware Valley." *New Jersey Historical Society Proceedings,* n.s., vol. 11, no. 1 (January 1926): 18-45.

Holcomb discusses two early Dutch maps which delineate New Jersey during the period the Dutch held the New Netherlands. One of the maps was made by Nicholas J. Visscher and the other by Van der Donck, and both were made in 1655-1656. In discussing the maps, Holcomb describes Dutch and Indian settlements, Indian place names, the Indian network of trails, Indian trade, and Indian-white relations. In a section entitled "Some of the Early Land Titles," passages are quoted from a patent granted to some twenty Dutch applicants to purchase land in Minisink country, February 9, 1696, and from a patent granted to Arent Schuyler in 1697 who secured land from Pompton Indians in the Jerseys. Circumstances of other patents are also discussed.

**439.** Holden, James Austin. "Influence of the Death of Jane McCrea on the Burgoyne Campaign." *New York State Historical Association Proceedings, Fourteenth Annual Meeting,* vol. 12 (Lake George, 1913): 249-310. Illustrated.

A long biography of McCrea precedes a conventional account of McCrea's death at the hands of Indians. Holden deals with inconsistencies in the story and mentions five of the differing sources. He argues that the weight of the evidence is against the theory that the Americans killed McCrea, and he gives evidence as to why she was killed by the Indians. He offers as true a version of the death of the woman as can be adduced from the varying stories which time, tradition, and historians have accumulated since the crime was committed. Holden discusses the effects of the killing on the public mind. In the appendix, there is an essay entitled "The Location of the Jane McCrea Tree and Spring" and a lengthy bibliography of the works consulted by the author in preparing this article, divided into the following categories: Individual and Family Bibliography, Early Histories of the Affair, Authorities: 1822-1850, 1850-1880, 1880-1900, 1900-1912, the Tragedy Mentioned, McCrea Poems and Ballads, News Accounts, and the Burgoyne Campaign.

**440.** Holm, Thomas Campanius. "Of the American Indians, in the Province of New Sweden, Now Called Pennsylvania." In *A Short Description of the Province of New Sweden, Now Called, by the English, Pennsylvania, in America. Historical Society of Pennsylvania Memoirs,* vol. 3, part 1 (Philadelphia, 1834): 112-143.

Published in 1702, "Book 3" tells of the origin and language of the

**440** *(continued)*
Indians in Virginia and New Sweden, and describes their personal appearances and morals, clothing, food and cookery, dwellings and furniture, marriages and education of children, occupations, trade and money, government and laws, warfare and weapons, funerals, religion, and difficulties in converting Indians to Christianity. "Book 4" entitled "Vocabulary and Phrases in the American Language of New Sweden," pages 144–156, contains the vocabularies and also discourses which took place at a council held by Indians in 1645. The "Addenda," pages 157–159, discusses the "Minques, or Minckus, and Their Language."

**441.** Honeyman, A. Van Doren. "Two Interesting Letters About New Jersey Indians." *New Jersey Historical Society Proceedings*, n.s., vol. 13, no. 4 (October 1928): 405–414.

The topic of the first letter written by Albert L. Kelly in 1884 is the life of eighty-year old Ann Roberts, an Indian. The other letter written by a great-granddaughter of Wequalia, Marion Peters, is prefaced with remarks about Peters and the death by hanging of Wequalia for murdering a prominent white farmer [*See New Jersey Historical Society Proceedings*, n.s., vol. 12, no. 4 (October 1927): 385–405]. The woman gives a more exact account of the reason for the murder of Captain Leonard by Wequalia than appears elsewhere. Peters's letter is dated June 20, 1864, at which time she was an old woman.

**442.** Hooke, Francis. "Letter from Captain Francis Hooke, Advising of Danger from the Indians." *New Hampshire Historical Society Collections*, vol. 8 (Concord, 1866): 255–256.

In his letter dated August 13, 1685, Captain Hooke warns Captain Barefoot that Indians may be planning to attack. The report describes the peaceful disposition of the Penacooks and their fears of the Mohawks who have declared they would kill all Indians from Mt. Hope to the eastward as far as Pegypscot.

**443.** Hoopes, Alban W. "Preliminary Report Upon the Correspondence of the Indian Rights Association in the Welsh Collection." *Pennsylvania Magazine of History and Biography*, vol. 67, no. 4 (October 1943): 382–389.

Hoopes briefly surveys the portion of the Welsh Collection which is designated as "Correspondence of the Indian Rights Association," which covers the years from 1877 to 1934 with the items numbering around 2000. Hoopes samples the collection of the organization founded in 1882, citing letters describing destitution and food shortages among Navajos, 1894–1895, and the role of the IRA in improving the situation. He discusses the letters that deal with the work of the IRA in opposing "home rule," or the appointment of local people as Indian agents.

**444.** Hope-Hood. "Deed of Indians to Peter Coffin." *Massachusetts Historical Society Proceedings*, ser. 1, vol. 17 (1879–1880): 352–355.

Hope-Hood, an Abenaki, is the first-named grantor in this deed, dated January 18, 1709, by which he and three others grant land to Peter Coffin for seven pounds.

**445.** Hopkins, Gerard T. "A Quaker Pilgrimage; Being A Mission to the Indians from the Indian Committee of the Baltimore Yearly Meeting, to Fort Wayne, 1804." *Maryland Historical Magazine,* vol. 4, no. 1 (March 1909): 1–24.
  Before the journal begins, there is the text of a letter signed by Little Turtle, Miami, and Five Medals, Potawatomi, dated September 18, 1803, in which the two chiefs ask the Indian Committee of the Baltimore Yearly Meeting to come and visit them. They complain about the deterioration of their peoples and the Indians' disinterest in farming. The journal of Hopkins, a member of the delegation appointed to visit Little Turtle and Five Medals, dated February 23 to April 15, 1804, tells how he and a few others traveled to the Wabash to visit the Indians. The journal is followed by an Appendix written in 1862 which recounts the work of the Society of Friends of the Baltimore Yearly Meeting for Indians after the Revolutionary War and which briefly outlines the history of tribes northwest of the Ohio River, discussing the views of Little Turtle. There are extracts from the Committee of the Baltimore Yearly Meeting from 1795 to 1804.

**446.** How, Jemima. "Letters Relating to Mrs. Jemima How, Who Was Taken by the Indians at Hinsdale, New Hampshire, in July, 1755." *New Hampshire Historical Society Collections,* vol. 5 (Concord, 1837): 256–258.
  In a letter dated January 20, 1758, Ebenezer Hinsdale writes to Governor Wentworth of New Hampshire asking him to help redeem Indian captives in New Hampshire. Dr. Benjamin Stiles writes to Hinsdale on December 23, 1757, reporting that he saw Mrs. How and her six children in Canada and that the woman begs for help to return home. An extract from another Hinsdale letter, dated December 24, 1757, explains the method by which Mrs. How can be ransomed from the French.

**447.** Hubbard, John. "Letter from Reverend John Hubbard." *Massachusetts Historical Society Collections,* ser. 1, vol. 2 (Boston, 1793): 30–32.
  In his letter dated September 1, 1792, Reverend Hubbard describes the destruction caused by the Indians in their war against the town of Northfield that occurred from the late 1670s until 1700.

**448.** Hubley, Adam, Jr. "His Journal, Commencing at Wyoming, July 30th, 1779." *Pennsylvania Magazine of History and Biography,* vol. 33, no. 2 (1909): 129–146. Illustrated.
  The journal of Colonel Adam Hubley, Jr., whose regiment was involved in Major General Sullivan's expedition to punish the Six Nations in western New York, dated May 24 to August 13, 1779, describes the order of march and the battles with Indians and destruction of their crops and settlements. The journal also contains observa-

**448** *(continued)*

tions on the countryside and its inhabitants. There are reproductions of drawings of the encampments and a brief biography of Hubley that prefaces the journal. [*Continued in Pennsylvania Magazine of History and Biography*, vol. 33, no. 3 (1909): 279–302. Illustrated. In entries dated August 14 to September 13, 1779, Hubley gives the text of a speech by General Sullivan to the army on the need to ration supplies and food. He also tells of the marks on trees made by Indians allied with the British and explains the meaning of inscriptions on the trees. *Continued in Pennsylvania Magazine of History and Biography*, vol. 33, no. 4 (1909): 409–422. Illustrated. This portion of the journal is dated from September 14 to October 7, 1779.]

**449.** Huden, John C. "The Abnakis, the Iroquoians, and Vermont." *Vermont History*, vol. 24, no. 1 (January 1956): 21–25.

Huden discusses the Abenakis, a subgroup of the Algonquian language stock and one of thirty tribes which spoke similar languages. He discusses how place names can be used to trace linguistic stocks. He tells of English advances into northern New England and the flight of Abenakis and other Indians to Canada in the first half of the eighteenth century. Huden discusses the Mahicans who hunted in southwestern Vermont prior to 1650 but were later forced by the Mohawks to move to Stockbridge, Massachusetts. He argues that after 1600, Algonquians used Vermont more than the Iroquoians and that the chief Algonquian influence in Vermont from 1600 to 1670 was Abenaki. He recounts several Abenaki legends and explains that Indian place names are scarce in Vermont compared with Connecticut and Massachusetts. The Abenakis left no written records such as deeds which would give insights into the place names.

**450.** Huden, John C. "Abstract of 'An Abenaki Village on the Missisquoi River.'" *Vermont History*, vol. 31, no. 3 (July 1963): 193–195.

Huden gives a précis of a translation of an article by Reverend Thomas Marie Charland concerning a work on the Abenakis of St. Francis from the late 1600s to 1765 and the experience of these Indians, living on the Missisquoi River, with the French and the English. There are footnotes.

**451.** Huden, John C. "Adventures in Abnaki Land." *Vermont History*, vol. 25, no. 3 (July 1957): 185–193.

In a letter to Dr. Wood, Huden comments on his research trying to decipher Abenaki names on a French map dated 1650 to 1750. He describes his exploratory trips to Ottawa, St. Regis, Caughnawaga, Quebec, and Odanak (which was headquarters of the St. Francis Abenakis for many years). There are footnotes with historical sources, information, and names of the people who assisted him in his research.

**452.** Huden, John C. "Indian Groups in Vermont." *Vermont History*, vol. 26, no. 2 (April 1958): 112–115. Illustrated.

Huden gives a list of the four large Indian divisions in Vermont from ancient times to 1790 including pre-Algonquians, Old Algonquians, Recent Algonquians with thirteen subgroups speaking Algonquian dialects (Abenakis, Coosucks, Mahicans, Penacooks, Pocumtucks, etc.), and Iroquoians. The derivation of each of the thirteen Algonquian subgroup names is given and where they have been located in Vermont and elsewhere. There are brief notes for each of the four large divisions and a map of Algonquian groups and Mohawk sites in Vermont, New Hampshire, and across the Canadian border.

**453.** Huden, John C. "Indian Place Names in Vermont." *Vermont History*, vol. 23, no. 3 (July 1955): 191–203.

Huden gives a glossary of seventy Indian place names in Vermont. There are introductory notes explaining how the meanings of Vermont Algonquian place names were ferreted out. [*Continued* in "Additional Indian Place Names." *Vermont History*, vol. 24, no. 2 (April 1956): 168–169. These thirteen names supplement the list given in the July 1955 issue.]

**454.** Huden, John C. "Indian Troubles in Early Vermont: Part 1." *Vermont History*, vol. 25, no. 4 (October 1957): 288–291.

Huden gives the text of a speech presented "At a Meeting of a Deputation from the Seven Confederate Indian Nations in the Province of Quebec with Their Excellencies, the Governors of New York and Quebec, in the North End of Lake Champlain the 8th of September, 1766" in which the Iroquoian Indians ask that their hunting and fishing rights be preserved by the British, who have taken possession of their lands from the French. The governors reply that they will discourage attempts made in New York and Quebec to undermine the rights and privileges already confirmed to the Indians. There are explanatory footnotes.

**455.** Huden, John C. "Indian Troubles in Early Vermont: Part 2." *Vermont History*, vol. 26, no. 1 (January 1958): 38–41.

Huden gives the text of the "Missiskoui Indians to the Governor of Quebec in the North End of Lake Champlain, the 8th Sep.ʳ 1766," in which the Indians ask the governor to inquire into English attempts to take their lands and request that traders be forbidden to come among them. There is also the text of a letter written by Sir Guy Carleton, dated October 18, 1766, which indicates how the Missisquoi Abenakis feel about the boundary line established by the governors. There are explanatory footnotes.

**456.** Huden, John C. "Indian Troubles in Vermont: Part 3." *Vermont History*, vol. 26, no. 3 (July 1958): 206–207.

**456** *(continued)*

Huden quotes the text of a letter from Luc Schmid, commander at the St. Francis Village, to General Frederick Haldimand, dated September 22, 1781, which tells of Abenaki activity during the Revolutionary period and explains that the Indians of St. Francis, who were under suspicion because many of them espoused the colonial cause, wanted permission to go hunting. Schmid also says he sent two Yankee prisoners to Haldimand. There are explanatory footnotes.

**457.** Huden, John C. "Indians in Vermont—Present and Past." *Vermont History,* vol. 23, no. 1 (January 1955): 25–28.

Huden discusses how very few Indians lived in Vermont in 1955 and that of those who did, the greatest number indicated they were of Algonquian stock. He discusses Jacob Fowler, a Montauk, and Samson Occom, a Mohegan, who have white descendants in Vermont and New York. Huden explains that since the late 1600s there have been no large, permanent Indian settlements in Vermont, most Indians having moved to Canada. He tells of the small trickle of Algonquians down from Canada and of Canadian Indians who claim payment for ancestral lands in Vermont.

**458.** Huden, John C. "Iroquois Place Names in Vermont." *Vermont History,* vol. 25, no. 1 (January 1957): 66–80. Illustrated.

In the first part, Huden cites documentary evidence that shows how the Vermont side of Lake Champlain was home to many Mohawks before 1600. In the second and third parts, he discusses Charles A. Cooke, a Mohawk, who aided in translating Iroquoian designations and who observed that Iroquoian names were generally common-sense descriptions usually concerned with an action. Huden therefore concludes that most Iroquois names as applied to Vermont's mountains, lakes, rivers, and islands, were action words. He provides examples of Iroquois names, for example, George Washington and each succeeding president of the United States was called *A na da ga' rias,* "the destroyer of towns"; General Sullivan was called *De gah nah da rih' tha,* "he smashes villages," after his campaigns of 1779. The Indian words which have been grouped under present-day town names have detailed derivations. There is a section of footnotes, a map showing the approximate distribution of Iroquois tribes around 1525, and photographs of Iroquois artifacts.

**459.** Huden, John C. "The Problem Indians and White Men in Vermont When and Where (1550–)?" *Vermont History,* vol. 24, no. 2 (April 1956): 110–120. Illustrated.

Huden theorizes that white explorers may have visited Lake Champlain before 1609, perhaps in the middle of the 1500s. He cites historical documents and old maps as he discusses the locations of Vermont tribes: the Penacooks, Coosucks, Pocumtucks, Mahicans. He tells of Algonquian migrations from New England to Canada between 1640 and 1790 as the English edged northward. There are two maps with a list of place names and commentary dealing with the 1713 French map. There are extensive notes listing Canadian historical sources.

**460.** Huden, John C. "The White Chief of the St. Francis Abenakis—Some Aspects of Border Warfare 1690–1790." *Vermont History*, vol. 24, no. 3 (July 1956): 199–210. Illustrated.

Huden discusses Joseph-Louis Gill, born in 1719, whose parents were captured by Indians in 1697. He explains how Joseph-Louis was adopted and raised by the St. Francis Abenakis, married an Indian woman, and was elected a sagamore of the Abenakis. Huden describes the 1759 British raid on the Abenakis at Odanak which resulted in the capture and eventual death of Gill's wife and children, and gives variant stories as to details of the capture and deaths. Huden reviews pre-Revolutionary history and explains that Gill sided with the rebels against England. There is a map prepared by the author including places, place names and notes.

**461.** Huden, John C. "The White Chief of the St. Francis Abenakis—Some Aspects of Border Warfare, 1690–1790: Part 2." *Vermont History*, vol. 24, no. 4 (October 1956): 337–355. Illustrated.

Huden discusses rebel and British espionage and counter-espionage from 1777 to 1783 involving Joseph-Louis Gill and other Indians in Canada and Vermont. He explains that Gill probably aided the rebels in Vermont, and reprints a lengthy passage which shows Gill as a rebel partisan. Huden theorizes that Gill steered Indians in their efforts to aid the Green Mountain Boys, soldiers of General Jacob Bayley's Northern Department. There is a map by Huden and extensive footnotes, many of which refer to French Canadian archival materials.

**462.** Hudson, Verne R. "The Naming of Marshfield, Vermont." *Vermont History*, vol. 23, no. 1 (January 1955): 56–57.

Hudson tells how eighteen Stockbridge Indians deeded the township of Marshfield to Isaac Marsh of Stockbridge, Massachusetts, on July 29, 1789. The names of the eighteen Indians, who were then residents of New Stockbridge in New York, are given.

**463.** Hull, William. "Letter of William Hull to Isaac McLellan." *Massachusetts Historical Society Proceedings*, vol. 62 (1928–1929): 25–27.

In his letter dated December 11, 1806, Hull describes Indian resentment towards government measures which would distribute lots to the inhabitants of Detroit. He also discusses the trial of Mashonee, a Potawatomi tried for murder of one of his nation, later judged not guilty by the jury.

**464.** Hunter, Joseph. "Letter of Joseph Hunter, of Carlisle, Pennsylvania, to His Cousin, James Hunter, of Philadelphia, Relating to Indian Depredations." *Pennsylvania Magazine of History and Biography*, vol. 28, no. 1 (1904): 108–109.

111

**464** *(continued)*
In his letter dated July 24, 1768, Hunter writes of people murdered by Indians and describes their defenseless state. He argues that the poor judgment of the Assembly and governor in failing to raise men to fight on the frontier makes a long war a certainty.

**465.** Hunter, William A. "First Line of Defense. 1755–1756." *Pennsylvania History*, vol. 22, no. 3 (July 1955): 299–255. Illustrated.

Hunter discusses an open breach between Pennsylvania's white settlers and her once friendly Indians in 1755 and the first attempts to organize the frontier defenses against the attack of French and allied Indians. He explains how, with the signing of the Supply Act, November 27, 1755, provincial officials began to plan for an effective system of defense and that by January of 1756, the province relied on a chain of forts garrisoned by paid troops who were to patrol constantly between the forts. There are two maps and a sketch of Benjamin Franklin's plan of Fort Allen.

**466.** Hunter, William A. "The Horses in the Moon." *Pennsylvania History*, vol. 22, no. 2 (April 1955): 176–178.

Hunter tells of a partial eclipse in May of 1760 and the reactions of a small party of Indians headed by Teedyuscung, a Delaware, and accompanied by the Moravian missionary, Christian Frederick Post, and John Hays, as recorded in the journals of Post and Hays.

**467.** Hunter, William A. "The Ohio, The Indian's Land." *Pennsylvania History*, vol. 21, no. 4 (October 1954): 338–350. Illustrated.

Hunter discusses how, by 1700, the upper Ohio region westward to present-day Indiana had become by conquest the hunting lands of the Iroquois and new home to displaced groups of Indian immigrants associated with and dependent upon the League. He tells of the Iroquois' practical political arrangements for these Ohio peoples and explains diplomatic arrangements between the Iroquois and the Delawares. Hunter explains the reactions of the Iroquois, Ohio Indians, and Delawares to white intrusion in Ohio country. [*See* the two preceding articles entitled "The French Occupy the Ohio Country" by Donald H. Kent, pages 301–315, and "The English Eye the French in North America" by Lois Mulkearn, pages 316–337. Both tell of the Anglo-French contest for the Ohio region and the struggle between British and French traders for control of the area which profoundly affected Indians of this area. The Hunter article has a map of Ohio country in 1754 and a facsimile of a translation of a Seneca message to Governor Gordon in 1730.]

**468.** Hunter, William A. "Provincial Negotiations With the Western Indians, 1754–1758." *Pennsylvania History*, vol. 18, no. 3 (July 1951): 213–219.

Hunter discusses other less effective and less documented negotiations that preceded the successful work of Christian Frederick Post.

Post made two trips in 1758 to the Ohio to persuade the Delawares to end their alliance with the French.

**469.** Hunter, William A. "Victory at Kittanning." *Pennsylvania History*, vol. 23, no. 3 (July 1956): 376–410. Illustrated.

Hunter discusses the meaning and effectiveness of Lieutenant Colonel John Armstrong's attack on Kittanning, headquarters of Shingas, and Captain Jacobs, both Delaware Indians, on September 8, 1756. He considers military events of the French and Indian war and Delaware raids, particularly their successful attack on Fort Granville in which Lieutenant Edward Armstrong was killed. Drawing on contemporary accounts, he details John Armstrong's plans for the attack of Kittanning in which Captain Jacobs was killed, and describes subsequent events at Kittanning and the troops' retreat. Hunter argues that the success should be measured against its intended purposes, to give a setback to the Indians and to shore up the morale of the province, both of which were, to a large measure, successfully accomplished. There is a portrait of John Armstrong, two maps, and a photo of Kittanning medals.

**470.** Hutchinson, Elmer T. "And We Replied." *New Jersey Historical Society Proceedings*, vol. 72, no. 1 (January 1954): 48–49.

Hutchinson provides information on an Indian reservation named Brotherton, the first Indian reservation in the United States, established by New Jersey and presided over by John Brainerd, a Presbyterian missionary. One hundred Indians went to live at Brotherton when it was laid out around June of 1759, eight months after the Indians waived all claims and demands on land in New Jersey except for hunting and fishing rights. The Brotherton Indians petitioned the state to sell their reservation after they received an invitation in 1801 from their kin, the Mahicans, to live with them at New Stockbridge, near Oneida Lake, New York.

**471.** Ibbotson, Joseph D. "Samuel Kirkland, the Treaty of 1792, and the Indian Barrier State." *New York History*, vol. 19, no. 4 (October 1938): 374–391.

Ibbotson discusses the Canadian plan first suggested in 1783, for an independent Indian Barrier State, which would separate Canada from the "Yankees." He explains how Canadian leaders, hoping to restore the United Empire, encouraged the Indians to continue their war against the U.S. In discussing Wayne's victory over the Indians at Fallen Timbers in 1794, he argues that Wayne succeeded because the Six Nations had decided not to support the Shawnees in their de-

471 *(continued)*
mands, largely the result of Samuel Kirkland's activities from 1790 to
1792 among the Iroquois. He tells of a treaty with the Six Nations that
convinced the Indians of the goodwill of the United States.

472. "An Indian at Princeton." *New Jersey Historical Society Proceedings,* vol. 56,
no. 3 (July 1938): 232.
This brief article discusses the arrangements made for three Delawares to attend Princeton, at government expense. Only one of the
three boys, George W. White Eyes, actually entered Princeton and he
failed to graduate.

473. "Indian Bible." *Massachusetts Historical Society Proceedings,* ser. 1, vol. 13
(1873–1875): 307–311.
This article contains a discussion of a copy of John Eliot's 1663
translation of the Bible into the language of American Indian, the
copy having survived burning by Indians. An extract from the journal
of Jasper Dankers in 1680 describes his visit with Eliot who was
instructing Indians in the Christian religion and recounts Eliot's observation that there were Indians who had "true conversions of the
heart."

474. "Another Interesting Indian Deed." *New Jersey Historical Society Proceedings,* n.s., vol. 10, no. 2 (April 1925): 232–234.
On June 8, 1677, Indians deed land situated in Bergen County and
extending over New York State towards the Hudson. A number of
Indians deed land to David Des Marets on June 22, 1677. They
received wampum, blankets, firelock guns, kettles, clothes, and other
items in payment. The boundaries of the tract are defined.

475. "Indian Deed." *New Jersey Historical Society Proceedings,* ser. 2, vol. 13, no. 3
(1895): 140–142.
On August 13, 1708, Indians deed a tract of land to Peter Sonmans for
money and merchandise. The tract extended from the vicinity of
Morristown south through Somerset County.

476. "Indian Deed." *New Jersey Historical Society Proceedings,* ser. 2, vol. 1, no. 1
(1867): 10–11.
On November 6, 1708 Indians deed a tract of land in New Jersey. The
boundaries are spelled out and the thirteen grantees listed.

477. [Indian Deed for Nauset, Massachusetts] *Massachusetts Historical Society
Proceedings,* vol. 44 (1910–1911): 257–260. Illustrated.
In a deed, dated November, 1666, Indians grant to purchasers of
Nauset several tracts of land, and they are paid with coats, wampum,
kettles, and knives. There are explanatory remarks that tell which
names of localities are still to be found on maps and a facsimile of
Native "signatures."

**478.** "Indian Deed for Petty's Island, 1678." *Pennsylvania Magazine of History and Biography,* vol. 89, no. 1 (January 1965): 111–114.

In a deed, dated July 12, 1678, four Indians turn over the island in the Delaware River to Elizabeth Kinsey. The woman agrees, in the deed, to allow the Indians to hunt and fish on the island, located opposite Kensington, and the Indians promise not to kill her hogs or set fire to her hay fields. Kinsey's promise to give them rum and powder yearly ran counter to the law of 1682 which forbade giving Indians liquor.

**479.** [Indian Deed for Salem, Massachusetts] *Massachusetts Historical Society Collections,* ser. 1, vol. 6 (Boston, 1800): 278–281.

On October 11, 1686, thirteen Indians deed a tract of land, the township of Salem, to selectmen.

**480.** "Indian Deed to Johannis Halenbeeck." *New York Historical Society Collections for the Year 1918, Cadwaller Colden Papers,* vol. 2 (New York, 1919): 87–89.

On February 9, 1732, four Indians from Albany country deed a certain tract of land to Johannis Halenbeeck and his heirs. Following this deed, there is a memorandum dated May 12, 1733, written by Martin Hoffman, one of the witnesses to the above document, noting that several Indians had been paid in full by him and others for a tract of land. This is followed by another brief deed, dated May 12, 1733, by which three Indians quit all claims to lands they sold to Martin Hoffman and several others.

**481.** "Example of Indian Fidelity." *Massachusetts Historical Society Proceedings,* ser. 1, vol. 3 (1855–1858): 304–305.

This story concerns the tenacity of an Indian in fulfilling his obligations to Major Schuyler who had sent him to deliver a letter and bring back an answer. The Indian was required to travel one hundred miles because Schuyler had become ill and was forced to leave the Six Nations country.

**482.** "Indian Fish Weir." *Rhode Island Historical Society Collections,* vol. 30, no. 1 (January 1937): cover. Illustrated.

The cover has a photograph of an Indian fish weir, a stone structure, at Anthony, Rhode Island, visible when water in the mill pond has been lowered.

**483.** "Indian Graves Unearthed at Charlestown." *Rhode Island Historical Society Collections,* vol. 15, no. 1 (January 1922): 18–19.

The contents of an old Indian burial ground are described, including objects and human and animal skeletons.

**484.** "Indian Implements Found in Rhode Island." *Rhode Island Historical Society Collections,* vol. 27, no. 4 (October 1934): 125–127. Illustrated.

These pages contain photographs of a bird stone, pendant, jasper

**484** *(continued)*
spear head, a knife, and a gorget all found in Rhode Island; some of
these artifacts show European influence. The locations where the
objects were found are noted.

**485.** "An Indian Makes History." *Vermont Historical Society News and Notes,* vol.
2, no. 11 (July 1951): 4–7. Illustrated.
The discovery of an Indian skeleton found at a site in Rhode Island is
discussed. There are photographs both of the site and of parts of the
skeleton.

**486.** "Indian Necropolis in West Medford, Massachusetts; Discovered October
21, 1862." *Massachusetts Historical Society Proceedings,* ser. 1, vol. 6 (1862–1863):
362–364.
These pages contain a discussion of the discovery of five Indian
skeletons, a soapstone pipe, and other articles on the farm of Edward
Brooks in West Medford, Massachusetts. There is some speculation
that one skeleton was that of Nanepashemit, a Pawtucket who was
killed in 1619.

**487.** "Indian Pottery." *Rhode Island Historical Society Collections,* vol. 25. no. 2
(April 1932): 45. Illustrated.
Three drawings of fragments of Indian pottery unearthed at Charlestown show artistic adornment by early Narragansett potters. The
fragments were found in 1873 and 1921.

**488.** "Indian Slaves of King Philip's War." *Rhode Island Historical Society Publications,* n.s., vol. 1 (Providence, 1893): 234–240.
The text of several documents, dated 1676, deals with the sale, transportation, and delivery of Indian slaves. A document entitled "Note
on the Transaction of Roger Williams and Others In Selling Indians
into Slavery" points out that in seventeenth century New England
there were no doubts about the right of selling captives taken in war or
of slavery as a fit punishment for crime. Quoted statements show that
slavery was considered a merciful alternative to death and a possible
means of conversion to Christianity. Roger Williams's signature on
some of the documents shows that his views, with regard to the
justification of slavery in the case of captives taken in war, did not
differ from those held in the colonies.

**489.** "Indian Speeches." *Historical Society of Pennsylvania Memoirs,* vol. 1, part 2
(Philadelphia, 1826): 328–333.
The contents of seven speeches, dating from 1724 to 1776, are briefly
identified. All are dated and some have tribal affiliation identified.

**490.** "Indian Terms and Definitions." *Maine Historical Society Collections,* ser. 1,
vol. 5 (Portland, 1857): 427–429.
The Lord's Prayer in the tongue of Norridgewock and Penobscot
Indians of New England and Nova Scotia is given as it was translated

for their use by a French Jesuit and attested to by four Indians on January 22, 1720. There is a list of definitions of Indian words from the manuscript of Paul Dudley, a general scientist.

**491.** [Indian Testimony Concerning Pequot Lands] *Massachusetts Historical Society Collections*, ser. 5, vol. 9 (Boston, 1885): 121–122.

On May 5, 1684, several Indians testify that in the Pequot war, "Sascoe" and "Pequonock" Indians fought with the Pequots against the English and that the English told those Indians they would stay alive if they peacefully surrendered. [*See also* "Testimony of Netorah Concerning Pequot Captives," page 118. Netorah tells about the surrender of Sascoe and "Paquamuck" Indians.]

**492.** "Indian Translation of the 23rd Psalm." *New Jersey Historical Society Proceedings*, n.s., vol. 9, no. 2 (April 1924): 195.

This page contains the full text of the Indian translation, in English, of the Twenty-third Psalm: "The Great Father above is a Shepherd Chief. I am His, and with Him I want not. . . ."

**493.** "Indian Treaties." *New Hampshire Historical Society Collections*, vol. 2 (Concord, 1827): 235–267.

This collection of sixteen documents consists of extracts from the Treaty at Fort William Henry, 1693; the treaties of 1702 and 1703; the full text of a letter from Governor Dudley to the Council of New Hampshire, dated April 6, 1713, regarding the dangers of giving rum to Indians; extracts from the Treaty at Pascataqua, July 13, 1713; a letter of Governor Dudley to the Council of New Hampshire regarding trade; extracts from Assembly records, 1714 and 1717, regarding trade and treaties; the text of the 1717 treaty at Georgetown; extracts from the 1775 treaty at Boston; the 1727 treaty of Casco Indian Articles of Peace, July 25, 1727; an extract from a message of Governor Wentworth to the Assembly of New Hampshire, July 14, 1747, regarding keeping the Six Nations allied to the British; a letter referring to the Falmouth Treaty of 1749 written by Governor Shirley; and a copy of a 1698 Indian submission of Maine and Massachusetts to the British crown.

**494.** "Indian Treaty at Deerfield, Massachusetts, 1735." *Maine Historical Society Collections*, ser. 1, vol. 4 (Portland, 1856): 123–144.

These pages contain the proceedings of a treaty conference between Massachusetts Bay and the Caughnawaga Tribe and the St. Francis, Scaticook, and other Indian groups in August of 1735 in which the Indians agree to be subject to King George. The text of the Indians' request for English trade goods, missionaries, and exemption from severe laws is given. The marks of the Indians are reproduced.

**495.** "Indian Treaty, Falmouth, Maine, 1726." *Maine Historical Society Collections*, ser. 1, vol. 3 (Portland, 1853): 378–405.

**495** *(continued)*
These pages contain the proceedings of a conference between Governor Dummer of Massachusetts Bay and the Eastern Indians at the peace treaty conference held at Falmouth in July and August of 1726. The conversations center on reasons the Norridgewocks did not attend the treaty conference and on the way disputes and controversies between Indians and the English should be settled. The Indians insisted that two houses built at Kennebeck and St. George's River be removed. The English insisted they had deeds for the land on which the houses were built. The text of the ratification of the treaty by the Penobscots and Governor Dummer on August 5 to August 6, 1726, is given. The conference continues on August 9, and Dummer explains that since the Norridgewocks and other tribes have not ratified the treaty, people on the frontier will be hesitant to make improvements. The Indians respond that they will try to get the other tribes to live peacefully and will resist them if they do not.

**496.** "Indian Treaty, Falmouth, Maine, 1727." *Maine Historical Society Collections,* ser. 1, vol. 3 (Portland, 1853): 407–447.
These pages contain the proceedings of a conference held July 17 to July 27, 1727, between Governor Dummer of Massachusetts Bay and the Eastern Indians, or the Penobscots, Norridgewocks, Wowenocks, and "Arresaguntacooks." The text of the treaty made with the Penobscots in August of 1726 is given as well as the conversations about the 1727 treaty which relate to mutual assistance between Indians who sign the treaty and the colony in matters of defense, restoration of English captives, and trade. The treaty was ratified on July 25, 1727.

**497.** "Indian Treaty, Falmouth, Maine, 1749." *Maine Historical Society Collections,* ser. 1, vol. 4 (Portland, 1856): 145–167.
These pages contain the proceedings of a treaty conference held between Massachusetts Bay and Eastern Indians, the Norridgewocks, Penobscots, and others, in September of 1749. Some of the conversations center on whether the few Norridgewocks are empowered to speak for the whole tribe, on whether the Indians are resolved to keep peace with the English during a war with France, on the restoration of Indian captives, and on the placement of trading houses. Text of the treaty is given.

**498.** "Indian Treaty, Georgetown, Maine, 1717." *Maine Historical Society Collections,* ser. 1, vol. 3 (Portland, 1853): 361–375.
These pages contain the proceedings of a conference between Governor Dummer and the sachems and chief men of the Eastern Indians (including the Kennebecs, Penobscots, Pigwackets, and Sacos) at Georgetown on Arrowsick Island August 9 to August 12, 1717. Included are the governor's speech to the Indians and his conversations with them about their necessary compliance with British demands for

their lands and about forts being built. The remarks by Indians are given, their promises of mutual assistance, and the articles of peace signed August 12.

**499.** "Indian Treaty, St. George's Fort, Maine, 1752." *Maine Historical Society Collections,* ser. 1, vol. 4 (Portland, 1856): 168–184.

These pages contain the proceedings of a treaty conference between Massachusetts Bay and the Eastern Indians (Norridgewocks, St. Johns, and Penobscots) in October of 1752. The conversations center on the treaty the tribes made in 1749 at Falmouth, which had been broken by the Norridgewocks, and on whether the Indians at the present conference are empowered to appear on behalf of the whole tribe. The commissioners reread the 1749 treaty, discuss trade, intemperance, end the restoration of captives and insist that Norridgewocks keep to the terms of the treaty.

**500.** "Indian Troubles in Maine, 1702–1704." *Maine Historical Society Collections,* ser. 1, vol. 3 (Portland, 1853): 343–350.

This article includes five letters that concern conflicts with Indians. The first letter, which is dated August 4, 1702, and is from John Wheelwright to the governor of Massachusetts Bay, explains that the town of Wells needs men to protect it from the threat of Indians and the French. The second letter, dated May 10, 1703, and the third, dated May 17, 1703, are both from Cyprian Southack who tells of French and allied Indian hostility. The fourth letter, from Governor Partridge and dated August 12, 1703, is a commission ordering Captain Thomas Parker to kill or take prisoners of French and allied Indians who oppose him. The last letter, dated February 24, 1704, and from Shadrock Walton to Governor Dudley, states that Indians in his company want leave to go home and explains that people have heard rumors that the Indians are planning to attack the army.

**501.** "Indians" in "A List of Documents in the Public Record Office in London, England, Relating to the Province of New Hampshire." *New Hampshire Historical Society Collections,* vol. 10 (Manchester, 1893): scattered pagination.

A number of references are sublisted under "Indian" in the index to this list including the following: address of, to king, captives taken by, conference with, presents to, sale of powder to, submission of, treaties with, and troubles with.

**502.** "A Message from the Indians at Paumittunnawseu, A Place Near Detroit, to the River Indians, of the County of Albany, & also Them of New England." *New York Historical Society Collections for the Year 1920, Cadwallader Colden Papers,* vol. 4 (New York, 1921): 12.

In a communication dated February of 1747, the Indians near Detroit tell the River Indians that they have tried to attack the French but cannot circumvent their fortifications so they can only hope to starve

**502** *(continued)*
them out over a period of time. The River Indians respond that they must revenge the injuries done to their allies according to the terms of their relationship.

**503.** "Indians' Testimony Concerning Title to Sasqua Lands." *Massachusetts Historical Society Collections,* ser. 5, vol. 9 (Boston, 1885): 122–123.

On May 5, 1684, several Indians testify that Romonock was a stranger at Fairfield, that his daughter was not a Sascoe, and that title of lands, according to Sascoes, is in the male line.

**504.** Irvine, James. "Letter of Captain James Irvine, Commanding Officer at Fort Allen, to the Indian Missionary, Christian Frederick Post, at Bethlehem, Concerning his Contemplated Journey to Ohio, with Teedyuscung, the Delaware Chief." *Pennsylvania Magazine of History and Biography,* vol. 24, no. 3 (1900): 392.

In a letter dated February 9, 1769, Captain Irvine tells Post that Teedyuscung wants the governor to supply clothing and wampum for him and the other Indians who will go on a journey to Ohio.

**505.** Jackson, Halliday. "Halliday Jackson's Journal to the Seneca Indians, 1798–1800: Part 1." Edited by Anthony F.C. Wallace. *Pennsylvania History,* vol. 19, no. 2 (April 1952): 117–147. Illustrated.

In his journal entitled "A Short History of My Sojourning in the Wilderness," Jackson gives an account of the circumstances surrounding Handsome Lake's visions in the years 1799 to 1800. The first part describes the planting of the Quaker educational mission among the Seneca Indians on the Upper Allegheny River and the first visions of Handsome Lake. [*Continued* in "Part 2," *Pennsylvania History,* vol. 19, no. 3 (July 1952): 325–349. In this part, Jackson discusses how the Friends' mission became firmly established, how the new Seneca religion, promulgated by Handsome Lake, emerged as one aspect of the spiritual renaissance which the Quakers had hoped to usher into being. Jackson's narrative conveys the Quaker belief that Handsome Lake's messages were worthy of their support.]

**506.** Jackson, Richard. [Letter to William Pitkin] *Connecticut Historical Society Collections,* vol. 19 (Hartford, 1921): 68–71.

In a letter dated February 6, 1767, Jackson reviews and discusses the situation regarding the Mohegan lands, claimed by certain people. He discusses the proposal that all Mohegans and other Indians should be removed from Connecticut to a grant of land obtained for them in a new colony to be erected in Illinois country.

**507.** Jacobs, Wilbur R. "Unsavory Sidelights on the Colonial Fur Trade." *New York History,* vol. 34, no. 2 (April 1953): 135–148.

Jacobs discusses the methods used by the fur traders to secure advantages in trade, particularly those who induced Indians to drink rum before bartering began so the Indians could be swindled out of their skins, those who kept Indians in a permanent state of debt, those who paid unjust prices for skins, and those who weighed fur at only one-third of the actual weight. He concludes with an extract from the first act of a play entitled *Ponteach* which portrays traders with callous attitudes toward Indians. There are lengthy notes.

**508.** Jennings, Francis P. "The Delaware Interregnum." *Pennsylvania Magazine of History and Biography,* vol. 89, no. 2 (April 1965): 174–198.

Jennings discusses the Delaware interregnum, the interval from 1747 to 1752 when there was no Delaware of outstanding importance to negotiate with colonial officials. He discusses the intrigue against Pisquetomen, a Delaware living on the Schuylkill River, conducted by James Logan, Conrad Weiser, and Shikellamy who succeeded in depriving him of legitimate succession to the leadership of his people. After being forced to evacuate his home valley, Pisquetomen migrated to Ohio and organized political alliances with other Delaware leaders which in effect became a resistance to the Iroquois. Eventually, in a crisis beginning in 1751, the Iroquois capitulated to the resistance, withdrawing from their attempt to impose a puppet. The Delawares succeeded in choosing Shingas their own leader in 1752.

**509.** Jennings, Francis. "Incident at Tulpehocken." *Pennsylvania History,* vol. 35, no. 4 (October 1968): 335–355.

Jennings discusses James Logan of Pennsylvania, who was empowered to allot, survey, and patent Pennsylvania's lands, and how he schemed to obtain lands that Indians claimed. In 1713, Logan talked Chief Sassoonan into "giving" 500 acres in Tulpehocken to some Palantines who had already settled on the land. In addition, he cheated the chief out of the full payment for the land. Thomas Penn caught up with Logan in 1732 and took away his power.

**510.** Jennings, Francis. "The Scandalous Indian Policy of William Penn's Sons Deeds and Documents of the Walking Purchase." *Pennsylvania History,* vol. 37, no. 1 (January 1970): 19–39.

This article focuses on the series of events that preceded the Walking Purchase, or Indian Walk, of 1737, documented in part by deeds and patents of land that destroy the proprietary case. The Penns' dilemma, according to Jennings, was that to discharge their family's debt they needed to sell lands, but to sell those lands they had to obtain money to make the prerequisite Indian purchase. The Penns, who recognized Indian ownership, tried to negotiate for conveyance of

510 *(continued)*

that ownership to themselves and in 1734 devised a tactic, an old deed of 1686, to seize Indian property. The Penns argued that the heirs of the Indians had been paid in full by their father but that the boundaries had not been measured off. Jennings describes the formal walk the Penns organized and how they compelled the Indians to agree to the outcome. He tells how the men released a "flood of patents" they had been holding for sale after the Walk freed up Indian lands.

511. Jennings, Francis P. "A Vanishing Indian: Francis Parkman Versus His Sources." *Pennsylvania Magazine of History and Biography,* vol. 87, no. 3 (July 1963): 306–323.

Jennings considers the nineteenth century historian Francis Parkman's version of the story of the many-sided negotiations in 1758 by which peace was restored between the British and Indians after colonial Pennsylvania's first Indian conflict. He argues that Parkman's account of the events leading to the Easton peace conference and of the conference itself in *Montcalm and Wolfe* (1884) is erroneous. Jennings compares Parkman's text with his own cited sources disclosing serious discrepancies even in statements put within quotation marks and altering the role of Indians in the proceedings.

512. Jennings, John. "Journal from Fort Pitt to Fort Chartres in the Illinois Country, March-April, 1766." *Pennsylvania Magazine of History and Biography,* vol. 31, no. 2 (1907): 145–156.

In his journal dated March 8 to April 6, 1766, Jennings describes Indian towns and encampments he passed through on his journey. [*See* Jennings's "Journal at Fort Chartres, and Trip to New Orleans, 1768." *Pennsylvania Magazine of History and Biography,* vol. 31, no. 3 (1907): 304–310. In entries for May 5 to July 8, 1768, Jennings tells how Indians allied either with the French or English were pitted against one another or against rival nations. He describes his trip to New Orleans and the Indians he observed along the way.]

513. Jennings, John. [Petition to the General Assembly of Connecticut] *Connecticut Historical Society Collections,* vol. 21 (Hartford, 1924): 184–185.

Jennings petitions the Connecticut General Assembly on October 13, 1668, to allow him to keep a gift of a tract of land given him by Nesahegen, an Indian.

514. Picquet, *Abbe* François. Edited and translated by John V. Jezierski. "A Journal of Abbe François Picquet." *New York Historical Society Quarterly Bulletin,* vol. 54, no. 4 (October 1970): 361–381.

This diary kept by Abbé François Picquet during his tour of Lake Ontario in June and July of 1751 comments on the attempts of the French and English to enhance their influence among the Six Nations. The Indians held the nominal balance of power in the Ohio Valley and Great Lakes region, and their allegiance was important in the event of war. There is a brief biography of Picquet and his work among Indians in New France. Jezierski analyzes the situation in the Great Lakes region in the early years before the outbreak of the Seven Years' War and comments on the influence of France and England among the Six Nations. Picquet undertook his trip to Lake Ontario to attract Iroquois Indians to his mission as well as to report to the governor-general of New France on the state of affairs in the area. There are footnotes throughout, a plan of Picquet's fort, a map of Lake Ontario, and engravings that illustrate the text.

515. Joselyn, John. "On Maine Indians." *Maine Historical Society Collections,* ser. 1, vol. 3 (Portland, 1853): 93–96.

In his journal published in 1675, John Joselyn gives an account of the appearance and habits, houses and religious beliefs of the Maine Indians.

516. Johnson, Mrs. James. "Mrs. Johnson's Story of her Vermont Journey." *Vermont Historical Society News and Notes,* vol. 2, no. 8 (April 1951): 1–4. Illustrated.

In August 1749, Mrs. James Johnson and others were captured by Indians at Charlestown, New Hampshire, and taken to Canada. This article includes an account of her giving birth along the way, and offers information about Mrs. Johnson's arrangements for commemorating the spot where she had her child. There is a photograph of the stones that were erected.

517. Johnson, Joseph E. "A Quaker Imperialist's View of the British Colonies in America, 1732." *Pennsylvania Magazine of History and Biography,* vol. 60, no. 2 (April 1936): 97–130. Illustrated.

In a lengthy introduction, Johnson discusses why he believes James Logan was the author of an essay written in 1732 and entitled "Of the State of the British Plantations in America: A Memorial." The essay discusses the importance of the American colonies to Great Britain, the dangers that France presents, the colonies' capability of defense, and the Indians as defenders of the British colonies. The essayist discusses the Five Nations Indians who protect New York province from France and feels that Indians in other provinces could be of service. There is a facsimile of the Delisle map of 1729 which shows the location of Indian nations.

518. Johnson, Walter R. "Description of a Specimen of Engraving by the Aboriginal Inhabitants of North America." *Historical Society of Pennsylvania Memoirs,* vol. 4, part 1 (Philadelphia, 1840): 92–103.

Johnson discusses the inscriptions on a block of gray sandstone which seem to represent a map of the country, probably containing directions regarding the haunts of deer, elk, and other game. He also relates some incidents in the history of the early settlers and Indians on the west branch of the Susquehanna River.

**519.** Johnson, Sir William. [Letter to Cadwallader Colden] *New York Historical Society Collections for the Year 1922, Cadwallader Colden Papers,* vol. 6 (New York, 1923): 11–14.

In a letter dated February 20, 1761, William Johnson informs Colden that the Mohawk Indians have been defrauded of their lands which, he argues, is one of the major reasons they are alienated from the British interest. He entreats Colden not to give patents for any lands that were not given or sold with the consent of the whole Indian "castle" because the Indians maintain that the whites "often make a few of their foolish People drunk, then get them to sign Deeds, while the rest, and those even whose property it is, know nothing at all of the affair." Johnson illustrates the Indians' assertion with examples of George Klock and Eve Pickard who both defrauded Indians of land and explains how the Indians are extremely upset. He urges that justice be done swiftly to forestall serious consequences.

**520.** Johnson, Sir William. [Letter to Cadwallader Colden] *New York Historical Society Collections for the Year 1922, Cadwallader Colden Papers,* vol. 6 (New York, 1923): 17–20.

In a letter dated March 19, 1761, Johnson tells how glad the Mohawks will be to hear that Colden resolves that only land purchases made openly and fairly with Indians can be allowed. Johnson reports that a minister and his congregation of Caughnawaga petition for the permission to build a church, that the Mohawks of the lower castle request having another minister, and that the Indians of Canajoharie have deeded him a gift of a tract of land which he knows is not the method of purchasing land. He petitions on behalf of himself and thirty-nine others for a license so the tract can be surveyed immediately. Johnson indicates he knows that other people in New York petitioned to purchase the tract but says that the Indians will not give the land to anyone else.

**521.** Johnson, Sir William. [Letter to Cadwallader Colden] *New York Historical Society Collections for the year 1922, Cadwallader Colden Papers,* vol. 6 (New York, 1923): 43–46.

In a letter dated June 18, 1761, Johnson claims the land given him by the whole castle of Canajoharie fulfills the king's intentions and he objects to the New York Council having so much trouble giving him a license for the tract. He explains that the Mohawks will not make any substantial grants of their land to people until justice is done regarding fraudulently secured lands. Johnson explains that if some lands around Lake George are surveyed for grants to certain white people, the British risk losing the Six Nations as friends and he advises that surveying be prevented, at least for the present.

**522.** Johnson, Sir William. [Letter to Cadwallader Colden] *New York Historical Society Collections for the Year 1922, Cadwallader Colden Papers,* vol. 6 (New York, 1923): 174–175.

In a letter dated May 15, 1762, Johnson renews the alliance with

Senecas at a conference and explains how they have turned over their prisoners. He also describes the unease of the Six Nations over the impending settlement of lands by Connecticut people; these are the lands claimed by virtue of an illegal purchase made years ago by John Lydius of Albany.

**523.** Johnson, Sir William. [Letter to Cadwallader Colden] *New York Historical Society Collections for the Year 1922, Cadwallader Colden Papers*, vol. 6 (New York, 1923): 225–226.

In a letter dated July 13, 1763, Johnson discusses the troubles with western Indian nations in whose country France and England have posts. He tells of the Indian suspicions (goaded by the French) toward British posts, and explains how he is trying to keep the Six Nations neutral. He discusses the Senecas who, under French influence, have declared themselves against the British.

**524.** Johnson, Sir William. [Letter to Cadwallader Colden] *New York Historical Society Collections for the Year 1922, Cadwallader Colden Papers*, vol. 6 (New York, 1923): 228–231.

In a letter dated July 25, 1763, Johnson tells Colden about the meeting he had with the Five Nations, except for the Senecas. He tells of the Five Nations' resolve to remain allied with the British, their intention to try to win back the Senecas, and their ultimatum that if a disputed tract not to be returned to the Mohawks, they will leave the alliance. He briefly discusses George Klock who has divided the Indians into parties, keeping one group drunk. Johnson discusses the hardships of the militia service on the frontier and the need to pay troop expenses because they march at harvest time quite frequently.

**525.** Johnson, Sir William. [Letter to Cadwallader Colden] *New York Historical Society Collections for the Year 1922, Cadwallader Colden Papers*, vol. 6 (New York, 1923): 265–269.

In a letter dated December 24, 1763, Johnson tells Colden about the meeting he had with the Six Nations, including some friendly Senecas. He explains that it is best not to go after hostile Senecas because it would alarm the other Five Nations. Johnson criticizes the English policy which he says never cultivated Indian friendship with the attention and expense that French policy has. As examples he explains how the French have told the Indians that the English would neglect them, hem them in with forts, encroach upon their lands, and destroy them. He also tells how the French have bestowed large gifts on Indians before the reduction of Canada and after it they attempted to divert the fur trade to the Mississippi. He claims that his work has preserved the whole Confederacy and other Inidan nations to the British cause.

**526.** Johnson, Sir William. [Letter to Cadwallader Colden] *New York Historical Society Collections for the Year 1922, Cadwallader Colden Papers*, vol. 6 (New York, 1923): 269–271.

**526** *(continued)*
In a letter dated December 30, 1763, Johnson tells Colden that there is hope for peace on the frontier because Indians expect they will get what they want by being peaceful rather than by being hostile. He explains that the friendship of the Five Nations saved the frontier and therefore trouble should be avoided by allowing them ammunition.

**527.** Johnson, Sir William. [Letter to Cadwallader Colden] *New York Historical Society Collections for the Year 1922, Cadwallader Colden Papers,* vol. 6 (New York, 1923): 276–279.
In a letter dated January 12, 1764, Johnson relates his conversations with the Six Nations, including his desire to give ammunition to those Indians he can trust, excluding Senecas, and to jail a man stirring up troubles among the Indians. He explains where enemy Indians are located and says he needs well-equipped troops to attack them in winter; he suggests that trade be carried on only at principal posts where it is secure and traders can be watched in order to prevent deceit, extortion, or possibly murder; and he says that mercenaries are selling ammunition to Senecas and that it should be prevented.

**528.** Johnson, Sir William. [Letter to Cadwallader Colden] *New York Historical Society Collections for the Year 1922, Cadwallader Colden Papers,* vol. 6 (New York, 1923): 280–281.
In a letter dated January 27, 1764, Johnson tells Colden that French Jesuits are dangerous; they should be abolished and Protestants endowed with their property. He reports that several friendly Conestogas were murdered by Pennsylvanians and that this incident may anger the Five Nations with whom the Conestogas are allied.

**529.** Johnson, Sir William. [Letter to Cadwallader Colden] *New York Historical Society Collections for the Year 1922, Cadwallader Colden Papers,* vol. 6 (New York, 1923): 293–295.
In a letter dated March 16, 1764, Johnson informs Colden that a party of Delawares was defeated by the English and allied Indians. He discusses the distribution of prisoners to the Five Nations to replace deceased persons of the tribes, an Indian custom; he discusses the effects on enemy Indians of employing Indian allies against them; he tells how he has provided guards for Oneida villages while the warriors are away; and he discusses asylum for the "Wialoosings" at Burlington Barracks.

**530.** Johnson, Sir William. [Letter to Cadwallader Colden] *New York Historical Society Collections for the Year 1922, Cadwallader Colden Papers,* vol. 6 (New York, 1923): 296–298.
In a letter dated April 6, 1764, Johnson tells Colden that the Senecas agree to peace terms with the British and that they will deliver up their prisoners, cede land to the British, and accompany them on excursions against the Shawnees and the Delawares. He raises the subject of the dispute over the tract of land given to him by the Canajoharies in 1760, the king's objection to the gift, his own payment, and his desire

to receive the patent which he believes is due to him. He concludes by promising Colden a share of his land.

531. Johnson, Sir William. [Letter to Cadwallader Colden] *New York Historical Society Collections for the Year 1922, Cadwallader Colden Papers,* vol. 6 (New York, 1923): 302–303.

In a letter dated April 20, 1764, Johnson reports that the Five Nations have attacked the Delawares, burning their homes, destroying their corn, seizing their implements and saddles, killing horses and cattle, and chasing the fleeing Delawares. He reports that the scalp of a Delaware chief's nephew has been brought in as well as a Raritan Indian who had been captured by the Delawares.

532. Johnson, Sir William. [Letter to Cadwallader Colden] *New York Historical Society Collections for the Year 1922, Cadwallader Colden Papers,* vol. 6 (New York, 1923): 314–317.

In a letter dated June 9, 1764, Johnson discusses how trade with Indians at war with England should be prohibited for some time to inconvenience them and to reward those Indians who make peace with a renewal of trade. He discusses fraud and abuses committed by traders and argues that traders should be strictly regulated and restricted to principal posts and their abuses prevented on pain of being banished from the posts and cut off from future trade. [*See* Johnson to Colden, December 18, 1764, pages 398–399, in which he discusses how traders should be bound to follow regulations on pain of forfeiting their license.]

533. Johnson, Sir William. [Letter to Cadwallader Colden] *New York Historical Society Collections for the Year 1922, Cadwallader Colden Papers,* vol. 6 (New York, 1923): 344–347.

In a letter dated August 23, 1764, Johnson reports on the large number of Indians who came to the Indian conference at Niagara. He names the nations that attended and those who did not, and discusses the conciliatory actions of the Hurons, Senecas, Delawares, and western nations. He discusses the need for honest people to trade with the Indians, so that peace is ensured. He tells how the Mohawks are being mistreated by Cobus Maybe who has no title but refuses to get off their land, and he describes how whites abuse Indian corn fields, women, and children.

534. Johnson, Sir William. [Letter to Cadwallader Colden] *New York Historical Society Collections for the Year 1922, Cadwallader Colden Papers,* vol. 6 (New York, 1923): 350–351.

In a letter dated September 21, 1764, Johnson discusses the need to answer Mohawks regarding the Kayaderosseras Patent and the need to regulate Indian trade, suggests that a general trade with Indians be forbidden until the conclusion of peace, and says that a small amount of trade should be allowed with the Six Nations since this was promised to them as part of the ratification of peace with the Senecas.

535. Johnson, Sir William. [Letter to Cadwallader Colden] *New York Historical Society Collections for the Year 1922, Cadwallader Colden Papers*, vol. 6 (New York, 1923): 365–367.

In a letter dated October 9, 1764, Johnson discusses the volume of Indian trade on the frontier and the number of traders who are guilty of fraud. He estimates the quantity of goods sold in his district which extends from Nova Scotia, Canada, to the mouth of the Ohio River. He recommends and explains the necessity of allowing the sale of rum and argues for the necessity of procuring justice for Indians in a summary way before the governor and himself.

536. Johnson, Sir William. [Letter to Cadwallader Colden] *New York Historical Society Collections for the Year 1922, Cadwallader Colden Papers*, vol. 6 (New York, 1923): 386–387.

In a letter dated November 20, 1764, Johnson complains about all the troubles George Klock has caused him including most recently his efforts to send two Mohawks to Europe with his son. Johnson complains that Klock has made trouble between Indians and whites as well as among Indians themselves, that he debauches Indians, that drunkenness is a constant scene at his house, and that he has undermined firm friends of the English. He asks Colden for steps to be taken against him in his department.

537. Johnson, Sir William. [Letter to Cadwallader Colden] *New York Historical Society Collections for the Year 1922, Cadwallader Colden Papers*, vol. 6 (New York, 1923): 396–398.

In a letter dated December 11, 1764, Johnson tells Colden he possesses a copy of an Indian purchase of Kayaderosseras Patent which he says is both absurdly worded and asserts wrongly that Indians do not have rights to the land. He talks about the need for speedy justice in regard to Indian property rights and in regard to people like Klock who entice Indians to Europe for purposes of exhibition and for his profit.

538. Johnson, Sir William. [Letter to Cadwallader Colden] *New York Historical Society Collections for the Year 1923, Cadwallader Colden Papers*, vol. 7 (New York, 1923): 19–21.

In a letter dated February 27, 1765, Johnson explains that the Kayaderosseras Patent is causing uneasiness among the Mohawks who, believing an injustice has been done in this matter, are determined to make their complaints public, an act which will cause trouble among other Indian nations. He suggests that to avoid trouble justice should be done speedily.

539. Johnson, Sir William. [Letter to Cadwallader Colden] *New York Historical Society Collections for the Year 1923, Cadwallader Colden Papers*, vol. 7 (New York, 1923): 24–25.

In a letter dated March 21, 1765, Johnson discusses the need to annul the Kayaderosseras Patent because of its obvious illegalities. He explains that the tract was acquired illegally and because it was so obvious, the first patentees never occupied or surveyed the land. He explains how Indians have registered complaints about the Patent since 1750. [*See* Johnson's letter to Colden again on March 21, 1765, pages 25–27, in which he says he will inform the Mohawks both that steps are being taken to vacate the patent and that Colden is taking steps to obtain speedy justice hereafter.]

**540.** Johnson, Sir William. [Letter to Cadwallader Colden] *New York Historical Society Collections for the Year 1923, Cadwallader Colden Papers*, vol. 7 (New York, 1923): 34–37.

In a letter dated May 29, 1765, Johnson discusses the opposition of the Six Nations to the Kayaderosseras Patent and explains why they feel the English did not deal fairly with them. Johnson observes that there were many fraudulent grants obtained with the Indians, discussing an Oneida example, and tells Colden that Kayaderosseras is a fraud, that the Six Nations consider it to be so, and that it should never have been undertaken, but questions whether it might still be legally valid.

**541.** Johnson, Sir William. [Letter to Cadwallader Colden] *New York Historical Society Collections for the Year 1923, Cadwallader Colden Papers*, vol. 7 (New York, 1923): 44–45.

In a letter dated July 5, 1765, Johnson tells Colden how the Shawnees, Delawares, and Mingos have arrived to enter into a peace treaty, how the Delawares and the Senecas have delivered prisoners, and how he has sent a party of Chippewa Indians to the western Indian nations to warn them not to start troubles or else they will be attacked and to inform them that peace has been established. The matter of the Kayaderosseras Patent is briefly mentioned.

**542.** Johnson, Sir William. [Letter to Cadwallader Colden] *New York Historical Society Collections for the Year 1923, Cadwallader Colden Papers*, vol. 7 (New York, 1923): 49–51.

In a letter dated August 15, 1765, Johnson explains that Mr. Croghan, his deputy agent for Indian affairs, was wounded and two white and three Shawnee chiefs with him were killed during a French-inspired attack by Kickapoos and Mascoutens. He further explains that the same Kickapoos and Mascoutens were repentant and wanted Croghan to mediate between them and the Shawnees and Six Nations of whom they are in dread.

**543.** Johnson, Sir William. [Letter to Cadwallader Colden] *New York Historical Society Collections for the Year 1923, Cadwallader Colden Papers*, vol. 7 (New York, 1923): 92.

In a letter dated November 9, 1765, Johnson informs Colden about the success of George Croghan's journey to make peace with the

543 *(continued)*
Illinois Indians. He explains that Croghan's success is due to the repentance described in the incident above. [*See* the previous letter.]

**544.** Johnson, Sir William. [Letter to Cadwallader Colden] *New York Historical Society Collections for the Year 1923, Cadwallader Colden Papers*, vol. 7 (New York, 1923): 149–152.

In a letter dated January 26, 1769, Johnson discusses the necessity for a change in the management of Indian affairs. He explains how the whole system of Indian politics has been changed since the reduction of Canada and the enlarged number of new allies. He tells of Indian suspicions regarding the treaty made at Fort Stanwix on November 5, 1768 and of the New England missionaries who opposed the Indian boundaries set in the treaty.

**545.** Jones, William. [Letter to Governor William Leete] *Connecticut Historical Society Collections*, vol. 21 (Hartford, 1924): 242–244.

In a letter dated May 2, 1676, Jones describes the murder of a man at Branford by two Indians and of the search for the Indian killers resulting in the holding of several innocent Indians.

**546.** Jones, William, and Bishop, James. [Letter to Deputy Governor William Leete] *Connecticut Historical Society Collections*, vol. 21 (Hartford, 1924): 223–225.

In a letter dated August 31 and September 2, 1675, Jones and Bishop report that danger from armed Indians approaching Paugusset and neighboring towns is not as great as was originally feared.

**547.** Kalm, Peter. "Selections from *Travels in North America* by Peter Kalm." *Vermont Quarterly*, n.s., vol. 19, no. 3 (July 1951): 159–171.

Dated July 2 to July 20, 1748, these selections from *Travels in North America* bear on Vermont history. Peter Kalm, a Swede, discusses forest fires owing to the carelessness of the Indians, tells of an Indian avenging the death of one of his brethren, discusses Indian diseases, their use of bear fat, and their food.

**548.** Kaufman, Martin. "War Sentiment in Western Pennsylvania: 1812." *Pennsylvania History*, vol. 3, no. 4 (October 1964): 436–448.

Kaufman questions the evidence from western Pennsylvania that indicates nationalism and hatred were causes of war sentiment which led to war in 1812. He argues that the causes of war as espoused by Julius W. Pratt were only partially correct as applied to western Pennsylvania, since though nationalism was the cause of war, in this area the feeling was directed neither towards acquisition of territory nor towards removal of the Indian menace. He explains further that there was no fear of Indians and therefore little interest in the removal of a menace which probably did not exist.

**549.** "Indian Deed for Kayaderosseras Patent" and "Grant of Kayaderosseras Patent." *New York Historical Society Collections for the Year 1922, Cadwallader Colden Papers,* vol. 6 (New York, 1923); 359–364.

By the deed of Kayaderosseras Patent, dated October 6, 1704, several Mohawks grant this tract of land located in the county of Albany to the attorney general of New York province for £60. The grant of Kayaderosseras Patent, dated November 2, 1708, follows, in which Queen Anne grants different sections of the tract to thirteen people. The boundaries of each of the thirteen portions of the tract are carefully defined for each patentee.

**550.** Keck, Jeremiah. "Sir William Johnson." *New York State Historical Association Proceedings, Fifth Annual Meeting,* vol. 4 (Lake George, 1904): 54–67.

Keck discusses how Sir William Johnson evolved from a land agent to a great representative of the British Empire, trying to win Indians from the French and confirm them in their alliance with the British. He quotes from letters written by Johnson that illustrate his conscientious discharge of duties towards the Indians and his domestic life until his death in 1774.

**551.** Keith, Charles P. "The Bishop of London and Penn's Indian Policy." *Pennsylvania Magazine of History and Biography.* vol. 31, no. 4 (1907): 385–392.

Keith discusses Henry Compton, Bishop of London, who, he argues, advised Penn to buy, not take away, the Indians' land. He briefly reviews Compton's background and considers attitudes held by other English on property rights of Indians. Keith theorizes that Compton wanted Penn to do justice to the Indians.

**552.** Kellogg, Elijah. "Vocabulary of Words in the Language of the Quoddy Indians." *Massachusetts Historical Society Collections,* ser. 3, vol. 3 (Boston, 1833): 181–182.

The vocabulary of about 130 words contains two columns, one in English and the other containing the Passamaquoddy equivalent.

**553.** Kellogg, Martin. [Letter to Roger Wolcott] *Connecticut Historical Society Collections,* vol. 16 (Hartford, 1916): 159–161.

In a letter dated April 14, 1752, Kellogg reports on information he has received from a Mohawk informer who told him the Six Nations have learned that the Taweetauwees' plan to go to war against the French and that the Six Nations and other tribes at the council are willing to join in this war against the French.

**554.** Kelsay, Isabel T. "Joseph Brant: The Legend and the Man, A Foreword." *New York History,* vol. 40, no. 4 (October 1959): 368–379.

554 *(continued)*
While working on a biography of Brant, a Mohawk chief, Kelsay tells about his life in Canada discussing various contradictions and anomalies, explaining the many kinds of published and unpublished materials she has used as sources, and repeating some of the legends that exist about Brant's life and character.

555. Kenny, James. "James Kenny's Journal to Yᵉ Westward, 1758–1759." *Pennsylvania Magazine of History and Biography*, vol. 37, no. 4 (1913): 395–449.
   In journal entries dated December 10, 1758 to November 8, 1759. Kenny, who traveled via York, Frederick, Cumberland, and Braddock's Road to Pittsburgh, reports on the trade of Indians, fighting between Indians and Whites, the movements of French Indians, English-French rivalry over Indians, and the reputation of Quakers among Indians as pacifists.

556. Kenny, James. "Journal of James Kenny, 1761–1763." *Pennsylvania Magazine of History and Biography*, vol. 37, no. 1 (1913): 1–47.
   In journal entries dated April 13, 1761 to April 6, 1762, Kenny gives details on Indian traders and the trading store, established by the Commissioners of Indian Affairs, that he operates. He describes the work of Christian Frederick Post, Moravian missionary to the Indians, the movements of the Indian "kings" of Pennsylvania and Ohio tribes, the British-French rivalry for Indian allies, intertribal fighting, Indian-white hostilities, and Indian prisoners. He tells of the Delawares' religion, which envisions no whites. [*Continued* in *Pennsylvania Magazine of History and Biography*, vol. 37, no. 2 (1913): 152–201. This part of the journal is dated April 7, 1762 to June 15, 1763.]

557. Kent, Donald H. "Contrecoeus's Copy of George Washington's Journal for 1754." *Pennsylvania History*, vol. 19, no. 1 (January 1952): 1–32. Illustrated.
   An introduction by Kent precedes the text of one version of a journal kept by George Washington during his march toward the Ohio to aid Captain Trent in constructing fortresses and defending British possessions against the French and describing the skirmish with the French under Jumonville. Kent discusses different versions of the journal and variations that arise from the process of translation. The journal, dated March 31 to June 27, 1754, fell into the hands of the French July 3, 1754. It tells of British intentions, the likelihood of an attack on Fort Duquesne, and the feelings of Indians regarding the French and the British, revealing the diplomatic tactics used in attempts to win over the Delawares as British allies. The texts of speeches by Delawares and Iroquois are recorded as well as those by Washington to the Indians. The journal also reveals how Indian spies were used by both British and French to learn each other's plans. Two maps and explanatory notes are included.

558. Kent, Donald H. "The Myth of Etienne Brulé." *Pennsylvania History*, vol. 43, no. 4 (October 1976): 291–306. Illustrated.

Kent finds no available evidence to prove either that Etienne Brulé was the first man to explore the Susquehanna Valley or the existence of the site of an Indian village of Carantouan which Brulé claimed to have visited in 1615–1616. Kent believes that even if Brulé's story of exploring the Susquehanna Valley is true, it led to no French claims and it had no effect on the historical development of Pennsylvania. Brulé did serve Champlain on his 1615 expedition to the Huron country. There are two maps dated 1616 and 1632, both part of Champlain's map of New France.

**559.** Kerr, Wilfred B. "Fort Niagara, 1759–1763." *New York History*, vol. 15, no. 3 (July 1934): 281–301. Illustrated.

Based on the papers of General Amherst, commander-in-chief of the British forces in America, Kerr describes the capture and occupation of Fort Niagara by British forces, the Indians who fought as British or French allies, trade at the fort with Indians, the poor treatment of Indians from traders at Toronto, troubles with Indians at Detroit during the summer of 1763, and the Indian attack on the British convoy at Devil's Hole in September of 1763. Included is an illustration of Fort Niagara.

**560.** Kidder, Frederick. "The Abenaki Indians: Their Treaties of 1713 and 1717, and a Vocabulary With a Historical Introduction." *Maine Historical Society Collections,* ser. 1, vol. 6 (Portland, 1859): 229–263.

Kidder describes the tribes all known as Abenakis, who inhabited the territory now constituting Maine and New Hampshire. He sketches their early history, various emigrations of Abenakis to Canada, and their hostile relations with Whites. He considers the locations of eight distinct tribes in Maine and New Hampshire: the Penobscots, Passamaquoddies, Wawenocks, Norridgewocks, Assagumticooks, Pigwackets (Sokokis), Penacooks, and St. Johns (Maliseets). There are extracts from a spelling book published in 1830 in the Abenaki language and texts of treaties of 1713 and 1717. All the marks of the Indians are reproduced.

**561.** Killbuck, William Henry. "Killbuck Island, Pittsburgh." *Pennsylvania Magazine of History and Biography,* vol. 10, no. 1 (1886): 116–119.

These pages contain the complete text of the original draft of a petition by William Henry Killbuck, a Delaware known as Gelelemend, to Governor Thomas McKean of Pennsylvania. Dated January 8, 1805, it concerns Killbuck's claim to Killbuck's Island near Pittsburgh, recounts how the island has been granted to him by Colonel Gibson in the name of Pennsylvania, and tells of the services he has performed for the United States. Killbuck requests an indisputable title to the island.

**562.** Kinnicutt, Lincoln N. "The Plymouth Settlement and Tisquantum." *Massachusetts Historical Society Proceedings,* vol. 48 (November 1914): 103–118.

562 *(continued)*
Kinnicutt discusses a series of events between 1605 and 1621 in which Tisquantum, or Squanto, Sir Ferdinando Gorges, Captain Thomas Dermer, Captain John Smith, and Captain George Weymouth all figure and considers the difference in opinion as to when Tisquantum first appears. He argues that the Pilgrims had at least a half-formed intention of settling in the vicinity of Cape Cod before they left England, that Sir Ferdinando, probably unknown to them, used every possible measure to accomplish this purpose, and that Captain Dermer and Tisquantum were to have played important roles in his scheme.

**563.** Kirkland, Samuel. "Fragment of a Letter by Samuel Kirkland." ed. George Fenwick Jones. *New York Historical Society Quarterly Bulletin,* vol. 53, no. 4 (October 1969): 385–389. Illustrated.

In a letter written around 1768, Kirkland tells of the hardships he has endured living among Indians and trying to convert and "civilize" them. He tells how he stopped his many forms of labor, such as growing his own food, because it lowered his status in the eyes of the Indians and explains that once he stopped, the Indians' opinion indeed changed. A portrait of Kirkland is included.

**564.** Kirkland, Samuel. [Letter to James Bowdoin] *Massachusetts Historical Society Collections,* ser. 7, vol. 6 (Boston, 1907): 75–76.

In a letter dated August 23, 1785, Kirkland tells of his missionary work with Indians and explains that the Commissioners of New York made a large purchase of land (around 500,000 acres) from the Oneidas in June. There was difficulty in making the purchase because the Indians originally had refused to cooperate. Kirkland describes the boundaries of the purchase.

**565.** Kirsch, George B. "Jeremy Belknap and the Problem of Blacks and Indians in Early America." *Historical New Hampshire,* vol. 34, nos. 3 and 4 (Fall and Winter 1979): 202–222.

Kirsch discusses Belknap's analysis of race relations which shows the latter had some benevolence and sensitivity along with a strong bias in favor of his own way of life. The brief biography of Belknap focuses on his *History of New Hampshire,* researched in the early 1780s, in which the minister devotes attention to the treatment of natives by the English and to the Indian wars, trying to present both sides fairly. He discusses Belknap's interest in U.S. Indian policy including his pessimism that Indians can be converted to Christianity and civilization. Belknap's interest in the role of blacks in America reveals many of the same themes apparent also in his study of Indians; his comparisons of native Americans and blacks in America reveal that he never accepts either culture as equal to that of whites.

**566.** Klingberg, Frank J. "The Anglican Minority in Colonial Pennsylvania, with Particular Reference to the Indian." *Pennsylvania Magazine of History and Biography,* vol. 65, no. 3 (July 1941): 276–299.

Klingberg discusses the complicated new society in Pennsylvania based on various European heritages, each of which was divided into many sects. He describes how German, British, and Scots-Irish sects disputed over the treatment of Indians. He examines the records of the Society for the Propagation of the Gospel, from the early 1700s through the 1760s, when it established itself as a strong Anglican minority. He studies the part played by the Society in Pennsylvania before the Revolution, problems facing the Society missionaries in converting Indians and its conflicts with the dominant Quaker party. Extracts from letters of missionaries document the Society plans for educating and converting Indian children and demonstrate the Society foresaw that the "Indian problem" would have to be an imperial, later a federal, responsibility.

**567.** Koier, Louise E. "The Tale of Moses Pierson's Blockhouse." *Vermont Historical Society News and Notes,* vol. 6, no. 7 (March 1955): 49–51. Illustrated.
    Koier discusses Indian raids in Vermont and tells specifically of the pioneer family of Moses Pierson whose members succeeded in fighting off attacking Indians in March of 1778. Included is an illustration of a pioneer family fighting off raiding Indians.

**568.** Labaree, Leonard W. "Benjamin Franklin and the Defense of Pennsylvania, 1754–1757." *Pennsylvania History,* vol. 29, no. 1 (January 1962): 7–23. Illustrated.
    Labaree discusses Franklin's role during the French and Indian War, including his efforts in helping Pennsylvania defend itself against French incursions and in building and garrisoning a series of forts beyond the Blue Mountains to protect the country from Indian attacks. There is a map of the scene of Franklin's frontier service, dated 1755–1756.

**569.** Lacey, John. "Memoirs of Brigadier-General John Lacey of Philadelphia." *Pennsylvania Magazine of History and Biography,* vol. 25, no. 1 (1901): 4–10.
    In this section of his memoirs, Lacey recalls a journey he made with his uncle to a Delaware town on the Ohio River, the capital of the Delaware nation, between July 7 and September of 1773. He describes the daily life of the Delawares and reports about the Indian girls, housekeepers at his lodging, who play "jute harps."

**570.** Lafayette, Marquis de. "Lafayette's Address to the Indians." *Pennsylvania Magazine of History and Biography,* vol. 14, no. 3 (1890) 319–320.
    In his 1784 address at Fort Stanwix, Lafayette tells the Indians that the American cause is just, that they should keep the peace among them-

**570** *(continued)*

selves, that the American-French alliance is durable, and that the Indians should trade with the Americans and sell them land.

**571.** LaFantasie, Glenn W. "Murder of an Indian." *Rhode Island History*, vol. 38, no. 3 (August 1979): 67–77. Illustrated.

LaFantasie discusses the murder in 1638 of "Penowanyanquis," a Nipmuck, by a group of white men, an incident which had repercussions on Indian-white relations. He tells how the murdered Indian, a messenger for the Narragansett Mixanno, was bearing a gift for the English when he was robbed and attacked by four men. Roger Williams unsuspectingly provided the men with refuge, but the Indians eventually captured them. LaFantasie discusses the confusion over what to do with the prisoners and the anger of the Narragansetts over Penowanyanquis' death; he describes the trial of three of the men (one escaping), and their hanging which averted the eruption of a frontier war. Footnotes and pictures accompany the text.

**572.** LaFantasie, Glenn W., and Campbell, Paul R. "Covenants of Grace, Covenants of Wrath: Niantic-Puritan Relations in New England." *Rhode Island History*, vol. 37, no. 1 (February 1978): 15–23.

The authors discuss the historiography of Indian-European relations, concluding that historians cannot reconstruct the history of New England Indians without relying solely on white sources of information. They explain how studies of Indian-white relations in New England have perpetuated the tradition of choosing sides without a critical examination of each culture's effect on the other, discuss the cultural reasons for Puritan policy toward the Niantics within a context of American Puritanism, and describe Puritan beliefs about law, pride and covenants of grace. They conclude by evaluating the Puritan treatment of Indians and though they consider it difficult to defend, they argue that understanding that policy, recognizing its complexities, and explaining its motivation may lead to a more balanced notion of Indian-white relations in the seventeenth century. Along with footnotes there is a 1677 map of New England and a sketch of Mather.

**573.** Lampee, Thomas C. "The Missisquoi Loyalists." *Vermont Historical Society Proceedings*, n.s., vol. 6, no. 2 (June 1938): 81–139. Illustrated. Bibliography.

Lampee traces the establishment of an Abenaki village on the banks of the Missisquoi River at the beginning of the seventeenth century and tells how the Abenakis remained there undisturbed until the mid-eighteenth century when the French and the government of New Hampshire attempted to secure their land. Included is the text of a lease between James Robertson and some Abenakis, dated July 13, 1765, concerning negotiations for a portion of the land. Lampee explains how the Abenaki Indians and the Missisquoi village were used by the French in their campaign against the frontiers of New York and New England during the several colonial wars. He summarizes the situation in regard to land titles on both sides of the international boundary as it existed at the close of the American Revolution, and he explains how the Abenakis, whose lands lay wholly in Vermont, finally abandoned the locality and retired to Canada. Lampee tells how a group of Loyalists began a settlement at Missisquoi Bay around 1784 on Indian lands that were the subject of claims, how they refused to leave, and how they eventually obtained titles to the land, angering the Abenakis. There are five maps and a bibliography of sources.

574. Lathrop, John. "Letter of John Lathrop." *Massachusetts Historical Society Proceedings*, ser. 1, vol. 10 (Boston, 1867–1869): 114–116.
  In a letter dated August 10, 1809, Lathrop discusses the inscription on a rock in the Taunton River, i.e., the Dighton Rock, and argues it was made by Indians rather than by people of Oriental or Occidental origins. He briefly explains the Indian way of recording transactions, either in war or in hunting.

575. Laurent, Stephen. "The Abenakis: Aborigines of Vermont." *Vermont History*, vol. 24, no. 1 (January 1956): 3–11.
  Laurent, an Abenaki, discusses the reasons why the Indians felt superior to whites and records a sample of story-telling in the Abenaki language that describes an encounter between a party of Iroquois and a small group of Abenakis from Missisquoi. [The tape is available at the Vermont Historical Society in its Living Voice Archives.] He discussses Abenaki religious beliefs dealing with the functions of shamans. Lastly, he describes illness and medicine among Indians.

576. Laurent, Stephen. "The Abenakis: Aborigines of Vermont: Part 1." *Vermont History*, vol. 23, no. 4 (October 1955): 286–295.
  Laurent, an Abenaki, explains how his tribe, a subdivision of the Algonquians, relates to other groups, and is further divided into smaller groups according to names of regions, rivers, or lakes near their villages. He discusses characteristics of the Abenaki language and tells of the missionaries' difficulties with the language, particularly their problem with obtaining Abenaki equivalents for religious abstractions.

577. Law, Jonathan. "The Law Papers: Correspondence and Documents During Jonathan Law's Governorship of the Colony of Connecticut, 1741–1750." vol. 1: *Connecticut Historical Society Collections*, vol. 11 (Hartford, 1907); vol. 2: *Connecticut Historical Society Collections*, vol. 13 (Hartford, 1911); vol. 3: *Connecticut Historical Society Collections*, vol. 15 (Hartford, 1914).
  Indians are mentioned throughout the three volumes. The first volume covers October, 1741 to July, 1745; the second volume covers August, 1745 to December, 1746; and the third volume covers January, 1747 to October, 1750.

**578.** Leach, Douglas Edward. "A New View of the Declaration of War Against the Narragansetts, November, 1675." *Rhode Island History,* vol. 15, no. 2 (April 1956): 33–41.

Leach examines documentary evidence surrounding the decision to begin hostilities against the Narragansetts. He discusses the disagreement over the true date the commissioners of the United Colonies officially decided to go to war (between November 6 and November 12, 1695), the question of when Rhode Island agreed to cooperate with the United Colonies in their attack on the Narragansetts, and the tensions characterizing relations among the colonies of Massachusetts, Plymouth, and Connecticut at the time of King Philip's War, rivalries which hampered the common war effort.

**579.** Leach, Douglas Edward. "Away to Rhode Island From Their Cellars." *Rhode Island History,* vol. 11, no. 2 (April 1959): 43–55.

Leach discusses the burden King Philip's War placed on the mainland population of Rhode Island with the destruction of property and the abandonment of towns. He also discusses the burden on Aquideck Islanders who were obliged to provide a haven for refugees and wounded soldiers from the mainland. The author tells how the people intended to stand their ground in Warwick and in Providence.

**580.** Lee, Charles. [General Lee's Remarks on Indians] *New York Historical Society Collections for the Year 1874, Lee Papers,* vol. 4 (New York, 1875): 70–72.

In these undated remarks, Lee suggests that Indians have no rights to land and should be driven from it because they have not used it for hundreds of years, that they are devils, that they depart from the law of nature when they take prisoners, and that they are murderers who should be exterminated. He writes that Indians who do not go to war should be permitted to live but those who do not refrain from attacking and fighting, should not be allowed to exist. Lee comments that several young Indians taken "from the woods" and sent to public schools still "retain the temper of their race" and were not made useful members of society. He refers to John Mentour as an example of an Indian who, though educated in a seminary, nevertheless remained a "savage."

**581.** Le Roy, Marie, and Leininger, Barbara. "Narrative of Marie Le Roy and Barbara Leininger For Three Years Captive Among the Indians." *Pennsylvania Magazine of History and Biography,* vol. 29, no. 4 (1905): 407–409.

The circumstances of the capture of both girls on October 16, 1755 are given, as well as descriptions of other whites who were killed, the route taken to Kittanning and other places, their treatment, the work they were forced to do, descriptions of tormenting of the captive English, and the circumstances of their escape to Pittsburgh. The authors conclude with a long list of names and circumstances of prisoners whom they met at various places where they were taken in the course of their captivity. There are footnotes.

582. Lewin, Howard. "A Frontier Diplomat: Andrew Montour." *Pennsylvania History*, vol. 33, no. 2 (April 1960): 153–186.

Lewin discusses how Andrew Montour, the son of an Oneida chief, played an important part in British-Indian relations as an interpreter and diplomat between 1742 and 1768, being employed by Pennsylvania and Virginia to mediate between them and the Indians. He discusses how Montour's importance stems from the influence he had at Onondaga. Montour is viewed through the eyes of those who knew and wrote about him since he could neither read nor write and so left no record of his own.

583. Lincoln, Benjamin. "Journal of a Treaty Held in 1793, With the Indian Tribes Northwest of the Ohio." *Massachusetts Historical Society Collections,* ser. 3, vol. 5 (Boston, 1836): 109–176. Illustrated.

Benjamin Lincoln, one of three U.S. commissioners dealing with Indians northwest of the Ohio, was unsuccessful in his peace negotiations. Dated April 23 to September 9, 1973, the journal quotes speeches by the commissioners, Cat's Eyes (a Shawnee), Carry-One-About (a Wyandot), and by other assembled Indians who declare they will not agree to any boundary other than the Ohio River. Lincoln observes the condition of the Indians and argues that they have not been destroyed by intemperance, drinking being more prevalent among the whites. Many of Lincoln's discussions center on why the Ohio River cannot be the boundary between the Indians and the United States. Included is a sketch of the scene at the conference, the Indians being drawn by a British officer present at the scene.

584. Lincoln, Benjamin. [Letter to Jeremy Belknap] *Massachusetts Historical Society Collections,* ser. 6, vol. 4 (Boston, 1891): 512–517.

In a letter dated January 21, 1792, Lincoln theorizes on how civilization would ultimately and naturally conquer "barbarism," that war, which he regards as an unrighteous measure, should not be used to remove the present generations of Indians. He theorizes that the number of inhabitants is controlled by the means of subsistence, *e.g.,* if fish and game which are essential to life are eliminated from a territory, the number of Indians that the food supports will consequently decrease. He also argues that when one attempts to enlarge borders faster than they are enlarged by the natural retirement of Indians, the consequence is death, injury, and sickness. Lincoln believes that where Indians have not transferred their land rights, their rights remain "complete."

585. Lincoln, Benjamin. "Observations on the Indians of North America; Containing an Answer to Some Remarks of Doctor Ramsey." *Massachusetts Historical Society Collections,* ser. 1, vol. 5 (Boston, 1798): 6–12.

In a response dated October 29, 1795, Lincoln replies to Dr. Ramsey's remarks concerning the causes which have combined to check the population of Indian tribes, the impracticability of the Indians' being

**585** *(continued)*
civilized, and on the prediction that soon they would cease to be a
nation. Lincoln disagrees with Ramsey's reasons being the principal
causes for the population decline of Indians. He agrees with Ramsey
that Indians will never be civilized; however, Lincoln does not agree
that the consequences of their remaining "untutored" will be annihila-
tion.

**586.** Lincoln, Enoch. "Remarks on the Indian Language." *"Maine Historical
Society Collections,* ser. 1, vol. 1 (Portland, 1865): 412–427.
　　Governor Lincoln discusses the general properties of the Abenaki
language and describes the language of the Norridgewocks and Micmacs. He cites examples of sentence composition and a vocabulary of
words in the Norridgewock tongue and explains how the vocabularies
of the Abenakis and Micmacs differ. He discusses the "hieroglyphics"
or picture-writing of Maine tribes.

**587.** Lincoln, Enoch. "Some Account of the Catholic Missions in Maine." *Maine
Historical Society Collections,* ser. 1, vol. 1 (Portland, 1865): 428–446.
　　Governor Lincoln gives the history of the Catholic missions and missionaries who tried to Christianize Maine Indians from the early
seventeenth century to the mid-nineteenth century. He tells of missionaries Biart and Massé, Druillettes, Vincent and Jacques Bigot,
Thury, Sebastien Rasles, and Romagne.

**588.** Lindesay, John. [Letter to Cadwallader Colden] *New York Historical Society
Collections for the Year 1934, Cadwallader Colden Papers,* vol. 8 (New York, 1937):
341–342.
　　In a letter dated September 5, 1746, Lindesay discusses his own
prestige among Indians and tells why Indians have petitioned the
king to have him transferred to Oswego. He relates two instances
which have elevated him in the Indians' estimation.

**589.** "List of Scalping Knives Sent to Captain Abercrombie." *New York Historical Society Collections for the Year 1921, Cadwallader Colden Papers,* vol. 5 (New
York, 1922): 234.
　　An itemized list dated June 10, 1758, describes 496 scalping and other
kinds of knives, which have been sent to Captain James Abercrombie
from Captain Wilmot. Number one on the list is "50 Bon hefted large
Scalping knifes."

**590.** Little, Reverend Daniel. "Penobscot Indians." *Massachusetts Historical Society Proceedings,* ser. 1, vol. 3 (Boston, 1855–1858): 305–306.
　　Reverend Little of Kennebunk, ordered by the General Court to meet
with the Penobscot Indians and to command the Indians to ratify an
1857 treaty, records their reasons for refusing to sign. He informs
them that after breaking such an agreement, they cannot expect
favors from the government.

591. Livermore, Daniel. "Military Journal of Major Daniel Livermore." *New Hampshire Historical Society Collections,* vol. 6 (Concord, 1850): 308–335.

In entries dated May 17, 1779 to April 6, 1780, Livermore describes the march of General Poor's Brigade from Soldier's Fortune in the expedition against the Six Nations, commanded by General Sullivan. Livermore, a captain in the Third New Hampshire Regiment, commanded a company of foot soldiers. His journal tells of destroying Indian crops and towns, taking Indian prisoners, and of resistance by Indians.

592. Livingston, Robert. "The Livingston Indian Records, 1666–1723." *Pennsylvania History,* vol. 23, no. 1 (January 1956): 1–240. Illustrated. Bibliography.

In an introductory article by Lawrence H. Leder entitled "Robert Livingston (1654–1728), Secretary for Indian Affairs, and His Papers," the mystery of the location of the Livingston Indian records is resolved. This is followed by an essay entitled "The Iroquois: A Brief Outline of Their History," by Paul W. Wallace, followed by the records, edited by Leder. The documents detail Iroquois negotiations with the English colonies from Massachusetts to Virginia, 1666–1723, with principal Iroquois trouble centering in New York, Maryland, and Virginia receiving most of the attention. There is an early map of the Susquehanna River in 1683 and other papers concerning Pennsylvania. The records document trade rivalry among the English colonies, movements of Shawnees both before and after they were given homes by the Iroquois in Pennsylvania, and clashes between white settlers and Indians along the Appalachian border. There is a glossary of Indian tribal names, two maps, and portraits of Livingston and Schuyler. At the bottom of pages 28–199, Ray Fadden's pictographic symbols are reproduced, with translation in English; these relate the history of the founding of the Five Nations and appear one to a page.

593. Lobdell, Jared C. "Some Indian Place Names in the Bergen-Passaic Area." *New Jersey Historical Society Proceedings,* vol. 84, no. 4 (October 1966): 265–270.

Lobdell discusses a group of names (Acquackanonk, Pompton, and Preakness in Passaic County, and Hackensack, Paramus, Pascack, Ramapo, Sicomac, and Tappan [Old Tappan] in Bergen County) that help to explain Indian history of the area. Footnotes are included.

594. Lockwood, Luke Vincent. "The St. Memin Indian Portraits." *New York Historical Society Quarterly Bulletin,* vol. 12, no. 1 (April 1928): 3–26.

Lockwood discusses watercolors done by St. Memin, born in 1770. He briefly discusses the history of Great and Little Osages and Mandan Indians and describes the arrival of a party of Osages in Washington, D.C., in 1804 to see President Jefferson. The full text of Jefferson's address to the Osages is quoted as well as the text of a message by H. Dearborn to the Indians dealing with bonds of friendship and docu-

594 *(continued)*
ments, particularly newspaper reports, that describe the Osage visit to other eastern cities. There are thirteen black-and-white reproductions of the water colors or crayon sketches of the Osage, Iowa, Mandan, and Delaware men or women all drawn by St. Memin and brief remarks under each sketch or watercolor.

595. Logan, James. "Letter of James Logan to Conrad Weiser, 1736." *Pennsylvania Magazine of History and Biography*, vol. 23, no. 3 (1899): 392–393.
In a letter dated January 22, 1737, Logan asks Weiser to inform the Iroquois Council that the Virginia governor wishes to negotiate a peace in April between the northern Indians and their enemies, the Cherokees and Catawbas, and to ask them meanwhile neither to attack the southern Indians nor to approach the inhabitants of Virginia.

596. Logan, James. "Names of Indian Chiefs, 1723–1734." *Pennsylvania Magazine of History and Biography*, vol. 18, no. 4 (1894): 510.
In extracts copied from James Logan's accounts with various proprietors between 1723 and 1725 he furnishes the names of some Indians prominent in that period of the history of Pennsylvania Province. The extracts cite the kinds of goods given to the Indians on certain occasions, such as the death of a husband.

597. Lords of the Committee of Council for Plantation Affairs. "Report of the Committee of Council." *Connecticut Historical Society Collections*, vol. 18 (Hartford, 1920): 227–228.
In the report dated March 3, 1763, the Committee discusses the resolution of a problem relating to the intent of some Connecticut people to settle on the Susquehanna River at Wyoming. Since this site is part of the Delaware hunting grounds, there might be trouble caused with the Six Nations. The Committee explains that the governor of Connecticut and Sir Jeffrey Amherst, commander in chief of English forces in America, are charged with preventing the settlement. [*See* "Thomas Fitch to Committee for Trade and Plantations," pages 258–259, dated November 10, 1763. Governor Fitch reports that a Connecticut Commissioner has been appointed to act in concert with a similar person in Pennsylvania to carry out the royal instructions. The governor reports that the Connecticut Commissioner has intelligence that the settlement at Wyoming had been destroyed by Indians.]

598. Lords of Trade. [Letter to Cadwallader Colden] *New York Historical Society Collections for the Year 1923, Cadwallader Colden Papers*, vol. 7 (New York, 1923): 23.
In a letter dated March 16, 1765, the Lords explain they are sending back to New York by boat, immediately, two Mohawks named Hermannus and Joseph who had been brought to London by a man

named Myers. The Indians were exhibited at a tavern in London and a complaint was made to the House of Lords. [*See* Alexander Colden's letter to William Johnson, June 1, 1765, pages 38–39, in which he reports the arrival of the two Mohawks from London and tells of their complaints against Myers. Colden explains their travel arrangements to Abany where they are to see Johnson.]

**599.** McAdams, Donald R. "The Sullivan Expedition: Success or Failure?" *New York Historical Society Quarterly Bulletin,* vol. 54, no. 1 (January 1970): 53–81.

The Sullivan Expedition was a two-pronged expedition of over 4000 Continentals who in the late summer of 1779 traveled to the heart of Indian country to punish the Iroquois for their raids on New York and Pennsylvania frontiers during the summer and fall of 1778. The army joined at Tioga and systematically proceeded to burn crops and destroy forty Indian towns in the heartland of the Six Nations. McAdams argues that instead of disabling the Indians, the Sullivan Expedition only served to exasperate them, as evidenced by Indian border raids in 1780 and 1781, which proved to be more destructive than the raids of 1778. McAdams argues that the Expedition failed completely in its main objective to bring peace to the frontier and that still undetermined are the long-term effects the Sullivan campaign had on the power of the Iroquois. He concludes by asserting that "the Iroquois' power would have died with or without the Sullivan Expedition." Included are a map showing Butler's line of march from the Schoharie to Indian and Tory settlements on the Susquehanna, dated October 1778, and other illustrations.

**600.** McClure, David. [On the Narragansett Indians, 1768] *Rhode Island Historical Society Publications,* vol. 7 (Providence, 1899): 136–238.

This extract relating to the condition of the Narragansetts in 1768 is taken from a book by Reverend David McClure. He describes an Indian meeting on the Sabbath in the summer of 1768 and focusing on how the Indians "exhorted."

**601.** McCorison, Marcus A. "Colonial Defenses of the Upper Connecticut Valley." *Vermont History,* vol. 30, no. 1 (January 1962): 50–62. Bibliography.

This article contains a survey of regional military activities between the French and allied Indians and the British and allied Indians preceding the establishment of the state of Vermont. McCorison recounts Indian raids on the towns in Maine, New Hampshire, Vermont, and Massachusetts from the late seventeenth through the mid-eighteenth century.

**602.** McHugh, Thomas F. "The Moravian Mission to the American Indian: Early American Peace Corps." *Pennsylvania History*, vol. 33, no. 4 (October 1966): 412–431.

McHugh discusses the general philosophy of the Moravian missionary and explains his daily life, showing that Moravians realized they had to work from within the Indian culture, accepting an Indian way of life, if they were to succeed in missionary work with Indians. He claims that the Moravian missionary work which differed from other religious groups was enlightened and modern for the eighteenth and nineteenth centuries and that the use of a systematic and functional method with the Indians resembled in many ways the twentieth century Peace Corps.

**603.** Mack, John Martin. "Reverend John Martin Mack's Narrative of a Visit to Onondaga in 1752." *Pennsylvania Magazine of History and Biography*, vol. 29, no. 3 (1905): 343–358.

In entries dated August 12 to September 23, Mack narrates his visit with Zeisberger and Rundt to Onondaga for the purpose of learning the dialects of the Five Nations. He tells of passing through different Iroquois towns, the hostility of the Oneidas to the missionaries, and the cooperation of different Iroquois along the route. Upon their arrival at Onondaga, they witness the Indian Council's meeting at which a request from the governor of South Carolina for peace between the Six Nations and the Catawbas is being considered. The Iroquois Council accepted the missionaries' proposal to learn the dialects of the Five Nations. Footnotes include explanatory materials.

**604.** McKendry, William. "Journal of William McKendry." *Massachusetts Historical Society Proceedings*, ser. 2, vol. 2 (1885–1886): 442–478.

McKendry's journal, dated October 25, 1777 to January 3, 1780, deals with General Sullivan's campaign against the New York Indians in 1779. McKendry gives testimony about the houses in the Indian towns.

**605.** McMahon, Reginald. "The Achter Col Colony on the Hackensack." *New Jersey History*, vol. 89, no. 4 (Winter 1971): 221–240. Illustrated.

McMahon discusses the Achter Col (Dutch) colony and Joannes Winckelman, Manager around 1641. He describes the boundaries of the colony, the location of Winckelman's house at Bogota, and the location of the Hackensacks about three miles away. Details of the building of Winckelman's house, which was subsequently burned by Indians, and the polarization between the lower Hudson Indians and the Dutch are given. Hostile relationships that led to bloodshed in 1642 and later a peace treaty in 1643 resulted in no white settlement in northern New Jersey until the English conquest in 1664. Extracts (undated) from a journal by David DeVries, a neighbor of the Achter Col colony and the Hackensack village, are cited. McMahon discusses how the placement of Winckelman's house at Bogota was ascertained through an Indian deed of 1664. There are maps of the Achter Col Colony, plans of Winckelman's house, and a photograph of an Indian dugout canoe.

**606.** M'Roberts, Patrick. "Patrick M'Roberts Tour Through Part of the North Provinces of America." *Pennsylvania Magazine of History and Biography*, vol. 59, no. 2 (April 1935): 170–175.

In observations dated May 1755, M'Roberts comments on Indians in New York and gives descriptions of clothing, shelter, food, temperament, and handiwork, all based on contacts with three groups—the Iroquois, Micmacs, and Delawares.

**607.** Madokawando. "Covenant of Lands With Sir William Phips, by Madokawando, Sagamore of Penobscot." *Maine Historical Society Collections, Documentary History of the State of Maine*, ser. 2, vol. 8 (Portland, 1902): 11–15.

Madokawando, sagamore of the Penobscots, released his lands on both sides of the St. George River to Sir William Phips in this covenant dated May 9, 1694.

**608.** Maine Commissioners. "Bond Given to the Penobscot Tribe of Indians, By Commissioners of the State of Maine, June 10, 1833." *Maine Historical Society Collections, Documentary History of the State of Maine*, ser. 2, vol. 8 (Portland, 1902): 303–305.

This text of a bond (dated June 10, 1833) given to the Penobscot Tribe by the commissioners of Maine was for $50,000 to be deposited for the use of the tribe in lieu of townships purchased from them by the commissioners.

**609.** Maine Commissioners. "Cession of Lands to the State of Maine for the Support of the Indians by the Commissioners Under the Act of Separation, December 28, 1822." *Maine Historical Society Collections, Documentary History of the State of Maine*, ser. 2, vol. 2 (Portland, 1902): 234–236.

This is the text of an act which ceded lands within Maine valued at $30,000 for the support of the Indians in accord with an article in the Act of Separation of June 19, 1819.

**610.** "Maine Indians, 1689–1701, Documents." *Maine Historical Society Collections, Documentary History of the State of Maine*, ser. 2, vol. 5 (Portland, 1897), various pages.

In this collection there are nearly 200 documents, letters, petitions, testimonies, depositions, instructions to committees, etc., that contain references to Indians in Maine from August 14, 1689 to February 1701 or lengthy texts such as the text of the "Agreement w[th] Indians at Wells, 1.3.91." with the marks of Indians reproduced. The documents tell of Indian hostilities, alliances, conferences, etc. [*See* "Indians, 1641–1689, Documents," *Maine Historical Society Collections, Documentary History of the State of Maine*, ser. 2, vol. 6 (Portland, 1900). This volume, dated September 2, 1641 to June 27, 1689, contains over one

610 *(continued)*
hundred references to Indians in petitions, journals, Massachusetts
council minutes, letters, etc. The documents largely tell of Indian
hostilities, the seizing of captives or the exchanging of prisoners, and
alliances.]

611. Mamoosin. "Commission for the Trial of Mamoosin, an Indian." *Massachusetts Historical Society Proceedings*, ser. 2, vol. 1 (1884–1885): 220–221.
This is the text of a commission of oyer and terminer dated November
24, 1703, for the trial for murder of Mamoosin, at Salem. This
commission was formerly issued to the royal judges empowering them
to hear and determine felonies on special occasions. The justices are
assigned to enquire into "all Felonies, Murders, homicides, and man-
slaughters committed by a certain Indian named *Mamousin* now in
Custody. . . ."

612. Manley, Henry S. "Buying Buffalo from the Indians." *New York History*,
vol. 28, no. 3 (July 1947): 313–329.
Manley discusses the period of 1837 to 1840, describing the maneu-
verings of the Ogden Land Company which, in attempting to remove
Senecas from their reservations, coerced the chiefs into signing a
treaty and in 1838 a deed, which surrendered all New York Seneca
reservations to the Company. Manley tells of the treaty's political
ramifications in Washington. A long bibliographical note is included.

613. Manley, Henry S. "Red Jacket's Last Campaign and an Extended Bibliographical and Biographical Note." *New York History*, vol. 31, no. 2 (April 1950):
149–168.
Manley discusses Red Jacket's final defense of his people's land,
describes charges against the 1826 Buffalo Creek Treaty, the removal
in 1827 and reinstatement of Red Jacket as chief and explains Seneca
factionalism. The article is followed by an annotated bibliographical
and biographical note.

614. Mann, James. "Account of the Surprise and Defeat of a Body of Indians,
Near Wrentham." *Massachusetts Historical Society Collections*, ser. 1, vol. 10 (Bos-
ton, 1809): 138–142.
In an account dated August 22, 1806, Mann repeats the story heard
from various persons regarding the defeat of Indians by settlers of
Wrentham.

615. Marsh, Philip. "Indian Folklore in Freneau." *New Jersey Historical Society
Proceedings*, vol. 71, no. 2 (April 1953): 125–135.
Marsh discusses the primitivism in Freneau's poetry as depicted by the
poet's advocacy of the environment and customs of American Indians. He also discusses Freneau's attachment to Rousseau's ideas of
primitivism including his belief in the renunciation of civilization for
the simple life and the solitude of the forest. Marsh analyzes the
poems and prose in which Freneau propagandizes for Indian customs

and primitivism, surveys the literature that he speculates Freneau read, and concludes that this primitivism was the product of a generally rising romantic imagination, which in the eighteenth century insisted on making Indians into noble savages who were both heroes of "ingenious humanity" and victims of "the evils of civilization."

**616.** Marshall, John. "John Marshall's Diary: Indians." *Massachusetts Historical Society Proceedings,* ser. 2, vol. 14 (1900–1901): 27–30.

In brief entries dated 1697 to 1708, Marshall tells of Indian hostilities, perfidy, murders, and captures. The attacks on Lancaster, Deerfield, and Haverhill are noted.

**617.** Marshall, John. "Chief Justice Marshall's Opinions of Indians." *Massachusetts Historical Society Proceedings,* ser. 2, vol. 14 (1900–1901): 337–338.

In a statement on October 29, 1828, Marshall considers that the time has arrived for the present government to be guided by the principles of humanity and justice in its conduct towards the Indians. He perceives that the conduct of our forebears may have been justified but believes that oppression and disreputable conduct towards Indians is no longer necessary and stains the American character.

**618.** Marshe, Witham. "Witham Marshe's Journal of the Treaty Held with the Six Nations by the Commissioners of Maryland and Other Provinces, at Lancaster, Pa., June, 1744." *Massachusetts Historical Society Collections,* ser. 1, vol. 7 (Boston, 1807): 171–201.

In entries dated June 16 to July 8, 1744, Marshe tells of the efforts of the Commissioners to settle land claims between the Six Nations and Maryland. He discusses the goods given to the Indians in exchange for their agreeing to release the claims and right to any lands now held by the inhabitants of Maryland and he names the chiefs who signed the deed giving Maryland some hundred thousand acres of land. Some Indian customs such as their refusal to stay in houses of white people and their placement of cabins according to rank of the nation in the grand council are also pointed out.

**619.** Marye, William B. "An Account of the Collections of Indian Artifacts Belonging to the Maryland Historical Society." *Maryland Historical Magazine,* vol. 33, no. 3 (September 1938): 262–271.

Marye describes the two collections of Indian artifacts owned by the Maryland Historical Society and then lists the objects of special interest under the following headings: banner stones, grooved axes, celts, gorgets, pipes, discoidal stones, folsom darts, cache blades, and spearheads. The seventy listed artifacts were found in Anne Arundel County.

**620.** Marye, William B. "The Annacostin Indian Fort." *Maryland Historical Magazine,* vol. 33, no. 2 (June 1938): 134–135.

Marye first discusses the site of the old Annacostin Indian fort and

**620** *(continued)*

then considers whether this was the Indian fort where Nacostines and Annacostins, acting as intermediaries, furthered trade between the Indians and the white people of Virginia.

**621.** Marye, William B. "The Baltimore County 'Garrison' and the Old Garrison Roads." *Maryland Historical Magazine,* vol. 16, no. 2 (June 1921): 105–149.

This is a discussion of the Baltimore County "rangers," a small body of men which patrolled the "wilderness in the seventeenth century and guarded or forewarned the frontier plantations of the county against incursions and raids of Indians." Marye gives an account of the fort, called "The Garrison," of the routes of the roads laid out through the forest, and of locations of outposts created at intervals on the roads. The article also contains a theory of Indian roads explaining the motives which determined the choice of the site of the Garrison. There are extensive notes. [*Continued* in *Maryland Historical Magazine,* vol. 16, no. 3 (September 1921): 207–259.]

**622.** Marye, William B. "Notes on the Primitive History of Western Maryland." *Maryland Historical Magazine,* vol. 38, no. 2 (June 1943): 161–166.

Marye includes notes intended to supplement his articles on a map. He discusses Will's Town, an Indian town on Will's Creek, and tells of a 1746 record in which the Upper (Shawnee) Old Town is mentioned. He also modifies an earlier statement concerning the extent of Indian fields on the north of the Potomac River.

**623.** Marye, William B."The Old Indian Road." *Maryland Historical Magazine,* vol. 15, no. 2 (June 1920): 107–124.

Marye describes a highway, evidently of Indian origin, that is referred to in a number of eighteenth century records of Old Baltimore County. By interpreting the references and allusions to the course of the Old Indian Road and to places situated along it, Marye determines the road's route over many miles. There are detailed explanatory notes. [*Continued* in *Maryland Historical Magazine,* vol. 15, no. 3 (September 1920): 208–229, and *Maryland Historical Magazine,* vol. 15, no. 4 (December 1920): 345–395.]

**624.** Marye, William B. " 'Patowmeck Above Ye Inhabitants.' A Commentary on the Subject of an Old Map. Part 1." *Maryland Historical Magazine,* vol. 30, no. 1 (March 1935): 1–11. Part 2, *Maryland Historical Magazine,* vol. 30, no. 2 (June 1935): 114–137; Part 3. *Maryland Historical Magazine,* vol. 32, no. 4 (December 1937): 293–300; Part 4. *Maryland Historical Magzine,* vol. 34, no. 3 (September 1939): 325–333.

In "Part 1," Marye attributes to Philemon Lloyd the drawing of the map of western Maryland and western Virginia circa 1721. He gives the full text of the "memoranda" that accompanies the map. In "Part 2," Marye reviews Indian towns and trails located on the map. He focuses on the Tuscarora Indian town, King Opessa's Town on the

Warriors' Path, a Shawnee Indian town, and evidences of Shawnee settlements in Baltimore County. In "Part 3," Marye discusses the land carriage between the Susquehanna and the waters of the Potomac. He argues that Indians used a "back way" for canoe travel that formerly existed. There is a map of the area he discusses. In "Part 4," Marye describes several Shawnee Indian "Old Towns" on the Upper Potomac River. He goes into some detail about Thomas Cresap, who acquired land at Old Town.

**625.** Marye, William B. "Piscattaway." *Maryland Historical Magazine*, vol. 30, no. 3 (September 1935): 183–240.

Marye discusses the Piscataways who lived near the Potomac River, reviews the nature of their ruling powers, and the domain of their three leaders (or "tayacs") called "emperors" by the English. He discusses the numbers of Piscataways and their allies in the period 1608 to 1697 and gives reasons for a population decline. Using documentary sources that reveal two seats of the tribe, a town known as Aquakeeke and a fort on Piscataway, he discusses which is the principal one. He describes the Indians' manners and customs, considers the location of Zachiah Fort where the Piscataways sought refuge from other Indian groups around 1680, and he also tells of the flight of the Piscataways from Maryland in the spring of 1697. An appendix of land notes is included.

**626.** Mashantatak. "Indian Deed of Mashantatak." *Rhode Island Historical Society Collections*, vol. 10 (Providence, 1902): 62–64.

Writing on June 23, 1662, Mashantatack quotes the text of a deed granting land in Providence to two Sweet brothers by the author and several Cohassiac Indians.

**627.** Mason, John. "Brief History of the Pequot War." *Massachusetts Historical Society Collections*, ser. 2, vol. 8 (Boston, 1826): 120–153.

Mason explains why the English fought the Pequots, centering on the murder of Captain Stone and incidents of Pequot violence in Connecticut. He gives a history of the Pequot War which began in May, 1637, and in which he was a principal actor as the commander of the Connecticut forces. Mason explores the reasons behind certain military actions, the alliance with Uncas, a Mohegan, and the assistance of the Narragansetts. He tells of war battles and explains the attack against the Niantics who were allied with the Pequots. An introduction by Thomas Prince written in 1735 discusses Mason.

**628.** Mason, John. "Captain John Mason's Memorial." *Connecticut Historical Society Collections*, vol. 5 (Hartford, 1896): 384–397.

Writing on May 13, 1725, Mason discusses the expenses he incurred while defending the Mohegans. This is followed by two reports of the Committee of the General Assembly which review Mason's memorial

**628** *(continued)*
in May, 1726. Following is a letter dated June 22, 1725, from Governor Talcott to Captain John Mason in which Talcott discusses Mason's memorial.

**629.** Mason, John. [Letter to Governor Talcott] *Connecticut Historical Society Collections,* vol. 4 (Hartford, 1892): 290–291.
Writing on October 8, 1733, Mason discusses intemperance among the Mohegans and suggests a plan to prevent drinking.

**630.** Mason, John. [Letter to John Allyn] *Connecticut Historical Society Collections,* vol. 21 (Hartford, 1924): 240
Writing on April 27, 1676, Mason asks that the Mohegans and Pequots be supplied with ammunition to protect them from enemy Indian attacks.

**631.** Mason, John. [Letters to John Winthrop] *Massachusetts Historical Society Collections,* ser. 4, vol. 7 (Boston, 1865): 411–427.
Writing between 1643 and 1669, Mason tells of Narragansett plotting against England, suggests that the Mohawks will not join the Narragansetts against the English, and questions why Wequashcooke has been captured. He describes Indian attacks on English houses and says that Ninigret has been arrested.

**632.** Mason, Samuel. "Petition of Samuel Mason and His Brother." *Connecticut Historical Society Collections,* vol. 5 (Hartford, 1896): 139–159.
In this undated petition, Mason and his brother argue that the Mohegans have been betrayed by Connecticut. In 1704 the Commission had declared that lands still held by Mohegans could not be conveyed without the consent of Samuel Mason, but this was not upheld and when the Commission met in 1738 to review various injustices (e.g., the taking of Ben Uncas's land), the Commissioners from Rhode Island abused the King's Commission of Review and did not allow the Indians to make a proper defense on their own behalf. The petition asks for restoration of Mohegan lands, especially to Uncas, the present sachem.

**633.** Mason, Samuel. "Samuel Mason's Petition to the King." *Connecticut Historical Society Collections,* vol. 15 (Hartford, 1914): 433–435.
Mason reviews the debts he has incurred as the trustee and guardian of the Mohegans in their dispute with Connecticut. He petitions the Lords of the Treasury for the money owed him as well as for money to give relief to impoverished Mohegans.

**634.** Mason, Thaddeus. "List of Names of the Indians Old and Young." *Massachusetts Historical Society Collections,* ser. 1, vol. 10 (Boston, 1809): 134–136.
A census, taken on June 16, 1749, lists Indian parents and the number of their children, both male and female, who live in Natick.

635. Massachusetts Colony. "Answer of the Agents of Massachusetts to the Complaints of Sir Edmund Andros, 1688." *Maine Historical Society Collections,* ser. 1, vol. 5 (Portland, 1857): 389–398.

On May 30, 1690, the agents of Massachusetts Colony answer Sir Andros' account of the forces raised in New England for the defense of the country against the Indians. The agents evaluate the forts built by Andros at several locations (Pemaquid, New Dartmouth, New Towne, Segadehock, Falmouth, Saco River, etc.) and deem them useless for purposes of defense.

636. Massachusetts Colony. "Instructions from Massachusetts Colony to John Winthrop, Governor of Connecticut to Treat with the Pequots." *Massachusetts Historical Society Collections,* ser. 3, vol. 3 (1833): 129–131.

In a communication written on May 4, 1636, Massachusetts Colony instructs the governor of Connecticut to deal with the Pequots on its behalf. Massachusetts requests a conference with the Pequots to discuss their role in the murder of a few English.

637. Massachusetts Commissioners. "An Intended Speech to be Made at Our Last Conference with the Indians in August, 1746." *New York Historical Society Collections for the Year 1919. Cadwallader Colden Papers,* vol. 3 (New York, 1921): 243–246.

The text of a speech by the Commissioners of Massachusetts Bay concerns the mounting of an expedition, with the assistance of Indians, against the French in Canada. The Commissioners describe French incitement of certain Indians against the British, and how the British King is resolved to avenge the wronged colonists. The speech is intended to rouse the Indians to help in fighting the king's battles.

638. Massachusetts Commissioners. "Massachusetts Commissioners' Proposals." *Connecticut Historical Society Collections,* vol. 11 (Hartford, 1907): 194–195.

In a memorandum dated June 20, 1744, the Massachusetts commissioners propose methods of mutual defense for New York, Massachusetts, and Connecticut. They consider how to deal, in case of confict, with Indians allied with the French.

639. Massachusetts and Connecticut Commissioners. "Commissioners from Massachusetts and Connecticut to the River Indians." *Connecticut Historical Society Collections,* vol. 11 (Hartford, 1907): 185–186.

In an undated message, the commissioners tell the Indians they wish to maintain friendship with them and that they want the Indians to keep their eyes on the French and to warn the British of French attempts to attack. The commissioners promise to defend the River Indians.

640. Massachusetts and Connecticut Commissioners. "Commissioners from Massachusetts and Connecticut to the Six Nations." *Connecticut Historical Society Collections,* vol. 11 (Hartford, 1907): 188–189.

**640** *(continued)*
In an undated message, the commissioners tell the Six Nations that because war has been declared between Great Britain and France, it is necessary for them to unite with the British colonies against the French.

**641.** Massachusetts General Court. "Act Conferring Treaty with Penobscot Tribe of Indians, by the General Court of Massachusetts, October 11, 1786." *Maine Historical Society Collections. Documentary History of the State of Maine,* ser. 2, vol. 8 (Portland, 1902): 80–82.
The text of the act passed by the General Court of Massachusetts on October 11, 1786 confirms a treaty made with the Penobscot Indians on August 30, 1786.

**642.** Massachusetts General Court. "Minutes About Indian Captives." *Massachusetts Historical Society Proceedings,* ser. 2, vol. 5 (1889–1890): 115.
In the minutes of the Massachusetts General Court of 1749–1750, there are brief items about certain captives taken either by the Indians or the French.

**643.** "Defense of Frontier Towns Against Indian Incursions in 1694–1695." *Massachusetts Historical Society Proceedings,* vol. 43 (1909–1910): 504–519.
Fifteen letters, dated December 3, 1694 to March 18, 1695, addressed to the executive authorities of Massachusetts, concern the defenses of the frontier towns against Indian incursions in 1694–1695, the aftermath of the outbreak of 1692.

**644.** "Massacre at Dover, 1689." *New Hampshire Historical Society Collections,* vol. 8 (Concord, 1866): 403–405. Illustrated.
This is a brief note about the massacre at Dover on June 27, 1689, and the death of Major Waldron. A 1689 map of Cochecho (Dover) gives an idea of the situation of the garrisons at that time. There is a discussion of one of the captives, an infant named Christina Baker, taken by the Indians at Dover. [*See also* her adult petition to Governor Belcher of New Hampshire for a tract of land, dated March 16, 1737. She cites her early captivity, loss of her estate, and hardships as reason for her petition. On pages 426–427 of same volume.]

**645.** Mather, Cotton. [Diary of Cotton Mather, 1681–1708, 1709–1724.] *Massachusetts Historical Society Collections,* ser. 7, vols. 7 and 8 (Boston, 1911): 1912.
There are brief references to Indians throughout the diary of Cotton Mather. "Indians" and the "Society for Propagating the Gospel Among Indians" are terms in the index.

**646.** Mathews, Vincent. [Letter to Cadwallader Colden] *New York Historical Society Collections For the Year 1921, Cadwallader Colden Papers,* vol. 5 (New York, 1923): 128–130.
Writing on March 12, 1757, Mathews informs Colden about the contents of a letter written by his nephew, Garret Abeels, concerning

the treaty renewed between the French and Five Nations of Indians that allows unmolested trade to Oneida Lake. Abeels provides information on the number of Indians and French troops and the plans of the Five Nations to attack frontier settlements in New York and Pennsylvania as well as their intention to take prisoners. Mathews requests help from Governor Hardy to protect the frontiers.

**647.** Matthews, Albert. "Tradition." *Massachusetts Historical Society Proceedings*, vol. 42 (1908–1909): 194–195.

Matthews recollects an incident involving an atrocity against the Indians committed by American officers, soldiers of Sullivan's campaign of 1779. He quotes from journals kept during the expedition substantiating the story that American soldiers skinned Indians and used the skin for boot-legs. He concludes that barbaric deeds were not just confined to one side in the Revolutionary War.

**648.** May, John. "Journal of Colonel John May, of Boston, Relative to a Journey to the Ohio Country, 1789." *Pennsylvania Magazine of History and Biography*, vol. 45, no. 2 (1921): 101–179.

Written between April 23 and December, 1789, the journal of John May contains many references to Indian attacks and killings of settlers. There are also descriptions of the shooting of an Indian, Indians signaling to one another, the capture of two boys and their escape, and the capture and release of a woman.

**649.** Mayer, Brantz, "Tah-gah-jute or Logan and Captain Michael Cresap." *Maryland Historical Society Publication*, no. 15 (Baltimore, 1851): 1–86. Illustrated.

Mayer discusses the elements of a story that has converted a Maryland man, Michael Cresap, into a "monster" for allegedly murdering the family of Logan, a Cayuga Indian. Mayer begins by telling of the Indians who lived and hunted in the Susquehanna Valley: Shawnees, Conoys, Nanticokes, Monseys, and others presided over by Shikellamy, a Cayuga of the Six Nations who lived at the Indian village called Shamokin and his son Tah-gah-jute, or Logan. He sketches the background of Lord Dunmore's War (known in Maryland as Cresap's War), a conflict between Virginians and Shawnees in which, the writer argues, Cresap was unjustly accused of acting "a bloody part." Mayer considers three reasons for the war that broke out in 1774, including the hostility of Indians towards Virginians since 1764, Pennsylvania-Virginia disputes over territorial limits and jurisdiction, and Lord Dunmore's desire to start a war which would ally the Indians with the British against the Americans. Mayer argues that Cresap had peaceful intentions when he settled in the Ohio Valley, but the bloody battles between Logan and the settlers, and the raid of April, 1774, in which Logan's family was murdered, changed him. He describes the circumstances in which Logan made a famous speech blaming Cresap for the murder of his family, although Mayer contends that others

649 *(continued)*
actually committed the crime. He writes of Cresap's death in 1775 and the aftermath of Logan's life through 1780 dealing with his intemperance. Logan's accusation against Cresap has since been endorsed by writers, historians, and even Jefferson. The appendix contains pertinent letters and other evidence supporting or refuting Logan's accusation. Mayer also provides six versions of Logan's speech and their sources. Pictures of colonial officials are included.

650. Mayhew, Thomas. "Letter to Governor Prince." *Massachusetts Historical Society Collections,* ser. 1, vol. 6 (Boston, 1800): 196–197.
    Writing on June 19, 1671, Mayhew informs Governor Prince that he knows of no plots by Martha's Vineyard Indians against the English. He writes that the Indians affirm their obedience to British authority and their willingness to fight British enemies. Mayhew tries to justify his mild treatment of the Indians.

651. Maylem, John. "Draft of Gallic Perfidy: A Poem." *Massachusetts Historical Society Collections,* vol. 80 (Boston, 1972): 416–422.
    Maylem's poem is entitled "Transactions of the Savages at the Capitulation of Fort William Henry, August 9, 1757." Maylem, who was at the fort when it fell to the French, was captured by Indians. He describes their physical appearance when they attacked, tells how the troops "fall hapless Victims to the Savage Fury!," and how some troops escaped or were captured and taken to Canada.

652. Mechacksitt. "Indian Bill of Sale of Bombay Hook, Delaware, 1679." *Pennsylvania Magazine of History and Biography,* vol. 14, no. 1 (1890): 75–76. Illustrated.
    Mechacksitt sells Bombay Hook to Peter Bayard in May, 1679, for gun powder, several coats, liquor, and a kettle. The boundaries of the tract are spelled out.

653. Melven, Eleazer. "Journal of Captain Eleazer Melven, with Eighteen Men Under His Command, in the Wilderness Towards Crown Point, 1748." *New Hampshire Historical Society Collections,* vol. 5 (Concord, 1837): 207–211.
    The journal by a survivor of the company of Captain John Lovewell who fell at Pigwacket in 1725 is dated May 13 to May 31, 1748. He describes marching from Fort Dummer, encounters with Indians, and firing between soldiers and Indians. Melven tells how the Indians fought with guns, hatchets, and knives, and lists the wounded or killed.

654. Melyn, Cornelis. "Purchase of Staten Island from Indians Described by Cornelis Melyn." *New York Historical Society Collections For The Year 1913, Publication Fund,* vol. 46 (New York, 1914): 123–127.
    On January 30, 1659, Melyn writes what he knows of the Dutch purchase of Staten Island from the Indians in New Netherland. He explains that the Indians were satisfied with the sale and agreement

until 1649 when they began to talk of the island's being theirs again and of wanting a new bargain. Melyn explains that he refused to pay for the island and that the Indians accepted his offer of small gifts to maintain a good relationship. He adds that the Indians were satisfied until Lubbert Vant Dincklagen again started up "mischiefs" by speaking to them about buying Staten Island. He names seven Indians who sold Staten Island to the Dutch. There is testimony by William Bogardus, notary public, dated June 27, 1672, regarding the dispute and resolving the question by allowing the Indians to hunt on Staten Island after its sale.

**655.** Michaelius, Jonas. "Portion of a Letter of Dominie Jonas Michaelius, First Minister of the Reformed Protestant Dutch Church in North America to Dominie Adrianus Smoutius, Minister of the Dutch Reformed Church of Amsterdam, Dated at Manhattan, New Netherland, August 11, 1628." *New York Historical Society Collections For the Year 1879 Publication Fund* vol. 12 (New York, 1880): 380–383.

A portion of Dominie Jonas Michaelius' letter deals with his low opinion of the Indians of Manhattan/New Netherland and his uncertain feeling whether they can be "led to the true knowledge of God. . . ." He discusses the Indians' language and claims that they are deliberately concealing much of their language from the Dutch. He suggests that in order to facilitate converting the Indians adults must be ignored and attention given only to children. He proposes that children be separated from parents, with parental consent, by means of presents and promises and that they be placed in the care of a schoolmaster who will instruct them to speak, read, and write in the Dutch language and learn the fundamentals of the Christian religion. He realizes the difficulty of the separations, since Indians maintain strong affection for their children. He suggests that the children be allowed to keep their Indian language because it will be a means of spreading religion throughout the whole nation.

**656.** Middletown Townbook. "Indians of Middletown." *New Jersey Historical Society Proceedings*, ser. 2, vol. 3, no. 1 (1872): 44–46.

These pages include the entries relating to Indians from the townbook of Middletown. Dated 1667 to 1670, entries deal with rewards for Indians' killing wolves, the order that no person shall sell or trade any sort of liquor to Indians within the limits of the township and that Indians who are drunk shall be put in the stocks till sober. Text of the proceedings of September 9, 1670, concerning a man's refusal to participate in a night watch for drunken Indians is included.

**657.** Miles, Elizabeth. "Deposition of Elizabeth Miles, 1754." *New Hampshire Historical Society Collections*, vol. 1 (Concord, 1824): 227–279.

In a deposition dated May 21, 1754, Mrs. Miles tells of two St. Francis Indians who, in May of 1752, while lodged at her house in her husband's absence, terrorized her, stole one of the Miles' slaves and

657 *(continued)*
another belonging to a neighbor, disappeared and a year later reappeared. She explains that the Indians returned because they have been required either to raise £500 or to obtain an English slave in order to redeem a kinsman being held for the murder of yet another Indian.

658. Miller, Ernest C. "Pennsylvania's Last Indian School." *Pennsylvania History,* vol. 25, no. 2 (April, 1958): 99–108. Illustrated.
One hundred and fifty years of Indian education, carried on at the elementary school on the Cornplanter Indian Grant, finally ended when the school closed in 1953. Miller describes the school and its importance, the career of Cornplanter, a Seneca, and tells how this land was granted to him in 1791 as a fee for his services.

659. Milton, J. E. "Fort Brewerton." *New York State Historical Association Quarterly Journal,* vol. 7, no. 2 (April 1926): 96–113.
Milton tells of traces of aboriginal occupation found near Brewerton. He describes French-English struggles with the Six Nations over their lands from the beginning of the eighteenth century and tells of a fort built in 1759 on the north side of the Oneida River claiming that it was abandoned around 1767.

660. "Ministers' Proposal for a Mission to the Eastern Indians." *Massachusetts Historical Society Collections,* ser. 3, vol. 1 (Boston, 1825): 133–134.
Writing in October, 1693, seven ministers solicit the king and council to encourage a plan of Christianizing the Indians in order to counter proselytizing by the French.

661. Mitchell, John. Letter to Cadwallader Colden. *New York Historical Society Collections For The Year 1935, Cadwallader Colden Papers,* vol. 9 (New York, 1937): 87–90.
Writing on April 5, 1781, Mitchell sends Colden a list of questions whose answers will provide proofs for the Five Nations of Indians' claims to lands that the French occupy.

662. Mohawk Indians. "Indian Deed to John H. Lydius." *New York Historical Society Collections For The Year 1918, Cadwallader Colden Papers,* vol. 2 (New York, 1919): 52–54.
Several Mohawk Indians deed John Henry Lydius of Albany two tracts of land lying northward of the English colonies of New England near Lake Champlain. On February 1, 1732, the Indians gave the land to Lydius in gratitude for his instructing them in Christianity.

663. Mohegan Indians. "Declaration of Indians of the Mohegan Tribe." *Connecticut Historical Society Collections,* vol. 5 (Hartford, 1896): 485–489.
Writing on April 24, 1738, two of Ben Uncas' sons and other Mohegan Indians review and confirm the lands deeded to Connecticut and

claim Mahomet was not sachem of the Mohegans at the time. Indians' marks are reproduced.

**664.** Mohegan Indians. "Memoir of Mohegan Indians." *Massachusetts Historical Society Collections,* ser. 1, vol. 9 (Boston, 1804): 75–99.

The memoir begins with an account by A. Holmes, dated February 1, 1804, of the present number of the Mohegan Tribe situated between Norwich and New London. The list is entitled "The Families of the Tribe of Mohegans and Number of Each Family." This is followed by "Additional Memoir of the Mohegans, and of Uncas, Their Ancient Sachem" which tells of the tract claimed as their hereditary country. Also discussed are the exploits, motives, and claims of Uncas. A long section on the language of the Mohegans is included.

**665.** Mohegan Indians. "Memorial of Mohegan Indians to the General Assembly." *Connecticut Historical Society Collections,* vol. 11 (Hartford, 1907): 88.

Writing on May 17, 1743, the Mohegans ask the General Assembly to approve a list of counselors chosen by Ben Uncas in July, 1742, and approved by the tribe. [*See also* page 50 of the same volume for the names of the Mohegan Indians chosen to be counselors. See "Memorial of Mohegan Indians to the General Assembly," vol. 11: 287–289: dated May 8, 1745. The Mohegans complain of English intrusions on their land and explain they cannot improve their lands because they are in an impoverished state and need relief. Mohegan names are listed.]

**666.** Mohegan Indians. "Petition of Mohegan Indians, 1739." *Connecticut Historical Society Collections,* vol. 5 (Hartford, 1896): 159–163.

A large number of members of the Mohegan Tribe petition the king of England to nominate John and Samuel Mason as their trustees and representatives to fight against the tyranny of the Connecticut government and to help restore Mohegan lands to them. In this petition, the Mohegans assert that they were denied the opportunity to defend themselves at the Commission of Review, June, 1737 and they argue that Ben Uncas was given a money bribe by the Connecticut government for giving a quit claim to all the lands seized from the Mohegans by the government.

**667.** Mohegan Indians. "Two Indian Deeds." *Connecticut Historical Society Bulletin,* vols. 1 and 2, no. 2 (February 1935): 2–4.

In the first Indian deed, dated July 4, 1665, a Mohegan man and woman deed land in Saybrook; in the second, dated April 10, 1666, Uncas, his wife, and three sons confirm a 1641 land sale to inhabitants of Saybrook. Pictographic marks of the Indians are reproduced.

**668.** Moll, John. "John Moll's Assignment of Indian Purchase in Delaware to William Penn." *Pennsylvania Magazine of History and Biography,* vol. 23, no. 1 (1899): 111–112.

**668** *(continued)*
In the first document dated July 10, 1680, several Indians deed land to John Moll. In the second document, dated February 21, 1682, John Moll assigns his Indian purchase to William Penn.

**669.** Monahon, Clifford P. "The Wooden Indian." *Rhode Island History,* vol. 14, no. 4 (October 1955): front cover, inside front cover, and 108–110.
Monahon relates the origin of cigar-store Indians to the history of trade symbolism. He describes how wooden figures were used in eighteenth and nineteenth century America to advertise shops and businesses, and he explains that the wooden Indian is one of a few types of shop signs surviving in the twentieth century. Monahon tells of the tradition regarding the first tobacco Indian. He discusses the carvers and significance of wooden Indians, citing, as an example of folk art, those acquired by the Rhode Island Historical Society. The article is illustrated with a photograph of the Indian figure that guarded the door of James M. Anthony and Company's tobacco store in Providence.

**670.** Montresor, John. "Journals of Captain John Montresor, 1757–1778: Bradstreet's Expedition to Niagara and Detroit, 1764." *New York Historical Society Collections For The Year 1881. Publication Fund* vol. 14 (New York, 1882): 252–322.
Throughout this section of the journals, there are numerous day-to-day references to Indians. For example, on July 23, 1764, the captain cites the numbers of sachems, warriors, women, and children attending the Niagara Congress from fifteen tribes, itemizes the costs of provisions and presents for the Indians at the July conference, and lists briefly the five terms of peace concluded between Colonel Bradstreet and the Delawares, Shawnees, Six Nations, and Hurons on August 12, 1764.

**671.** "Moravian Indian Converts and the Quakers." *Historical Society of Pennsylvania Memoirs,* vol. 13 (Philadelphia, 1891): 352–353.
Extracts from four eyewitness accounts indicate that Quakers armed themselves to defend Indian Moravian converts in February of 1764.

**672.** Moravian Missionaries. "Six Months On the Frontier of Northampton County, Pennsylvania, During the Indian War, October, 1755 to June, 1756." *Pennsylvania Magazine of History and Biography,* vol. 39, no. 3 (1915): 345–352.
A brief introduction discusses Indians who engaged in predatory warfare along the northern boundaries of old Northampton County after Braddock's July 1755 defeat. Incidents connected with Indian raids into the upper north county in the winter of 1755–1756 are recorded in entries dated October 31, 1755 to May 12, 1756. Footnotes are included.

**673.** Morgan, Jacob. "Life in a Frontier Fort During the Indian War." *Pennsylvania Magazine of History and Biography,* vol. 39, no. 2 (1915): 186–191.

The diary of Captain Jacob Morgan, written in April, 1758, describes daily life in a frontier fort. Morgan was commander of one of the forts in the cordon of blockhouses erected during the Indian war for the protection of the frontiers along the line of the Blue Mountains from the Delaware to the Susquehanna.

**674.** Morgan, John. [Letter to Governor Talcott] *Connecticut Historical Society Collections,* vol. 5 (Hartford, 1896): 351–352.

In a letter dated May 26, 1741, Captain John Morgan, overseer of the Pequot Indians, complains that Captain James Avery interferes with his attempts at dealing out justice to the Indians and recommends that Avery be dismissed.

**675.** Morris, David H. "General Harmar's Campaign Against the Northern Indians in 1790." *New Jersey Historical Society Proceedings,* vol. 60, no. 4 (October 1942): 238–246.

This first-hand account of General Josiah Harmar's campaign against Indians near the present city of Fort Wayne, Indiana, was first published in the *Troy Times* of Miami, Ohio on January 29, 1840, by David H. Morris, a member of Harmar's expedition. Morris recounts the daily movements of the troops and the battles with Indians.

**676.** Morris, Lewis. [Letter to the Lords of Trade] *New Jersey Historical Society Collections,* vol. 4 (Newark, 1852): 158.

In a letter dated December 20, 1742, Lewis Morris tells of "An Act for Regulating Purchasing of Lands from the Indians," that made illegal the purchase of lands without a license from the proprietors.

**677.** Morrison, Kenneth M. "Sebastien Racle [sic] and Norridgewock, 1724: The Eckstorm Conspiracy Thesis Reconsidered." *Maine Historical Society Quarterly,* vol. 14, no. 2 (Fall 1974): 76–97.

Morrison argues that it is simplistic to credit the presence of Jesuit Sebastien Rasles, who served the Norridgewock Abenakis from 1694 to 1724, rather than the arrogant English treatment of the Indians for the cause of troubles between the Abenakis and the English from 1688 to 1727, resulting finally in the war of 1721–1727. He explains in detail the fallacies of Fanny Hardy Eckstorm's 1934 article, which suggests that Rasles was a French political agent who coerced the Abenakis into warring against the English settlers. He concludes that conflicting interpretations stem from the polarization of the secondary sources and only a partial consideration of primary testimony. There are extensive notes.

**678.** Morton, Louis. "How the Indians Came to Carlisle." *Pennsylvania History,* vol. 29, no. 1 (January 1962): 53–73. Illustrated.

Morton discusses the Indian school at Carlisle in existence from 1879 until World War I, when it was converted into an Army hospital. Founded by R. H. Pratt, the school was a unique experiment in Indian

678 *(continued)*

education. He tells of Pratt's relationship with the Indian prisoners he took from Fort Sill, Oklahoma, to Fort Marion prison in Florida in 1875. He mentions Pratt's proposal to educate in the Northeast those Indians who refused to return to their tribes and describes his work in founding Carlisle, recruiting Indian children from the "fiercest tribes," many from families of the chiefs, for the first class at Carlisle. Morton presents Pratt's views concerning the relations between Indians and whites. There are photographs of Pratt, children at Carlisle, and an Indian family at Fort Marion.

679. "Specimen of the Mountaineer, or Sheshatapooshshoish, Skoffie, and Micmac Language." *Massachusetts Historical Society Collections,* ser. 1, vol. 6 (Boston, 1800): 16–33.

The vocabulary is transcribed from Gabriel, a Mountaineer Indian. There is a column of English words and three columns headed Micmac, Mountaineer, and Skoffie with equivalent words. Brief notes are given for the vocabulary.

680. Munro, William Bennett. "The Coureurs de Bois." *Massachusetts Historical Society Proceedings,* vol. 57 (1923–1924): 192–205.

Munro discusses the *coureurs-de-bois,* individual forest traders, the most active figures in the fur trading system of the French, who were organizers, promoters, and pilots of the trade, acting as the liaisons between the tribes of the West (Ohio, Illinois, Iowa, Wisconsin, Michigan, and the Great Lakes and Upper Mississippi) and the commercial enterprises maintaining warehouses at Montreal. Munro tells of the large numbers of *coureurs-de-bois* involved after 1660, reviews the ways in which they established relations with tribes, organized trade at its source, gathered large groups of Indians, and piloted them down trade routes to Montreal. He describes the summer fairs at which fur and French goods, particularly brandy, were exchanged, lists the sale prices for furs, and tells of the decline of trade after 1730. Munro concludes by noting the numerous and far-reaching effects of the French fur trade on the Indians and the eventual disastrous effects of the fur trade on the French.

681. Nalty, Bernard C. and Strobridge, Truman R. "Emmet Crawford, Pennsylvania Volunteer Turned Indian Fighter." *Pennsylvania History,* vol. 33, no. 2 (April 1966): 204–214.

Crawford became a cavalryman after the Civil War and spent the remaining years of his life either fighting Indians or attempting to educate them to peaceful ways. His career ended with his death during the Geronimo Campaign, 1885–1886. Nalty tells of Crawford's long association with the Plains Indians and describes his varied experiences with the frontier army.

**682.** Narragansett Indians. "Indian Confirmation of Narragansett Deeds." *Massachusetts Historical Society Collections,* ser. 5, vol. 9 (Boston, 1885): 34–36. Writing on September 11, 1662, four Indian witnesses confirm that Scuttup, a Narragansett, sold his land to Edward Hutchinson, William Hudson, and Richard Smith. This is followed by a second deposition dated September 22, 1662 confirming again that Scuttup sold his land.

**683.** "Lineal and Collateral Descent of the Narragansett Sachems." *Massachusetts Historical Society Collections,* ser. 5, vol. 9 (Boston, 1885): 104–108. The lineal and collateral descent of the chief sachems of Narragansett country begin with Canonicus, showing how the chief sachems were descended and related. This is followed by a narrative which explains how English proprietors derived title to Narragansett lands.

**684.** Narragansett Sachems. [Mortgage Deed of Narragansett Sachems] *Massachusetts Historical Society Collections,* ser. 5, vol. 9 (Boston, 1885): 25–26. Writing on September 29, 1660, three of the Narragansett sachems sell "all our whole country" to the Commissioners of the United Colonies for 595 fathoms of wampum.

**685.** Nash, Gary B. "The Quest for the Susquehanna Valley: New York, Pennsylvania, and the Seventeenth Century Fur Trade." *New York History,* vol. 48, no. 1 (January, 1967): 3–27. Nash discusses the events which frustrated William Penn's Susquehanna plans: intertribal Indian conflicts, inter-colonial rivalries, and international war in the late seventeenth century. He focuses on the Iroquois and their allegiance to the English in this period.

**686.** Nedacocket. "Ancient Deed." *New Hampshire Historical Society Collections,* vol. 8 (Concord, 1866): 453. Nedacocket deeds his tract of land along the Merrimack River to Jeremiah Belcher on March 28, 1659.

**687.** Nelson, William. "Indian Place Names: Loantica." *New Jersey Historical Society Proceedings,* ser. 2, vol. 11, no. 3 (1891): 120–123. Nelson reviews the Indian method of naming places and then suggests the meaning of "Lowantaka" from the Delaware language.

**688.** Nelson, William. "Some Notes on Matinneconk, or Burlington Island." *Pennsylvania Magazine of History and Biography,* vol. 10, no. 2 (1886): 214–216. Nelson discusses the history of Burlington Island, recording the Dutch, French, Swedish and English interest in it and the warfare between Indians and whites. Footnotes are included.

**689.** "New England's First Fruits: The Geneal Court and Indians." *Massachu-setts Historical Society Proceedings*, vol. 42 (1908–1909): 259–261.

This is a discussion concerning authorship of the first section of a tract entitled *New England's First Fruits*, the tract is about the conversion of Indians and actions of the General Court of Massachusetts towards civilizing and Christianizing them during the period 1644–1646.

**690.** "New Jersey: First Hundred Years: Excerpts from the New Jersey Archives." *New Jersey Historical Society Proceedings*, vol. 82, no. 1 (January 1964): 1–28.

The excerpts include "Journal of Captain Arent Schuyler's visit to the Minisink Country" written February 3–10, 1694, which reports that no French or French-allied Indians had been in the Minisink country. Another piece, "Letter from William Franklin, governor of New Jersey, to the Lords of Trade, containing an account of his proceedings with the Assembly with respect to the means of repelling the hostilities of the Indians," is dated December 5, 1763.

**691.** "A New Jersey Tribute to an Indian Chief.'" *New Jersey Historical Society Proceedings*, n.s., vol. 11, no. 1 (January 1926): 114. Illustrated.

This brief article discusses the first real monument to an Indian chief in New Jersey, erected by citizens of Flemington on October 18, 1925. It honors Tuccamirgan, a Delaware chief who is believed to be buried on the exact spot. There is a photo of the marble obelisk at the beginning of the journal.

**692.** New Hampshire Council. "Copy of a Letter from the Council to Governor Dongan." *New Hampshire Historical Society Collections*, vol. 8 (Concord, 1866): 252–253.

In a letter written on March 21, 1684, the Council of New Hampshire asks Governor Dongan of New York province to help protect the people of New Hampshire from sudden Indian attacks by sending a number of Mahicans or other Indians experienced in warfare to assist New Hampshire.

**693.** New Hampshire Council. "Employment of Seneca and Mohawk Indians, 1684." *New Hampshire Historical Society Collections*, vol. 2 (Concord, 1827): 199–200.

In a document written on March 20, 1684, the Council of New Hampshire indicates that it would like the governor of New Hampshire to meet with Governor Dongan to persuade him to send Mohawks, Senecas, and other Indians to New Hampshire to help in defense against the Indian attacks there and in other New England colonies.

**694.** Newkerk, Johannis. [On Defending the Frontiers] *New York Historical Society Collections For The Year 1921, Cadwallader Colden Papers*, vol. 5 (New York, 1922): 51–53.

There are two letters by Newkerk. Written on December 20, 1755, the first letter discusses the treatment of Indians suggesting that certain ones should be brought before the justices to be examined and others should be asked to live in well-settled towns, not in the woods or in thinly settled parts, so that they can be watched. This is followed by a second letter written by Captain Newkerk and two others, dated December 22, 1755, in which they present proposals for guarding the frontier in Ulster County against Indian attacks.

**695.** New Milford and Potatuck Indians. "Memorial of New Milford and Potatuck Indians to the General Assembly." *Connecticut Historical Society Collections*, vol. 11 (Hartford, 1907): 42–43.

On May 13, 1742, these Indians declare they wish they knew how to read English and ask to be instructed in the principles of Christianity. They request that Connecticut provide money to support some teachers.

**696.** New York Assembly. "Deliberations on the Kayaderosseras Patent." *New York Historical Society Collections For The Year 1922, Cadwallader Colden Papers,* vol. 6 (New York, 1923): 356–358.

Meeting in October, 1764, New York Assembly members tell why it is inadvisable to inquire into the title of the Kayaderosseras Patent. The Assembly points out it is common for Indians to deny their ancestors' and their own sales of land and for them to renew their claims and attempt to force repeated payments for the same lands. The Assembly argues that the Indians claiming patented lands do so because they are indigent and neglect arts and agriculture, that they know witnesses are dead and, therefore, proof of prior sale is weakened. The Assembly concludes that it is dangerous to start an inquiry and that annulling crown grants undermines officials who have the power to make grants, renders property insecure, alarms British subjects, and discourages settlement and cultivation of colony lands. The Assembly confirms its opposition to the patent being vacated and suggests that Johnson pacify the Mohawks.

**697.** New York Council. "Address of a Member of the Council at a Conference of the Council with the General Assembly of New York." *New York Historical Society Collections For The Year 1934, Cadwallader Colden Papers,* vol. 8 (New York, 1937): 307–309.

Speaking on September 5, 1744, the council member explains that it is necessary for the English to secure and defend the garrison at Oswego to aid in preserving the friendship of the Five Nations and other western Indians and to help defeat the plans of the French. The member offers several reasons for securing a certain pass: to send relief to the Oswegos, to keep open communication between Oswego and the Five Nations and New York province in order to receive and send necessary intelligence and supplies, etc., and to secure a retreat in all emergencies.

**698.** New York Council. [Council Meeting] *New York Historical Society Collections For The Year 1869. Publication Fund,* vol. 2 (New York, 1870): 373–374.

At a meeting on April 16, 1675, the governor resolves that the English befriend the Mohawk Indians and that the French be warned not to molest them without cause. He also asks the Jesuits or other French residing with the Mohawks to give an account to the governors of their actions.

**699.** New York Council. [Council Meeting] *New York Historical Society Collections For The Year 1869. Publication Fund,* vol. 2 (New York, 1870): 376.

At a meeting on October 11, 1676, the governor of New York proposes that the English meet with the Mohawk sachems to thank them for their assistance in fighting the "North" Indians.

**700.** New York Council. [Council Meeting] *New York Historical Society Collections For The Year 1869. Publication Fund,* vol. 2 (New York, 1870): 378–383.

At a meeting on October 9, 1683, the governor insists that the Mohawks should not deal with the French without the permission of the British, that they should not permit any French, other than the Jesuits, to live among them, that they should negotiate peace and trade with Indian enemies, and that they should inform the British of French demands in return for the governor's "promissing them that he will allways look upon them as his children and treat them with all respect and kindness accordingly. . . ." A speech by Odianah, a sachem, follows in which he agrees to all the governor's requests and informs him that the Indians are not selling their beaver pelts to another government but rather that beaver supplies are diminishing.

**701.** New York Council. [Council Meeting] *New York Historical Society Collections For The Year 1869. Publication Fund,* vol. 2 (New York, 1870): 383–384.

At a meeting on June 26, 1684, Governor Dongan of New York informs the governor of Canada which Indians are under his government's jurisdiction, tells him to prevent the French from crossing onto English territory and promises he will likewise prevent the English from crossing over into French land. He suggests that neither the English nor French commit hostilities in North America and that the kings, not governors, are the proper decision makers.

**702.** New York Council. [Council Meeting] *New York Historical Society Collections For The Year 1869. Publication Fund,* vol. 2 (New York, 1870): 384–386.

At a meeting on August 30, 1686, the governor chastises the Indians for trading with the French which he says is contrary to the promise they made at Albany and "contrary to the obedience which children owe to their parents." He warns the Indians that the French refrain from making war against the Indians because they fear "disobliging the Great King of England who is your King allso." The governor reaffirms the demand that the Indians not make war against the French except in self-defense, and he indicates that neither the English nor the French should hunt or trade among Indians without his approval. He also tells the Indians to allow white prisoners of Indians to be christened before they are put to death. [*See also* New York Council meeting, September 1, 1686, pages 387–389. Several Indians of the Five Nations respond to the governor's requests of the day before.]

**703.** New York Council. [Council Meeting] *New York Historical Society Collections For The Year 1869. Publication Fund,* vol. 2 (New York, 1870): 389–390.

At a meeting on September 9, 1687, the governor informs the Council that the French in Canada have provided 1500 pairs of snowshoes for troops. He orders the wives, children, and old men of the Five Nations of Indians to be resettled near English forces and orders that only young men remain in their homeland. He commands that all the Indian corn that can be spared be sent to the English forces. [Two days earlier, on September 7, 1687, pages 389–390, he had discussed a proclamation being drawn up prohibiting the taking of any Indian corn or peas out of Albany or Ulster Counties.]

**704.** New York Council. [Council Meeting] *New York Historical Society Collections For The Year 1869. Publication Fund,* vol. 2 (New York, 1970): 392–393.

At a meeting on May 7, 1688, the governor orders that a messenger be sent to the Minisinks and to the Indians of New York, ordering them to send their young men to Albany for fighting against the French and allied Indians.

**705.** New York Council. [Council Meeting] *New York Historical Society Collections For The Year 1869. Publication Fund,* vol. 2 (New York, 1870): 394–395.

At a meeting on January 11, 1691, the commander in chief reports that a letter from Albany reports on the number of Mohawks killed by the French at Corlaers Lake. One warrant is issued to encourage Indians of New York to fight against the French and allied "praying" Indians of Canada; another deals with giving white wampum to friends and relatives of those Indians killed at the lake.

**706.** New York Council. [Council Meeting] *New York Historical Society Collections For The Year 1869. Publication Fund,* vol. 2 (New York, 1870): 395–396.

At a meeting on March 19, 1691, the commander in chief reports on a letter from Albany that tells of the Onondagas killed by the French; it also reports on threats of desertion by garrison inhabitants. To forestall desertion, the commander orders that Albany send money to pay the soldiers.

**707.** New York Council. [Council Meeting] *New York Historical Society Collections For The Year 1869. Publication Fund,* vol. 2 (New York, 1870): 393–394.

At a meeting on September 3, 1691, the governor produces a "Bill of Exchange" sent by the governor and council of Virginia as a present to

**707** *(continued)*
the Five Nations of Indians to "ty the knott of friendship with them on their behalf."

**708.** New York Council. [Council Meeting] *New York Historical Society Collections For The Year 1869. Publication Fund,* vol. 2 (New York, 1870): 399–400.

At a meeting on February 15, 1692, the Council orders letters sent to Virginia, Maryland, New Castle, Pennsylvania, Connecticut, and Boston asking for contributions to help the expenses of the New York expedition against those French and allied Indians who had invaded two of the New York Indians' homelands. The Council agrees that the expedition is for the common safety.

**709.** New York Council. [Council Meeting] *New York Historical Society Collections For The Year 1869. Publication Fund,* vol. 2 (New York, 1870): 396–97.

At a meeting on August 12, 1692, the mayor of Albany is directed to give parchment or vellum passes with the official seal of the city of Albany to Indians traveling or hunting south of Virginia in order that they may pass safely.

**710.** New York Council. [Council Meeting] *New York Historical Society Collections For The Year 1869. Publication Fund,* vol. 2 (New York, 1870): 397–398.

At a meeting on September 17, 1692, the River Indians and Shawnees indicate their wish to settle in the Minisink country. The governor tells them they must first make peace with the Five Nations. A Minisink Indian replies that the River Indians and Shawnees are friends and relatives.

**711.** New York Council. [Council Meeting] *New York Historical Society Collections For The Year 1869. Publication Fund,* vol. 2 (New York, 1870): 401–402.

At a meeting on July 28, 1693, Governor Fletcher informs the council that the Five Nations, without English knowledge, have planned a meeting of their sachems to consider an answer to the governor of Canada, who has sent them a belt of peace. The New York governor, surprised that the Five Nations have disregarded their vows to the British, proposes to dissuade the Five Nations from holding the meeting. He intends also to exhort the Oneidas to deliver their prisoner, the Jesuit Milet, who has been in intrigue with the French. [*See also* New York Council meeting, dated August 3, 1693, page 403. This page contains a brief list of the warrants issued for the messenger who brought the intelligence from Albany regarding the meeting of the sachems, for presents to Indians, and for other creditors.]

**712.** New York Council. [Council Meeting] *New York Historical Society Collections For The Year 1869. Publication Fund,* vol. 2 (New York, 1870): 403–404.

Three warrants are issued on August 17, 1693: one for ammunition for the Indians at Albany, one for the expenses of maintaining three Indian boys at Reverend Godfrey Dellius', and the last for a widow.

713. New York Council. [Council Meeting] *New York Historical Society Collections For The Year 1869. Publication Fund,* vol. 2 (New York, 1870): 404.

In a report on his journey to the Five Nations dated September 4, 1693, Major Wessells, who is trying to prevent their making peace with the French, informs the council that the Indians have declared that they will not make peace despite their inclination to do so.

714. New York Council. [Council Meeting] *New York Historical Society Collections For The Year 1869. Publication Fund,* vol. 2 (New York, 1870): 406.

At a meeting on September 25, 1693, the governor informs the council that Sir William Phips, the governor of Massachusetts, refuses assistance to New York in spite of the king's command, and that Connecticut denies assistance also. [*See* New York Council meeting, dated September 20, 1693, page 405; this meeting deals with the same issue of assistance.]

715. New York Council. [Council Meeting] *New York Historical Society For The Year 1869. Publication Fund,* vol. 2 (New York, 1870): 407.

At a meeting on December 11, 1693, Governor Fletcher informs the council that the French Governor Frontenac has sent another belt of wampum, as a peace offering, to the Five Nations.

716. New York Council. [Council Meeting] *New York Historical Society Collections For The Year 1869. Publication Fund,* vol. 2 (New York, 1870): 415–416.

At a meeting on August 6, 1694, Governor Fletcher discusses rejecting the belt of wampum sent to him for the Five Nations by Governor Frontenac of Canada because he feels it is a trick intended to deceive the Indians into thinking that the English have broken a peace agreed upon earlier with France.

717. New York Council. [Council Meeting] *New York Historical Society Collections For The Year 1869. Publication Fund,* vol. 2 (New York, 1870): 408–409.

At a meeting on August 13, 1694, Governor Fletcher rejects the idea of giving presents to the Five Nations in the name of individual provinces or colonies. He argues that this might anger Indians against other colonies. Governor Phips of Massachusetts wanted to give a present to the Five Nations on behalf of his own province; Fletcher wants presents given to Indians "in the name of his Master and Mistresse the King and Queene and includ [ing ] all the neighboring Provinces and Colonies in the covenant chain . . .".

718. New York Council. [Council Meeting] *New York Historical Society Collections For The Year 1869. Publication Fund,* vol. 2 (New York, 1870): 409–415.

At a meeting on August 14, 1694, the sachems of the Five Nations of Indians answer the question of Governor Benjamin Fletcher of New York who wants to know who will be for him and who will be against him. A sachem of Onondaga, Sadekanahtie, speaks for the Five Na-

**718** *(continued)*
tions and explains that ever since the Indians made a covenant with
the English, they have had trouble from their own enemies and the
French. He explains why the Indians were disobedient and went to
Canada to ally with the French; he concludes by asking for cheaper
ammunition, lead, and guns.

**719.** New York Council. [Council Meeting] *New York Historical Society Collections
For The Year 1869. Publication Fund,* vol. 2 (New York, 1870): 416–417.
   At a meeting on August 20, 1694, Governor Fletcher argues that it is
not safe to make a treaty on behalf of only one province since this
might endanger the other provinces. Fletcher resolves to inform the
New York Indians that the Indians of New England have broken the
peace; he further intends to offer them a belt of wampum to gain their
assistance in persuading the New England Indians to bury their
hatchets. Flectcher argues that 500 men are needed to defend the
frontiers of New England, Connecticut, and the Jerseys against the
French.

**720.** New York Council. [Council Meeting] *New York Historical Society Collections
For The Year 1869. Publication Fund,* vol. 2 (New York, 1870): 418–419.
   At a meeting on March 13, 1695, Governor Fletcher informs the
council of terrible consequences for the New York Indians if the
French repossess Cadaracqui. The Indians would then be compelled
to negotiate peace with the French, and the enemies of the English
would then control Indian trade. The governor indicates that requested assistance must be given to the Indians and the council agrees
with him. The expenses of the expedition are discussed. [*See also* New
York Council meeting, dated September 9, 1694, pages 417–418, at
which Governor Fletcher reports on the intelligence that there are
movements of large numbers of French by water and that they intend
to settle Cadaracqui.]

**721.** New York Council. [Council Meeting] *New York Historical Society Collections
For The Year 1869. Publication Fund,* vol. 2 (New York, 1870): 420–421.
   At a meeting on April 8, 1695, the Onondaga sachem Sadekanahtie
makes a speech thanking Governor Benjamin Fletcher for his assis-
tance in providing ammunition. He explains that the governor of
Canada is false and seeks to divide the Five Nations.

**722.** New York Council. [Council Meeting] *New York Historical Society Collections
For The Year 1869. Publication Fund,* vol. 2 (New York, 1870): 421–422.
   At a meeting on April 13, 1695, Sadekanahtie, Dekanisore (both
Onondagas), and others are given presents by the council and
cautioned to keep the covenant with the British and to ignore the
French. Sadekanahtie promises to be steadfast to the English and
explains how the French are making inroads into Indian lands.

**723.** New York Council. [Council Meeting] *New York Historical Society Collections
For The Year 1869. Publication Fund,* vol. 2 (New York, 1870): 423–424.

At a meeting on July 11, 1695, the governors of Massachusetts and Pennsylvania refuse the assistance asked for by New York. Governor Fletcher wants to prohibit the River Indians from visiting frontier towns of Massachusetts on their return home from hunting.

**724.** New York Council. [Council Meeting] *New York Historical Society Collections For The Year 1869. Publication Fund,* vol. 2 (New York, 1870): 425–426.

At a meeting on August 18, 1695, Governor Fletcher indicates that the Indians need assistance in resisting those French trying to resettle Cadaracqui. He explains that he has sent forces to help the Indians. He discusses Connecticut's refusal to assist New York, and the council suggests that Fletcher write again and report on the French actions. [*See also* New York Council meeting, dated September 6, 1695, page 427, in which the governor discusses the intelligence that the French have repossessed Cadaracqui and that the Indians of Albany demand assistance of the British to expel the French. The governor communicates that no assistance is expected from New England.]

**725.** New York Council. [Council Meeting] *New York Historical Society Collections For The Year 1869. Publication Fund,* vol. 2 (New York, 1870): 428–429.

At a meeting on November 1, 1695, Governor Fletcher tells the Council of receiving insolent demands for assistance from the Indians. The council recommends that Fletcher send a copy of the Indian sachems' propositions to the Lords of the Committee for the king's information. The council also indicates that the governor is not obliged to assist the Indians whenever there is French aggression towards them; and that it has been recommended to the upper nations that they defend themselves with the arms, ammunition, and clothing supplied by the British for that purpose.

**726.** New York Council. [Council Meeting] *New York Historical Society Collections For The Year 1869. Publication Fund,* vol. 2 (New York, 1870): 429.

At a meeting on July 9, 1696, Governor Fletcher reports that the governor of Canada plans to reduce the Five Nations in the summer and that all men between the ages of fifteen and fifty are ordered to be ready for war.

**727.** New York Council. [Council Meeting] *New York Historical Society Collections For The Year 1869. Publication Fund,* vol. 2 (New York, 1870): 431–434.

At a meeting on August 7, 1696, Governor Fletcher discusses the need to renew the covenant with the Five Nations, now that the French have left the Indian country. When the French invaded, the Senecas and Cayugas were not disturbed, but the French destroyed corn planted by the Onondagas and Oneidas. As a result, the Onondagas and Oneidas set their lands on fire and fled. They, along with the Mohawks, have come to Albany for food, provisions, and ammunition. The governor resolves that during the next winter these Indians should be supplied with corn at government expense; he also lists four methods for reuniting them with the others in renewing the covenant.

**727** *(continued)*
He recommends that in the future small parties of troops should be sent out to protect farms at harvest time.

**728.** New York Council. [Council Meeting] *New York Historical Society Collections For The Year 1869. Publication Fund,* vol. 2 (New York, 1870): 434.
At a meeting on November 5, 1696, Governor Fletcher asks the council to reward the three officers who killed seven French and their Indian guide.

**729.** New York Council. [Council Meeting] *New York Historical Society Collections For The Year 1869. Publication Fund,* vol. 2 (New York, 1870): 437–439.
At a meeting on August 17, 1698, Richard, Earl of Bellomont, explains to the council that Count Frontenac of Canada refuses to give up some Oneida prisoners and that the French threaten to continue the war if the Indians do not submit and make a separate peace with them. The Earl notes that the Five Nations plan to meet at Onondaga and that they desire assistance. Dekanisore, an Onondaga, indicates that if the Onondagas cannot be protected from the French, they will be forced to negotiate peace because other Indians are too far away to help them. The Earl promises to protect the Onondagas in case the French should break the peace. The governor advises the Onondagas to send their women and children to Albany for safety if they cannot resist the strong French forces.

**730.** New York Council. [Council Meeting] *New York Historical Society Collections For The Year 1869. Publication Fund,* vol. 2 (New York, 1870): 439–441.
Written on October 6, 1698, this document contains an audit of more than twenty charges incurred by Richard, Earl of Bellomont's, expedition to Albany. Linens, guns, kettles, blankets, tobacco, and other gifts are itemized. One example is "Ordered a warrant issue for payment of forty pounds one shilling to Samuel Bayard for Guns for the Indians and Pewter for a Travelling chest."

**731.** New York Council. [Council Meeting] *New York Historical Society Collections For The Year 1869. Publication Fund,* vol. 2 (New York, 1870): 443–444.
Dated November 7, 1698 and May 31, 1699, these documents contain three warrants issued for the payment of sundries delivered to the Indians and to the French prisoners at Albany.

**732.** New York Council. [Council Meeting] *New York Historical Society Collections For The Year 1869. Publication Fund,* vol. 2 (New York, 1870): 444.
Dated July 31, 1700, this document orders payment to three men who brought a message from Albany telling of ten Frenchmen from Canada who have gone to the Onondagas to seduce them into an alliance and states that the person in charge of Indian affairs at Albany had instructed them not to make a treaty with the French.

**733.** New York Council. [Council Meeting] *New York Historical Society Collections For The Year 1869. Publication Fund,* vol. 2 (New York, 1870): 445–447.

Dated September 13, 1700, these council minutes contain a document dated January 27, 1696, in which William III, King of England, appoints Robert Livingston of New York Secretary or Agent to the Indians and discusses his salary.

**734.** New York Council. [Council Meeting] *New York Historical Society Collections For The Year 1869. Publication Fund,* vol. 2 (New York, 1870): 452–453.

Dated January 20, 1701, this document contains a voucher for payment to William Teller for hiring his sloop to carry the governor to Albany to visit the Five Nations in July of 1700. There is also a voucher for payment to Johannis Schuyler for "sundry necessaries provided by for the messengers sent to the Onondaga Indians. . . ." [*See also* New York Council Meeting, dated November 6, 1700, pages 447–448, for other issues of payments to six men for their various services to Indians.]

**735.** New York Council. [Council Meeting] *New York Historical Society Collections For The Year 1869. Publication Fund,* vol. 2 (New York, 1870): 448–449.

At a meeting on August 22, 1701, the governor reads a letter dated August 19 sent to him from Albany by men who manage Indian affairs. In it is a message from Onondaga sachems requesting English representatives to accompany the seven French representatives planning to attend some meetings. These managers from Albany have told the sachems not to listen to any proposals of the French until they receive an answer from the governor.

**736.** New York Council. [Council Meeting] *New York Historical Society Collections For The Year 1869. Publication Fund,* vol. 2 (New York, 1870): 449–450.

At a meeting on September 16, 1701, the House of Representatives of the province of New York commends John Nanfan, Lieutenant Governor and commander in chief of New York, for his negotiations with the Five Nations and requests that only Laurence Claesson be chosen interpreter with the Indians.

**737.** New York Council. [Council Meeting] *New York Historical Society Collections For The Year 1869. Publication Fund,* vol. 2 (New York, 1870): 457.

At a meeting on April 19, 1708, the Five Nations send a message that they plan to meet "four Nations of Waganhaes with whom they were in warr" and request John Lord Lovelace, Baron of Hurley, to send a representative, as well as provisions to the treaty proceedings.

**738.** New York Council. [Council Meeting] *New York Historical Society Collections For The Year 1869. Publication Fund,* vol. 2 (New York, 1870): 453.

At a meeting on July 6, 1708, the managers of Indian affairs at Albany inform Lord Edward Cornbury of French intentions to build two forts at the chief hunting places of the Indians. The managers report that the Indians want the English to prevent this by building a garrison. They explain that the French are giving gifts daily to the Indians in order to alienate them from the British.

**739.** New York Council. [Council Meeting] *New York Historical Society Collections For The Year 1869. Publication Fund,* vol. 2 (New York, 1870): 453–455.
The council minutes of September 7, 1708, contain Queen Anne's appointment of Robert Livingston as Town Clerk in Albany County and confirm his position as Secretary or Agent for the government of New York to the Indians. Salary figures are given.

**740.** New York Council. [Council Meeting] *New York Historical Society Collections For The Year 1869. Publication Fund,* vol. 2 (New York, 1870): 456–457.
At a meeting on December 1, 1708, the council discusses payment to Colonel Schuyler for his journey to Onondaga in 1703, for scouts sent out when the French appeared to be on the march into Indian country, and for building a fort in Mohawk country.

**741.** New York Council. [Council Meeting] *New York Historical Society Collections For The Year 1869. Publication Fund,* vol. 2 (New York, 1870): 457–459.
The minutes of May 6, 1709 contain two of the more than one hundred instructions given to New York by the Court at Kensington, dated June 27, 1708. One deals with trade and the other with Indian affairs. The instructions read that Indians must be induced to trade with the British rather than with other Europeans, that the Five Nations must be submissive to the British and assured that they will be protected from the French, that River and other Indians in the neighborhood should be united with the Five Nations and submissive to the British, and that New York should be discreet if Indians are offering to sell great tracts of land for small sums.

**742.** New York Council. [Council Meeting] *New York Historical Society Collections For The Year 1869. Publication Fund,* vol. 2 (New York, 1870): 460–461.
At a meeting on March 29, 1711, Robert Hunter informs the council that he disapproves of the Five Nations' war against the "Waganhaes"; he advises that the Indians' demand for ammunition be rejected because it is not a just war.

**743.** New York Council. [Council Meeting] *New York Historical Society Collections For The Year 1869. Publication Fund,* vol. 2 (New York, 1870): 461–462.
At a meeting on April 24, 1711, Governor Robert Hunter reports that a group of French have arrived at Onondaga. The council wants Colonel Peter Schuyler to go to Onondaga with instructions to thank the Indians for apprising the British of the French presence. He is to tell them also that Governor Hunter expects their allegiance, that the British must attend all meetings with the French and Indians, and that the French should leave Indian country and be warned against interfering with the Indians. Schuyler is also instructed to send reliable Indians to Canada to check on the movements of the French and to inform the governor of any proceedings between the French and allied Indians.

**744.** New York Council. [Council Meeting] *New York Historical Society Collections For The Year 1869. Publication Fund,* vol. 2 (New York, 1870): 463.

At a meeting on June 15, 1713, Governor Hunter reports that the Tuscarora Indians who are at war with British subjects in Carolina are coming to settle with the Five Nations. The council advises that a letter be sent to the Commissioners of Indian Affairs at Albany directing them to tell the Five Nations not to receive any Tuscaroras among them or permit them to settle with them or give them assistance until they have made peace with the Carolinians. The council also instructs the commissioners to forbid the Five Nations committing hostilities against the Flatheads who are allied with British Carolinians and at war with the Tuscaroras.

**745.** New York Council. [Council Meeting] *New York Historical Society Collections For The Year 1869. Publication Fund,* vol. 2 (New York, 1870): 463–464.

At a meeting on June 19, 1713, Governor Hunter reports that the Five Nations have returned a wampum belt they were given to dissuade them from warring with the Flatheads. Even so, the council feels it is necessary to send some Albany notables to Onondaga with presents for Five Nations Indians to keep them from allying with the Tuscaroras in a war against the Flatheads. The Flatheads are allies of the British in Carolina and Virginia.

**746.** New York Council. [Council Meeting] *New York Historical Society Collections For The Year 1869. Publication Fund,* vol. 2 (New York, 1870): 464–465.

The council minutes for August 6, 1714 authorize money for presents to the Five Nations. The council directs that a letter be written to the Commissioners of Indian Affairs to summon the Five Nations to Albany to meet with Governor Hunter who wishes "to take the Hatchett out of their hands and renew the covenant chain."

**747.** New York Council. [Council Meeting] *New York Historical Society Collections For The Year 1869. Publication Fund,* vol. 2 (New York, 1870): 465–466.

At a meeting on June 24, 1717, the governor lists several conferences he has had with the Five Nations at Albany. The governor tells the council that he has received a letter from Governor Spotswood of Virginia who complains of a "grievous Insult" done by some of the Five Nations to Indians under his protection.

**748.** New York Council. [Council Meeting] *New York Historical Society Collections For The Year 1869. Publication Fund,* vol. 2 (New York, 1870): 467.

Dated June 17, 1718, this list of three expenses is for the governor's quarterly salary, for the Commissioners of Indian Affairs for "Spies Intelligence" and other incidentals, and for money to be used in giving presents to the Five Nations. [*See also* Councils of September 16, 1717, pages 466–467; June 13, 1719, page 469, and June 15, 1727, page 493 for similar expenses.]

**749.** New York Council. [Council Meeting] *New York Historical Society Collections For The Year 1869. Publication Fund,* vol. 2 (New York, 1870): 468.
At a meeting on August 23, 1718, the governor reports on a letter from the Commissioners of Indian Affairs at Albany which contains the propositions of the sachems of the Five Nations that they are to be cut off by "Christians" and that they need the governor's assistance with arms and other necessities.

**750.** New York Council. [Council Meeting] *New York Historical Society Collections For The Year 1869. Publication Fund,* vol. 2 (New York, 1870): 469–470.
At a meeting on June 24, 1719, the Commissioners of Indian Affairs at Albany tell of Oneida Indians' complaints of a lack of ammunition and a great famine. The governor reports that he sent off powder and lead according to the commissioners' request.

**751.** New York Council. [Council Meeting] *New York Historical Society Collections For The Year 1869. Publication Fund,* vol. 2 (New York, 1870): 470–471.
At a meeting on July 9, 1719, the Commissioners of Indian Affairs at Albany enclose a written message from Consora, one of the Five Nations Indians, informing that the French are building a fort near a certain pass in order to intercept trade with the Indians who travel by that route through Five Nations country on their way to Albany with their pelts. The council directs the commissioners to visit the Indians, particularly the Senecas in whose land the fort lies, to inform them that the fort will obstruct their hunting and that they should try to hinder the French from settling in their country or on the frontiers. The commissioners are also directed to tell the Five Nations not to jeopardize the peace existing between the crowns of Great Britain and France.

**752.** New York Council. [Council Meeting] *New York Historical Society Collections For The Year 1869. Publication Fund,* vol. 2 (New York, 1870): 471–474.
At a meeting on June 19, 1720, the sachems of the Five Nations say that they will not war against the "far" Indians nor fight the English-allied Indians to the south unless they are antagonized and that they will endeavor to keep the peace. The sachems report that they opposed the French building a fort and that they will inform the British of any prejudicial actions against them but ask that the British be quick to respond and assist in the event of Indian need.

**753.** New York Council. [Council Meeting] *New York Historical Society Collections For The Year 1869. Publication Fund,* vol. 2 (New York, 1870): 474–475.
Dated July 28, 1720 the council minutes list several gifts to the Five Nations, as well as their costs. Such items as guns, strouds, shirts, kettles, blankets, ammunition, tobacco, pork, Indian corn, wampum beads, hats, etc. are listed. An example of a listed item is: "50 Guns computed at £65."

**754.** New York Council. [Council Meeting] *New York Historical Society Collections For The Year 1869. Publication Fund,* vol. 2 (New York, 1870): 478–479.

At a meeting on October 9, 1721, the council advises that a letter be written to the governor of Massachusetts Colony informing him that no treaty should be made nor presents given to the Five Nations without the previous consent and other advice of the governor of New York. [*See also* New York council meeting, September 20, 1721, pages 476–478, for a letter from Josiah Willard, Secretary of Massachusetts Colony, which tells the governor of New York that some men from his colony have been appointed to meet the Five Nations with a present and requests that New York notify the Indians to be in Albany October 6th. At this council meeting, a letter is also written to the governor of Boston informing him that New York will not consent to commissioners from any neighboring colony meeting, treating, or giving presents to the Five Nations in its name because the Five Nations are a branch of New York province. A list of the minutes of the council in which this policy has been stated is supplied.]

**756.** New York Council. [Council Meeting] *New York Historical Society Collections For The Year 1869. Publication Fund,* vol. 2 (New York, 1870): 479–482.

The council minutes of August 9, 1722 contain two letters. The first, from Governor Spotswood of Virginia, asks the New York governor for permission to confer with him and the council about making a treaty between Virginia and the Five Nations. The second letter, from Governor Keith of Pennsylvania, indicates that Pennsylvania wants to renew a "league of friendship" with the Five Nations. Keith writes that he wishes to discuss the killing of an Indian by traders and wishes to prevent the Five Nations from going to war and making a path through Pennsylvania settlements along the Susquehanna River. The New York Council says it will confer with the governors of Virginia and Pennsylvania on measures to be taken with the Five Nations to secure a general peace between them and the Indians and their neighboring colonies.

**756.** New York Council. [Council Meeting] *New York Historical Society Collections For The Year 1869. Publication Fund,* vol. 2 (New York, 1870): 482–483.

At a meeting on August 28, 1722, Governor Burnet indicates he has chosen Major Abraham Schuyler and eight other men to live among the Senecas in order to promote British trade directly with the Indians. The governor and council discuss the expenses involved in this proposal.

**757.** New York Council. [Council Meeting] *New York Historical Society Collections For The Year 1869. Publication Fund,* vol. 2 (New York, 1870): 185–187.

The Council minutes of October 27, 1726 contain a list of sums allowed by the council for services in Indian country for the purpose of securing the Indians to the British interest. The sums listed are for

**757** *(continued)*

services of smiths, for tools, for presents given to Indians, for provisions, birch canoes, and for transporting sachems by horse hire, etc.

**758.** New York Council. [Council Meeting] *New York Historical Society Collections For The Year 1869. Publication Fund,* vol. 2 (New York, 1870): 493–495.

At a meeting on July 31, 1727, Governor Burnet tells the council that the governor of Canada has insisted on stopping the building of a fort at Oswego as it is contrary to the Treaty of Utrecht. Burnet explains that the fifteenth article of the treaty does not relate to the Five Nations, who are subjects of Great Britain, that the Five Nations used and possessed Oswego, and that they had granted this land to the British crown in order to be protected there. The council orders the work at Oswego to proceed, states that the French had themselves infringed on the Utrecht Treaty by building a fort at Niagara, and that the Five Nations be informed of French threats to disturb the trading house at Oswego and expel any disruptive Indians. [*See also* New York Council meeting, September 14, 1727, page 506, in which Governor Burnet tells the council that the Six Nations of Indians have agreed to defend Oswego and to warn all Indians in Canada not to start trouble against the fort.]

**759.** New York Council. [Council Meeting] *New York Historical Society Collections For The Year 1869. Publication Fund,* vol. 2 (New York, 1870): 511–513.

The council minutes of June 14, 1744 contain the reaffirmation of the Six Nations' promises to keep the peace unless the enemy attacks and to guard against the French and keep their people home. The sachems tell Governor Clinton that the trading house at Oswego, which initially had cheap goods, now has goods that are too expensive. They ask that the prices be lowered to the earlier rates. The Indians promise to try to remain friends with the "far" Indians.

**760.** New York Council. [Council Meeting] *New York Historical Society Collections For The Year 1922, Cadwallader Colden Papers,* vol. 6 (New York, 1923): 355–356.

At a meeting on September 26, 1764, the council orders the king's attorney general to begin a suit to recover lands rightfully belonging to the Southold Indians, if those in possession of the land do not satisfy the demands of the Indians.

**761.** New York Council. "The Examination of an Indian." *New York Historical Society Collections For The Year 1919, Cadwallader Colden Papers,* vol. 3 (New York, 1920): 231–232.

At a meeting on July 26, 1746, the New York Council questioned an Indian about the killing of a French man and about the reasons the man was imprisoned and later released by the French. The Indian is also asked about other prisoners taken by the French and about the movements of other Indians.

**762.** New York Council. "Representation to Clinton of Seven Members of the Council in Reference to Colden's Pamphlet on the Treaty With the Six Nations." *New York Historical Society Collections For The Year 1919, Cadwallader Colden Papers,* vol. 3 (New York, 1920): 294–305.

At a meeting on December 16, 1746, seven members of the New York Council, in an effort to vindicate themselves, claim that Cadwallader Colden misrepresented facts about his and their roles in getting Indians to join an expedition against Canada. This is all discussed in Colden's pamphlet entitled, "A Treaty Between Your Excellency and the Six United Nations Depending on the Province of New York." Council members discuss what they feel is Colden's surprising behavior and their unhappiness at not being privy to information about his influence on Indian affairs.

**763.** New York Council and Commissioners of Massachusetts, Connecticut, and Pennsylvania. "Conference Between the Committee of the Council and the Commissioners from the Neighboring Governments (Massachusetts Bay, Connecticut, and Pennsylvania) at Albany." *New York Historical Society Collections For The Year 1869. Publication Fund,* vol. 2 (New York, 1870): 516–522.

At a meeting on October 7, 1745, the New York Council moves that Governor George Clinton speak to the Six Nations, on behalf of the governments, about their intentions in a war between England and France. The Pennsylvania commissioners indicate that they want to speak to the Six Nations separately about matters of concern to their province. The Massachusetts Commissioners feel that the Six Nations are bound by treaty to join immediately with the British in a war against the French and allied Indians. The Six Nations answer, except for the absent Senecas, on October 12, 1745, that they reaffirm their allegiance to the British and their willingness to fight the French and allied Indians but not until they inform their allies, the "far" Indians, about it. The Six Nations indicate that if the "far" Indians refuse to avenge the wrongs done to the British, they will fight them whenever the governor of New York orders them to do it. The Indians request that goods be sold at a cheaper rate; Clinton answers that the goods were expensive since prices depend on quantity available and during war goods were scarce.

**764.** New York Historical Society. "Drawings by George Catlin." *New York Historical Society Quarterly Bulletin,* vol. 26, no. 1 (January 1942): 12–16. Illustrated.

On January 23, 1872, the New York Historical Society purchased 220 original pencil and ink drawings of North American Indians by George Catlin, 1796–1872. There is a brief biography of Catlin and his resolve to use his "art and so much of the labors of future life as might be required in rescuing from oblivion the looks and customs of the vanishing races of native man in America." There are a list of the tribes represented in the Society collection and one illustration of Catlin's Green Corn Dance.

**765.** New York Indian Commissioners. [Letter to George Clinton] *Connecticut Historical Society Collections,* vol. 13 (Hartford, 1911): 16–19.

In a letter dated August 12, 1745, the commissioners report that the Canadian Indians have taken up arms against the English, signifying the end of Indian neutrality. They also complain of the French governor's conspiracy with the New York Indians. The commissioners suggest that the Six Nations be prevailed on to fight the French, that the governor give more than ordinary presents to the Indians and that he help to raise money for a fort to protect the frontiers.

**766.** New York Indian Commissioners. [Meeting] *New York Historical Society Collections For The Year 1920, Cadwallader Colden Papers,* vol. 4 (New York, 1921): 68.

At a meeting on June 27, 1748, the commissioners recommend two missionaries, Mr. Elihu Spencer and Mr. Job Strong, for the Six Nations. The commissioners urge that Governors Clinton and Shirley (of Massachusetts) try to influence the Six Nations to receive the two missionaries or any others sent; they suggest that, if they refuse, the governors try to get the Six Nations to persuade other Indians to receive the men.

**767.** Niantic Indians. "Memorial of Niantic Indians to the General Assembly." *Connecticut Historical Society Collections,* vol. 11 (Hartford, 1907): 81–84.

In a document dated May 9, 1743, the Niantics describe ways in which some English are encroaching on their lands, causing damages, and appear to want to drive them away. They petition the Assembly to investigate the matter. Names are listed. [*See* "Memorial of Niantic Indians to the General Assembly," pages 86–87, dated May 13, 1743. The Niantics name the English and others of Lyme who are causing them trouble. *See also* "General Assembly Report on Herbage in Niantic Indian Lands," pages 127–129. The commissioners report on the rights of the English to herbage of the Indian fields, how the lands ought to be improved, and on Indian rights that have been violated.]

**768.** Nicholson, John P. "Forts in Pennsylvania." *Pennsylvania Magazine of History and Biography,* vol. 15, no. 2 (1891): 250–255.

Nicholson lists and discusses the historical locations of Fort Augusta, Bethlehem, Bigham, Appleby, Anderson, Adam Carson, Armstrong, Beversrede, Bedford, Antes, and Allen and relates each fort to Indian history from the seventeenth through the eighteenth centuries.

**769.** Niemcewicz, Julian. "Journey of Niagara, 1805: From the Diary of Julian Niemcewicz." Edited by Metchie J. E. Budka. *New York Historical Society Quarterly Bulletin,* vol. 44, no. 1 (January 1960): 73–113. Illustrated.

Niemcewicz, a Polish aristocrat who came to America as Kosciuszko's aide, wrote a day-by-day account of his journey from Elizabeth, New Jersey, to Niagara Falls, New York. On October 15, 1805 (pages 94–100 and 102–105) he observes the Oneidas, describing their clothing, physical characteristics, housing, and life styles. On October 12, 1805, he tells of a Cayuga Indian who killed a white man because he had "a pressing need to shed blood." He describes an impoverished reservation he traveled through on October 21, 1805, and Senecas he observed on October 23. There is a photograph of a print of an Indian by a salt lake.

770. Niles, Samuel. "History of the Indian and French Wars." *Massachusetts Historical Society Collections*, ser. 3, vol. 6 (Boston, 1837): 154–279.

Originally published before 1762, the history is a narrative of the wars in New England from 1634 to 1760 and offers some information that antedates the first war with the Indians. Niles tells of the Pequot War of 1637 and King Philip's War of 1675 and gives an account of the numbers of English slain in both wars; he lists all the English "slaughtered" by the French and Indians under their influence in northern and more eastern parts of New England. [*Continued* as "A Summary Historical Narrative of the Wars in New England with the French and Indians in the Several Parts of the Country." *Massachusetts Historical Society Collections*, ser. 4, vol. 5 (Boston, 1861): 309–589.]

771. Ninigret. "Nenegrate's Petition." *Massachusetts Historical Society Collections*, ser. 5, vol. 9 (Boston, 1885): 206–209.

In a document dated October 1705, Ninigret petitions the Rhode Island General Assembly regarding some lands, contained in the mortgage deed of October 13, 1660, that the colony has not disposed of. He offers to pay off the mortgage and grant deeds at reasonable rates also to people already settled on the land without the colony's order; in addition he promises not to withhold other land that remains to him but to sell it to people of the colony. The petition is followed by questioning of Ninigret about his plans.

772. "The Ninigret Portrait." *Rhode Island Historical Society Collections*, vol. 18, no. 3 (July 1925): 99–100. Illustrated.

This brief discussion of a portrait of Ninigret, a Niantic sachem, considers its date (either 1637 or 1647) and the artist (unknown). A photograph of the oil painting is provided.

773. Nixon, Lily Lee. "Colonel James Burd in the Forbes Campaign." *Pennsylvania Magazine of History and Biography*, vol. 59, no. 2 (April 1935): 106–133. Illustrated.

Nixon discusses Burd's work in the Braddock and Forbes campaigns and gives varying interpretations of the attack on Loyal Hanna by French and Indians. She tells of English defeats in the Ohio country, and describes the successful English attack on Fort Duquesne in November of 1758. The actions of the Cherokees in the campaign suggest that the French would not have had to evacuate Fort Duquesne had their Indian allies stood by them. Nixon gives four reasons for the French Indians' decision to go hunting. There are

773 *(continued)*
footnotes and a map of Burd's work in the Braddock and Forbes campaigns. [*See* "Henry Bouquet: Professional Soldier." *Pennsylvania Magazine of History and Biography*, vol. 62, no. 1 (January 1938): 11–51. This is a biography of this soldier and his role in the Forbes Expedition.]

774. Noe, S. D. "Indian Medal of 1750." *New York Historical Society Quarterly Bulletin*, vol. 8, no. 1 (April 1924): 3–9. Illustrated.

Noe discusses the medal presented to General Philip Schuyler by one of the last chiefs of the Mohawks, probably after the close of the American Revolution during the period Schuyler was commissioner to the Indians. Noe describes the images on both sides of the medal, examines two inscriptions (one of which is in the Native Language) and discusses the two figures on the obverse of the medal, concluding the medal is English-made and is a palimpsest. Noe also reviews a few facts that governed the giving of these Indian peace medals and conjectures about the alterations undergone by the medal under study. There are a few remarks about the presence of "smiths" or "metal workers" among the Indians in colonial days. There are photographs of the obverse and reverse of Schuyler's medal and a painting of the general.

775. Nolan, J. Bennett. "Peter Williamson in America, a Colonial Odyssey." *Pennsylvania History*, vol. 31, no. 1 (January 1964): 23–29.

Nolan explains how Peter Williamson fabricated the story of his capture by a raiding party of Iroquois, written in a narrative embellished with horrors and decorated with a woodcut of Peter in Indian dress. The story was published and went through ten reprints. There is a copy of the engraving of Peter Williamson in Indian garb.

776. Norridgewock Tribe. "On Norridgewock Tribe and Reverend Hugh Adams." *Massachusetts Historical Society Proceedings*, ser. 1, vol. 3 (1855–1858): 324–325.

There is a discussion of how Reverend Hugh Adams, who cured the arthritic pain of Sebastien Rasles, a French Jesuit missionary to the Norridgewock Tribe on the Kennebec River in 1716, was surprised to learn the Jesuit was not obligated to prevent the Indians from further hostilities against the eastern settlers. There is also a discussion of how in 1718 Adams planned to prevent war with the Norridgewocks.

777. Norris, Isaac. "Journal of Isaac Norris, During a Trip to Albany in 1745, and An Account of a Treaty Held There in October of That Year." *Pennsylvania Magazine of History and Biography*, vol. 27, no. 1 (1933): 20–28.

In entries dated September to October, 1745, Norris, a Pennsylvania commissioner who met with the Indians at a treaty conference in Albany, tells of conferring with the Indians and commissioners from several colonies to decide whether to negotiate jointly or separately with the Indians. The journal tells of the commissioners' debates about whether the Five Nations should fight the French and Canadian Indians.

**778.** Notley, Thomas. "From Book of Entries Letter CN 18–1682/1683 Entered for Henry Coursey Esquire this following Commission, May 31, 1677." *New York Historical Society Collections For The Year 1869. Publication Fund,* vol. 2 (New York, 1870): 377–378.

Thomas Notley, governor of Maryland, commissions Henry Coursey to deal with the Susquehannocks and other northern Indians who committed murders and other outrages within the colony. Since most of the Indians were now living under the protection of Indians residing in New York, Notley asks the governor of New York for permission to allow Coursey to travel through New York to conclude a treaty and to assist him.

**779.** Nottingham, Earl of. [Letter to the Governor of Pennsylvania] *New York Historical Society Collections For The Year 1869. Publication Fund,* vol. 2 (New York, 1870): 400–401.

In a letter dated October 11, 1692, the Earl of Nottingham says that it is necessary that the several colonies and provinces of New England, Virginia, Maryland, and Pennsylvania aid and assist New York with troops in its war against the French and allied Indians. He tells Pennsylvania that it must agree with the other colonies on a quota of men or other assistance to be given to help defend New York.

**780.** Nowwaquanu. [Petition to the General Assembly] *Connecticut Historical Society Collections,* vol. 21 (Hartford, 1924): 252–253.

In a document dated October 1676, Nowwaquanu, brother-in-law of Ninigret, tells how two Mohegans stole his sister's goods; he petitions for the restitution of the property.

**781.** Noyes, James. [Letter to John Allyn] *Connecticut Historical Society Collections,* vol. 21 (Hartford, 1924): 255–257.

In a letter dated October 1676, Noyes first reviews his war service to the English without pay and then discusses his desires for using Indian captives as servants. He tells of one Indian sent to him who was returned because he was not used to work, was sick and lame, and was of little use.

**782.** "The Number of Indians in Connecticut." *Massachusetts Historical Society Collections,* ser. 1, vol. 10 (Boston, 1809): 117–118.

The number of Indians in Connecticut was taken from "An Account of the Number of Inhabitants" taken in Connecticut January 1, 1774. The Indians are numbered by categories including Indian males under and above twenty years old and Indian females under and above twenty years old.

**783.** "The Number of Indians in Rhode Island." *Massachusetts Historical Society Collections*, ser. 1, vol. 10 (Boston, 1809): 119.

The number of Indians in Rhode Island came from "An Account of the Number of Inhabitants in That Colony" taken between May 4 and June 14, 1774. The Indians are divided by towns and categories including males and females above and under sixteen years old.

**784.** Oaks, Robert F. "The Impact of British Western Policy on the Coming of the American Revolution in Pennsylvania." *Pennsylvania Magazine of History and Biography*, vol. 101, no. 2 (April 1977): 171–189.

Oaks reviews the minimal influence of British western policies, the Proclamation of 1763 and the Quebec Act of 1774, on Pennsylvanians and tells of the colony's resistance to independence. He avers that the Proclamation of 1763 was designed to prevent expensive Indian wars by reserving the trans-Appalachian region for the Indians and by centralizing the regulation of Indian trade. He explains that many Pennsylvanians supported this policy either out of disdain for frontier inhabitants or because it served political or economic interests. People in the eastern area of the province, particularly Philadelphia merchants eager to trade with the Indians, supported the proclamation but were apprehensive about frontier people who they feared would move into western areas and arouse Indian hostilities. Oaks blames the settlers, who moved into the frontier areas and abused Indians, for increased tensions. He concludes by explaining events that divided Virginia and Pennsylvania over Pennsylvania frontier interests and tells of the Quebec Act, Britain's final attempt to establish a western policy.

**785.** O'Brien, Michael Charles. "Grammatical Sketch of the Ancient Abenaki, Outlined in the Dictionary of Father Sebastian Rale, S. J. Part 1. The Abnaki Noun." *Maine Historical Society Collections*, ser. 1, vol. 9 (Portland, 1887): 259–294.

O'Brien discusses the *Dictionary of the Abnaki* written by Father Rasles which consists of about 7500 distinct Abenaki words, nearly all of them in French. The paper is concerned with the etymology, or source, of the ancient Abenaki noun. He describes the properties of the noun under classification, distribution of all objects into two general classes, and inflection by number, conjugation, and accidents, certain affixes and changes at the end of words as well as three personals. He gives examples of the conjugation of each of the two classes into which nouns are divided. He tells of irregular nouns, vocative plural, the past, obviatives, the locatives, and case.

**786.** Occum, Samson. "Mr. Occum's Account of the Montauk Indians." *Massachusetts Historical Society Collections*, ser. 1, vol. 10 (Boston, 1809): 105–111.

Occum, a Mohegan, wrote an account of the Montauks in 1761. He describes some of their ancient customs and ways, focusing on marriage, naming of children, gods, powwows, burial, mourning, and ideas of the future state. He lists families and numbers of members in them.

**787.** O'Gorman, J. Leo. "Journals of Early Travel in Vermont: A Bibliography." *Vermont Historical Society Proceedings*, n.s., vol. 7, no. 4 (December 1939): 263–278.

This bibliography lists published journals or narratives of explorers and travelers in the region now known as Vermont from the earliest days, around 1609, up to 1830. The list is arranged chronologically according to the year of travel followed by an index of travelers. The earliest travels are of four kinds: exploratory, missionary (mainly French Jesuits), accounts of Indian captives who are taken through Vermont to Canada by Indians, and military reports of scouting parties and excursions. The journals indicate that Vermont and Lake Champlain were a battleground of warring Indian tribes and clashing French and English until well into the eighteenth century. [*See also* "The Journals of Early Travels in Vermont-Resume of Remarks by J. Leo O'Gorman . . ." *Vermont Historical Society Proceedings*, n.s., vol. 8, no. 3 (September 1940): 288–289. There are additional comments on the same subject.]

**788.** Olmstead, Captain. "Testimony of Captain Olmstead and Sergeant Tibbals About the Pequots." *Massachusetts Historical Society Collections*, ser. 5, vol. 9 (Boston, 1885): 117.

On September 20, 1683, these two men testify about a fight between the English and the Pequots in which eight or nine score surrendered to the English and were made captives. They tell how the Sascoe Indians also were with the Pequots.

**789.** Olsen, Godfrey J. "Archaeology of Ticonderoga." *New York History*, vol. 15, no. 4 (October 1934): 407–411.

Olsen discusses the preliminary survey of archaeological remains in and about Fort Ticonderoga and tells of the location of sites and of Algonquian and Iroquoian materials found in them.

**790.** Oneiga. "Oneiga, Indian Messenger to General Sullivan, September, 1779." *New Hampshire Historical Society Collections*, vol. 15 (Concord, 1939): 115–116.

Oneiga reports of his informing the Oneidas about Sullivan's battle with Butler's party near Newtown and of the Oneidas' joyous reaction. Onegia also reports on a speech by the Oneida chief warriors who ask Sullivan not to destroy Cayuga crops because they are looking for those Cayugas who are willing to make peace with the Americans.

**791.** Onohaghguage Chiefs. "Chiefs of Onohaghguage to General Abercrombie." *New York Historical Society Collections For The Year 1921, Cadwallader Colden Papers*, vol. 5 (New York, 1923): 192.

**791** (*continued*)
In a message dated October 5, 1757, the chiefs report news of some Cayugas and Delawares going to war against the English and efforts by them and the Nanticokes to prevent the attack. The Indians tell the English to alert the towns to this news and that there is another group of Indians and French also planning to attack along the western frontiers.

**792.** Orton, Vrest. "No Indians Lived in Vermont." *Vermont Historical Society News and Notes,* vol. 2, no. 6 (February 1951): 5–7. Illustrated.
Orton argues that no Indians ever lived in Vermont and points to the state's arctic weather as a factor. He argues that Indians hunted, fished, and fought all over Vermont and therefore left artifacts and other evidence of occupancy but in each instance it was only for a few nights and never for permanent occupancy. A letter from A. W. Peach follows to Orton telling him to "eat his words" because evidence has been found that Indians did live in Vermont. There is an example of a Vermont Historical Society cartoon regarding the controversy over Indians living in Vermont.

**793.** "Oswego." *New York State Historical Association Proceedings, Fifteenth Annual Meeting,* vol. 13 (Lake George, 1914).
There are a number of articles dealing with Oswego, whose location within the disputed lands between the English and French made it important; Indians are mentioned in all of these articles in a peripheral way. The articles are: W. H. Bertsch, "The Defenses of Oswego," pages 108–127; Frederick W. Barnes, "The Fur Traders of Early Oswego," pages 128–137; Franklin D. Roosevelt, "Montcalm's Victory and Its Lesson," pages 138–142; Avery W. Skinner, "Old Trail from the Mohawk to Oswego," pages 199–209; George T. Clark, "Oswego," pages 321–338; and W. L. Grant, "Capture of Oswego in 1756," pages 339–370.

**794.** "Onondaga Names of Months." *Pennsylvania Magazine of History and Biography,* vol. 14, no. 3 (1890): 323–344.
The Onondaga names of the months were obtained by Albert Cusick from John Jacobs, or Ke-nent-too-te. The year begins in the fall, October, when the Indians went out to hunt. From the same source, the names of the days of the week, probably of recent origin, are given.

**795.** Paltsits, Victor Hugo. "The Depredation at Pemaquid in August, 1689." *Maine Historical Society Collections,* ser. 3, vol. 2 (Portland, 1906): 261–274.
Paltsits discusses the exposed condition of Pemaquid and the weak state of the garrison at Fort Charles, the Indian hostilities and the role

of Father Thury, a Catholic missionary at Pentagoet, who urged Indians to attack the English at Pemaquid. The author describes the Indians' attack and the capitulation of the fort August 2, and tells of the fate of the captive John Gyles who was eventually released in 1698.

**796.** Parker, Arthur C. "The Iroquois Wampums." *New York State Historical Association Proceedings, Tenth Annual Meeting*, vol. 8 (Lake George, 1909): 205–208.

Parker briefly discusses one feature of the Iroquois system important to Indians and to the historical development of the colonies of New York and New England: wampum. He discusses its uses, particularly as money and, for the Iroquois, as memorials of their laws and treaties.

**797.** Parker, Arthur C. "The Senecas in the War of 1812." *New York State Historical Association Proceedings, Seventeenth Annual Meeting*, vol. 15 (Lake George, 1916): 78–90. Illustrated.

Parker, a Seneca, discusses how the Iroquois became allies of the U.S. in the war of 1812 against Britain, citing the tribe's loyalty to America, and its declaration of war against the British after the latter's siege on Grand Island in 1812. He tells of Red Jacket, who argued for war, and of an Oneida woman who went to war. Parker reviews how the War of 1812 estranged the Canadian and New York branches of the Iroquois. He also describes the uniforms and clothing worn by the Iroquois. There are photos of Fort Putnam and of a chapel.

**798.** Parker, Arthur C. "Sources and Range of Cooper's Indian Lore." In *James Fenimore Cooper: A Re-Appraisal. New York History*, vol. 25 (Cooperstown, N.Y., 1954): 447–456.

Parker discusses how Cooper received many of his ideas about Indians from one source that had a great impact on him. It was a book written by the Reverend John G. E. Heckewelder, a Moravian missionary who worked among the Delawares, his favorite tribe, and who had little love for the Iroquois. Parker reveals that Cooper missed opportunities to write authentic stories and that his dependence on Heckewelder's accounts made him essentially a fiction writer, not a historian or an anthropologist. Parker also cites Cooper's ethnographic mistakes and the facts he chose not to include.

**799.** Parker, Arthur C. "The Unknown Mother of Red Jacket." *New York History*, vol. 24, no. 4 (October 1943): 525–533. Illustrated.

Parker discusses the records that show Ah-wey-ne-yonh, a member of the Wolf clan born about 1733, was Red Jacket's mother. He describes events she doubtlessly witnessed. He tells of a monument which is the first and only one erected to an Indian mother. There is a photograph of the monument.

**800.** Parker, James. "Letter from James Parker to the Governor and Council of Boston." *New Hampshire Historical Society Collections*, vol. 3 (Concord, 1832): 100.

**800** *(continued)*
Parker's letter, dated January 23, 1677, reports that an Indian named Wonnalanset informed him that he discovered fifteen Indians he supposed to be Mohawks on the Merrimack River.

**801.** Parker, Robert. "Journal of Lieutenant Robert Parker, of the Second Continental Artillery, 1779." *Pennsylvania Magazine of History and Biography,* vol. 27, no. 4 (1903): 404–420.
Writing from June 14 to September 6, 1779, Parker deals with General Sullivan's march against the Indians in 1779. The journal contains accounts of battles with Indians. [*Continued in Pennsylvania Magazine of History and Biography,* vol. 28, no. 1 (1904): pages 12–23. This part of the journal is dated September 7 to December 6, 1779.]

**802.** Parrish, John. "Extracts from the Journal of John Parrish, 1773." *Pennsylvania Magazine of History and Biography,* vol. 16, no. 4 (1892): 443–448.
Parrish visited the western Indians in 1773 and recorded details of his journey including his contacts with Indians along the way.

**803.** Parsons, John E. "Gunmakers for the American Fur Company." *New York Historical Society Quarterly Bulletin,* vol. 36, no. 2 (April 1952): 181–193. Illustrated.
Parsons discusses the orders, first recorded in 1828, of the American Fur Company for firearms for the "American" or "Lancaster" pattern rifles, for rifles of the "English" pattern, and "North West" guns. These firearms were used in the Indian trade. Parsons discusses the gunsmiths, kinds of rifles, size of the order, and how they were shipped. There are illustrations of Indians with rifles, trade cards, and documents from the American Fur Company.

**804.** Parsons, John E., ed. "Letters on the Chickasaw Removal of 1837." *New York Historical Society Quarterly Bulletin,* vol. 37, no. 3 (July 1955): 273–283. Illustrated.
Bowes Reed McIlvaine's letters to his wife, dated November-December, 1837, record the Mississippi River crossing at Memphis of thousands of Chickasaws, their baggage, dogs, and ponies. The letters describe how the Indians dressed and comported themselves. They tell of the murder of one Indian by another and how it was resolved. Photographs of the McIlvaines in 1833 and in later life are included. There is a map showing the area visited by McIlvaine and the overland routes of Chickasaws to the Mississippi crossing, 1837.

**805.** Parsons, Phyllis Vibbard. "The Early Life of Daniel Claus." *Pennsylvania History,* vol. 29, no. 4 (October 1962): 357–372. Illustrated.
Daniel Claus worked in Pennsylvania Indian affairs and was appointed to the British Indian Service in 1756 to explain the British government and policies to Indians. Parsons tells that Claus spoke their language and was honest in his dealings with the Indians. She describes how, after the fall of Canada, 1763, Claus, a deputy agent in Indian affairs in charge of Canadian Indians in Montreal, tried to

convert the Iroquois from French loyalties to British alliance. There is a portrait of Claus and his wife.

**806.** Partridge, Samuel. [Letter to Fitz-John Winthrop] *Massachusetts Historical Society Collections,* ser. 6, vol. 3 (Boston, 1889): 170–172.

In a letter dated February 21, 1704, Partridge tells of an attack on Haverhill and Exeter by Indians. He warns that Deerfield and Brookfield need relief and garrisoning.

**807.** Patrick, Daniel. [Letter to the Governor and Council of War in Massachusetts] *Massachusetts Historical Society Collections,* ser. 4, vol. 7 (Boston, 1865): 322–324.

In a letter dated June 19, 1637, Patrick tells of the Pequots' flight from their country to "Quinnopiage" where it might be possible to surprise them at night with some Narragansett help.

**808.** Paumahtukquasuk. "Will of Paumahtukquasuk." *Massachusetts Historical Society Proceedings,* ser. 1, vol. 2 (1835–1855): 290–291.

The text of Paumahtukquasuk's will, dated August 1673, is copied from the probate records of Plymouth Colony; it divides his property among his surviving family.

**809.** Pawpeqwenock. "Pawpeqwenock's Engagement." *Connecticut Historical Society Collections,* vol. 21 (Hartford, 1924): 265–267.

On August 16, 1677, Pawpeqwenock acknowledges that he acted treacherously toward the English by leading away some ninety surrendered Indians; he now promises to be true to the English and reveal any evil plans the Indians may have against them. He also promises to surrender to the English the Indians he encouraged to desert and to get them to settle wherever they are appointed. This is followed by Uncas' statement, dated August 13, 1677, that he promises to do what is right regarding the surrendering Indians.

**810.** Peckham, Howard H., ed. "Thomas Gist's Indian Captivity: 1758–1769." *Pennsylvania Magazine of History and Biography,* vol. 80, no. 3 (July 1956): 285–311.

Peckham describes Gist's capture by Hurons and discusses the authenticity of the journal. The captivity narrative, dated September 9, 1758 to September 30, 1759, clarifies the participation of the Detroit Indians in western Pennsylvania hostilities, illuminates the battle of Grant's Hill during the Forbes Expedition of 1758, and underscores certain characteristics of the Indians. The journal tells how Gist was carried to Fort Pont Chartrain, Detroit, where he was adopted by an Indian family and was well treated until his escape in 1759.

**811.** Peekskill, William Wait. "The Hudson, Its Aboriginal Occupation, Discovery, and Settlement." *New York State Historical Association Proceedings, Thirteenth Annual Meeting,* vol. 11 (Lake George, 1912): 152–165.

Peekskill discusses the traditional history of two aboriginal nations in

811 *(continued)*
the Hudson Valley before white contact, the Mingos and the Lenapes.
He describes the Indians of Lenape stock, as recorded by Hudson in
his journal. He argues that "savage life" was debauched by advancing
civilization. The article also describes the journey of the Half-Moon
on the Hudson River.

812. Penhallow, Samuel. "Penhallow's Indian Wars." ed. Nathaniel Adam.
*New Hampshire Historical Society Collections*, vol. 1 (Concord, 1824): 13–133.
Adam provides a biographical sketch of Penhallow on pages 2–13.
This is followed by the entire text of Penhallow's book entitled, *The
History of the Wars of New England with the Eastern Indians, or a Narrative
of Their Continued Perfidy and Cruelty. From the 10th of August, 1703, to the
Peace Renewed the 13th of July, 1713, and from the 25th of July, 1722, to
Their Submission the 15th of December, 1725, Which Was Ratified August 5,
1726.* The book was originally published in 1726.

813. Penn, Granville John. "Presentation to the Historical Society of Pennsylvania of the Belt of Wampum Delivered by the Indians to William Penn at the
Great Treaty Under the Elm Tree, in 1682." *Historical Society of Pennsylvania
Memoirs*, vol. 6 (Philadelphia, 1858): 204–263. Illustrated.
This document by Penn, great-grandson of William Penn, discusses
the belt of wampum given to the founders of Pennsylvania by the
Indian chiefs at the 1682 treaty. He describes the customs of Indians
in their use of wampum, including treaty-making. Penn presented the
belt to the Historical Society. The acceptance speech discusses Penn
and the treaty of Shackamaxon and is followed by the text of three
letters by William Penn (dated October 18, 1681, April 21, 1682, and
June 21, 1682), the text of Secretary James Logan's conference with
the Indians, June 27, 1720, and Governor Gordon's conference with
the Indians, May 26, 1728. There is a sketch of the belt.

814. Penn, John. [Letter to Cadwallader Colden] *New York Historical Society
Collections For The Year 1922, Cadwallader Colden Papers*, vol. 6 (New York,
1923): 274–275.
In a letter dated January 5, 1764, Governor Penn reports that
Pennsylvania whites have killed Indians who have been living under
government protection for sixty years in an Indian town near Lancas-
ter and that now the whites are threatening to kill a number of
Indians whom the governor had permitted to live near Philadelphia.
The latter Indians want to go to join the Susquehannocks. Governor
Penn asks Colden to protect these Indians on their journey to Sir
William Johnson. [*See also* Sir William Johnson's letter to Cadwallader
Colden, dated February 28, 1764, page 292, in which he suggests the
best route to send the Indians to Albany.]

815. Penacook Indians. "Penacook Papers, 1659–1668." *New Hampshire Historical Society Collections*, vol. 3 (Concord, 1832): 212–224.
Three documents pertain to the examination of a group of Indians

regarding their knowledge of the murder of an Englishman by an Indian in 1668. Eight depositions and affidavits report on one man's trading liquor to Indians in violation of the law and point to the intemperance of the Indians as contributing to the killing of the Englishman.

**816.** Pennsylvania. "An Act Appointing the Commissioners to Meet with the Commissioners Who are or May be Appointed by the Legislatures of the Neighboring Colonies to Form and Agree on a General Plan for the Regulation of the Indian Trade." *New York Historical Society Collections For The Year 1922, Cadwallader Colden Papers,* vol. 6 (New York, 1923): 167–169.

The Pennsylvania act, dated March 6, 1770, appoints commissioners who will confer with the colonies of Quebec, New York, New Jersey, Maryland, and Virginia and the three lower counties on the Delaware about regulations for the Indian trade.

**817.** Pennsylvania. "Frontier Forts of Pennsylvania." *Pennsylvania Magazine of History and Biography,* vol. 20, no. 2 (1896): 257–264.

Based on the "Report of the Committee to Locate the Sites of the Frontier Forts of Pennsylvania," this article points out that the "Report" refutes the commonly held opinion that the Quakers refused to erect forts or raise troops for the defense of the inhabitants of the frontier against the French and allied Indians. The report states that no fewer than 207 forts, large and small, were erected on the frontier during the campaigns of 1755–1758 and 1763, Pontiac's War. This construction, at the expense of the Assembly where the Quakers held a majority, is counter to the assertion that the colony was defenseless.

**818.** "Depredations of Indians in Pennsylvania." *Pennsylvania Magazine of History and Biography,* vol. 52, no. 3 (1928): 272–276.

A lengthy footnote to an article about a pre-Revolutionary episode in Pennsylvania discusses the depredations of Indians in western Pennsylvania after Braddock's defeat in July of 1755. It includes an extract from the text of a petition entitled, "A Representation to the General Assembly of the Province of Pennsylvania, by some of the Principal Inhabitants of the City of Philadelphia, in the said Province," dated November 12, 1755, in which the citizens demand a law for the defense of the province. There are quotations from the address of the Quakers of the Assembly in November, 1755, protesting payment of a tax for destructive purposes.

**819.** Pennsylvania Indians. Petition of Pennsylvania Indians to Governor Markham. *Historical Society of Pennsylvania Memoirs,* vol. 3, part 2 (Philadelphia, 1836): 206–207.

On October 8, 1681, four Indians, whose marks are reproduced and explained, petition Governor Markham to rescind prohibition of selling liquor in Pennsylvania until liquor is also prohibited in New Castle, Delaware.

820. "Lists of Pennsylvania Settlers Murdered and Taken Prisoners by Indians, 1755–1756." *Pennsylvania Magazine of History and Biography*, vol. 32, no. 3 (1908): 309–319.

The lists made of names during the French and Indian War are from the present-day counties of Berks, Dauphin, Lancaster, Lebanon, Monroe, and Northampton, and the valley of the Lehigh.

821. Pequot Indians. "Agreement of Pequot Indians with the Commissioners of the United Colonies." *Massachusetts Historical Society Proceedings*, ser. 1, vol. 16 (1878): 401–402.

On October 16, 1654, captive Pequot Indians agree to go to such a location as might be selected by the Commissioners of the United Colonies. The Pequots, who agree to disown the jurisdiction of Ninigret, also agree not to join in any war with Ninigret or others without the full consent of the commissioners. There are 108 Pequot names listed. A facsimile of the agreement is included.

822. Pequot Indians. "Memorial of Pequot Indians to the General Assembly." *Connecticut Historical Society Collections*, vol. 11 (Hartford, 1907): 36–38.

On May 5, 1742, the Pequots tell how they wish to learn to read the Bible. They request that Captain Morgan be appointed to care for them and their lands. [*See also* "Owen and Croswell to the General Assembly," pages 38–39. On May 6, 1742, these two confirm the intent of some Pequots to learn to read and also comment on the miserable state of the Pequots.]

823. Pequot Indians. "Pequot Indians' Petition." *Massachusetts Historical Society Collections*, ser. 5, vol. 9 (Boston, 1885): 144.

The Pequot Indians, who took no part in shedding blood of the English but fled their country on the advice of Wequash, petition the English to designate some place where they may live peacefully under English government. The petition is undated.

824. Pequot Indians. "Petition of Pequot Indians." *Connecticut Historical Society Collections*, vol. 4 (Hartford, 1892): 319–321.

On September 22, 1735, the Pequots inform Governor Talcott of a number of English encroachments and damage on their lands and petition him to stop these actions. [*See* "Captain James Avery to Governor Talcott," dated October 8, 1735, page 323. Avery claims he cannot find any real damage done to the Indians by the English.]

825. Pequot and Narragansett Indians. "Indian Depositions Relative to Pequot and Narragansett Bounds." *Massachusetts Historical Society Collections*, ser. 5, vol. 9 (Boston, 1885): 158–159.

On September 15, 1679, some Pequots and elderly Narragansetts answer questions regarding the boundaries of their lands.

826. Perepole. "The Indian Perepole's Deposition." *Maine Historical Society Collections*, ser. 1, vol. 3 (Portland, 1853): 333.

Perepole testifies that the Indian name of a specific river is "Pejepscook" and that Indians used to catch salmon at a certain falls on the river. The affidavit was taken in order to prove Richard Wharton's title to land at Pejepscot. The Indian's mark is reproduced.

**827.** Perkins, George Henry. "Prehistoric Vermont: Evidences of Early Occupation by Indian Tribes." *Vermont Historical Society Proceedings For the Year 1905–1906,* ser. 1, 89–101.

Perkins discusses the lifestyle of the early inhabitants of Vermont, their lines of travel, and some kinds of Vermont Indian relics, particularly pottery, stone chisels or celt, and other varieties of implements and ornaments.

**828.** "Examination of the Messenger of Pessicus." *Connecticut Historical Society Collections,* vol. 21 (Hartford, 1924): 241–242.

In a document written April 29, 1676, the messenger of Pessicus, a Narragansett, reports that Pessicus is pleased the English want peace, blames the Indians rather than the English for the death of so many English, and holds Ninigret and others responsible for the death of Nanantenoe. The messenger states that Pessicus wants those Narragansetts who surrender to the English to be kept in Hartford, reports that the Dutch are supplying ammunition to Narragansetts, and describes Mohawk hostility towards Narragansetts.

**829.** Peters, Richard. [Letter to Governor Monckton] *Massachusetts Historical Society Collections,* ser. 4, vol. 10 (Boston, 1871): 508–511.

Writing on January 19, 1764, Peters reports how a number of Conestego Indians, under protection of Pennsylvania, were killed by some Paxton inhabitants and the survivors threatened. Although the killings were savage, Peters asserts that a review of the facts might justify the crime. In addition, he describes government protection of Moravian Indians who committed crimes against frontier people.

**830.** Peters, Richard. [Letter to Governor Sharpe] *Maryland Historical Magazine,* vol. 4, no. 4 (December 1909): 348–353.

Writing on May 18, 1761, Peters asserts it would be a breach of faith to take possession of Wyoming lands given to the Delawares in negotiations between the Six Nations and Sharpe's agent and, furthermore, any white settlement there would cause hostilities. Also included are three letters from William Johnson, dated January 29 and May 1, 1767 and March 25, 1768, which tell the governor about disposing of the Nanticokes' lands that are situated in the Maryland province.

**831.** Peters, Richard. "Some Selections from the 'Peters Papers' in the Library of the Historical Society of Pennsylvania." *Pennsylvania Magazine of History and Biography,* vol. 29, no. 4 (1905): 451–456.

Writing from February, 1741 to October, 1750 Richard Peters and Governor George Thomas tell Conrad Weiser about the matter of properly entertaining Indians who come to Philadelphia to trade

**831** *(continued)*
lands for goods. The letters discuss possible lapses by Count Zinzendorf when he entertained Indians at his house, and also describes the lamentable condition of Indian affairs.

**832.** Philadelphia Citizens. "Seven Hundred Dollars Reward." *Pennsylvania Magazine of History and Biography*, vol. 39, no. 4 (1915): 500.

The people of Philadelphia raised reward money for the heads of Shingas and Captain Jacobs, two chiefs of the Delaware nation who were largely responsible for alienating the affections of the Delaware Indians towards both the British crown and the Pennsylvanians. This is undated.

**833.** Philadelphia Citizens. "Two Petitions of Citizens of Philadelphia County to the Governor of the Province, for Protection Against Indian Incursions, 1728." *Pennsylvania Magazine of History and Biography*, vol. 29, no. 2 (1905): 228, 230. Illustrated.

Two 1728 petitions to Governor Patrick Gordon of Pennsylvania from settlers living on the frontiers of Philadelphia County, now Montgomery County, seek protection from threatened Indian incursions.

**834.** Philhower, Charles A. "The Aboriginal Inhabitants of Monmouth County." *New Jersey Historical Society Proceedings*, n.s., vol. 9, no. 1 (January 1924): 22–40.

Philhower draws on archaeological research to discuss three subdivisions of the Lenapes and their locales within the state, particularly Monmouth County. He lists the divisions and locales of each of the subtribes—the Munsees, Unamis, and Unilachtigos—explaining that his classification does not agree with other authorities and giving linguistic and geographic data on the divisions. He quotes passages from Giovanni Verrazano who was the first to touch the coast of New Jersey in 1524 and whose account has been found to be the earliest known description of the Lenapes. The author also quotes Henry Hudson's 1609 descriptions of the Indians and DeVries' 1642 notes about the New Jersey Indians. Philhower briefly discusses the negative nature of New Jersey Indian-white relations, which only ended when the last of the Delawares moved westward.

**835.** Philhower, Charles A. "The Aboriginal Inhabitants of Union County." *New Jersey Historical Society Proceedings*, n.s., vol. 8, no. 2 (April 1923): 124–238.

Citing archaeological and linguistic evidence, Philhower asserts that the Lenapes have possessed land in New Jersey, "as far back as tradition takes us." He mentions implements and pottery found in New Jersey which suggest that people have lived in this area thousands of years. He discusses the geographic location of Lenape subtribes in New Jersey and the early records which help determine these places as well as the complexity of translating native names and their equivalents into other languages, variant spellings, extant Indian names, and the origins of geographic and Indian names. Philhower also examines the land transactions between Indians and whites which illustrate the generally deceitful policy whites followed when dealing with Indians. He describes the physical characteristics and culture of the Raritan and other Indians in the seventeenth century.

836. Philhower, Charles A. "The Aborigines of Hunterdon County, New Jersey." *New Jersey Historical Society Proceedings*, n.s., vol. 11, no. 4 (October 1926): 508–525.

Philhower mentions Indian place names in Hunterdon County, most of which were determined by the character of the terrain. He explains that Hunterdon lay within the domain of the Lenapes, and discusses their three main subtribes, giving the location of each within the state. He describes some of the important purchases of land from the Indians in Hunterdon County between 1680 and 1760, as well as rock shelters, the network of Indian paths, local Indian traffic in argillite, and the few noteworthy Hunterdon Indians, such as Moses Totamy and Tuccamirgan. He defines several Indian words used in the county and concludes with some traditional stories concerning conflicts between Indians and whites in Hunterdon.

837. Philhower, Charles A. "Agriculture and the Food of the Indians of New Jersey." *New Jersey Historical Society Proceedings*, vol. 58, no. 2 (April 1940): 93–102.

Philhower discusses the agriculture and food of the New Jersey Indians, reporting what the Lenapes ate and how they cultivated corn, their principal crop. He mentions their cultivation of beans, an important vegetable food to Lenapes, wild rice, sunflowers, squash, and other vine growths such as pumpkins. [*Continued* in *New Jersey Historical Society Proceedings*, vol. 58, no. 3 (July 1940): pages 192–202. Philhower discusses other foods the Lenapes used, such as ground nuts, wild artichokes, Indian turnips, wild potato vines, hog peanuts, American lotus, and root foods. He mentions how saps and barks were used as food as well as nut and fruit trees, giving the Indians' method of preparing these plants for human consumption.]

838. Philhower, Charles A. "The Art of the Lenape." *New Jersey Historical Society Proceedings*, vol. 50, no. 3 (July 1932): 249–256.

Philhower discusses the Lenapes' stone objects, showing that these Indians were not content with merely utilitarian artifacts. He mentions their most elaborate stone specimens and explains that wood was used largely for utilitarian objects. He also describes basketry, vegetable dyes, utensils made from bones and antlers, pottery, clothing, and the decoration of the human body. He concludes that Lenape implements and ornaments made of stone, wood, bone, and other materials express an artistic sense.

**839.** Philhower, Charles A. "Did the Minisink Trail Go By Way of Lake Hopatcong?" *New Jersey Historical Society Proceedings,* n.s., vol. 11 no. 3 (July 1926): 397–490.

Philhower describes the path of the Minisink Trail, one of the Indian trails in the East which seldom takes a straight route but follows instead the valley of a river or avoids a meadow; he terms it, "a meandering sort of route of travel." The author takes issue with a point raised in an article by Holcomb who writes that the Minisink Trail, "goes wide of Lake Hopatcong." [*See New Jersey Historical Society Proceedings,* n.s., vol. 11, no. 1 (January 1926): 18–45.]

**840.** Philhower, Charles A. "Indian Currency and Its Manufacture." *New Jersey Historical Society Proceedings,* n.s., vol. 13, no. 3 (July 1928): 310–318.

Reviewing Indian currency and its manufacture, Philhower describes the development of a medium of exchange among Indians before the arrival of whites and explains that it was not used universally to obtain products or property. He discusses "Wampum," the derivation of the word, the two distinct black and white varieties, the various shapes, the materials from which it was made, how and where it was manufactured, and its eventual obsolescence.

**841.** Philhower, Charles A. "Indian Days in Middlesex County." *New Jersey Historical Society Proceedings,* n.s., vol. 12, no. 4 (October 1927): 385–405.

Philhower discusses the groups of Indians living in Middlesex County in the seventeenth century. He quotes a passage from *Remonstrance of New Netherlands,* printed in 1649, which describes the Raritan Indians and then explains their conflict with the Dutch in the mid-seventeenth century. He mentions county trails and scrutinizes the route of the missionaries, Danker and Sluyter, who crossed the state from 1679 until 1680. He cites evidence of Indian villages, burial grounds, campsites in Middlesex County, and the mission at Cranbury, which was the work of the Brainerd brothers. He reviews the meaning of the few Indian names used in the county and then refers to the traditional story that says Wequalia, a Middlesex resident during the last quarter of the seventeenth century and the first quarter of the eighteenth century, was induced into signing over vast stretches of his land. Philhower quotes several sources that claim Wequalia murdered the white man deceiving him and was subsequently hanged for this crime.

**842.** Philhower, Charles A. "The Indians of Morris County Area." *New Jersey Historical Society Proceedings,* vol. 54, no. 4 (October 1936): 249–267.

Philhower quotes the transaction made at the Easton Treaty on October 23, 1758, the last transfer of Indian lands in northern New Jersey. He mentions Indian archaeological findings, villages, campsites, paths, trails, and place names in the county and then discusses the Indians living in present-day Morris County.

**843.** Philhower, Charles A. "The Indians of Somerset County." *New Jersey Historical Society Proceedings,* n.s., vol. 10, no. 1 (January 1925): 28–41.

Philhower discusses the Narraticongs, or Raritans, and other groups comprising the Unami subtribe of the Lenapes who lived in what is now Somerset County, drawing on linguistics, archaeological findings, and tradition to tell his story. He describes the Indian occupation of Green Brook and other areas of Somerset County, the paths that crossed the county, and Indian names linked to several early county purchases of land. He explains how difficult it is to translate Indian names and gives linguistic interpretations of many Somerset Indian names. He concludes with a passage from DeVries describing the customs of New Jersey Indians.

844. Philhower, Charles A. "A Letter From a Gentleman of New Brunswick, To His Friend in Elizabeth-Town." *New Jersey Historical Society Proceedings*, vol. 53, no. 4 (October 1935): 239–249.

This letter of August 31, 1752 justifies the claims made in the "Elizabeth Town Bill in Chancery," a legal document defending the rights of the East Jersey proprietors against certain Elizabeth Town inhabitants who claimed the lands through settlement and direct purchases from Indians. The letter not only contains a copy of Augustine Herman's December 26, 1651 deed showing he had bought lands from Indians, but it also refers to the controversy concerning land purchases from Indians which were made as early as 1651 under the Dutch, overlapping claims for West Jersey lands, bad bargains with the Indians, and the priority of proprietary claims over individual purchases.

845. Philhower, Charles A. "The Minisink Indian Trail." *New Jersey Historical Society Proceedings*, n.s., vol. 8, no. 3 (July 1923): 199–205.

The most notable network of Indian paths in New Jersey, the Minisink Trail is two to three feet wide and was used by the Indians as late as 1820. Philhower discusses the main purposes of the trail, gives a detailed description of the course of the main path and the other smaller paths that led into it, and lists eighteen place names of Indian origin along the path that are still extant, citing the archaeological and linguistic sources of his information.

846. Philhower, Charles A. "Minisink—Its Use and Significance." *New Jersey Historical Society Proceedings*, vol. 11, no. 2 (April 1926): 186–190. Illustrated.

Philhower discusses the numerous definitions of the word "Minisink." Drawing on linguistics and archaeology for his analysis, he lists nine variant spellings of "Minisink," dating when they were used and by whom. He concludes that "Minisink" may mean, "they who worship Living Solid Face," citing a photograph of an archaeological find which yields evidence of the worship of a Living Solid Face or "make-being."

847. Philhower, Charles A. "Some Personal Characteristics of the Lenape Indians." *New Jersey Historical Society Proceedings*, vol. 16, no. 2 (April 1931): 138–161.

**847** (*continued*)

Philhower dispels misconceptions about the Lenapes when he discusses the three distinctive subtribes, the Munsees, Unamis, and Unalachtigos, giving their personal characteristics and territorial limits. He describes their physical traits, particularly their hair, facial decorations, ornamentation, and dress, pointing out the distinctions among the three groups. Philhower also mentions the diet, medicines, shelter, language, dialects, recreation, and religion of these Indians.

**848.** Philhower, Charles A. "South Jersey Indians on the Bay, the Cape, and the Coast." *New Jersey Historical Society Proceedings*, vol. 16, no. 1 (January 1931): 1–21.

Drawing on several seventeenth century sources containing the observations of the first Europeans who saw the Indians, Philhower studies the early Indians of south Jersey. He describes the Indians who occupied New Jersey during and immediately preceding contact with Europeans, discussing the domain of these Indians and their political divisions. He focuses on the subtribe, the Unalachtigos of southern Jersey, and describes their legends, well-known individuals, villages, physical traits, clothing, skills, children, language, war, shelter, subsistence, medicine, death practices, as well as their enemies, the Susquehannas. He mentions the Indian trails in New Jersey particularly in the southern part of the state, Indian dugouts and pipes, Indian names in southern Jersey, several great people of the subtribe, and the fate of the Unalachtigos after the second half of the eighteenth century.

**849.** Philhower, Charles A. "Wampum, Its Use and Value." *New Jersey Historical Society Proceedings*, n.s., vol. 15, no. 2 (April 1930): 216–223.

Philhower discusses wampum of wood and shell which was made by Indians and became the universal currency in America. He describes how wampum was strung, its size, colors and kinds, and the units of measure and their values. For example, "One yard equalled eighteen pence in Virginia." He quotes Conrad Weiser's complete memo which lists the sizes of eight wampum belts and gives a table showing how wampum varied in value in selected years during the seventeenth century in New England and New Netherlands. Philhower also does some linguistic analysis of words dealing with wampum.

**850.** Philip, *King of Pokanoket*. "Letter from King Philip to Governor Prince." *Massachusetts Historical Society Collections*, ser. 1, vol. 2 (Boston, 1793): 40.

Probably writing about 1660 or 1670, King Philip tells the magistrates that they should ask the English not to talk about any of his land because he promised he would not sell it for seven years.

**851.** "On King Philip." *Rhode Island Historical Society Proceedings, 1874–1875*. (Providence, 1875): 60–68.

This is a discussion of a bead belt, said to have belonged to King Philip of Pokanoket, that was presented to the Rhode Island Historical

Society. The not very favorable descriptions historians have given of Philip indicate that his characteristics may have been drawn by the pens of prejudiced writers. A suggestion is offered that Philip was more pacific in his behavior than writers have given him credit for being. There is an argument that history should be written impartially. The plan of Judge William R. Staples for Indian monuments is included.

**852.** [On King Philip's Day] *Rhode Island Historical Society Proceedings, 1876–1877.* (Providence, 1877): 54–70.

The planting of a memorial tree on the summit of Mount Hope commemorated the 200th anniversary of the death of King Philip of Pokanoket. The remarks of Governor Lippitt and Samuel G. Arnold, the full text of William J. Miller's paper reviewing the circumstances which led to the death of Philip, and an anonymous lengthy poem written for the occasion are quoted. Also included is a brief discussion of "The Swamp Fight" in South Kingston on December 19, 1675 during which the Narragansetts fought against Massachusetts, Plymouth, and Connecticut forces which resulted in the destruction of the Narragansetts and their corn.

**853.** Pickering, John. "The Massachusetts Language." *Massachusetts Historical Society Collections,* ser. 2, vol. 9 (Boston, 1832): 223–242.

An introductory statement tells how to distinguish Indian languages from other languages, particularly in the construction of compound words. Pickering cites John Eliot, Heckewelder, and others concerning the character of the languages of the Indians living in the middle region of the continent (Mexico, Chile, and, "more civilized parts of the continent") and argues, "yet the dialects of the more barbarous nations must be extremely poor and deficient . . . ." The author explains that the numerous dialects used in North America east of the Mississippi River can be reduced to three or four classes or families. He names five principal nations of Indians in New England existing at the time of the first settlement of the country who, he argues, have one principal dialect which he calls the Massachusetts language.

**854.** Pierson, Abraham. [Letter to the Commissioners of the United Colonies] *Connecticut Historical Society Collections,* vol. 21 (Hartford, 1924): 158–160.

Writing on August 29, 1664, Reverend Pierson describes his travels among the Indians when he went to teach them religion and reports that the slow progress made is partially due to the liquor the Indians are obtaining from the English.

**855.** Pierson, Abraham. "Some Help for the Indians: A Catechism." *Connecticut Historical Society Collections,* vol. 3 (Hartford, 1895): 1–67.

The text of the catechism, originally published in 1658, is preceded by an introduction discussing Pierson, his work, and his catechism which is in the dialect of the Quiripi Indians, who lived near Long Island

**855** *(continued)*
Sound, with interlinear notations in the original English. The full title of Pierson's catechism is, "Some Help for the Indians Shewing them How to improve their natural Reason, to know the True God, and the true Christian Religion. 1. By leading them to see the Divine Authority of the *Scriptures*. 2. By the Scriptures the Divine Truths necessary to Eternal Salvation."

**856.** Pierson, Adrian H. "The Prehistoric Indian in Otsego and His Immediate Successor." *New York State Historical Association Proceedings, Eighteenth Annual Meeting*, vol. 16 (Lake George, 1917): 103–119.
Pierson reveals that neither the aboriginal population of Otsego County in prehistoric times nor that of the Iroquois in historic times was ever large during any one period. He describes the occupation of the county by successive tribes of the Algonquian family. Further, he mentions that the Iroquois, the successors of the Algonquians, never had much to do with Otsego County until historic times, that occupation by the Iroquoians and Algonquians was mainly temporary in character, and that villages were, with few exceptions, of minor importance. He also argues that there was an Indian village at the present site of Cooperstown. A bibliography is included.

**857.** Pike, John. "Journal of Reverend John Pike." *Massachusetts Historical Society Proceedings*, ser. 1, vol. 13 (1873–1875): 121–150 and *New Hampshire Historical Society Collections*, vol. 3 (Concord, 1832): 40–62.
Writing from November 1, 1678 to November 22, 1709, Reverend Pike describes countless Indian attacks on settlements, including the killing or capture of individuals, and gives the names and locations involved. Long, explanatory footnotes regarding the tribes participating in the raids are provided.

**858.** Pintard, John. [Letters from John Pintard to His Daughter] *New York Historical Society Collections For The Year 1937. Publication Fund*, vol. 70; *1938. Publication Fund*, vol. 71; *1939. Publication Fund*, vol. 72; *1940. Publication Fund*, vol. 73 (New York, 1938–1941).
Scattered throughout the four volumes are letters which contain remarks about the possibility of the Indians' attaining a certain degree of civilization and education. Pintard explains that Indians will attain this degree only when they are, "herding by themselves," under White supervision, because they degenerate when they intermix with the white settlers.

**859.** [Pitkin, William]. "Narrative of the Service of Connecticut in the Indian Wars." *Connecticut Historical Society Collections*, vol. 24 (Hartford, 1932): 65–70.
Presumably written by William Pitkin on September 25, 1693, this piece recounts the service of Connecticut in the wars against the Indians and is presented as evidence against the charge that the militia should be removed from Connecticut's jurisdiction. Pitkin describes Connecticut's role in the Pequot War of 1637, in the troubles with the

Narragansetts, and in King Philip's War of 1675. He argues that Connecticut has done more than its duty and has come to the aid of New York and Massachusetts during their troubles with the Indians, while Rhode Island and New York have done little during the most recent Indian war.

**860.** Pitkin, William. "The Pitkin Papers: Correspondence and Documents During William Pitkin's Governorship of the Colony of Connecticut, 1766–1769, With Some of Earlier Date." *Connecticut Historical Society Collections,* vol. 19 (Hartford, 1921).

Indians are discussed briefly in the papers, and Indian items are noted in the index.

**861.** Plumer, William. "A Deed from Four Indian Sagamores, to Reverend John Wheelwright and Others: Remarks on the Authenticity of the Wheelwright Deed." *New Hampshire Historical Society Collections,* vol. 1 (Concord, 1824): 298–304.

Plumer cites the reasons why one writer feels that the Wheelwright deed of May 17, 1629 is a forgery and notes that writer's objections to the reasons given for the authenticity of the deed. Plumer, however, asserts his own reasons for supporting the authenticity. [*See New Hampshire Historical Society Collections,* vol. 2 (Concord, 1827): pages 137–138 which contains a letter and three pieces of testimony that deal with the authenticity of the Wheelwright deed. The testimony, copied from a paper filed in the records of Norfolk County Court, proves that a purchase from the Indians, similar to the one expressed in the deed, was actually made.]

**862.** Podunck Indians. [Petition to the General Assembly] *Connecticut Historical Society Collections,* vol. 21 (Hartford, 1924): 288–289.

Petitioning in October, 1686, Poduncks report the danger of their losing their lands by reason of drink and other "follies." They petition the Assembly to investigate the legality of former sales and to appoint a guardian who will prevent the Poduncks from giving away any of their lands without his consent. Eight Poduncks are named.

**863.** "Pomham and His Fort." *Rhode Island Historical Society Collections,* vol. 11, no. 1 (January 1918): 31–36. Illustrated.

Pomham, sachem of the Shawomet tribe which deferred to Miantonomo, chief sachem of the Narragansetts, sought an alliance with the English as a step toward emancipation from Narragansett authority. This description of Pomham's efforts to get the Massachusetts Bay Colony to protect him and build a fort includes information about his role and death in King Philip's War, 1675–1676. There is a photograph of the tablet erected at Pomham's Fort in Warwick, Rhode Island, which reads: "Pomham's Fort. Erected for the Indian Sachem in 1644 by his English Allies as a Defense Against the 'Bluddy Mindedness' of the Narragansetts." Views of the fort are included.

**864.** Porter, Frank W., III. "A Century of Accommodation: The Nanticoke Indians in Colonial Maryland." *Maryland Historical Magazine,* vol. 74, no. 2 (June 1979): 175–192. Illustrated.

Porter discusses Lord Baltimore's Indian policy after 1632, the primary objectives of which were to procure land for the colonists from the Indians, to establish trade relations with them, and to Christianize them. He explains that the most severe problem which continually confronted the Nanticokes and other tribes in Maryland was the encroachment on their lands. Porter mentions the friction between the Nanticokes and the Maryland settlers despite treaties, the reservation established for the Nanticokes which was antithetical to their seasonal subsistence strategy, and the settlers' disregard of the Indians' right to occupy the reservation lands. The author describes how groups of Nanticokes began to emigrate to Pennsylvania in the 1740s, explains their northward movements away from encroachments, and their amalgamation with other tribes, such as the Iroquois, until 1768 when the Nanticokes sold their remaining land in Maryland. Porter concludes by attributing the decline of the Nanticoke population to contact with European settlers. Extensive notes and two maps are included.

**865.** Potman, Aaron *et al.* "Deposition of Aaron Potman, Abraham Quackenbos, Lewis Davis & William Printup, in Relation to the Kayaderosseras Patent." *New York Historical Society Collections For The Year 1922, Cadwallader Colden Papers,* vol. 6 (New York, 1923): 371–375.

Well acquainted with Mohawk complaints about the Kayaderosseras Patent, Aaron Potman mentions families settling on the tract. Quackenbos relates that the Indians have complained to him about the, "great injustice of the patent . . . which they looked upon to be fraud [ul]ently obtained . . ." and reports two families settling on the land. He also repeats an old story told to him by Ariva, a Mohawk, concerning Visscher, an Albany man whom the Indians suspected might want to cheat them of their lands. Davis explains that he knows little about the grant, but he has heard Mohawks deny selling the lands. Printup, a Mohawk interpreter, reports a conversation between his father and Hendrick, a Mohawk chief, forty years earlier concerning Dekouwyadirha, a Mohawk who privately sold some land in the Kayaderosseras Patent to Visscher without the consent or knowledge of the Mohawk chiefs. Furthermore, the Mohawks universally deny selling the patent lands yet two families have now settled on lands which may possibly be contained within the limits of the patent.

**866.** Potter, C. E. "Appendix to 'Language of the Abnaquies'." *Maine Historical Society Collections,* ser. 1, vol. 4 (Portland, 1856): 185–193.

In his letter of November 10, 1855, Potter furnishes definitions of familiar Indian place names and defines common Indian terms.

867. Potter, Elam. "An Account of Several Nations of Southern Indians. In a Letter from Reverend Elam Potter to Reverend Stiles." *Massachusetts Historical Society Collections,* ser. 1, vol. 10 (Boston, 1809): 119–121.

Writing on September 12, 1768, Potter briefly describes the Indians in Virginia, the Carolinas, Georgia, and the Floridas and pays particular attention to the Cherokees, Catawbas, Creeks, Cheraws, Choctaws, and Chickasaws.

868. Potter, Elam. "The Early History of Narragansett." *Rhode Island Historical Society Collections,* vol. 3 (Providence, 1835): 1–100.

This history of the Narragansett Tribe after 1621 describes their allies and enemies, population figures, important sachems, and relations with the Rhode Island settlers. Potter reviews the events of the war which destroyed the Pequots in 1637, the sale of Warwick by Miantonomo, other Indian land grants to Rhode Island, the Narragansetts' role in King Philip's War, the eventual sale of most of their lands by 1746, and the emigration of a considerable part of the tribe to New York. The appendix contains the July, 1675 treaty with the Narragansetts, a brief description of the Indian sachems in Rhode Island, the 1638 treaty between the English in Connecticut and two sachems, Miantonomo and Uncas, and papers regarding the Pettiquamscut purchase. Indian and place names are listed on pages 302 to 307.

869. Pownall, Thomas. "Journal of the Voyage of Governor Thomas Pownall from Boston to Penobscot River." *Maine Historical Society Collections,* ser. 1, vol. 5 (Portland, 1857): 363–387.

The May, 1759 journal entries of Governor Thomas Pownall of Massachusetts Bay record his intention to build a fort at Penobscot as well as his observation that Indians are violating the conditions of treaties. He states his requirement that the whole tribe must put themselves under his protection near the fort to insure their safety.

870. Pownall, Thomas. "Thomas Pownall's Speech to Indians." *Massachusetts Historical Society Proceedings,* ser. 2, vol. 63 (1929–1930): 267–270.

In a May, 1759 speech to four Indians at Fort St. George, Pownall, an Englishman who went to America to get an understanding of the conditions in various provinces, warns that unless the local families put themselves under his protection, he will not be responsible for their safety. An extract from the speech is included.

871. Pratt, George D. "Presentation of an Indian Statue to the New York State Historical Association." *New York State Historical Association Quarterly Journal,* vol. 3, no. 1 (January 1922): 30–55. Illustrated.

Pratt's speech describes the sculpture of an Indian of peace, a hunter halting for a moment in his quest for game, who has been depicted by A. Phimister Proctor, a sculptor. The piece will be located at Lake George Battleground. An acceptance speech on behalf of the Associa-

871 *(continued)*
tion follows which explains that the function of the monument is to
instruct about the past. A photograph of the sculpture is included.

872. Preston, Howard W. "The Defenders of Providence during King Philip's
War." *Rhode Island Historical Society Collections,* vol. 21, no. 2 (April 1928):
56–62.
    Preston discusses the Narragansetts' attacks on Rhode Island during
    King Philip's War from 1675 to 1676. The author quotes contempor-
    ary sources to describe the war in Providence and mentions twenty-
    seven defenders of that city.

873. Prevost, Augustine. "Turmoil at Pittsburgh: Diary of Augustine Prevost,
1774." ed. Nicholas B. Wainwright. *Pennsylvania Magazine of History and Biography,* vol. 85, no. 2 (April 1961): 111–162.
    This chapter of Prevost's diary for the period from April 16 to Sep-
    tember 24, 1774 describes his experiences in Pittsburgh with his
    father-in-law, George Croghan, with whom he had become involved
    in real estate speculations. The chapter also contains the 1774 letters
    and documents written by George Croghan, Lord Dunmore, John
    Connolly, and Prevost as well as the speech by several chiefs of the Six
    Nations and the Delawares to Lord Dunmore followed by his reply.
    These materials mention the Indian-white conflicts caused by the
    encroachments of Virginians, Croghan's efforts to preserve peace,
    frontier turmoil resulting from the Indian disturbances provoked by
    Lord Dunmore's agent, Connolly, and Dunmore's plan to chastise the
    Shawnees.

874. "Proportion of Presents to be given to the Catawba, Nottowa[y] & Tuscarora Indians." *New York Historical Society Collections For The Year 1921, Cadwallader Colden Papers,* vol. 5 (New York, 1923): 264–265.
    This undated list of the presents given to Catawba, Nottaway, and the
    Tuscarora Indians includes combs, scissors, flannel, garters, stock-
    ings, and jewelry, other items of clothing.

875. Pynchon, John. [Letters to Governor John Winthrop or John Allyn]
*Connecticut Historical Society Collections,* vol. 21 (Hartford, 1924): 221–223.
    In his August 6, 1675 letter, Pynchon mentions that because Brook-
    field needs help in defending itself against the attacks of hundreds of
    Indians, troops, both Indians and non-Indians, are being sent there.
    In his August 25, 1675 letter, Pynchon speculates that the Indians had
    preplanned King Philip's War and that the Quabaugs might be taking
    part in the hostilities.

876. Pynchon, William. [Letter to Stephen Day] *Massachusetts Historical Society
Collections,* ser. 4, vol. 6 (Boston, 1863): 376–378.
    Writing on August 8, 1644, Pynchon comments that it is cheaper to
    use English messengers than Indian ones. He discusses wampum

prices and predicts that Indians will soon charge too much for corn, beans, and deer.

**877.** Pynchon, William. "Letters of William Pynchon." *Massachusetts Historical Society Proceedings,* vol. 48 (October 1914): 35–56. Illustrated.

William Pynchon, a member of the General Court of Connecticut, writes letters to present his side of a controversy involving his contract to deliver at least 500 bushels of good corn at five shillings a bushel in Hartford and the fine he received for undue practices in trading corn. The letters from 1639 to 1644 describe the endeavor to regulate the trade in corn with the Indians, quote the text of the April 20, 1641 purchase of land by Pynchon from a party of Indians in exchange for goods, and contain the April 17, 1651 deed in which he grants this land to his son and two others. Also included is a paper written by Pynchon on the corn trade with Indians and a facsimile of the signatures on the 1641 deed.

**878.** Quanapaug, James. "James Quanapaug's Information." *Massachusetts Historical Society Collections,* ser. 1, vol. 6 (Boston, 1800): 205–208.

On November 24, 1675, Quanapaug, an Indian who had spied on enemy Indians, reports that some anti-English Narragansetts wish to kill the English. He specifies the number of Narragansetts, their allies, prisoners, and amount of ammunition they possess.

**879.** Quattrocchi, Anna M. "Thomas Hutchins in Western Pennsylvania." *Pennsylvania History,* vol. 16, no. 1 (January 1949): 31–38.

Quattrocchi describes Thomas Hutchins and his role in compiling an inventory of abandoned French forts in the upper Ohio Valley in 1759, his service at Fort Pitt to Bouquet, and his work as an assistant in the Department of Indian Affairs after 1761. She reviews his performance during the 1793 siege of Fort Pitt, one of the few major British forts that did not succumb to Indians. She discusses the maps and sketches made by Hutchins for a proposed expedition against Indians in 1764 and his subsequent work until his death.

**880.** Race, Henry. "Historical Sketch of Miss Jane McCrea."*New Jersey Historical Society Proceedings,* ser. 2, vol. 9., nos. 1 and 2 (1886): 93–104.

Race reviews the circumstances of Jane McCrea's murder on July 27,

880 *(continued)*

1777 near Fort Edward, New York during the Revolutionary period. He discusses the British policy of isolating the New England frontier colonies and using Indian allies in the campaign against the Americans. The author describes David Jones, Jane's fiancé who fought the British, and her brother, who was a patriot. Citing eyewitness accounts, Race describes Jane's capture and subsequent murder by Le Loup, an Indian allied with the British. In an appendix, Race evaluates the conflicting accounts and evidence of the murder, noting the traditional stories of the McCrea and Jones families which say Jane McCrea was killed by Indians, not by American pickets.

881. Rafn, Carl Christian. "On Indian Place-Names." *Massachusetts Historical Society Proceedings,* ser. 1, vol. 8 (1864–1865): 193–198.

Writing on April 26, 1839, Professor Rafn mentions the derivation from the Icelandic of Indian place names. He believes that the local names he analyzes furnish proof that the "ancient Northmen" have inhabited New England for several centuries because, "It is established custom, that places retain the names which have been imposed on them by their first civilized discoverers."

882. Ramsey, *Dr.* "Observations on the Indians in the Southern Parts of the United States, in a Letter from the Honorable Dr. Ramsey." *Massachusetts Historical Society Collections,* ser. 4, vol. 4 (Boston, 1795): 99–100.

Writing on March 10, 1795, Ramsey claims that because Indians cannot be civilized, they will cease to be a people. He asserts that climate has had no effect on southern Indians, citing the point that their manners and habits differ little from those of the northern Indians. The population of the southern tribes is included.

883. Rankin, Edward S. "Oraton, Sachem of Hackensack." *New Jersey Historical Society Proceedings,* n.s., vol. 10, no. 4 (October 1925): 383–387.

Rankin discusses Oratamin, an Indian for whom a parkway in Essex County was named and whose tribe lived in that region at the time of the whites' settlement there. The author cites references to Oratamin in New York colonial documents from 1643 to 1664 and considers both his peaceful attitudes and his opposition to the Dutch sale of liquor to his people, quoting Oratamin's March 30, 1662 prohibition statement. Rankin mentions this Indian's role in the purchase of land by the founders of Newark and his relations with the Dutch.

884. Rankin, Edward S. "The Purchase of Newark from the Indians." *New Jersey Historical Society Proceedings,* n.s., vol. 12, no. 4 (October 1927): 442–445.

Rankin discusses the purchase of Newark from the Indians by a group of settlers, listing the things the Indians received as payment. He compares this purchase to others of a similar nature made at about the same time, 1666. Using a "Table of Land Purchases, Prices, Etc.," he determines the approximate cost per square mile paid for the eight tracts of land during the period from 1626 to 1702. Rankin concludes there was no standard value for Indian lands, and Newark people paid far more than the average price for the lands they bought from the Indians.

885. Rankin, Edward S. "The Ramapo Tract." *New Jersey Historical Society Proceedings*, vol. 50, no. 4 (October 1932): 375–379.

Rankin quotes the complete text of the original November 18, 1709 Indian deed for the Ramapo tract of land in which Indians granted land to a group of men from New York. He mentions two Indian women who signed the deed. The tract comprised the present townships of Franklin, Hohokus, and Ridgewood, a small part of Passaic County, and a section of Rockland County, New York.

886. Ranney, Charlotte T. "Letters and Journal of Charlotte T. Ranney." *Vermont Quarterly*, n.s., vol. 21, no. 4 (October 1953): 279–288.

Timothy and Charlotte Ranney were assigned by the American Board of Commissioners of Foreign Missions to be missionaries to the Pawnees. In letters written from December 25, 1845 to January 30, 1847, Charlotte Ranney describes Sioux hostilities against the Pawnees, the Indians' intemperance, and daily life at the mission with the Indians. [*Continued* in *Vermont History*, vol. 22, no. 1 (January 1954): pages 42–51. Written from February 1, 1842 to March 21, 1847, these letters and extracts from Charlotte Ranney's journal describe the dangerous conditions the couple faced when they lived among the Indians and the final decision to return to Vermont.]

887. Ranney, Timothy E. "Letters of Timothy E. Ranney." *Vermont History*, vol. 22, no. 3 (July 1954): 212–222.

From October 23, 1848 to April 2, 1860, Timothy Ranney writes letters from the Cherokee Nation where the Ranneys are missionaries. His letters compare Cherokee country to Vermont, describe the Ranneys' preference for the Pawnees, and mention the Cherokee influence on the Ranneys' children. A brief statement explaining the historic background behind the events happening in Missouri and Arkansas during the spring of 1861 is included in an extract from Charlotte Ranney's journal for the period from May 27 to July 4, 1861. It also states that the Ranneys are being recalled from the mission because of the approaching Civil War and the deteriorating conditions of the country through which they must travel north by horseback to return.

888. Rasles, Sebastien. "Biographical Memoir of Father Rasles." *Massachusetts Historical Society Collections*, ser. 2, vol. 8 (Boston, 1826): 250–263.

Rasles' biography was compiled principally from the letters he wrote during the twenty-six years from 1698 to 1724 when he was a Jesuit missionary to the Abenaki Indians in a village called Norridgewock. His letters describe how he learned the Abenaki language, his mission to the Illinois tribe and others, his work among the Abenakis, the

**888** *(continued)*
chapel he built, his labors, the Indians' mode of living, his troubles which embittered his later years, and English attempts to seize him because of his influence with the Indians. Father de la Chasse's account of the day Rasles was murdered is included, as well as two letters, one written by Father Rasles on November 18, 1712 to Captain Moody and the other written by the Eastern Indians on July 27, 1721 to the governor. The latter includes a reproduction of the Indians' marks. [*See* "Intercepted Letter from Ralle, 1724," pages 266–267. The letter mentions the attack on an English fort in winter by the Abenakis and their subsequent retreat to Canada for fear of English retaliation to Norridgewock.]

**889.** Rasles, Sebastien. "The Mission of Father Rasles." ed. E. C. Cummings. *Maine Historical Society Collections,* ser. 2, vol. 4 (Portland, 1893): 146–169.

Cummings discusses Rasles' thirty-seven years as a Jesuit missionary to the Abenakis and other Indians and the events of historical significance in which he participated. Rasles' October 15, 1722 letter to his nephew is quoted in which he describes the Indians he instructed, the other work he did with them, their village in which he lived, and the food he ate. Rasles considers the ideas that unite the Indians to the French rather than to the English as well as English actions in New England aimed at seducing the Indians away from the French. He reports Abenaki-English hostilities from 1721 to 1722 and English designs on Rasles himself. The text of the lengthy October 12, 1723 letter from Rasles to his brother, quoted on pages 265 to 301 of this volume, provides descriptions of the country the Jesuit lived in, the Abenaki culture, Rasles' visits to other Indian nations, his work among the Indians, and the dangers to which he was exposed, particularly from the English who he claimed were conspiring for his destruction. Father de la Chasse's October 29, 1724 letter to the Father of the Company of Jesus is quoted on pages 404 to 410, as well as his other letter, dated August 23, 1724, which describes the circumstances of Rasles' death which he insists was caused by the English.

**890.** Rasles, Sebastien. "Monsignor Ralley, the Romish Priest at Norridgewock, His Letter to his Reverend Father." *Massachusetts Historical Society Collections,* ser. 2, vol. 8 (Boston, 1826): 245–249.

Writing on August 12, 1724, the very day that Captain Harmon and his troops killed Rasles and a number of Indians at the mission, Rasles discusses the movements of the Indians at his mission against the English and the actions of the English and their allied Iroquois against the Jesuit. He describes the paucity of Indian provisions, the attempt to burn the fort at St. George, and the attacks on the English at Port Royal. This letter is a rough translation from the French.

**891.** Ratiocan, *et al.* "Deed of Horse or Lloyd's Neck from the Indians to Mayo, Whitehead, and Wright, 1654." *New York Historical Society Collections for the Year 1926, Lloyd Family Papers,* vol. 1 (New York, 1927): 1–3.

On September 20, 1654, Ratiocan, sagamore of Cow Harbor, sells his land to three men for three coats, three suits, three hatchets, three hoes, wampum, six knives, two pairs of stockings, and shoes. The marks of Ratiocan and fourteen other Indians are reproduced followed by a statement made on May 14, 1658 by Wyandanch, an Indian sachem who confirms the sale.

892. Rawle, William. "A Vindication of the Reverend Heckewelder's *History of the Indian Nations.*" *Historical Society of Pennsylvania Memoirs,* vol. 1, part 2 (Philadelphia, 1826): 258–275.

Rawle discusses the 1826 review in *North American Review* which attempts to strip Heckewelder of his fame in regard to his work entitled, *"An Account of the History, Manners, and Customs of the Indian Nations Who Once Inhabited Pennsylvania and the Neighboring States."* Although the 1826 reviewer notes ten errors in Heckewelder's work, Rawle maintains that Heckewelder was unjustly condemned.

893. Rawson, Grindal. "Account of an Indian Visitation." *Massachusetts Historical Society Collections,* ser. 1, vol. 10 (Boston, 1809): 129–134.

Reverend Rawson describes his visit to several Indian plantations in Massachusetts from May 30 to June 24, 1698. He names each town and its teacher or preacher and gives the Indian population, specifying the number of families involved.

894. Ray, Roger B. "Maine Indians' Concept of Land Tenure."*Maine Historical Society Quarterly,* vol. 13, no. 1 (Summer 1973): 28–51.

In order to shed light on their subsequent land claims, Ray discusses the Maine Indians' ideas about their land before their way of life was altered by Europeans. He explores the Indians' reasons for signing many deeds conveying most of coastal Maine, from Kittery to Pemaquid, to English colonists between 1625 and 1675. Maine maritime Indian myths and legends are reviewed to better understand these Indians' beliefs about the natural world. He mentions that the Indians developed a policy of land tenure best described as usufruct, not ownership. Ray studies the reports of explorers and missionaries for information on local Indian governments and their methods of land allocations to determine the Indians' policies before the Europeans arrived. Ray concludes that deeds meant one thing to the Maine Indians and quite another to the English from Massachusetts; the Indians assumed they could continue living in their habitats, drawing on the bounty of the land they conveyed in the deeds. Extensive notes are included.

895. "Red Jacket." *New York History,* vol. 23, no. 4 (October 1942): 458–460.

Indians in general and Red Jacket in particular are discussed in these extracts from the prologue to *Red Jacket,* the Society for the Preservation of Indian Lore's 1942 pageant presented at the Forest Theater in New York in celebration of the Annual Feast of the Green Corn.

**896.** Reeves, George W. "The Story of the North Country." *New York State Historical Association Quarterly Journal,* vol. 10, no. 2 (April 1929): 105–117.

Reeves discusses the history of the North Country, an area in Canada and New York State including Lake Champlain and the Richelieu westward to Lake Huron and from Ottawa southward to the line drawn from Lake George westward to the southern shore of Lake Ontario and the northern shore of Lake Erie. He describes Indians as being "like savage dogs" when studying the Iroquois, particularly the Mohawks, and mentions the French-English rivalry for the Iroquois' alliance, an allegiance that was divided during the American Revolution, with some Iroquois being pro-British, some pro-American, and others neutral.

**897.** "Relation of the Plott-Indian." *Massachusetts Historical Society Collections,* ser. 3. vol. 3 (Boston, 1833): 161–164.

Probably written in August, 1642, this anonymous essay concerns the plans of Miantonomo, the Narragansett sachem, to destroy the English, a conspiracy discovered by several Indians.

**898.** [Report of the Committee of the Rhode Island Historical Society on the Old Indian Steatite Pottery] *Rhode Island Historical Society Proceedings, 1779– 1880.* (Providence, 1880): 36–39.

The Committee that consulted with scholars and examined the quarry in Johnston, Rhode Island, reports on the excavation of the quarry, particularly the stratum of steatite discovered which contains an ancient Indian manufactory of stone pots and smoking pipes. Recommendations for preserving the old Indian steatite pottery and quarry are included.

**899.** Richard, Earl of Bellomont. "Speech of his Excellency Richard, Earl of Bellomont, Governor of Massachusetts and New Hampshire, to the Council and Assembly of the Province of New Hampshire, August 7, 1699." *New Hampshire Historical Society Collections,* vol. 4 (Concord, 1834): 251–253.

The governor describes ways in which the French are instigating the Eastern Indians to attack the English and are trying to "debauch Indians from forming subjections to the Crown of England." He tells the council and assembly that a fort is needed in order to secure the province.

**900.** Riddell, William Renwick. "Last Official Report on the French Posts in the Northern Part of North America." *Pennsylvania Magazine of History and Biography,* vol. 56, no. 1 (January 1932): 56–57.

This report on the French posts in Canada includes information on the vicinity near each fort as well as the area protected by it. Although the author and date of the report are unknown, Riddell speculates that it may have been compiled after 1758 to be used during the peace negotiations at the end of the Seven Years' War. The information concerns eleven posts and the Indians who traded there. Footnotes with explanatory material are included.

901. Ritchie, William A. "A Prehistoric Ceremony of Sacrifice in New York State." *New York History,* vol. 28, no. 4 (October 1947): 458–465.

Ritchie discusses the discovery of evidence of ceremonialism in the Owasco culture which flourished between the twelfth and sixteenth centuries. He describes the site and materials discovered and then hypothesizes about the types of food offered and the significance of the other items that were found.

902. Ritchie, William A. "The Present Status of Archaeology in New York State." *New York History,* vol. 22, no. 2 (April 1941): 170–179.

Ritchie briefly reviews New York prehistory, discussing the culture sequence, based on a solid foundation of excavated sites, that has had thirteen manifestations. He tells why the Iroquois have been assigned to the historic and a large part of the late prehistoric period. He discusses the Owasco culture assigned to the late prehistoric period, describes the principal discoveries relevant to the semiarchaic period, the Laurentian aspect, and the archaic period which was the earliest known period of occupation. Included are tables of classification of "Aboriginal Cultures of New York State" and "Aboriginal Cultures of New York in Historical Perspective."

903. Ritter, Woldemar H. "Archaeology for the Amateur." *Vermont Historical Society Proceedings,* n.s., vol. 10, no. 3 (September 1942): 162–170.

Ritter gives advice to aspiring young archaeologists who are trying to uncover evidence of Indian occupation and save the Indian relics from being destroyed. He discusses campsites, equipment needed, surface collecting, excavating, types of mounds, stratification, house sites, bone implements, burials, preservation of material, and cataloguing.

904. River Indians. "Answer of the River Indians to Governor George Clinton of New York." *New York Historical Society Collections For The Year 1919, Cadwallader Colden Papers,* vol. 3 (New York, 1920): 258–259.

On August 26, 1746, the River Indians state their resolve to shed the blood of the French and their allied Indians, vowing to live and die with the British in the "common cause." The River Indians indicate that they need British protection.

905. River Indians. "Answer of the River Indians to the Five Nations to a Message Delivered to Them." *New York Historical Society Collections For The Year 1919, Cadwallader Colden Papers,* vol. 3 (New York, 1920): 415–417.

On August 10, 1747, the River Indians "thank" the Five Nations for their information concerning both their forebears' agreement to help one another and that they both should fight the French.

906. Robert, John. "Petition of Settlers of Bebbers Township for Aid Against Indians." *Pennsylvania Magazine of History and Biography,* vol. 31, no. 1 (1907): 11–13.

This petition of May 10, 1728, written by John Robert, was signed by

**906** *(continued)*
the seventy-two people whose names are listed. It deals with the threat
of Indian attacks on the frontier and requests government protection.

**907.** Roelker, William Greene. "Samuell Gorton's Master Stroke." *Rhode Island
History*, vol. 2, no. 1 (January 1943): 1-10.
Roelker discusses Samuel Gorton's master stroke in negotiating a
treaty in 1644 with the Narragansett sachems which subjected them to
the King of England. This treaty strengthened Gorton's position with
the English authorities and played a role in protecting Rhode Island
from the aggression of Massachusetts and Connecticut authorities.
The treaty gave the king an indefeasible title to Indian land and
satisfied the desire for legalism so ingrained in the minds of the
seventeenth-century English. Roelker notes that this treaty received
official recognition when it formed the basis of Rhode Island's title to
its land.

**908.** Rooney, Gerald F. "Daniel Denton, Publicist of Colonial New York." *New
York Historical Society Quarterly Bulletin*, vol. 55, no. 3 (July 1971): 272-276.
Rooney summarizes Daniel Denton's twenty-two page *A Brief Description of New-York: Formerly Called New-Netherland*, the first description of
colonial New York published in English in 1670. He notes that almost
one third of this promotional tract concerns the Indian way of life.
Rooney remarks that Denton presents Indians as different, rather
than dangerous, and marvels at their customs, religion, methods of
warfare, burial ceremonies, medicine, marriage and family traditions,
feasts, clothing, and grooming. Denton discusses, in idyllic terms, the
settlers' trade with the Indians.

**909.** Rose, John [Baron Rosenthal]. "Journal of a Volunteer Expedition to
Sandusky, From May 24 to June 13, 1782." *Pennsylvania Magazine of History and
Biography*, vol. 18, no. 2 (1894): 129-157. Illustrated.
John Rose [Baron Rosenthal] kept a journal during an expedition
against Indian settlements on the Sandusky River led by Colonel
Crawford who was captured by the Indians during the march. This
part of the journal describes in detail the march of the army towards
Sandusky, encounters with Indians along the way, and battles with
Delaware and Shawnee Indians. The tactical manner in which volunteers fought Indians is described. The journal is prefaced by a brief
biography of Rose. There are drawings of the line of battle and a plan
of the encampment. [*Continued in Pennsylvania Magazine of History
and Biography*, vol. 18, no. 3 (1894): 293-328. Illustrated. The second part of this journal contains criticism of the campaign and an
estimate of the officers' value during the expedition. Rose suggests his
own military plans against the Indians. There are drawings of the
march across the plains and through the woods and a plan of the
upper Indian settlements on the Sandusky River which were de-
lineated by a Delaware Indian on June 30, 1782.]

910. Ross, Edward Hunter. "Antiques Are Where You Find Them." *New Jersey Historical Society Proceedings,* vol. 77, no. 4 (October 1959): 274–278. Illustrated.
Ross discusses the documentary value of antiques in existing ethnographical and archaeological collections. He explains how objects of European and American manufacture found in Indian sites differ from inventions made specifically for the Indian trade, such as the tomahawk pipe. He describes silver ornaments, particularly gorgets, that the British presented to chiefs after 1730 and the glass beads used in the Indian trade which are now valued as European antiques. He mentions hair pipes, ornaments used by Indians before white contact, and the role of the Campbell family of New Jersey in developing the tools and methods for quantity production of wampum. He analyzes the photograph of Red Cloud wearing a breast plate of hair pipes. Ross suggests that students of American and European antiques should study the artifacts of Indian trade.

911. Russ, William A. "The Export of Pennsylvania Place Names." *Pennsylvania History,* vol. 15, no. 3 (July 1948): 194–201.
In the portion of this article about the export of Pennsylvania place names and the influence that Pennsylvanians exerted on the place names of other states, Russ discusses the Pennsylvania Indians who did some of the earliest name carrying. He shows how the Eastern Shawnees and Delawares considerably influenced western nomenclature, especially in Ohio. Russ discusses the slight influence of the Pennsylvania Iroquois on western place naming.

912. Russell, Eber L. "The Lost Story of the Brodhead Expedition." *New York State Historical Association Quarterly Journal,* vol. 11, no. 3 (July 1930): 252–263.
Russell tells the stories and legends of the Iroquois Indians regarding the Brodhead Expedition, the western movement of Washington's effort to break British power that was directed against colonial frontier settlements. The author includes extracts from Brodhead's report to show the possibility of error in the report, to establish the geography of the region, and to disprove some popular misconceptions concerning the route of the expedition. He also tries to support the local belief prevalent among both Indians and non-Indians of the region which indicates that Brodhead did not make a full report, did not penetrate New York, and did receive some determined opposition.

913. Russell, Marvin F. "Thomas Barton and Pennsylvania's Colonial Frontier." *Pennsylvania History,* vol. 46, no. 4 (October 1979): 313–334.
Russell discusses the participation of Anglican missionary Barton in the pamphlet war which raged during the first half of 1764 in response to the Paxton Boys' massacre of Indians, the frontier peoples' anger with their lack of adequate defenses, and the use of government money to support reservation Indians. He explains how the pamphlet war focused on several key issues including the murder of Indians in

913 *(continued)*
Lancaster and the political struggles among Quakers, Presbyterians, and Anglicans. In his pamphlet, Barton, a political polemic, empathizes with the Paxtons because of his own years on the frontier. Russell mentions Barton's interest in training young boys to be missionaries for the Church of England and the assistance he received from Sir William Johnson.

914. Ruttenber, E. M. "Footprints of the Red Men: Indian Geographical Names in the Valley of Hudson's River, the Valley of the Mohawks, and on the Delaware: Their Location and the Probable Meaning of Some of Them." *New York State Historical Association Proceedings, Seventh Annual Meeting,* vol. 6 (Lake George, 1906): 241 pp. Illustrated.

This work contains a compilation of hundreds of Algonquian and Iroquoian geographical names from the Mohawk, Hudson, and Delaware River Valleys, the places and physical features to which these names belonged, and the meanings of these aboriginal names. The study begins with an explanation of linguistic methods used by the various European scribes of different languages to record the geographical names, the methods used to interpret them, the structure of polysynthetic Algonquian dialects with an explanation of their differences from Iroquoian constructions, and the problems in correctly pronouncing sounds as they were originally spoken in these two language families. The author also includes several obsolete names to illustrate either the dialect spoken in the valley or the local geography. The book is arranged by geographical regions and includes an alphabetical index of names, photographs of places to which certain names belonged, and two maps of the Hudson Valley in 1609 and 1666. Example: "Passaic is a modern orthography of Pasaeck (Unami-Lenape), German notation, signifying 'vale or valley.' Zeisberger wrote Pachsajeck in the Minsi dialect. The valley gave name to the stream. In Rockland County, it has been corrupted to Paskack, Pasqueck, etc."

915. Ryoncombome. "Confirmation by Sachem Wyandanch's Son of the Sale of Horse Neck." *New York Historical Society Collections For The Year 1926, Lloyd Family Papers,* vol. 1 (New York, 1927): 8.

On February 1, 1659, Ryoncombome, the son of Wyandanch, ratifies and confirms the bill of sale for a tract of land known as Horse Neck from Ratiocan to Mayo, Wright, and Whitehead.

916. Sainsbury, John A. "Miantonomo's Death and New England Politics, 1630–1645." *Rhode Island History,* vol. 30, no. 4 (November 1971): 111–123. Illustrated.

Sainsbury examines the circumstances surrounding the execution of Miantonomo, the Narragansett sachem, in light of the evolving policy of the English colonists towards Indians, a vivid example of the influence of intercolonial politics on Indian affairs. He evaluates the justice of Miantonomo's execution by Uncas, the Mohegan sachem. The author discusses the 1637 alliance between the Mohegans and officials of Massachusetts which disqualified the Narragansetts from making peace with the Pequots or taking Pequot refugees without the consent of the Massachusetts government. He tells of Uncas, a Mohegan, who wished to war against the Pequots in revenge for personal reasons, and explains how the Pequot War, although it brought Narragansetts and Mohegans into temporary alliance, was the major cause of the breach between the two tribes. Sainsbury describes how Uncas strengthened his tribe by taking in Pequot refugees and how he consolidated his friendship with the English in Connecticut and Massachusetts. The author mentions Miantonomo's disillusionment with the English as allies and considers the rumors of his plot. After Uncas captured Miantonomo in battle during the Narragansett-Mohegan War of 1643, the commissioners of the United Colonies found Miantonomo guilty of breaking an agreement by attacking the Mohegans without English consent and authorized Uncas to execute him. Sainsbury evaluates English policy towards the Mohegans and the Narragansetts as well as Miantonomo's alliance with Samuel Gorton in 1643 that partly contributed to his fall from grace with the English. Documents, statements by Indians and colonists, and sketches illustrate this article which also includes footnotes.

917. St. Clair, Arthur. [Letter from Arthur St. Clair to General Schuyler] *New York Historical Society Collections For The Year 1879. Revolutionary Papers*, vol. 2 (New York, 1880): 20–22.

Writing on June 24, 1777, St. Clair describes the numerous Indians reported to have been seen in the vicinity of Ticonderoga as, "the children of a disturbed imagination." St. Clair reports that he thinks these Indians have come to harass, not to attack, because if they were prepared for battle they would not remain at such a distance. Furthermore, they are in a part of the country where they can not sustain themselves. St. Clair writes that his scouts have not seen any enemy Indians but qualifies this observation by pointing out that it is not easy to estimate numbers in a distant encampment. [*See* St. Clair's letter to Honorable John Hancock, President of Congress, written on June 25, 1777, pages 22–23, in which he portrays the sorry state of his army and relays the information received from scouts that enemy troops are approaching.]

918. St. Clair, Arthur. [Letters from General Arthur St. Clair to Major General Schuyler] *New York Historical Society Collections For The Year 1879, Revolutionary Papers*, vol. 2 (New York, 1880): 14–17.

Writing on June 24 and June 25, 1777, St. Clair reports on the nearby

918 *(continued)*
encampments of numerous enemy Indians. He claims that he does not see how he can defend the post unless a militia is sent in. He adds that he will try to frustrate the Indians' plans, but it will be difficult because his troops are "ill-armed, naked, and unaccoutred."

919. Salter, Edwin. "Origin and Significance of Geographical Names in the Counties of Monmouth and Ocean and their Vicinity, in New Jersey." *New Jersey Historical Society Proceedings,* ser. 2, vol. 4, no. 1 (1875): 18–26.
Salter gives the origin of Navesink, Mannahaukin, West Creek, Squaw, Raritan, Matawan, and other places in the counties of Monmouth and Ocean as well as Cinnaminson in Burlington.

920. Samoset and Unongoit. "Brown Deed at Pemaquid by Samoset and Unongoit, Sagamores." *Maine Historical Society Collections, Documentary History of the State of Maine,* ser. 2, vol. 7 (Portland, 1901): 80–81.
From July 15 to 25, 1625, Samoset and Unongoit deed land at Pemaquid to John Brown in exchange for fifty skins.

921. Sandel, Andreas. "Letter from Andreas Sandel." *Pennsylvania Magazine of History and Biography,* vol. 84, no. 2 (April 1960): 209–218.
Writing on June 17, 1702, this Swedish pastor reviews his voyage from Stockholm to Philadelphia and describes the latter city. In one part of the letter, he gives his observations on tribes in Pennsylvania, noting their manners and customs, government, religion, clothing, and loyalty to Swedish warfare.

922. Sapio, Victor. "Expansion and Economic Depression as Factors in Pennsylvania's Support of the War of 1812: An Application of the Pratt and Taylor Theses to the Keystone State." *Pennsylvania History,* vol. 35, no. 4 (October 1968): 379–405.
Sapio discusses the original lack of fear of the "Indian menace" in Pennsylvania and the way in which stories of past and present Indian atrocities were widely circulated by the British as soon as war began. He explains that neither British intrigue among the Indians nor the desire to drive the British out of Canada for other reasons, such as more land, were considered to be causes of war. Although these factors did not contribute to the growth of pro-war sentiment in Pennsylvania, they did become issues after war was declared.

923. Samuel. "Fragment of a Journal Kept by Samuel, of Bucks County, While a Member of the Colonial Assembly of Pennsylvania, 1762-3-4." *Pennsylvania Magazine of History and Biography,* vol. 5, no. 1 (1881): 60–73.
Written from September 20, 1762 to February 7, 1763, the journal largely concerns the strife caused by frontier people who murdered Indians. Samuel reports the murders of Conestoga Indians by the Paxton gang, efforts of the Pennsylvania government to protect the remaining Indians from lawless frontier people, the public expenses involved in protecting Indians, and the frontier people's plans to murder Indians put under the protection of the king's troops. Samuel

discusses the bills passed by the assembly in response to the distur-
bances caused by the rioters.

**924.** Sargent, Harry G. "The Bradley Massacre." *New Hampshire Historical Society Proceedings*, vol. 2, part 2 (1889–1891) (Concord, 1891): 152–174.

Sargent discusses the August 11, 1746 massacre of Jonathan Bradley and others by Indians in the context of the French-English rivalry for mastery of North America which was intensified by Indian warfare. He reviews the expedition against Louisbourg, stronghold of the French, by the colonial militia of New England and the Canada Expedition, 1744 to 1746, which encouraged the French to ally with Indians in warfare against New England frontiers. He mentions the garrisoning of towns and gives the text of the original authority under which garrisons were established in 1746. Sargent conveys a picture of Rumford in 1746 and the circumstances which led to, and culminated in, the attack of Indians on Bradley. Reuben Abbott, who carried away bodies from the massacre site, briefly tells what is known about each of the dead and how they were buried.

**925.** Sascoe Indians. [Deed of Sascoe Indians] *Massachusetts Historical Society Collections*, ser. 5, vol. 9 (Boston, 1885): 108–110.

On June 14, 1680, Sascoe Indians confirm that they deeded their lands to the town of Fairfield on March 21, 1661, with the exception of some lands reserved for their subsistence needs.

**926.** Sattley, Robert. "Robert Sattley's Pike." *Vermont Quarterly*, n.s., vol. 19, no. 2 (April 1951): 103–104.

This Vermont folklore concerns Robert Sattley, an early settler in Ferrisburg, and tells how some Indians cooked in the ground, encased in muddy clay, a pike he had caught.

**927.** Scales, John. "The Oyster River Massacre." *New Hampshire Historical Society Proceedings*, vol. 5 (1907–1912) (Concord, 1916): 240–250.

Scales describes the July 18, 1694 Indian massacre in the Oyster River settlement. He discusses the French leadership of the attack and tells which houses were destroyed, who was killed, and which garrisons were successfully defended.

**928.** Schaghticoke and River Indians. "Schaghticoke and River Indians to George Clinton and the Commissioners from Massachusetts and Connecticut." *Connecticut Historical Society Collections*, vol. 11 (Hartford, 1911): 186–187.

Undated. The Schaghticoke and River Indians vow they will maintain friendship with the English and will warn them if harm might be coming from the French.

**929.** Schanck, George C. "An Inquiry Into the Location of Mount Ployden, the Seat of the Raritan King." *New Jersey Historical Society Proceedings*, ser. 1, vol. 6, no. 1 (1851): 26–29.

Schanck discusses the mountain range in the valley of the Raritan,

929 *(continued)*

designated by the English as "Mount Ployden," and former romantic
seat of the king of the Raritans before the whites encroached. He
reviews the various locations of the Raritans at different points in
history in an attempt to fix the former seat of "Indian royalty."

930. Schenck, Garret C. "Early Settlements and Settlers of Pompton, Pequan-
noc and Pompton Plains." *New Jersey Historical Society Proceedings*, ser. 3, vol. 4,
nos. 1–4 (January–October 1919): 48–51.

Reverend Schenck discusses the Munsee Indians of Pompton Valley
and the purchases of their lands by white settlers. He describes the
first recorded land sale by Mengooticus on April 1, 1694, quoting an
excerpt from the deed which delineates the boundaries. He mentions
other land purchases and quotes the June 6, 1695 deed for the
Indians' sale of a large tract of land to Arent Schuyler. The Indians
whose names appear on the deeds are listed.

931. "The Destruction of Schenectady." *New York Historical Society Collections
For The Year 1869. Publication Fund*, vol. 2 (New York, 1870): 165–176.

These pages contain three selections relating to the French expedition
into New York from 1689 to 1690 and the massacre in Schenectady.
First is "Propositions of the Maquas Sachems: at Albany, February 25,
1689–90." The Indians condoling the deaths of their comrades murdered in Schenectady by the French ask the major and aldermen of
Albany for advance notice in the future whenever the French are
coming. Second is "Answer by the Mayor, City of Albany, February
26, 1689–90." The mayor responds by stating that Indians at Schenectady should have been more aware of the French, reaffirms that the
British and the colonists in New York will pursue the war against the
French, and recommends that the Indians harass the French in
Canada. He also indicates that other colonies will be contacted for
help against the French. Third is "Examination of French Prisoners,
at Schenectady, March 3, 1689–90." Three of the Mohawks' French
prisoners are questioned by the mayor and others in Schenectady
concerning the murder of sixty men, women, and children in that city
and the transfer to the Jesuits of the other people who were captured.
The Mohawks' prisoners also explain that some French wanted to
attack Albany as well but were refused permission. Other Canadian
military affairs are reviewed during this discussion.

932. Schermerhorn, John F. "Report Respecting the Indians, Inhabiting the
Western Parts of the United States." *Massachusetts Historical Society Collections*,
ser. 2, vol. 2 (Boston, 1814): 1–45.

In 1812, Schermerhorn was commissioned by the Society for Propagating the Gospel to obtain information on the condition of the
Indians in the areas west of the Allegheny Mountains and near the
Mississippi River to determine the feasibility of future missionary
work. He reports on the Wyandots, Shawnees, Potawatomis, Delawares, Miamis, Weas, Eel Rivers, Kickapoos, Pinkashaws, Sauks, Win-

nebagos, Menominees, Chippewas, Cherokees, Chickasaws, Choctaws, Creeks, Caddos, Kiowas, Apaches, Osages, Kansas, Missourias,
Pawnees, Poncas, Mandans, Crows, Cheyennes, Sioux, Mountaineers,
and many others. He describes their locations, extent of their territories, population, language, schools, and the source and extent of
money they receive. He discusses whether the gospel has ever been
propagated among them, any existing churches and their denomina-
tions, schools, and their disposition to receiving religious instruction.
This information is followed by a "Historical Sketch of the Society for
Propagating the Gospel Among the Indians and Others in North
America," pages 45–48. [See "Remarks on Mr. Schermerhorn's Report Concerning the Western Indians." *Massachusetts Historical Society
Collections,* ser. 2, vol. 4 (Boston, 1816): 65–69. Writing on August 28,
1815, Ebenezer Hazard corrects an inaccuracy in Schermerhorn's
report on the Indian school established in Cherokee country, giving
facts and dates regarding the school.]

**933.** "Some Account of the Capture, Captivity, and Release from the Indians,
of a Little Girl, 1755." *Pennsylvania Magazine of History and Biography,* vol. 43, no.
3 (1919): 284.

The capture of Maria Christina Schmidt in 1755, her journey westward, the tortures she witnesses, and her release in 1757 as the result
of a treaty are all recorded in a church register.

**934.** Schoonmaker, Theodore. "Minisink." *New York State Historical Association
Proceedings, Eighth Annual Meeting,* vol. 7 (Lake George, 1907): 42–73. Illustrated.

Schoonmaker discusses the boundaries of the Minisink region from
1770 to 1790. He tells which Indians originally occupied the territory
and describes Iroquois and Delaware raids and massacres against
white settlements of New York and Pennsylvania which occurred at
about the time of the Revolution, particularly the Battle of the Conestoga in Pennsylvania. He mentions two raids in the Minisink region in
which Joseph Brant was involved and reviews the Battle of the
Minisink, July 22, 1779, as well as its aftermath. Correspondence
relating to the Battle of Minisink is quoted, and the monument
erected to mark the battle site is described. A map of the Minisink
Region, a diagram of its battlefield, and a sketch of the monument are
included.

**935.** Schuyler, David, Schuyler, Peter, and Pickert, Nicholas. [Letter from
David Schuyler, Peter Schuyler, Nicholas Pickert to Mr. Goolding] *New York
Historical Society Collections For The Year 1920, Cadwallader Colden Papers,* vol. 4
(New York, 1921): 412.

Writing on October 25, 1753, the three men implore Goolding to
survey immediately the land they plan to purchase because the Indians do not want to wait for their presents. If the surveying is not

935 *(continued)*
done until spring, the Indians may decide not to sell the land or they
may increase their demands for presents or money.

936. Schuyler, John. "Journal of Captain John Schuyler, on His Expedition to
Canada and Fort La Prairie, During the Latter Part of August, 1690." Translated by S. Alofsen. *New Jersey Historical Society Proceedings*, vol. 1, no. 2 (1845):
72–74.
> Written from August 13 to 30, 1690, the journal of Captain John
> Schuyler, a Dutchman, is a daily account of his expedition to Fort La
> Prairie and other places in Canada, an operation he commanded
> using Whites and Iroquois to fight the French.

937. Schuyler, Philip. Copy of Orders to Colonel Van Schaick. *New York Historical Society Collections For The Year 1879, Revolutionary Papers*, vol. 2 (New York,
1880): 107–109.
> Writing on June 14, 1777, Schuyler orders Van Schaick to march to
> Cherry Valley, not to attack any Indians unless attacked first, to treat
> them kindly at their posts, and to give them provisions, particularly
> rum. Schuyler instructs him to remind the "Ochquagues" to preserve
> their covenant with the Americans and to inform these Indians that he
> has orders to pursue Joseph Brant and others who kill or capture
> Americans. Van Schaick must also tell the Indians that Schuyler wants
> the Six Nations to meet the treaty commissioners July 15. Further-
> more, Van Schaick should emphasize the unlikely prospect of the
> English winning America because the colonists are gaining strength
> daily while the British are weakening.

938. Schuyler, Philip. [Copy of Orders to Mr. James Deane] *New York Historical
Society Collections For The Year 1879, Revolutionary Papers*, vol. 2 (New York,
1880): 101–102.
> Writing on June 10, 1777, Schuyler wants Deane to tell Thomas, an
> Indian, and other Indians to go into Canada to learn everything they
> can about the enemy forces and particularly to assess their effect on
> the Indians. He instructs Deane to assure the Canadians and the
> Indians of the Americans' lack of hostility towards them and of the
> Americans' friendly relationship with France which is offering resis-
> tance. Schuyler wants Thomas to tell the Canadian Indians that a
> treaty conference will be held with the Six Nations on July 15 in
> Albany to which all members are invited.

939. Schuyler, Philip. "Letter to the Board of War." *New York Historical Society
Collections For The Year 1879, Revolutionary Papers*, vol. 2 (New York, 1880):
206–207.
> Writing on June 27, 1778, Major General Schuyler observes that the
> object of the expedition, confined to chastising Senecas, is too narrow
> and should be expanded to include the Cayugas and some of the
> Onondagas who are equally insolent and hostile and also deserve
> punishment. He discusses troops to be used in the expedition and

where they should rendezvous. He orders that the reason for the expedition should be kept secret until the troops begin marching towards Seneca country.

**940.** Schuyler, Philip. [Letter to Colonel Bedel] *New York Historical Society Collections For The Year 1879, Revolutionary Papers*, vol. 2 (New York, 1880): 189–190.

On September 11, 1777, Schuyler writes that forty-five families of St. Francis Indians are inclined to settle near the Connecticut River. He tells the Colonel to persuade them, with provisions and ammunition, to settle on the Connecticut River near settlements. Explaining that it is important to "secure as many of the Indians to the interest of the American cause as possible, especially such as reside in Canada," Schuyler speaks of the need to impress the St. Francis Indians with the idea that the Americans expect assistance should it be necessary.

**941.** Schuyler, Philip. [Letter to Congress] *New York Historical Society Collections For The Year 1879, Revolutionary Papers*, vol. 2 (New York, 1880): 190–191.

On September 27, 1777, Schuyler reports that about three hundred Oneidas, Tuscaroras, Onondagas, and Mohawks arrived at Albany for a conference, that they were inclined to go to war, and that the warriors of each nation accepted the war belt. Schuyler describes how the warriors have already entered battle, taking thirty prisoners and intercepting British dispatches. He tells Congress that these Indians want the southern Indians to be notified by the Americans the northern Indians have taken up arms. Schuyler writes that the Americans are taking measures to induce the whole confederacy to join them and have reason to believe that they will.

**942.** Schuyler, Philip. [Letter to Congress] *New York Historical Society Collections For The Year 1879, Revolutionary Papers*, vol. 2 (New York, 1880): 198–200.

Writing on February 8, 1778, Schuyler mentions the Senecas', Cayugas', and possible Onondagas' hostility to the Americans and his belief that an expedition will be formed against the western frontiers of New York State, Virginia, and Pennsylvania by British troops, Ottawas, Chippewas, Wyandots, Mingos, and other tribes. He suggests that preparations be made to defend the frontiers and to invade the Indians' county in order to chastise them and convey the power and just resentment of the Americans. He says the Oneidas and Tuscaroras are still friendly but are apprehensive about taking an active part. They want American protection for their women and children because they fear reprisals from other Indians.

**943.** Schuyler, Philip. [Letter to Congress] *New York Historical Society Collections For The Year 1879, Revolutionary Papers*, vol. 2 (New York, 1880): 204–205.

Writing on May 17, 1778, Schuyler tells Congress that he thought it necessary to advise the Six Nations convened at Onondaga of the American alliance with France and of the rejection of the treaty

943 *(continued)*
proposed by Britain. The purpose of the British treaty with the
Americans was to effect reconciliation with them and to forestall U.S.
ratification of the French alliance.

944. Schuyler, Philip. [Letter to Congress] *New York Historical Society Collections
For The Year 1879, Revolutionary Papers,* vol. 2 (New York, 1880): 205.
  Writing on May 29, 1778, Schuyler suggests that the Cayugas and
some of the Senecas now being supplied arms by British troops in
Canada must be made aware of the power of the Americans. He
recommends that 1,000 men, half the garrison of Fort Schuyler,
militia from Tryon County, and some of the Oneida and Tuscaroras
would be sufficient to burn the Cayuga town and some of the Seneca
village.

945. Schuyler, Philip. [Letter to Congress and General Washington] *New York
Historical Society Collections For The Year 1879, Revolutionary Papers,* vol. 2 (New
York, 1880): 136–139.
  Writing on July 5, 1777, Schuyler relates that enemy Indians have
scalped two officers of Gansevoort's regiment, that Joseph Brant
threatens the Indians with a party of about 200 Indians, and that the
enemy's approaching by Oswego alarms the people of Tryon County.
Schuyler indicates his provisions are insufficient since he needs a
supply of goods for a meeting with the Six Nations. He has sent
someone to Boston with $10,000 to attempt to obtain a supply.

946. Schuyler, Philip. [Letter to the Council of Safety] *New York Historical
Society Collections For The Year 1879, Revolutionary Papers,* vol. 2 (New York,
1880): 175–176.
  Writing on July 21, 1777, Schuyler discusses difficulties with the
Indians in Tryon County and suggests that it would be prudent not
to cause a rupture with the Indians at this time. He tells the Council
that the people of Tryon County are too ready to lay down their arms
and take whatever terms the British offer.

947. Schuyler, Philip. [Letter to Mr. James Deane, Indian Interpreter] *New
York Historical Society Collections For The Year 1879, Revolutionary Papers,* vol. 2
(New York, 1880): 72–73.
  Writing on February 6, 1777, Schuyler tells Deane about the informa-
tion he is to get when he accompanies a group of Indians to Canada to
visit the Caughnawagas. Deane is instructed to find out how many
Indians may be expected to join the British forces in Canada, how they
will obtain provisions, and whether they will attack Ticonderoga in the
winter. He is to learn the date and location of the meeting to make a
treaty with the Six Nations as well as whether it will actually take place.
Schuyler asks Deane to have the Indians persuade some of the
Caughnawagas to give intelligence on the movements of the enemy.

**948.** Schuyler, Philip. [Letter to the President of the State of Massachusetts Bay] *New York Historical Society Collections For The Year 1879, Revolutionary Papers*, vol. 2 (New York, 1880): 131–132.

Writing on July 3, 1777, Schuyler asserts that it is of utmost importance to induce the Six Nations to abide by the neutrality they promised. To encourage the Indians' cooperation, presents will be given to them at the July 15 conference in Albany. Schuyler mentions he has sent someone to Massachusetts Bay with a memo listing the articles he needs.

**949.** Scots Society for Propagating Christian Knowledge. "Report of a Committee of the Board of Correspondents of the Scots Society for Propagating Christian Knowledge, Who Visited the Oneida and Mohekunuh Indians in 1796." *Massachusetts Historical Society Collections*, ser. 1, vol. 5 (Boston, 1798): 12–32.

Reporting in July, 1796, the committee answers twenty-four questions regarding their visit to the Oneida and Mahican Indians who were the objects of the Scots Society's missions. The answers deal with the number of Indians served by Reverends Kirkland and Sergeant, the number of Christians versus "pagans," the tribal affiliations of the Indians, their religious and political parties, the number instructed in the gospel, and the existence of any opposition to the missionaries' principles. In addition, there is information on the number who have renounced old habits, particularly intemperance, the character of white people who lived near the Indians, Native regulations to prevent the use of liquor, and Indian adoption of new methods of agriculture. The answers concerning Indians also deal with the manner in which money is granted by Congress to encourage husbandry, the effects of colonial civilization, the reasons for their developing lung diseases, individual ownership of land by Indians, sums of money received from the colonial government, population increases resulting from the missions, the slow change of habits, and the state of Oneida or Hamilton Academy.

**950.** Scott, John Alber. "Joseph Brant at Fort Stanwix and Oriskany." *New York History*, vol. 19, no. 4 (October 1938): 399–406. Illustrated.

Scott discusses Joseph Brant, who joined the 1776 expedition against Fort Stanwix which entrapped Herkimer and caused the Indians to stampede from the fort because of rumors of large numbers of American troops. The author evaluates Brant's command of the Indians at Oriskany and discusses reasons why Fort Stanwix did not fall immediately after Oriskany. There is an illustration of the fort.

**951.** Scott, Kenneth, and Baker, Charles E. "Renewals of Governor Nicholls' Treaty of 1665 With the Esopus Indians at Kingston, New York." *New York Historical Society Quarterly Bulletin*, vol. 37, no. 3 (July 1953): 251–272. Illustrated.

951 *(continued)*

Scott and Baker discuss the conflict between the Esopus Indians and the Dutch over Indian lands as well as the treaties imposed on the Indians by Director-General Stuyvesant. The authors mention Richard Nicholls, an English governor who negotiated the new treaty with the Esopus in October, 1665, and note the sixth article which required annual renewal of the treaty. Included are minutes of the January 22, 1676 Court of Sessions in Kingston regarding the Esopus renewal as well as the minutes of the 1712 renewal. Scott and Baker describe other proceedings during which Esopus sachems came before justices to ratify the treaty even after more than a century had passed since it was signed. The authors review additional treaty matters brought before the court, the relationship between the court and the governor, and the way in which the Ulster County Court of Sessions obtained an original copy of the treaty. A map of Kingston in 1695 is provided.

952. Scuttup. "Scuttup's Confirmation Deed." *Massachusetts Historical Society Collections,* ser. 5, vol. 9 (Boston, 1885): 8–9.

On August 9, 1659, Scuttup and Cosuequansh, chief Narragansett sachems, confirm by deed the transfer of two parcels of land in Narragansett County, one to John Winthrop bearing date of June 11, 1659 and the second to Humphrey Atherton bearing the date of July 4, 1659. [*See* pages 22 and 23 for another confirmation; pages 70 and 71 describing the December 28, 1664 confirmation of a Narragansett land sale by Scuttup and others; pages 74 to 76 quoting confirmatory Indian deeds to Humphrey Atherton and Company, signed May 8 and October 1, 1668; pages 82 and 83 confirming lands sold to Atherton and his associates on October 24, 1672.]

953. Sehr, Timothy J. "Ninigret's Tactics of Accomodation: Indian Diplomacy in New England 1637 to 1675." *Rhode Island History,* vol. 36, no. 2 (May 1977): 43–53. Illustrated.

Sehr discusses the tactics used from the 1630s to the 1670s by Ninigret, an Eastern Niantic, to handle the difficulties caused by the presence of the English in Massachusetts and Connecticut. Sehr describes how Ninigret used defiance, isolation, active personal diplomacy, and the submission of appeals to the Crown in order to maintain his autonomy, all of which failed to make the colonists respect his need for freedom in Indian-Indian relations. A painting of Ninigret, a map of the Niantic territory, other illustrations and footnotes are included.

954. Semmes, Raphael. "Aboriginal Maryland, 1608–1689. Part I: The Eastern Shore." *Maryland Historical Magazine,* vol. 24, no. 2 (June 1929): 157–172.

Semmes locates, discusses, and estimates the populations of the Maryland Indians' settlements on the eastern shore, specifically the areas north of the Pocomoke River or near the shores of the Chesapeake including its tributary rivers from the north up to the Susquehanna

River that were mentioned in explorers' accounts and other colonial sources. He locates and discusses in detail such groups as the Assateagues, Marumscos, Wicocomicos, Nanticoke River Indians, Choptanks, Matapeakes, Ozinies, Tockwoghes, Mattwas, and Susquehannocks. Semmes estimates the total Indian population of Maryland in the early seventeenth century. Explanatory notes are provided.

**955.** Semmes, Raphael. "Aboriginal Maryland, 1608–1689. Part 2: The Western Shore." *Maryland Historical Magazine*, vol. 24, no. 3 (September 1929): 195–209.

Semmes locates and discusses the seventeenth century Maryland Indians' settlements on the western shore between the Susquehanna and the Patuxent Rivers. He studies the Patuxents, Mattanpanients, Acquaskacks, Secowocomocos, Chopticons, Doags, Port Tobaccos, Piscataways, and Anacostans. He points out that the Anacostans were one of the few Indian tribes in Maryland of Iroquoian ancestry rather than the Algonquian stock from which most of the other Maryland tribes derived. Semmes mentions that Patuxents and other groups were settled on the reservation near the Wicomico River for their protection by the colonial officials around 1651. He estimates that 6,500 Indians lived on the western shore of Maryland in the early seventeenth century. Of these about 2,000 were of Iroquois stock, and the rest were of Algonquian origins. His figures are based on the accounts of Captain John Smith and other colonists.

**956.** Seneca, Cayuga, and Onondaga Indians. Indian Deed. *New York Historical Society Collections For The Year 1869. Publication Fund,* vol. 2 (New York, 1870): 487–489.

Signing on September 14, 1727, the principal sachems of the Senecas, Cayugas, and Onondagas deed a tract of land to the British in exchange for presents. The land and beaver hunting are to be protected by the British Crown for the three Indian nations and their descendants. The deed is signed with the marks of six sachems, two from each tribe.

**957.** Seruniyattha (Half King). "Speech of Half King to the Governors of Virginia and Pennsylvania." *Massachusetts Historical Society Collections,* ser. 1, vol. 6 (Boston, 1800): 143.

On April 18, 1754, Seruniyattha, a Seneca who is also known as Half King, announces that his Senecas are ready to strike the French and must join forces with the English to avoid defeat.

**958.** Seume, Johann Gottfried. "Adventures of a Hessian Recruit." *Massachusetts Historical Society Proceedings,* ser. 2, vol. 4 (1887–1889): 9–11.

In this letter written in 1782, Seume describes the Indians living in Nova Scotia, their appearance, habits, intemperance, clothing, birch bark boats, and food. He remarks that little conversion of these Indians has occurred.

**959.** Sewall, Samuel. [Letter] *Massachusetts Historical Society Collections*, ser. 6, vol. 1 (Boston, 1886): 400–403.

Sewall discusses the necessity of teaching English to the Indians, gives the reasons why some Indians wish to learn it, and specifies which Indians are divided over this issue. He asserts that it is advisable to print the Bible in English, because if it is printed in one Indian dialect it would be incomprehensible to Indians speaking a different dialect.

**960.** Sewall, Samuel. [Letter on Difficulties Translating the Bible into Indian Tongue] *Massachusetts Historical Society Proceedings*, ser. 1, vol. 12 (1871–1873): 372–374.

Writing in late 1710, Sewall attributes the difficulties of translating the Bible into Indian dialects to the point that Christian concepts have no meaning to the Indians. Furthermore, there are many different Indian dialects, and they are continually changing.

**961.** Sewall, Samuel. [Letters to Gurdon Saltonstall] *Massachusetts Historical Society Collections*, ser. 6, vol. 5 (Boston, 1892): 274–275.

Written in May and October of 1713, these two letters mention several Pequot Indians' complaints that they have been forced to leave Groton, the place where they have long dwelt that is necessary for their subsistence. Sewall asserts this is not a good time for them to receive the gospel and asks for relief for this "distressed" remnant which has been subject to English rule for more than seventy years.

**962.** Sewall, Samuel. [Letter to William Ashurst] *Massachusetts Historical Society Collections*, ser. 6, vol. 1 (Boston, 1886): 231–233.

Written on May 3, 1700, Sewall's letter suggests that missionaries be recruited from the ranks of the converted Indians. He further proposes that the Eastern Indians who survived the long war with the English be given tracts of lands which use natural objects as boundaries. Any encroachment on these reservations by the English should be considered a crime.

**963.** Sewall, Samuel. "A Memorial Relating to the Kennebeck Indians." *Maine Historical Society Collections*, ser. 1, vol. 3 (Portland, 1853): 351–353.

Writing on September 8, 1721, Sewall asserts that Maine has not done everything it could to prevent a rupture with the Kennebeck Indians. He stresses the need to settle the boundaries between the English and the Indians and gives the reasons why the province of Maine should negotiate peace with the Kennebec Indians.

**964.** Sewall, Samuel. "Samuel Sewall's Receipt Book." *Massachusetts Historical Society Proceedings*, vol. 67 (1941–1943): 78–110.

This index lists the people mentioned in the receipt book, 1708 to 1719, who received money from Samuel Sewall, disbursing agent for the New England Company, a London missionary society created for financial, not spiritual purposes. It lists the salaries of Indian preachers and teachers, the places in which they taught, the names of the English preachers and teachers, direct payments to Indians, and payments for expenses connected with Indians. Included with each entry is the name, date, amount, purpose, and location.

**965.** Sewall, Samuel. [Sewall Papers] *Massachusetts Historical Society Collections,* ser. 5, vols. 5, 6, 7 (Boston, 1878, 1879, and 1882).

The Sewall papers include his diary, 1674 to 1700, vol. 5, 1700 to 1714, vol. 6, and 1714 to 1729, vol. 7, as well as other papers. Numerous references to Indians are indexed under Bible, canoes, colleges, converts, dance, fights, preachers, sachems, scalps, schools, slaves, trade, warfare, captivities, atrocities, Indians, and French.

**966.** "Lord's Prayer in Shawnese."*Massachusetts Historical Society Collections,* ser. 3, vol. 5 (Boston, 1836): 287.

This page contains "The Lord's Prayer" in Shawnese.

**967.** "What is the Meaning of the Aboriginal Phrase Shawmut?" *Massachusetts Historical Society Collections,* ser. 2, vol. 10 (Boston, 1823): 173-174.

A number of native dialects are examined, and the word, "Shawmut" is defined as, "fountains of living waters."

**968.** Shea, John Gilmary. "Champlain's Expedition into Western New York in 1615, and the Recent Identification of the Fort by General J. Clark." *Pennsylvania Magazine of History and Biography,* vol. 2, no. 1 (1878): 103-108.

Shea discusses Champlain who joined a Hudson River war party in 1615 and whose history of the expedition was published in Paris in 1619. Widely varying opinions exist about the route the Hurons followed and the position of an Indian fort which Champlain depicts in his 1619 narrative. Shea discusses these opinions as well as John Clark's theory which possibly answers the question of the site of the fort.

**969.** Shippen, Joseph. "Military Letters of Captain Joseph Shippen of the Provincial Service, 1756-1758." *Pennsylvania Magazine of History and Biography,* vol. 36, no. 4 (1912): 385-463.

Written between June, 1756 and September, 1758, the military letters describe the movements of Indians allied with the British, battles fought by Indians allied with the French, Indian depredations, and trade with the Indians.

**970.** Shirley, William. Letter to Penobscot and Norridgewock Indians. *Connecticut Historical Society Collections,* vol. 11 (Hartford, 1907): 337-338.

Writing on July 12, 1745, Shirley sends intelligence to the Indians regarding the British victories over the French and warns the Indians not to be deluded by the French and not to break a friendship with England.

971. Shirley, William. [Letter to the Six Nations] *New York Historical Society Collections For The Year 1919, Cadwallader Colden Papers*, vol. 3 (New York, 1920):208–209.

Writing on May 29, 1746, Shirley urges the Six Nations to join an expedition against Canada. He tells the Indians of the plan to enter Canada by way of Albany as well as by a sea expedition. Cadwallader Colden would not allow this letter to be presented to the Six Nations at the meeting with them at Albany in August of 1746.

972. Shultze, David. "Letter: Indian Affairs in Eastern Pennsylvania, 1756." *Pennsylvania Magazine of History and Biography*, vol. 19, no. 3 (1895): 403–406.

Writing on January 18, 1756, Shultze tells of the lack of ammunition to fight Indians, gives news of Indian depredations against whites, discusses the need for a militia on the frontier to fight the small number of Indians, and suggests that these troops be unmarried men. He also explains that the rewards for scalps of chiefs and others are impractical because the Indians carry off their dead.

973. Shute, Samuel. "Letter from Governor Shute to Ralle the Jesuit."*Massachusetts Historical Society Collections*, ser. 1, vol. 5 (Boston, 1798): 112–119.

Writing on February 21, 1718, Governor Shute warns Rasles, the Jesuit priest situated in Maine, that the English would have lived in peace with neighboring Indians had it not been for the French instigating, protecting, supplying, and assisting Indians. He tells Rasles to keep the Indians peaceful and to remind them they are subjects of King George acknowledged by treaty. The governor also tells the missionary that his behavior should be dutiful towards the British government.

974. Silver, Walter T., and Silver, Helenette. "The Indian 'Fort' at Lochmere." *Historical New Hampshire*, vol. 17 (June 1962): 49–60. Illustrated.

The Silvers argue that the so-called "Indian fort" on the shores of Little Bay at Lochmere was not a fort but a fish trap almost identical in design to the one located at the Weirs that was abandoned before the advent of the whites. The authors consider features that led the observers to call the Lochmere structure a "fort," then try to determine whether these might not have been, instead, the features of a trap. There are three drawings on one modern topographical map of the "fort" site. Footnotes are provided.

975. Six Nations. [Answer of Six Nations to Governor B. Clinton and the Commissioners of Massachusetts Bay] *New York Historical Society Collections For The Year 1919, Cadwallader Colden Papers*, vol. 3 (New York, 1920): 255–258.

On August 23, 1746, the Six Nations declare they will use the hatchet against the French and their allied Indians as soon as possible. The Indians also report that a nation called the "Messessages" want to join the cause against the French and their allied Indians.

**976.** Six Nations. [Conference with the Six Nations.] *Connecticut Historical Society Collections,* vol. 17 (Hartford, 1918): 147–150.

On September 11, 1755, at Lake George, the Indians tell the English that they have assisted England in its war against France and they are now determined to go home to their families. The English reply that they are not happy that the Indians are going home and that the Caughnawagas are enemies because they joined the French. On September 12 the Indians reply that after an engagement in which they have any loss it is their custom to go home for a little while and then return with fresh vigor to attack enemies. [*See* "William Johnson to Sir Charles Hardy," pages 150–153, dated September 16, 1755. Johnson describes the battle in which the Six Nations sustained heavy losses, which is the reason why they wish to go home.]

**977.** Six Nations. "Extract of a Speech of a Chief of the Six Nations." *Vermont Historical Society Collections,* vol. 2 (Montpelier, 1871): 362–363.

On December 11, 1782, the principal chiefs and warriors of the Six Nations express their resentment and consequent determination to retaliate against the Virginians who destroyed the Shawnee settlement and its inhabitants. The Indians describe the attack on their villages by American rebels in 1779, in which women and children were put to death, and younger women carried off for their soldiers' use.

**978.** Six Nations. [Message to the Commissioners of Massachusetts and Connecticut] *Connecticut Historical Society Collections,* vol. 11 (Hartford, 1907): 193–194.

Writing on June 20, 1744, the Six Nations assure the commissioners that their Indians will assist Massachusetts, Connecticut, and New York in fighting the French.

**979.** Six Nations. "The Six Nations in the Revolutionary War." *Pennsylvania Magazine of History and Biography,* vol. 32, no. 3 (1908): 381–382.

The fidelity to the British Crown of the majority of the Six Nations is documented, with quotations from documents, as well as their neutrality until the Oneidas, Onondagas, and Tuscaroras aligned themselves with the Americans. Information is included concerning Carleton and Haldimand's 1779 pledge to the Mohawks to repair the rebels' damage to Indian property.

**980.** Slocum, H. Jermain. "Plans for Indian Archaeological Study and Exploration." *Vermont Historical Society Proceedings,* n.s., vol. 8, no. 3 (September 1940): 296–299.

Slocum attributes the minimal interest in the study of New England's archaeology in comparison with the work done in other parts of the country to the lack of surface indications of aboriginal occupation. He reports on the plan to do an archaeological survey of Vermont.

981. Smith, Edward P. "Communication from the United States Department of the Interior to Honorable Frederick T. Frelinghuysen Relating to Certain Delaware Indians." *New Jersey Historical Society Proceedings*, ser. 2, vol. 7, no. 3 (1883): 133–137.

Smith discusses the events befalling those Delaware Indians who became affiliated with the Stockbridge and Munsee Indians in 1802, many of whom moved in 1824 to a tract of land in Wisconsin. He tells how those Delawares who were west of the Mississippi requested permission in 1839 to relocate and eventually reached their destination in Kansas in 1840. He traces and documents the movements of these three tribes and concludes that few if any Delawares remained either with the Stockbridges in Wisconsin or with the Munsees or Chippewas in Kansas.

982. Smith, Horace J. "On Boydell's Engraving of West's Picture of William Penn's Treaty with the Indians." *Massachusetts Historical Society Proceedings*, ser. 2, vol. 15 (1901–1902): 365–366.

Written on December 13, 1901, Smith's letter discusses the family legends surrounding the people portrayed in *William Penn's Treaty with the Indians* by Benjamin West.

983. Smith, Peter. "Indian Personal Name Entries in Peter Smith's Indian Blotter." *New York History*, vol. 28, no. 4 (October 1947): 466–469.

Smith's ledger contains the names and the accounts of the Indians with whom Peter Smith did business at Old Ford Schuyler, Fort Stanwix, Canajoharie, and an Oneida village from 1788 to 1802. The Indians' names are listed under the appropriate locations.

984. Smith, Robinson V. "New Hampshire Remembers the Indians." *Historical New Hampshire*, vol. 8, no. 2 (October 1952): 1–36. Illustrated. Bibliography.

Smith describes in chronological order the confrontations between the colonists and the Indians from the early 1600s to the late 1700s, specifying the place and date of each. He adds a section on those events in which Indians captured New Hampshire settlers to sell to the French who then absorbed the captives and converted them to the religion of the French. Smith provides Indian names for places in New Hampshire. He claims that New Hampshire's first two hundred years were not ones of massacre and slaughter but were rather a time of treaties and trading with the Indians as well as the taking of captives for ransom. Included are photographs of weapons, colonial leaders, garrisons, Indians, and artifacts as well as a list of the author's sources of information.

985. Smoyer, Stanley C. "Indians as Allies in the Intercolonial Wars." *New York History*, vol. 17, no. 4 (October 1936): 411–422.

Smoyer investigates the methods used by English colonial government agents to enlist the support of Iroquois Indians in the face of continued rivalry with the French because of the vital role played by

Indians as allies in the intercolonial warfare in New York between 1700 and 1763. He describes ceremonies, giving presents and rewards, paying for scalps and heads of enemies, missionary work, and the effort made to convince Indians that English arms were superior. Self-recruitment was achieved by exposing small parties from the Six Nations to actual fighting in which warriors were killed thus bringing out the main Indian forces to avenge those killed. He also mentions the way English colonists undersold the French at trading posts. Smoyer discusses Indians as military aides, their style of fighting, and other ways in which they were used by colonial officers in wartime.

**986.** Society for the Propagation of the Gospel in New England. "Report of a Committee on the State of the Indians in Mashpee and Parts Adjacent." *Massachusetts Historical Society Collections,* ser. 2, vol. 3 (Boston, 1815): 1846. 12–17.

In this undated report supposedly written around 1767, the commissioners of the Society for the Propagation of the Gospel in New England describe the Indians in Mashpee and the adjacent area. The commissioners discuss the Indians they met, giving the number of families, and suggest the best places to preach.

**987.** Sosin, Jack M. "The Yorke-Camden Opinion." *Pennsylvania Magazine of History and Biography,* vol. 85, no. 1 (January 1961): 38–49.

Sosin discusses how the Yorke-Camden opinion of 1757, a specific answer to a question raised by the East India Company regarding lands in India, was altered and transmitted to America for use by land speculators as a rationalization for their activities in acquiring lands from the Indians in an area closed to settlement and reserved, by the Proclamation of 1763, for use by the Indians.

**988.** Southgate, William S. "The Saco Indians." In *The History of Scarborough from 1633 to 1783. Maine Historical Society Collections,* ser. 1, vol. 3 (Portland, 1853): 99–115.

Southgate draws on eyewitness accounts for descriptions of the appearance of the Saco Indians and tells of Indian-English relations in Maine until 1675 when peace ruptured between the Sacos and the English. He describes Indian depredations and the settlers' defense in Maine during King Philip's War. The author explains how Indians negotiated peace with the Massachusetts government and were dissatisfied with the treaty and the death of Mugg whom the English dreaded.

**989.** Kempe, John Tabor. "Report of John Tabor Kempe Concerning the Southold Indians." *New York Historical Society Collections For The Year 1922, Cadwallader Colden Papers,* vol. 6 (New York, 1923): 390–393.

Writing on November 27, 1764, Kempe, the attorney general of New York, gives his opinion about the claims of Southold Indians. He explains that he has not started a suit on behalf of these Indians

989 *(continued)*
because of insufficient evidence, a statute of limitations barring their right to lands at South Harbor, and other legal reasons that prevent their claim from being valid.

990. Southold, Long Island Proprietors. [Petition] *New York Historical Society Collections For The Year 1922, Cadwallader Colden Papers*, vol. 6 (New York, 1923) 353–355.

The Southold proprietors show cause why they cannot restore lands to certain Indians by drawing on legal reasoning and seventeenth century records concerning the lands. They cite the conditions under which these Indians, true descendants of the old Southold Tribe, can live and plant on Indian Neck.

991. Spangenberg, A. G. "Spangenberg's Notes of Travel to Onondaga in 1745." *Pennsylvania Magazine of History and Biography*, vol. 2, no. 4 (1876): 424–432.

A. G. Spangenberg, David Zeisberger, and John Jacob Shebosch, Moravian missionaries, traveled to Onondaga in 1745 to seek the Six Nations' permission for the Moravian Indians of Shecomeco, New York to move to Wyoming. Writing between May 24 and June 8, Spangenberg comments on encounters with Indians along the route to Onondaga. The journal is heavily footnoted with information on names of geographical places, Indian nomenclature, variant names of places in the Indian or English languages, and information about certain Indians and settlements. [*Continued in Pennsylvania Magazine of History and Biography*, vol. 3, no. 1 (1879): 56–64. Spangenberg describes Indian customs and settlements along the route. He discusses how the missionaries put their propositions before the Onondaga Council, Indian hospitality, the return journey, and contacts with Indians along the way.]

992. Speck, Frank G. "The Delaware Indians as Women: Were the Original Pennsylvanians Politically Emasculated?" *Pennsylvania Magazine of History and Biography*, vol. 70, no. 4 (October 1946): 377–389.

Speck examines the backgrounds of Indian cultures from northern New England to the Delaware Bay region, focusing on their tendency to give each other ratings of relationship according to a kind of consanguinity that one finds in extended branches of a large family. He studies records and oral testimony from Delawares then alive to learn the kinship terms used by the Delawares in their relations with other tribes during the period when the Delawares were independent of Iroquois control. He concludes that during the early colonial period, the Delaware Nation was highly esteemed as a patriarchal people by the Algonquians. He claims that the Five Nations did not regard the Delawares as highly as the other tribes because the Iroquois assigned the Algonquians to a lower position. He considers how the realtionship status became symbolized by gender, the Delawares becoming "women" to the Five Nations. Speck discusses the two opposing views concerning the interpretation of this status as "women," one which preserves the dignity and social supremacy of the Delawares and one which does not. He explains that the two views have remained irreconcilable in the subsequent histories of the two peoples.

**993.** Speck, Frank G. *The Nanticokes and Conoy Indians with a Review of Linguistic Material from Manuscript and Living Sources: An Historical Study. Delaware Historical Society Historical and Biographical Papers,* n.s., vol. 1 (Wilmington, 1927): 77 pp. Illustrated.

In this monograph, Speck gives a historical sketch of the Nanticokes and Conoys who lived in the northern portions of the Chesapeake area. He discusses the Conoys from 1634, when the colonists established a Catholic mission among them, until the mid-eighteenth century when their numbers were reduced. He comments on the Nanticokes from 1642 until 1777 when they became dependent on the Iroquois and disappeared from the public records. Speck considers the Nanticokes in the records of the Six Nations with regard to their social position among the Iroquois, Nanticoke matrons as electors of chiefs, proper names, and the relationship of the Nanticokes to the Delawares. A section reviews documentary sources of the Nanticoke language, including vocabularies as recorded by Williams Van Murray, 1792, on the Choptank River; by John Heckewelder, 1785, including his vocabulary list; the Jefferson Nanticoke Vocabulary, 1817; and the Nanticoke Vocabulary from the Six Nations Reserve, 1914, recorded by Speck.

**994.** Speck, Frank G. "The Wapanachki Delawares and the English; Their Past as Viewed by an Ethnologist." *Pennsylvania Magazine of History and Biography,* vol. 67, no. 4 (October 1943): 319–344.

Speck reviews the history of the eastern Algonquian tribes originally found along the Atlantic seaboard in terms of the culture and traditions of their present descendants, as of 1943. He describes traditional Delaware life culled from notes taken during conversations with elderly people, considers the matter of tribal names of the North Atlantic seaboard, the system of relationships among the tribes, and early relations between the Indians and colonial administrators. Speck discusses the reasons that some tribal people adopted new names while others preserved the old. He tells why the ethnological as well as a historical approach is necessary in order truly to understand Indian history. He discusses characteristics of contemporary Delawares as representative of Algonquian Indians encountered by the English from New England to Virginia. His discussion includes an evaluation of the war atrocities attributed to Indians in the East.

**995.** Spencer, Oliver. "Boy Captured by Indians." *New Jersey Historical Society Proceedings,* n.s., vol. 10, no. 4 (October 1925): 451–452.

This brief article discusses the lives and captivity narratives of both Colonel Oliver Spencer who was seized by Indians in Ohio in 1792 and

**995** *(continued)*
of Mary Kinnan who was taken captive in Virginia in 1791. The article tells where the texts of the narratives are located.

**996.** Stanton, John. Letter to Fitz John Winthrop. *Massachusetts Historical Society Collections,* ser. 5, vol. 9 (Boston, 1885): 140.
Writing on May 12, 1685, Stanton repeats the testimony of Wonkow that Ninigret has chosen Major Fitz John Winthrop to be a guardian of his children.

**997.** Stanton, John. [Letter to Fitz John Winthrop] *Massachusetts Historical Society Collections,* ser. 5, vol. 9 (Boston, 1885): 142–144.
In an undated letter, Stanton tells Fitz John Winthrop about hostile acts by the son of Ninigret and asks Winthrop, as the son's guardian and overseer, to stop him.

**998.** Staples, William R. "Purchases of the Natives, and Divisions of the Town." In *Annals of the Town of Providence From Its Settlement to the Organization of the City Government, In June 1832. Rhode Island Historical Society Collections,* vol. 5 (Providence, 1843): 562–576.
Staples discusses the ambiguity, vagueness, and uncertainty of the wording of many of the grants that the Providence colonists received from the Indians. The texts of several deeds from 1659 and 1661 are included with the marks of the Indians reproduced when the town paid for clearing away the Indian titles.

**999.** Stephenson, Clarence D. "The Wipey Affair: An Incident Illustrating Pennsylvania's Attitude During Dunmore's War." *Pennsylvania History,* vol. 23, no. 4 (October 1956): 504–512. Illustrated.
Stephenson tells of the murder of Joseph Wipey, a Delaware Indian, in 1774 during Dunmore's War. The author describes the war as one in which Lord Dunmore, governor of Virginia, was determined to make Ohio safe for land speculation. He discusses two of the people accused of the murder, neither brought to justice, and speculates on the motives for Wipey's murder. There is a facsimile of the proclamation by John Penn for apprehending Hinkston and Cooper, the two men.

**1000.** Stiles, Ezra. "Memoir of the Pequots." *Massachusetts Historical Society Collections,* ser. 1, vol. 10 (Boston, 1809): 101–103.
Stiles gives the population and other statistics for the Pequot for the years from 1775 to 1762. There is a list of the principal names and numbers of the families for the year 1762.

**1001.** Stiles, Ezra. "The Number of the Niantic Tribe of Indians." *Massachusetts Historical Society Collections,* ser. 1, vol. 10 (Boston, 1809): 103–105.
Stiles personally took this count on October 7, 1761. The names of families and the numbers of their sons and daughters are listed. This is followed by the number of Ninigret's tribes and the population of

the Indians on the Connecticut River. The tribes are named, and the locations and populations of each are given. [*See* "Account of the Potenummecut Indians. Taken By Dr. Stiles, On the Spot, June 4, 1762." pages 112–113. This is followed by the population figures for the Mashpee Indians in 1762, the Manamoyik Indians in 1762, and the Saconnet Indians, Eastern Indians, and those in Acacia in 1760. Included is a list entitled, "Names of the Indian Chiefs Inhabiting Acadie Coast," pages 113–116.]

**1002.** Stockbridge, Henry. "The Indian in the Archives of Maryland as Illustrating the Spirit of the Times of the Early Colonists." *Maryland Historical Society Fund Publication,* no. 22 (Baltimore, 1886): 43–59.

This selection cites acts, declarations, and journals to prove that Indians were always under suspicion in Maryland and had few rights that the colonists considered themselves bound to respect. Indians eventually were declared enemies of the province and subject to being shot or killed if not carrying a white flag. Stockbridge tells of expeditions against Indians, confining them to reservations, and binding them with treaties.

**1003.** Stockbridge Indians. "Extract from an Indian History." *Massachusetts Historical Society Collections,* ser. 1, vol. 9 (Boston, 1809): 99–102.

This is a discussion of Stockbridge Indians, the areas in which they were situated in New York, Massachusetts, and Vermont, their way of life in towns, and their manner of cultivating fields. Their tools, weapons, and hunting are described.

**1004.** Stoddard, Solomon. [Reverend Solomon Stoddard to Governor Joseph Dudley] *Massachusetts Historical Society Collections,* ser. 4, vol. 2 (Boston, 1854): 235–237.

Writing on October 22, 1703, Reverend Stoddard tells how the town of Deerfield suffered from Indian attacks and how people wished to train dogs to hunt Indians. He justifies the use of dogs by saying that Indians do not conduct themselves in a manner similar to other nations and do not appear openly in the fields to fight. He also proposes that the Deerfield people be exempted from taxes during war, and he asks the governor to try to obtain the release of two captives taken from Deerfield.

**1005.** Stone, Frederick D. "Penn's Treaty with the Indians. Did It Take Place in 1682 or 1683?" *Pennsylvania Magazine of History and Biography,* vol. 6, no. 2 (1882): 217–238.

Stone gives reasons which he documents to support his feeling that Penn's Treaty with the Indians was made in 1683 rather than in 1682. He cites many expressions found in the records of Indian experiences which point to the fact that the long friendship which existed between the Indians and the English in Pennsylvania began soon after Penn arrived in November of 1682. Stone submits his reasons for thinking

1005 *(continued)*
that this long and honorable relationship originated with a 1683 treaty
which is described in Penn's letter to the Free Society of Traders in
August, 1683. He connects the treaty with two purchases of land by
Penn, one deed showing that the first purchase was made on June 23
and the second on June 25 and July 14, 1683.

1006. Stone, Rufus. "Sinnontouan, or Seneca Land, in the Revolution."
*Pennsylvania Magazine of History and Biography*, vol. 48, no. 2 (1924): 201–226.
Illustrated.
  Stone writes of the peaceful union of six tribes into an essentially
representative federal republic, discusses the pressure put on the
Confederacy by the English in the East and the French in the West,
and reviews the history of the Seneca embitterment with the English.
He mentions the role of the Senecas in terrorizing the frontier settlements and describes Washington's plan to penetrate the heart of the
Senecas' land and drive them out. Stone tells the story of the destructive expedition against the Seneca Indians of the Allegheny Valley in
1779 and of Washington's and Brodhead's roles, and the subsequent
decline of the Senecas. There is a map showing the route of Brodhead's Expedition in 1779 to destroy the Indian villages.

1007. Stone, William L. "Joseph Brandt and His Raids." *New York State Historical Association Proceedings, Eighth Annual Meeting*, vol. 7 (Lake George, 1907):
21–25.
  Stone discusses Joseph Brant, Tha-yen-da-ne-gea, a Mohawk, the
raids and wars with which this Indian has been associated, and his
close relationship to the British. The author evaluates Brant's role
during the Wyoming Massacre in 1778, Cherry Valley in 1778, and at
Minisink in 1779. [*See* Alfred W. Abrams, "Schoharie in the Border
Warfare of the Revolution," pages 37–40, in which Brant's role at
Cobleskill in 1778 and Schoharie in 1780 are discussed. *See also* Henry
U. Swinnerton, "The Story of Cherry Valley," pages 79–87, in which
Brant's role at Cherry Valley in 1778 is discussed.]

1008. Stone, William L. "King Hendrick." *New York State Historical Association,
Second Annual Meeting*, vol. 1 (Lake George, 1901): 28–34.
  Stone discusses the life of Hendrick, a Mohegan adopted by the
Mohawks who were allies of the English. The author refers to Hendrick's most famous speech delivered to Congress in Albany on June
19, 1754 and gives its entire text. He explains Hendrick's disapproval
of the campaign plans developed in connection with the 1755 expedition of General Johnson against Crown Point and tells how the Indian
died during this expedition. Stone discusses how Hendrick's loss was
deeply lamented by Sir William Johnson and others. Stone also describes Hendrick's visits to the British king.

1009. Storer, Mary. "Letters of the Indian Captive, Mary Storer of Wells,
1725–1737." ed. Malcolm Storer. *Massachusetts Historical Society Proceedings*, vol.
55 (1921–1922): 228–233.

Malcolm Storer discusses Mary Storer, the prisoner taken by the Indians in 1703 and held captive in Canada for several months until a Jesuit convinced the Indians to turn their captives over to him. The letters, written between June, 1725 and 1764, do not refer to her experiences while with the Indians.

1010. Strickland, William. "Journal of a Tour in the United States of America: 1794–1795." *New York Historical Society Collections for the Year 1950,* vol. 83 (New York, 1971): 116–168.

In a letter dated October 22, 1794, Strickland explains how the state of Connecticut ended up with the right of preemption to lands reserved for Senecas in the Indians' sale of lands to New York. He tells how land speculators pursued the destruction of Indians "with atrocious pleasure" and predicts that any attempts by the government to improve the condition of Indians will not succeed because special interest groups prevail over all these efforts.

1011. "John Strong." *Vermont Historical Society Proceedings,* n.s., vol. 8, no. 2 (June 1940): 203–209.

In this biographical note about the John Strong family of Lake Champlain, there is a long passage about the "savageness" of Indians after the commencement of the Revolutionary struggle. The information is taken from the first volume of Hemenways's *Vermont Historical Gazetteer* published in 1868.

1012. Stryker, Melancthon Woolsey. "Samuel Kirkland and the Oneida Indians." *New York State Historical Association Proceedings, Sixteenth Annual Meeting,* vol. 14 (Lake George, 1915): 101–107. Illustrated.

Stryker briefly discusses Reverend Kirkland and his relations to the Iroquois and particularly to the Oneidas with whom he was closely associated after 1766. He describes Kirkland's patriotic views during the American Revolution, his efforts and subsequent failure to maintain the Six Nations' neutrality, and his work with the Indians until his death in 1808.

1013. Sturgis, William. "Memoir of William Sturgis on Northwest Coast Indians." *Massachusetts Historical Society Proceedings,* ser. 1, vol. 7 (1863–1864): 439–450.

Sturgis' diary, written about 1800, and his three lectures on the Northwest Coast Indians delivered in 1845 and 1846 describe the manners, customs, dwellings, and ornaments of the Indians of the Northwest Coast. These materials also intersperse anecdotes characteristic of Indian life with commentary on Sturgis' life. There is a lengthier discourse on the Indian character which Sturgis claims combines conflicting elements, noble impulses, and brutal propensities. He tells of the treatment of Indians on the Northwest Coast by aggressive whites.

**1014. Suffolk County.** "Indian Attack on Haverhill." *Massachusetts Historical Society Proceedings*, ser. 2, vol. 16 (1902–1903): 53–54.

This account of the Indian attack on Haverhill on August 29, 1708 comes from the County of Suffolk Register of Probate for 1639 to 1799. The murder of the father, mother, and youngest sister of Benjamin Rolfe are described.

**1015. Sullivan, James.** "History of the Penobscot Indians." *Massachusetts Historical Society Collections*, ser. 1, vol. 9 (Boston, 1804): 207–232.

Describing the Penobscot Indians, their manners, lack of civilization, and intemperance, Sullivan continually compares these Indians to Europeans and to Indians of South America. He discusses the French influence among Penobscots and gives the text of the treaty of October, 1749 which subjects the eastern Indians (Wawenocks, Anasaguntacooks, Norridgewocks, and Penobscots) to English authority and terminates their existence as independent tribes. He notes the impact of the French-Indian War on the eastern Indians, many of whom joined the French in Canada to fight against the English. Sullivan concludes by theorizing about the arrival of the Indian nations on this continent.

**1016. Sullivan, John.** [Address to Oneida Indians] *New Hampshire Historical Society Collections*, vol. 15 (Concord, 1939): 114–115.

Speaking on September 1, 1779, General John Sullivan informs the Oneidas that they could best demonstrate loyalty to the American cause by joining his forces, leading him through the country, and giving him intelligence about enemy movements.

**1017. Sullivan, John.** [Address to Oneida Indians] *New Hampshire Historical Society Collections*, vol. 15 (Concord, 1939): 116–119.

In an undated address, General John Sullivan responds to the Oneida request that Cayuga crops be spared destruction by recalling how the Oneidas and some friendly Tuscaroras and Onondagas adhered to the American request that the Six Nations remain neutral during the dispute between Great Britain and America. The Cayugas, however, planned to raid the frontiers, aided Butler, and only expressed friendship for the Americans after Butler was defeated. Sullivan concludes that the Cayugas are enemies to America and, therefore, concealing them constitutes an act of hostility.

**1018. Sullivan, John.** [Address to Oneida Indians] *New Hampshire Historical Society Collections*, vol. 15 (Concord, 1939): 137–138.

On October 1, 1779, General John Sullivan instructs the Oneidas to persuade the Cayugas, who profess friendship for the Americans, to incorporate with the Oneidas. He reveals that Congress plans to extirpate any Five Nations tribe that does not join the Oneidas. Sullivan tells the Oneidas to destroy the town of an unfriendly nation.

1019. Sullivan, John. "Letters and Papers of Major-General John Sullivan, Continental Army." ed. Otis G. Hammond. *New Hampshire Historical Society Collections*, vol. 15 (Concord, 1939): 661 pp.

The concluding volume of the Sullivan Papers (vol. 3, 1779–1795) covers his departure from Rhode Island, his command of the expedition against the western Indians, and his final campaign in which he destroyed the Indians' power and enabled General Washington to carry on the war in the South without fear of interruption from the North. Included is Sullivan's correspondence with Washington and others concerning the Sullivan Campaign.

1020. Sullivan, John. "Sullivan Sesquicentennial 1929." *New York State Historical Association Quarterly Journal*, vol. 9, no. 2 (April 1928): 217–220. Illustrated.

The author discusses the one hundred and fiftieth anniversary of the Sullivan Expedition, the military campaign planned by George Washington to destroy the Indian settlements, sever the English-Indian alliance, and conquer Canada. Second only to the Burgoyne Campaign, the Sullivan Expedition was the largest military operation within New York during the Revolutionary period. It lasted from April to October, 1779, and eventually involved New Jersey and Pennsylvania as well as New York. Suggestions are provided for commemorating the event. A Sullivan marker, shown in a photograph after page 156, will be placed in six locations in New York. It states: "Route Between Lakes, Sullivan Expedition 1779. This Campaign Severed the English-Indian Alliance and Checked English Aggression on our Western Frontier." A sketch of troop movements during the expedition is included. [*See* Grenville M. Ingalsbe, "A Bibliography of Sullivan's Indian Expedition," *New York State Historical Association, Seventh Annual Meeting*, vol. 6 (Lake George, 1906): 37–79.]

1021. Sullivan, John. "Supplies for General Sullivan: The Correspondence of Colonel Charles Stewart, May–September, 1779." eds. Marion Brophy and Wendell Tripp. *New York History*, vol. 60, no. 3 (July 1979): 245–281. Illustrated.

The correspondence concerns gathering supplies for General John Sullivan's Expedition into western New York. An editor's introduction, a map of the expedition's theater, and paintings of Sullivan and Stewart are provided. [*Continued* in *New York History*, vol. 60, no. 4 (October 1979): 439–467 and *New York History*, vol. 61, no. 1 (January 1980): 43–80.]

1022. Talcott, Joseph. [Letter to Colonel Adam Winthrop] *Connecticut Historical Society Collections*, vol. 5 (Hartford, 1896): 397–399.

Writing on September 20, 1725, Governor Talcott furnishes the

**1022** *(continued)*
population and locations of the Indians in Connecticut including the Pequots, Mohegans, and Narragansetts. In a letter of September 30, 1725 to Robert Ashurst, governor of the Society for Propagating the Gospel in America, Talcott provides similar information and comments on the best way to begin "civilizing" and Christianizing the Connecticut Indians.

**1023.** Talcott, Joseph. [Letter to Colonel Adam Winthrop] *Connecticut Historical Society Collections*, vol. 4 (Hartford, 1892): 338–344.

Writing on February 17, 1736, Governor Talcott insists Connecticut has protected its Indians and secured sufficient lands for the Pequots and Mohegans to practice their husbandry. He argues that Captain Mason's plan to depose Ben Uncas and replace him with Mahomet is an illustration of English meddling in Indian politics just to advance their own interest.

**1024.** Talcott, Joseph. [Letter to Francis Wilks] *Connecticut Historical Society Collections*, vol. 5 (Hartford, 1896): 195–208.

Writing on January 11, 1740, Governor Talcott refutes each of the complaints in the Masons' petition. He discusses the authority of the late Queen Anne's commission, the Rhode Island commissioners, Ben Uncas's title, the sachem's advocates, the deeds and releases of land by the Mohegans from 1640 to 1721, and the question of whether the Mohegans have inalienable title to the land. He informs Wilks that in March, 1738, seventeen Indians renounced Ben Uncas because of Mason's machinations. Talcott argues that a judgment in their favor would destroy half the colony because the Mohegans would regain title to lands in Connecticut.

**1025.** Talcott, Joseph. "The Talcott Papers: Correspondence and Documents During Joseph Talcott's Governorship of the Colony of Connecticut, 1724–1741." ed. Mary Kingsbury Talcott. vol. 1: *Connecticut Historical Society Collections*, vol. 4. Hartford: 1892. vol 2: *Connecticut Historical Society Collections*, vol. 5. Hartford: 1896.

Indians are mentioned briefly throughout these two volumes and are indexed under Indians, Mohegans, and John and Samuel Mason. The first volume covers the period from 1724 to 1736, the second from 1737 to 1741.

**1026.** Taukishke. [Deed] *Connecticut Historical Society Collections*, vol. 21 (Hartford, 1924): 137.

On February 20, 1662, Taukishke, a female sachem, and Hemumpam, her daughter, deed an island to Sam Wyllys in exchange for cloth and wampum.

**1027.** Thayer, Henry O. "The Last Tragedy of the Indian Wars: The Preble Massacre at the Kennebec." *Maine Historical Society Collections*, ser. 3, vol. 1 (Portland, 1903): 406–422.

Thayer discusses the mid-eighteenth century Indian raid on the Preble family in early June in which the parents were killed and the children taken captive. He examines the existing historical records for information about the raid, particularly the date of the event which was sometime in 1758, the recovery of some Preble captives from the French, and the aftermath of their lives. He concludes by placing this raid in the framework of the French and Indian War. A brief outline of the Prebles' descendants is provided.

1028. Thayer, Theodore. "The Friendly Association." *Pennsylvania Magazine of History and Biography*, vol. 67, no. 1 (October 1943): 356–376.

Thayer describes the Friendly Association started by the Quakers during the French and Indian War to restore peace with the Indians. He analyzes the Association's reform program to create permanent peace with the Indians of Pennsylvania and shows how the Association was involved with provincial politics from the outset. He explains why the frequent treaties with the Indians as well as all the payments, presents, and benefits conferred by the Association failed to assuage the Indians. Thayer asserts that the organization's support of provincial stores, legislated in 1755, which were designed to provide reasonably priced goods for the Indian trade was undermined by private traders who flouted the law and clinched their hold on the trade. After the Pontiac War of 1763, the Quaker influence in Indian affairs was slight.

1029. Thomas, George. "Letter of Governor George Thomas to Conrad Weiser." *Pennsylvania Magazine of History and Biography*, vol. 36, no. 4 (1912: 500.

Governor Thomas complains about Count Zinzendorf's treatment of Indians. Speculating on drunkenness as a bad trait for Christians and Indians, he judges that "the common sort of People amongst Christians are worse than the Indians, who are left to the Law of Nature . . . to guide them" and that Christianity has not improved people.

1030. Thomas, Nathaniel. "Letter from Nathaniel Thomas, in the Expedition Against Philip, to Governor Winslow." *Massachusetts Historical Society Collections*, ser. 1, vol. 6 (Boston, 1800): 36–37.

Writing on June 25, 1675, Thomas reports on both military actions against Philip and on Philip's exploits. [*See* other letters concerning King Philip's War: "Letter from John Freeman to Governor Winslow," dated April 3, 1675, page 91; "Letter from Governor Leverett to Governor Winslow," dated March 26, 1676, page 89; "Letter from Selectmen to Governor Winslow," dated January 26, 1676, page 92; and "Letter of Sachem Philip, His Answer to the Letter Brought to him from the Governor of New-Plymouth," no date, page 94.]

1031. Thompson, J. M. "Fort Niagara as the Base of Indian and Tory Operations." *New York State Historical Association Proceedings, Eighth Annual Meeting*, vol. 7 (Lake George, 1907): 15–20.

1031 *(continued)*
Thompson discusses the 1764 meeting of thousands of Indians at Niagara who pledged friendship to the British. He describes Fort Niagara as a base for Indian and Tory operations at the beginning of the Revolutionary War. Because it was secure from attacks, the fort was a good place to plan and begin raids. He notes two widely varying accounts of the social conditions at Fort Niagara. Americans took possession of the fort in 1796.

1032. Tinkcom, Harry M. "Presque Isle and Pennsylvania Politics, 1794." *Pennsylvania History,* vol. 16, no. 2 (April 1949): 96–121.
    Tinkcom discusses the controversial Erie triangle, the tract of land originally deeded to Pennsylvania by the Six Nations and finally sold to the state in 1792 by the United States. He describes the Indians' hostility toward the development of Presque Isle, their denial that they sold the Erie tract to Pennsylvania, and finally Washington's decision to suspend Presque Isle operations in order to keep the Six Nations at peace, a decision that was contrary to Governor Mifflin's wishes. Tinkcom also considers the British presence at the forts they promised to vacate in 1783 and their influence over the Indians. He concludes that the land development schemes for Presque Isle ended "happily" for all except the Indians.

1033. Tooker, William Wallace. "Indian Geographic Names, and Why We Should Study Them." *Rhode Island Historical Society Publications,* n.s., vol. 5 (Providence, 1897): 203–215.
    Tooker believes that names are often the only survivors of extinct languages whose analysis will increase our knowledge of the history of early settlements. He considers Rhode Island deeds as a source of the place names which he analyzes.

1034. Torrey, Joseph. "The Discovery and Occupation of Lake Champlain." *Vermont Historical Society Proceedings* (October 1860): 13–27.
    Torrey discusses Samuel Champlain's discovery of Lake Champlain in 1609 and Champlain's investigation of Indian life. The author gives a brief history of the Algonquian and Iroquoian tribes which shows their relationship to each other, based on Schoolcraft's findings. He describes Champlain's meeting with the Algonquians, an expedition they took together, and his discoveries along the way. Torrey claims that the battle with the Iroquois in which Champlain killed two men laid the foundation for the Iroquois hatred of the French. The author discusses the efforts to establish Jesuit missions among the Iroquois in the 1640s and 1650s. He explains that the long contest between the French and the Indians for possession of the Champlain Valley ended because of the imperial contest between France and England. [*See* Henry W. Hill, "Samuel Champlain and the Lake Champlain Tercentenary." *Vermont Historical Society Proceedings* (1907–1908): 41–61. This article covers the same period.]

1035. Torry, William. "Extracts from the Orderly Book of William Torry, Second Massachusetts Infantry, 1779." *Pennsylvania Magazine of History and Biography*, vol. 28, no. 3 (1904): 382.

> One piece, dated October 18, 1779, details the Sullivan Expedition. Torry congratulates the army on its success in destroying Seneca towns and cornfields despite some opposition by Indians.

1036. Towle, Edward L., and Rawlyk, George A., eds. "A New Baron de Lahontan Memoir on New York and the Great Lakes Basin." *New York History*, vol. 46, no. 3 (July 1965): 212–229.

> Written after 1713. The Baron de Lahontan analyzes the natural structure of the Great Lakes Basin and its separation of the English and the French. The Baron comments on the relationship between the Hudson River and the St. Lawrence River Indian fur trade, the logistics of the fur trade, water transportation, and Lake Ontario forts. He discusses the necessity of maintaining better relationships with the entire Iroquoian trading group because of New York's linkage to the trading system of the St. Lawrence and Great Lakes drainage basin.

1037. Tozzer, Alfred Marston. "Chronological Aspects of American Archaeology." *Massachusetts Historical Society Proceedings*, ser. 2, vol. 59 (1924–1926): 283–292.

> Tozzer discusses stratification as well as the development of stylistic methods of decoration on pottery, architecture, and crafted products as important chronological approaches to studying archaeology in America. He considers the migration of objects far from their original place of manufacture as another factor in establishing the relative chronology of a site or a series of sites. He argues that only by means of dated monuments, correlated with Christian chronology, is one on satisfactory historical ground. Tozzer focuses on the Mayan calendar hieroglyphic inscriptions and the steps used in supplying the historical development of Mayan civilization from the sixth century before Christ.

1038. "Tracts Relating to the Attempts to Convert to Christianity the Indians of New England." *Massachusetts Historical Society Collections*, ser. 3, vol. 4 (Boston, 1834): 1–261.

> Seven tracts published between 1647 and 1655 were written by different individuals attempting to convert Indians to Christianity. The authors of the tracts are the Reverends John Eliot, Thomas Shepard, Henry Whitfield, Thomas Mayhew, and Edward Winslow.

1039. Trask, Roger R. "Pennsylvania and the Albany Congress, 1754." *Pennsylvania History*, vol. 27, no. 3 (July 1960): 273–290.

> Trask discusses the Indian business conducted at the Albany Congress of 1754, particularly as it related to Pennsylvania. He briefly

**1039** *(continued)*
describes the four Pennsylvania commissioners who were closely involved with Indian affairs, originally meant to be the main concern of
the meetings. He notes the four commissioners' cooperation with the
rest of the colonies in renewing ties with the Six Nations. Trask judges
as superficial the renewal of friendship with the Indians; he believes
the successful negotiation of large land purchases from the Six Nations while Congress was in session was far more important for the
proprietors of Pennsylvania.

**1040.** Treat, Richard. "Richard Treat's Memorial." *Connecticut Historical Society
Collections,* vol. 5 (Hartford, 1896): 478–484.
Writing on May 11, 1737 to Governor Talcott, Richard Treat recounts
his service instructing Indians in Christianity at Middletown, beginning in December, 1734 and continuing for several months. He states
his reasons for leaving the Indians and asks for remuneration.

**1041.** [Treaty of Peace with the Delaware Nation] *New York Historical Society
Collections for the Year 1923, Cadwallader Colden Papers,* vol. 7 (New York, 1923):
29–32.
Signed on May 8, 1765, this peace treaty was made between the
Delaware Nation and Sir William Johnson, the Crown's sole agent and
Superintendent of Indian Affairs in the Northern Department of
North America. Twelve articles concern the exchange of prisoners,
British free passage on roads and waterways, the observation of British law, punishments for guilty people, disputes over lands, land
reparations for traders who were plundered and severely treated by
the Delawares in 1763, mutual observation of boundaries established
by the English and the Six Nations, and the protection of traders and
their goods. The last article mandates that all Delawares must observe
the treaty and not enter into any other engagements with any nation
without the knowledge of the superintendent or the king.

**1042.** [Treaty of Peace with the "Eastward Indian Enemy Sagamores"] *Massachusetts Historical Society Collections,* ser. 3, vol. 1 (Boston, 1825): 112–114.
Signed on November 29, 1690, the treaty of peace was made between
the English and the Indians. The exchange of captives is discussed,
and the Indians are told to convey French plans to the English. Five
Indians are listed.

**1043.** [Treaty with the Maine Indians] *Massachusetts Historical Society Collections,*
vol. 80 (Boston, 1972): 330–338.
On July 20 and 23, 1720, Indians are questioned by John Penhallow
concerning the threatening of the English and the killing of their
cattle. A July 24, 1720 letter from John Penhallow to Samuel Shute
concerns the Indians' behavior toward the English, commenting that
the Indians are inclined to be hostile despite efforts to extort peace
from them.

**1044.** [Treaty with the Mohawks and Senecas] *New York Historical Society Collections For The Year 1869. Publication Fund,* vol. 2 (New York, 1870): 336–338.
This September 24, 1664 treaty of peace was made among the Mohawks, the Senecas, and Colonel George Cartwright on behalf of Governor Nicols. The four articles deal with a mutual impact between the Indians, who were under the protection of the English, and the English. The Indians are guaranteed wares and commodities from the English, and offensive Indians or English are to be punished. There are five more articles agreed to by the Indians and the English which provide that the English would not assist three particular Indian nations whose members had murdered a Mohawk.

**1045.** [Treaty with the Passamaquoddy Tribe of Indians, by the Commonwealth of Massachusetts] *Maine Historical Society Collections, Documentary History of the State of Maine,* ser. 2, vol. 8 (Portland, 1902): 98–102.
By this treaty, dated September 29, 1794, Massachusetts established a reservation of land for the Passamaquoddy Tribe near a river and a lake. This treaty by Massachusetts was the basis for the relations which Maine held with the Indians of the same tribe in 1902.

**1046.** [Treaty with the Penobscot Tribe of Indians, By the Commonwealth of Massachusetts] *Maine Historical Society Collections, Documentary History of the State of Maine,* ser. 2, vol. 8 (Portland, 1902): 127–132.
The relationship which Massachusetts established with the Indians was continued under the constitution of Maine, in accordance with the Articles of Separation. Dated June 29, 1818, this treaty between Massachusetts and the Penobscot Tribe gives the details of the relationship. [*See* the text of the treaty between the Penobscot Tribe and Maine, dated August 17, 1820, by which Massachusetts is released from any further obligations under the treaty of June 29, 1818, and Maine is substituted in its place].

**1047.** [Treaty with the Sioux Indians] *New Jersey Historical Society Proceedings,* n.s., vol. 13, no. 1 (January 1928): 109–110.
This is a brief note concerning the 1816 treaty between the U.S. commissioners and several Sioux tribes. A list of more than forty Indians who signed the treaty and the meaning of their names is supplied.

**1048.** Trumbell, J. Hammond. "The Composition of Indian Geographical Names, Illustrated from the Algonkin Languages." *Connecticut Historical Society Collections,* vol. 2 (Hartford, 1870): 1–50.
Trumbell discusses Indian geographical names which he explains are not proper names but significant appellatives which have lost their original character when they were transferred to a foreign tongue. He tells how the names describe the localities to which they were affixed and can be topographical, historical, or natural products of the place.

**1048** *(continued)*
The names can reflect the geographic relationship to a place previously known. He reviews three classes of structure: Those formed by the union of two elements, those which have a single element, and those formed from verbs as participles or verbal nouns. He notes that most names belong to the first two classes. Examples are provided of each class taken from the Algonquian language, chiefly from the Natick, Massachusetts, Abenaki, Lenape, Chippewa, and Cree. At the close of the paper, Trumbell gives suggestions for analyzing a name as well as tests to judge the probability that the translation is accurate.

**1049.** Trumbull, Jonathan, Jr. [Letter to Jonathan Trumbull] *Massachusetts Historical Society Collections,* ser. 7, vol. 2 (Boston, 1902): 103–105.
Writing on August 6, 1777, Trumbull, Jr., describes how the Tories disguised themselves as Indians, Indian atrocities against Tories and innocent families, and Oneidas' loyalty to the Americans. He gives the number of Indian troops in the British army.

**1050.** Tuttle, Charles W. "On Supposed Massacre at Fox Point." *Massachusetts Historical Society Proceedings,* ser. 2, vol. 17 (1879–1880): 105–111.
This communication deals with Tuttle's discovery of substantial reasons for doubting that the destruction of Fort Point was done by a party of Indians in May, 1690 as alleged by Cotton Mather in his account which described a version of a massacre that has gone unchallenged. Tuttle reviews his researches that do not uncover anything relating to the tragedy near Portsmouth, New Hampshire, except for a letter from which he quotes. He concludes that the destruction never occurred.

**1051.** Tuttle, Charles W. [Remarks on the Name 'Pascataqua'] *Massachusetts Historical Society Proceedings,* ser, 1. vol. 16 (1878–1879): 377–379.
Tuttle discusses various interpretations of "Passataquack," or "Pascataqua," one of the Indian geographical names which first appeared in Captain John Smith's *Description of New England* printed in 1616. Smith collected about thirty names of Indians while exploring the coast between the Penobscot River and Cape Cod in 1614.

### «U»

**1052.** Uncas (Mohegan sachem). "Agreement Between Uncas and the Colony of Connecticut." *Massachusetts Historical Society Proceedings,* ser. 1, vol. 10 (1867–1869): 16–18.
On May 18, 1681, Uncas, sachem of the Mohegans, and the government of Connecticut agree that Uncas will not injure, damage, or plot against the people of Connecticut, that he will give up his lands and territories to Connecticut, that he will not make a friendship with any

enemies of the colony, and that he will supply Connecticut with men to fight against any enemy. The General Court of Connecticut promises the Indians equal justice, advice, farmland, and fairly-priced ammunition.

**1053.** Uncas (Mohegan sachem). [Indian Deed] *Connecticut Historical Society Bulletin,* vol. 4, no. 2 (January 1938): 10.

Signed on April 5, 1650, this is the earliest deed executed by the Indians that appears in the town records of New London. Uncas, sachem of the Mohegans, deeds land to Jonathan Brewster in return for his agreement to run a trading house with the Indians.

**1054.** Uncas (Mohegan sachem). "Genealogy and Lineage of Uncas, Sachem of Moheag." *Massachusetts Historical Society Collections,* ser. 5, vol. 9 (Boston, 1885): 101–104.

Written on October 19, 1692, this genealogy and lineage of Uncas begins with Tamaquawshad, great-grandfather of Uncas, and continues down to Uncas and his successors. Their native right to land is shown with respective boundaries.

**1055.** Uncas, Owaneco, and Attawanhood. [Indian Deed] *Massachusetts Historical Society Collections,* ser. 5, vol. 9 (Boston, 1885): 79–80.

On May 9, 1671, Uncas, Owaneco, and Attawanhood, all Mohegans, grant their lands to Major John Mason.

**1056.** Uncas, Ben. "Address of Ben Uncas to the King." *Connecticut Historical Society Collections,* vol. 5 (Hartford, 1896): 103.

Speaking on May 4, 1739, Uncas says the English have always treated the Mohegans with kindness, and the Indians have far more lands than they can improve. He also adds that many Mohegans are resolved to embrace Christianity.

**1057.** Uncas, Ben. "Declaration of Ben Uncas and His Tribe." *Connecticut Historical Society Collections,* vol. 5 (Hartford, 1896): 40–44.

On February 28, 1738, Ben Uncas and other Mohegans confirm that the English have duly paid the price for land according to the agreement and have the right and title to the lands they purchased. The Indians explain that Mahomet was not the rightful sachem of the Mohegans, that he complained to the king without consulting them, that his complaint was untrue when he claimed that Connecticut broke the league with the Mohegans and unjustly took their lands. The marks of the Indians are reproduced.

**1058.** Uncas, Ben. "Petition of Ben Uncas, Sachem of Mohegan Indians." *Connecticut Historical Society Collections,* vol. 4 (Hartford, 1892): 291–292.

In October, 1733, Uncas asks the General Court to take action and suppress the practice of English people selling great quantities of liquor to the Mohegans. Uncas's mark is reproduced.

**1059.** Underhill, John. "History of the Pequot War." *Massachusetts Historical Society Collections,* ser. 3, vol. 6 (Boston, 1837): 1–28.

Originally published in 1638, Underhill, one of the first planters of Massachusetts, gives his account of the history of the Pequot war, describing the "warlike proceedings that hath been in New England these two years last past." He suggests locations in New England that would be good places to plant.

**1060.** Underwood, Wynn. "Indian and Tory Raids On the Otter Valley, 1777–1782." *Vermont Quarterly,* n.s., vol. 15, no. 4 (October 1947): 195–221.

Underwood discusses the campaign of Burgoyne who, with the help of thousands of allied Indians, planned to invade Vermont and New York and terrorize people into submission. The author describes a series of Indian and Tory raids in the Otter Valley, particularly those showing signs of Tory leadership, association, or origin, including descriptions of Tories painting their faces to resemble Indians. Underwood tells how Tory spying, raiding, and burning continued until the end of the Revolution.

**1061.** Uring, Captain Nathaniel. " 'Indians' in Uring's Notice of New-England 1709." *New Hampshire Historical Society Collections,* vol. 3 (Concord, 1832): 145–150.

Uring's book is entitled *A Voyage to Boston in New England and the West Indies, in 1709, with a Short Description of New-England, Their Trade and Products, and the Nature and Manners of the Indians, Who are the Natives of that Country.* He describes the Indians in general and then retells a story Governor Dudley told him about the accidental death of an Indian by a tree felled by a carpenter, the Indians' insistence on the carpenter's being hanged, and the expedience of the governor hanging an old weaver in the place of the carpenter in order to satisfy the Indians. Uring repeats two other stories he heard about Indians.

**1062.** Vail, Robert W. G. "Certain Indian Captives of New England." *Massachusetts Historical Society Proceedings,* vol. 68 (1944–1947): 113–131.

Vail discusses the past popularity and present-day interest in Indian captivity narratives and illustrates with passages from the narratives. He examines and analyzes several narratives written between 1676 and 1867, pointing out their different features and discussing particular "adventures."

**1063.** Vail, Robert W. G. "The First Artist of the Oregon Trail." *New York Historical Society Quarterly Bulletin,* vol. 34, No. 1 (January 1950): 25–30. Illustrated.

Vail discusses Alfred Jacob Miller, the artist, who joined Captain Stewart on the latter's trip to the Rockies and the Plains. Miller sketched herds of buffalos and painted Rocky Mountain Indians before white contact altered their life. Vail describes a picture of a buffalo hunt by the Pawnees on the prairies between Council Bluffs and Fort Laramie, probably made during the expedition of 1837, and describes a similar 1840 sketch that the Society secured. Included is a photograph of the Society drawing entitled, "A Buffalo Surround in the Pawnee Country, 1837," painted by Miller in 1840.

**1064.** Vail, Robert W. G. "Sir William Johnson's Indian Testimonial." *New York Historical Society Quarterly Bulletin,* vol. 30, no. 4 (October 1946): 208–214. Illustrated.

A group of letters by Sir William Johnson concerns a certificate or testimonial designed to accompany his presentation of medals as gifts at Indian councils. The letters, written in 1770, concern the details and expenses of preparing engravings on copper plates to be printed on parchment. He discusses the cartouche for the Johnson testimonial. Included is a photograph of an Indian testimonial engraved by Henry Dawkins in 1770 and photographs of Indian silver gorgets and medals.

**1065.** Vail, Robert W. G. "Unknown Views of Old New York." *New York Historical Society Quarterly Bulletin,* vol. 32, no. 2 (April 1949): 97–101. Illustrated.

Vail discusses the Dutch view of North America, a copper plate reproducing part of the Restitutio View of New Amsterdam in 1673, and the recapture of the city of New York by the Dutch on August 24, 1673, published around 1700. In the article, illustrations are shown of the 1740 reproduction of the view, from the original 1674 edition, the drawing itself, the same reversed, and the reproduction of the finished print. The drawings of New Amsterdam show native peoples and their clothing.

**1066.** Vail, Robert W. G. "Unknown Views of Old New York: Purchase of Manhattan Island, 1626." *New York Historical Society Quarterly Bulletin,* vol. 39, no. 4 (October 1955): 380–381. Illustrated.

Vail discusses the cartoon by Will Crawford in *Puck,* April 14,1909, which records the event from the Indians' point of view. The cartoon is entitled "A Birchbark Record Depicting the Aboriginal Jubilation over Selling Manhattan Island for $24." There are quotations from the only contemporary account of the transaction, November 5, 1626, by Peter Jansen Schaghen.

**1067.** Vail, Robert W. G. "The Western Campaign of 1779: The Diary of Quartermaster Sergeant Moses Sproule of the Third New Jersey Regiment in the Sullivan Expedition of the Revolutionary War, May 17–October 17, 1779."

1067 *(continued)*
*New York Historical Society Quarterly Bulletin,* vol. 51, no. 1 (January 1957): 35–69. Illustrated.

> In 1778, Washington planned a campaign of retaliation to destroy the power of the Iroquois who had aided the British cause, to wipe out Indian crops planted to feed the British who were dependent on these acres of Indian farmlands for a large part of their food supply for their frontier forts and for garrisons in Canada, and to drive back the Iroquois in order to get their lands for the new republic. Vail explains that Sproule's diary is concerned with the main expedition, one of four deployed against the Iroquois. The main expeditionary force under General Sullivan's command assembled against Tioga in May, 1779. Sproule's diary, dated from May 17 to October 17, 1779, continues the story through the Sullivan campaign and along the return march until the expedition ended and his regiment returned to its winter quarters in New Jersey. The journal is edited throughout; there is a bibliographical note about the campaign, a discussion about the early days of the expedition, and some biographical material about Sproule. There are two maps of the Sullivan campaign of 1779, a copy of the first page of Sproule's journal, sketches of the orders of battle and march, and other illustrations.

**1068.** Vallandigham, Edward Nobel. "Lieutenant Colonel George Vallandigham." *Pennsylvania Magazine of History and Biography,* vol. 53, no. 2 (1929): 159–167.

> Vallandigham discusses his relative's long service in the struggle between the Indians and the whites from 1774 to 1794 along Pennsylvania's western frontier. The author describes the lieutenant colonel's role during the Revolutionary War in accompanying Colonel Brodhead on the punitive expedition along the Allegheny River, burning Indian towns and fighting the Delaware Indians in eastern Ohio.

**1069.** Van Epps, Percy M. "The Battle of 1669 at the Kinaquariones." *New York History,* vol. 13, no. 4 (October 1932): 420–430.

> Van Epps discusses the lengthy warfare between the Mohawks and the other eastern Indians during the seventeenth century. He describes the preparations made by the Algonquians of New England during the summer of 1669 to organize the expedition against the Mohawks, the Algonquians' futile seige at a Mohawk "castle," Gandawague, and the final battle at Kinaquariones where the Mohawks defeated the Algonquian nations. He mentions the Dutch ignorance of the battle and explains that current information exists because the events were recorded by contemporaries, Major Gookin and Father Pierron.

**1070.** Van Epps, Percy M. "The Place Names of Glenville, New York." *New York State Historical Association Quarterly Journal,* vol. 9, no. 3 (July 1928): 272–278.

Van Epps outlines place names in Glenville, a few of which are of Indian origin, specifying rivers, streams, hills, and roads, including the Mohawk Turnpike.

**1071.** Vaux, Roberts." "Anniversary Discourse." *Historical Society of Pennsylvania Memoirs*, vol. 2 (Philadelphia, 1827): 9–55.

Vaux contrasts the concern for the Indians' welfare shown after 1685 by the religious Society of Friends with the wrongs inflicted on the Indians by another class of people who settled in Pennsylvania. He notes that William Penn and some of his contemporaries and successors agreed with the Society and tried to be just to the Indians. Vaux believes the influx of settlers into Pennsylvania whose habits and principles were alien to those of the first immigrants caused serious differences with the Indians by 1727. The author describes the Moravians' and the Friends' pursuit of justice for the Indians between 1741 and 1757 despite proprietary injustices inflicted on the Indians.

**1072.** Vaux, Roberts. "A Memoir on the Locality of the Great Treaty Between William Penn and the Indian Nations in 1682." *Historical Society of Pennsylvania Memoirs*, vol. 1, part 1 (Philadelphia, 1826): 79–98.

Vaux discusses the question of the site where the first treaty was signed between William Penn and the Indians in 1682. He provides several letters and other proofs to confirm the traditional belief that Shackamaxon was the place.

**1073.** Vaux, Roberts; Fisher, J. Francis; and Tyson, Job R. [Report of the Committee on Indian Portraits] *Historical Society of Pennsylvania Memoirs*, vol. 3, part 2 (Philadelphia, 1836): 209–212.

The report describes two portraits of Indian chiefs, painted in 1737, that were presented to the Society and mentions that both Lapawinsa and Tishcohan signed the 1737 treaty known as the Walking Purchase.

**1074.** Vermeule, Cornelius C. "Early New Jersey Place-Names." *New Jersey Historical Society Proceedings*, n.s., vol. 11, no. 2 (April 1926): 151–160.

Vermeule discusses the Dutch, Indian, Dutch-Indian, English and English-Indian origins of the names of places in New Jersey, giving the dates when the places were named to show how these names reflect New Jersey history. An example of a Dutch-Indian compound word is "sandhocken." The Dutch "sand" and the Indian "hocken," or "hawken," combine to mean sandy, cultivated land. An English-Indian combination is "Pensauken" which links William Penn's surname with the Indian "hawken" to mean Penn's cultivated land.

**1075.** Vermeule, Cornelius C. "Raritan Valley, Its Discovery and Settlement." *New Jersey Historical Society Proceedings*, n.s., vol. 13, no. 3 (July 1928): 282–291.

Vermeule explains how the land in the Raritan Valley passed from the

1075 *(continued)*
Indians to the Dutch, English, and Scotch during the seventeenth
century.

1076. Vermeule, Cornelius C. "Some Early New Jersey Place-Names." *New
Jersey Historical Society Proceedings,* n.s., vol. 10, no. 3 (July 1925): 241–256.
Vermeule discusses the "Netherlandish" influence on the naming of
places and subtribes in New Jersey and New York. He indicates that
the Indians not only used the Dutch names for places, but the subtribes also named themselves with the Dutch words for the places they
frequented. He mentions that the whites rarely named places for an
Indian tribe, but rather these settlers named the subtribe for the
Indian place name of their habitat. He explains that this name is not
always Indian nor is it always applied to the same subtribe because of
the Indians' continuous mobility.

1077. Vetromile, Eugene. "The Abnaki Indians." *Maine Historical Society Collections,* ser. 1, vol. 6 (Portland, 1859): 203–227.
Vetromile gives the location of five of the Abenaki villages, a detailed
translation of the word, "Abenaki," and the number of nations or
tribes in the East included under the title "Abenaki." He explains how
their name and history indicate that the Abenakis are an ancient
original people who never acknowledged any ancestral tribe and
states that their manners and language support this theory. A short
history of the Abenaki method of writing and some sentences in the
Micmac (an Abenaki tribe) language are provided.

1078. Vetromile, Eugene. "Acadia and Its Aborigines." *Maine Historical Society
Collections,* ser. 1, vol. 7 (Portland, 1876): 337–349.
Vetromile discusses the public and domestic life of the Etchimins,
Micmacs, and Abenakis of Acadia as well as their astronomy and
division of time. He lists their names for the four seasons, thirteen
moons, nine parts of the month, the days of the week, and the parts of
day and night.

1079. Vincent, P. "History of the Pequot War." *Massachusetts Historical Society
Collections,* ser. 3, vol. 6 (Boston, 1837): 29–43.
Vincent, about whom no information is known, originally published
this in 1638. He describes the Pequot War between the Pequots and
the English in which approximately seven hundred Indians were
killed or taken prisoner. He also gives an account of the present state
of affairs in that area.

1080. "Virginia's Deplored Condition." *Massachusetts Historical Society Collections,* ser. 4, vol. 9 (Boston, 1871): 162–187.
The Susquehannock war against Virginia and Maryland is described
as well as Nathaniel Bacon's role in illegally leading discontented
people against the Pamunkey Indians despite the governor's orders to
stop. The narrative tells that the Indians reacted to Bacon's Rebellion

by murdering the English and pillaging their homes. This is followed by, "The Opinion of the Councl of Virginia Concerning Mr. Bacon's Proceedings," "Copy of Gloucester County's Petition," "The Governor's Answer to the Petition," and "Copy of Mr. Bacon's Declaration in the Name of the People, July 30, 1676."

1081. "Visit Paid by Four Indian Sachems to England."*New Jersey Historical Society Proceedings*, ser. 1, vol. 9, no. 1 (1860): 16–19.

These pages describe the visit to England by four Indian sachems and Colonel Schuyler in 1710 and their public audience with the Queen on April 19, 1710. Included is the speech delivered to the Queen by one of the four in which he claims that it is urgent for Britain to reduce Canada, that the French are courting the Indians, and that the Indians desire English instructors. Also printed is their speech to the Duke of Ormond in which they implore him to assist them in conquering the French.

1082. Vivian, James F, and Vivian, Jean H. "Congressional Indian Policy During the War for Independence: The Northern Department." *Maryland Historical Magazine*, vol. 63, no. 3 (September 1968): 241–274.

The Vivians compare Congress's resolve to form alliances with Indian tribes should the British attempt to enlist Indian services with the government's original policy of keeping the Six Nations neutral. The authors explain how Congress established the Northern, Middle, and Southern Departments of Indian Affairs in July, 1775 and how they conducted trade. Within a year of the initial declaration to cultivate Indian neutrality, Congress reversed itself and allowed active recruitment of Indians in 1776. The Vivians describe the debate over whether Congress or the states should exercise jurisdiction over the various tribes. In 1778, Congress had to cope with the problems of Indian hostility, the resumption of Indian trade which competed with British goods, the recruiting of Indians, and the defense of American frontier settlements. The Vivians discuss the formulation of plans by the Americans to destroy Indian towns and food, the Sullivan Expedition of 1779, and Indian raids along the frontier during 1781. Footnotes, photographs of Gates and Tilghman, and two maps are provided.

1083. Volwiler, A. T. "George Croghan and the Westward Movement, 1741–1782." *Pennsylvania Magazine of History and Biography*, vol. 46, no. 4 (1922): 273–311.

Volwiler describes the Indian fur trade and the role played by Croghan until 1754 in exploiting and developing the "vast wilderness" beyond the frontier. The author discusses Pennsylvania traders and immigrants who aggressively pushed westward from 1730 to 1775, the routes they traveled, the chief Indian tribes with whom the Pennsylvanians traded, and which English goods they traded for furs. Volwiler analyzes Croghan's Indian trade operations, probably the

**1083** *(continued)*

largest in all of Pennsylvania, his preeminence, the friendship the Indians felt for him, his bankruptcy, and finally his activities after 1754 as an Indian agent, land speculator, and western colonizer. The author focuses on French aggression in the Ohio country from 1749 to 1754 and efforts made after 1763 to secure restitution. Extensive footnotes are provided.

**1084.** Volwiler, A. T. "George Croghan and the Westward Movement, 1741–1782." *Pennsylvania Magazine of History and Biography,* vol. 47, no. 1 (1923): 28–57.

This chapter discusses Croghan's work in negotiating with the Ohio Indians and his role after 1747 in convincing colonial officials in Philadelphia of the need for an aggressive Indian policy in the "Far West," or Ohio and toward the Mississippi. He tells how Croghan checked the westward movement of settlers and temporarily diminished the danger of Indian hostilities. The competition between colonial traders as well as the French-English struggles for the Ohio Valley are portrayed. Volwilder argues that the English were losing the Indians' support principally because they did not erect forts and prepare for defense. Extensive footnotes are provided.

**1085.** Volwiler, A. T. "George Croghan and the Westward Movement, 1741–1782." *Pennsylvania Magazine of History and Biography,* vol. 47, no. 2 (1923): 115–142. Illustrated.

Volwiler discusses the ways in which Croghan assisted Major George Washington in securing supplies and transporting them through the "wilderness" and in maintaining favorable relations with the Indians. He reviews the ritual of giving presents to obtain the Indians' allegiance and to maintain their refugees in Pennsylvania. He discusses Croghan's assistance to Braddock's expedition by determining which roads he should use and by furnishing him with approximately one hundred Indians. The author mentions the July 9, 1755 battle in which Braddock was killed. Volwiler describes the subsequent Indian warfare in Pennsylvania, reviews the efforts of the colonial government to defend the frontiers, and tells that Croghan was commissioned as a captain but resigned after three months. Volwiler considers the attacks on Croghan's character and the reasons why colonial and imperial officers mistrusted him. A map illustrating Croghan's activities as an Indian trader and agent is included as well as footnotes.

**1086.** Voorhees, Ocar M., ed. "A New Jersey Woman's Captivity Among Indians, May 1791 to August 1793." *New Jersey Historical Society Proceedings,* n.s., vol. 13, no. 2 (April 1928): 152–165.

These pages contain the captivity narrative of Mary Kinnan, formerly of Basking Ridge, New Jersey, plus a preliminary statement by Voorhees about the woman's family and other information regarding the way in which the narrative came to be published. Kinnan, who was born in 1763, was captured by Indians and subsequently released.

The title of the fifteen-page pamphlet is, "A True Narrative of the Sufferings of Mary Kinnan who was Taken Prisoner by the Shawnee Indians on the thirteenth Day of May, 1791, and Remained with Them till the Sixteenth of August, 1794."

**1087.** Wadsworth, Benjamin. "Wadsworth's Journal." *Massachusetts Historical Society Collections,* ser. 4, vol. 1 (Boston, 1852): 102–110.

Written from August 6 to 31, 1694, Reverend Wadsworth's journal describes the conference in which the commissioners of Massachusetts met with representatives of the Five Nations of Indians at Albany.

**1088.** Wahatomacho (Delaware). [Speech] *New York Historical Society Collections For The Year 1871, Lee Papers,* vol. 1 (New York, 1872): 137–139.

Dated September 29, 1774, this speech at Fort Dunmore, formerly Fort Pitt, by Wahatomacho, a Delaware, was written by Charles Lee and given to the Earl of Dunmore. The chief discusses the murder of his people by whites who claim not to be at war with the Indians. He says that he wants peace, but if the whites do not stop killing Indians he will not be afraid to go to war. He says that if whites want more land they should pay for it, not take it. He also states that the Delaware women and children are safe with the Six Nations.

**1089.** Wainwright, Nicholas B. "George Croghan and the Indian Uprising of 1747." *Pennsylvania History,* vol. 21, no. 1 (January 1954): 21–31. Illustrated.

Wainwright discusses the French and English competition for control of the Indian trade, Croghan's trading activity in the Ohio country, and his work in keeping the Indians friendly toward the English while alienating them from the French. The author describes the origins of the Indian conspiracy which swept the West in 1747 and was aimed at destroying French posts. He speculates about Croghan's exact role in alienating the Indians from the French and in promoting their revolt. Wainwright argues that Croghan was well acquainted with the Indian conspiracy before the French knew about it. There is a map of the middle British colonies in 1755 as well as a copy of a letter from the Indians to Governor Thomas in 1747.

**1090.** Wainwright, Nicholas B. "Governor William Denny in Pennsylvania." *Pennsylvania Magazine of History and Biography,* vol. 81, no. 2 (April 1957): 170–198.

Wainwright discusses Indian affairs in Pennsylvania during the governorship of William Denny from 1756 to 1759. The author describes the Quakers' activities and their influence with Indians in

1090 *(continued)*
making treaties. He analyzes Governor Denny's conduct of Indian affairs and his attitude toward these people, the Indians' accusation of land fraud by the Pennsylvania proprietors, and the treatment of Indians by Pennsylvania.

1091. Wainwright, Nicholas B. "An Indian Trade Failure: The Story of the Hockley, Trent, and Croghan Company, 1748–1752." *Pennsylvania Magazine of History and Biography*, vol. 72, no. 4 (October 1948): 343–375. Illustrated.
Wainwright supplies brief biographies of the three men who formed the partnership and discusses Croghan's barter with the Indians for skins and his major role in alienating the Ohio Indians from the French. The author mentions how Trent controlled the shipment of skins to Hockley in Philadelphia who then dispatched the goods to Croghan on the Ohio River. Wainwright describes colonial rivalry in Virginia, the loss of prestige and leadership by Pennsylvania in the Ohio country, and the reasons for the failure of the Hockley, Trent, and Croghan Company by 1752.

1092. Waldo, Samuel. "Samuel Waldo's Interview with the Indians." *Massachusetts Historical Society Collections*, vol. 80 (Boston, 1972): 388–391.
Writing from November 2-11, 1735, Waldo tells of meeting with the Indians to inform them of his intent to settle on lands sold to him by Madokawando, their former sachem. After a Penobscot named Loren tells the English to desist from going farther into the country, Waldo threatens the Indians saying they had better not hinder the settlement. He explains to the Indians the advantages they would derive from the grist mill England would construct on a river.

1093. Waldron, Richard. "Indian Attack on Cocheco." *Massachusetts Historical Society Collections*, ser. 3, no. 1 (Boston, 1825): 87–88.
Writing on June 28, 1689, Waldron tells of an Indian attack on Cocheco.

1094. Walker, Edwin Robert. "The Lenni Lenape or Delaware Indians." *New Jersey Historical Society Proceedings*, n.s., vol. 2, no. 4 (1917): 193–218.
Walker discusses the names Delaware, Lenni Lenape, and Shejachbi, the Indian name for New Jersey. He also describes the Lenape sub-tribes, their origins, culture, political organization, religious beliefs, games, and gambling as well as the settlers' selling liquor to the Indians and conflicts between settlers and Indians. He briefly reviews title to lands in New Jersey and the contents of an Indian deed, dated November 11, 1703, granted by a few Indian sachems to the proprietors of West Jersey. He tells of the Brotherton Reservation organized around 1758 and the final dissolution of all Indian claims in New Jersey by 1832.

1095. Walker, Timothy. "Diaries of Reverend Timothy Walker." *New Hampshire Historical Society Collections*, vol. 9 (Concord, 1889): 123–191.

Written between 1746 and 1780, the diary entries report Indian raids, captures, and killings. They also describe life in New Hampshire on the Indian frontier during the French-English rivalry over the North American continent. There are explanatory notes.

**1096.** Wallace, Anthony F. C. "Origins of Iroquois Neutrality: The Grand Settlement of 1701." *Pennsylvania History,* vol. 24, no. 3 (July 1957): 223–235.

Wallace claims that the two treaties the Iroquois made in 1701 in Albany and in Montreal inaugurated a new era of Iroquois policy which survived in principle until 1795. This policy included peace toward the "far" Indians, political manipulation of nearby tribes, and armed neutrality between the contending Europeans, the English and the French. Wallace reviews the fifty-two-year period of incessant warfare which led to the 1701 settlement in which the Iroquois found a better system by playing off the French and British against each other, each nation protecting the Iroquois from any intrusion by the other.

**1097.** Wallace, Paul A. W. "Conrad Weiser and New York Contacts." *New York History,* vol. 28, no. 2 (April 1947): 170–179. Illustrated.

Wallace discusses Conrad Weiser's work in New York during the mid-1730s to 1750 in maintaining Iroquois allegiance to the English interest. Wallace describes as crucial the Iroquois role in the struggle between the two European rivals in America. He tells of France's efforts to wrest the Iroquois from the English colonies and how New York and Pennsylvania vied for the control of the Iroquois around 1750 until Weiser yielded to William Johnson of New York in 1755. There are maps of the Onondaga trail and of Indian country in 1755.

**1098.** Wallace, Paul A. W. "Conrad Weiser and the Delawares." *Pennsylvania History,* vol. 4, no. 3 (July 1937): 139–152.

Wallace discusses Weiser's relations with the Lenni Lenapes who were also known as the Delaware Indians. He first assesses Weiser's character and says that his work in holding together the Six Nations' alliance gave the English a decisive advantage over the French in the struggle for North America. Wallace argues that Weiser's policy emanated from a clear understanding of the situation facing the colonies and that he acted with the best intentions. The author suggests that Weiser's policy of acknowledging the suzerainty of the Six Nations over the Delawares and strengthening the authority of the Onondaga Council postponed a Delaware war and almost prevented it. Wallace states that Weiser's policy did not drive the Delawares to the French because the Indians were alienated before he appeared on the scene. Rather, Weiser tried to keep the Delawares in fear of the Six Nations while the French tried to undermine his policy. Wallace tells briefly of the Easton Peace Conference of 1758 during which Weiser's Indian policy was vindicated and the "revolution" of Teedyuscung, a Delaware, against the Six Nations collapsed.

1099. Wallace, Paul A. W. "Cooper's Indians." In *James Fenimore Cooper: A Re-appraisal. New York History*, vol. 35 (Cooperstown, New York, 1954): 423–440.

Wallace claims that the basic source of Cooper's theory about Indians was John Heckewelder's 1819 *Account of the History, Manners, and Customs of the Indian Nations Who Once Inhabited Pennsylvania and the Neighboring States.* This theory was that the woods of America were divided between Indians of two sorts, the noble savage and the savage fiend. He explains his belief that Cooper misunderstood the Iroquois who were for many years the chief Indian allies of the English colonies but are viewed as tools of the French. He briefly looks at Cooper's basic story line "The Mingoes and the Delawares are born enemies" through the five *Leatherstocking Tales.* Wallace suggests that the lack of authenticity in Cooper's Indians does not detract from the literary achievement. He reviews historical records for the causes of the "hullabaloo" about the Delawares being "women" and also examines the political relationship between the Six Nations and the Delawares. Footnotes are included.

1100. Wallace, Paul A. W. "The Covenant of Blood." *Pennsylvania History*, vol. 20, no. 3 (July 1953): 284–286. Illustrated.

Wallace tells the traditional story of the agreement made in 1760 between Colonel Benjamin Chambers and an Indian friend which stipulated that as long as heirs remained to either of them, a grove of trees at Chambersburg would serve as a burial place for whites and Indians alike. There is a photograph of the burial site and a painting of Chambers.

1101. Wallace, Paul A. W. "The Five Nations of New York and Pennsylvania." *New York Historical Society Quarterly Bulletin*, vol. 37, no. 3 (July 1953): 228–250. Illustrated.

Wallace searches for the reasons why we do not apply to the Iroquois the same criteria we apply to others whom we judge not by their worst but by their best human qualities. He argues that the answer lies in the support given by several Iroquois tribes to the British during the American Revolution viewed as disloyalty by some Americans, and to our massive ignorance of the history of the Six Nations. He considers the legend of the founding of the Five Nations by Deganawidah and Hiawatha, Iroquois political wisdom, and their wars of expansion. He discusses the settlement of the Susquehanna Valley with "displaced persons" who filled the vacuum after the dispersion of the Susquehannocks and who became "props to the Longhouse." These displaced persons were the Conoys, Tuscaroras, Nanticokes, and Delawares. Wallace analyzes the crushing of the Iroquois power in the Susquehanna Valley. There are photographs of the Hiawatha Belt and of the refugee peoples who became "props," as well as a map of the Five Nations country.

1102. Wallace, Paul A. W. "Historic Indian Paths of Pennsylvania." *Pennsylvania Magazine of History and Biography,* vol. 76, no. 4 (1952): 411–439. Illustrated.

Wallace evaluates Indians as road engineers and explains the principles of Indian trail location which value the dry, level, and direct pathways. He describes the complexity of the system and its adaptability to the changing seasons and varying conditions of travel. He discusses painted trees, the "billboards" of American Indians, the sizes of trails, and the problems involved in mapping Indian paths. There is a schedule of sixteen important Indian paths divided into five main paths from the Delaware to the Susquehanna, five main paths to the Allegheny River, and six main warrior paths. There is a map of the historic Indian paths of Pennsylvania limited to the postcontact period.

1103. Wallace, Paul A. W. "The John Heckewelder Papers." *Pennsylvania History,* vol. 27, no. 3 (July 1960): 249–262. Illustrated.

Wallace discusses the body of writings by the Moravian missionary John Heckewelder, "one of the best sources available for the study of Indians as they were one hundred and fifty or two hundred years ago." Wallace first considers Heckewelder's opportunities to observe Indians under all conditions, beginning with his first mission work in 1762, at the age of nineteen, until the end of the eighteenth century. The letters, mission diaries, and travel journals that record his experience among the Indians, particularly the Delawares and the Mohicans, are reviewed as well as the kinds of information about Indians Heckewelder provides. There is a portrait of Heckewelder.

1104. Wallace, Paul A. W. "The Return of Hiawatha." *New York History,* vol. 29, no. 4 (October 1948): 385–403.

Wallace examines the Five Nations, particularly their power and prestige which lasted until the end of the eighteenth century, their myths, and their religion. He tries to understand the success of their Confederacy which gave the Five Nations such an ascendancy over the surrounding peoples. He speaks of Hiawatha and Deganawidah and retells the legend of the way in which their Constitution was formulated. Wallace explains that there is no connection between Longfellow's Hiawatha and the Hiawatha who founded the League. The author reviews the dates of the founding of the Five Nations' Confederacy and concludes by recommending serious study of both the Hiawatha legend and Deganawidah's Constitution as a good introduction to the problem of collective security.

1105. "Attack of the Indians at Walpole in 1755." *New Hampshire Historical Society Collections,* vol. 2 (Concord, 1827): 49–58.

This discussion of the murders of Twitchell and Flint in 1755, the first incident which disturbed the security of whites in Walpole, de-

1105 *(continued)*
scribes how John Kilburn and several others repelled hundreds of Indians.

1106. Wampatuck. [Indian Deed of Boston] *Massachusetts Historical Society Proceedings*, ser. 1, vol. 17 (1879–1880): 51–55.
This is the text of the March 19, 1684 quitclaim deed for the peninsula of Boston which was given by Wampatuck and other Indians in exchange for a "valuable summe of money."

1107. "An Old Fathom of Wampum." *Pennsylvania Magazine of History and Biography*, vol. 39, no. 2 (1915): 231–232.
This is a discussion of a string of wampum given to Count Zinzendorf on August 3, 1742 by five Iroquois Indians to ratify a covenant of friendship between the Moravians and the Indians. The wampum was subsequently handed over to Bishop Spangenberg when the Count returned to Europe. The text of Spangenberg's March 10, 1743 receipt of this wampum is also given.

1108. Wampus, John. "John Wampus, Nipmunk Indian, and Dr. Sutton." *Vermont Quarterly*, n.s., vol. 21, no. 3 (July 1953): 260.
This is a brief note about John Wampus, a Nipmuck, from whom Sutton, Massachusetts, proprietors bought their township. There is an explanation that John Wampus suggested the name of Sutton because a Dr. Sutton had treated him in a health emergency on a return voyage to New England prior to 1704.

1109. Warner, Seth. "Deposition by Seth Warner." *Vermont Historical Society Proceedings*, n.s., vol. 11, no. 2 (June 1943): 103–104.
Possibly written 1839. Warner retells a conversation he had in 1817 with Sir John Johnson in which the latter explains how Captain John Warner had captured him during the Revolutionary War and then released him only because he promised not to allow his Indians to go on that tract of land or to hurt any inhabitants on that side of Lake Champlain.

1110. [Warrant of Survey] *New York Historical Society Collections for the Year 1935, Cadwallader Colden Papers*, vol. 9 (New York, 1937): 94–95.
This is the text of a warrant to survey a tract of land purchased by a group of people from Indian proprietors. The boundaries of the tract of about 25,000 acres are specified.

1111. [Warrants of Survey] *New York Historical Society Collections for the Year 1935, Cadwallader Colden Papers*, vol. 9 (New York, 1937): 113–116.
This is the text of two warrants to survey three tracts of land purchased by men from the Indian proprietors. Two of the tracts involve about 3,000 acres, and one involves 950 acres.

1112. Waterston, R. C. "Letter About Indians of California." *Massachusetts Historical Society Proceedings*, ser. 1, vol. 11 (1869–1870): 347–350.

Writing on August 29, 1870, Waterston discusses the domain of the missions extending from San Diego to San Francisco and the Indians who labored for the missions. He reviews the extent of the disappearance of the Indians in and around San Francisco, San Jose, Santa Clara, etc. He briefly tells of the visit to Mono and Pomo in which he saw the preparation of acorns for food.

1113. Watson, John F. "The Indian Treaty for the Lands Now the Site of Philadelphia and the Adjacent Country." *Historical Society of Pennsylvania Memoirs*, vol. 3, part 2 (Philadelphia, 1836): 129–140.

Watson discusses records which show that the actual treaty for the lands of present-day Philadelphia and the adjacent country was made in 1685 by Thomas Holme in the absence of William Penn. The texts are given for the treaty, dated July 1685, and for the agreement by Holme regarding surveying the tract, dated July, 1685.

1114. Watts, John. "Letter Books of John Watts, Merchant and Councillor of New York, January 1, 1762–December 22, 1765." *New York Historical Society Collections for the Year 1928, Publication Fund Series* vol. 61 (New York, 1929).

In brief paragraphs from letters, Watts discusses the capture of British forts, tells of skirmishes and hostilities between Indians and whites, cites the British officers killed and the settlers who were murdered, explains that British force was insufficient for the Indian wars, and describes the roles of the French to Pontiac.

1115. Wayne, Anthony. "Letters of Generals Wayne and O'Hara." *Pennsylvania Magazine of History and Biography*, vol. 14, no. 3 (1890): 327–328.

Written on July 4, 1794, Wayne's letter to O'Hara reports an attack by 1,000 to 1,500 warriors on an escort and on the Fort Recovery post. He cites the number of officers and soldiers killed or wounded during action. Wayne asks O'Hara for reinforcements. Colonel James O'Hara, in a letter dated July 5, 1794, reports on troops who were assaulted by Indians near Fort Recovery and tells how ten scalps were taken by soldiers.

1116. Wayne, Anthony. "Wayne's Western Campaign. The Wayne-Knox Correspondence, 1793–1794." *Pennsylvania Magazine of History and Biography*, vol. 78, no. 3 (July 1954): 298–341.

Major General Anthony Wayne was chosen in 1793 to quell the Indian resistance to American settlement in the Ohio Country after the failures of Harmar and St. Clair. These letters, dated from September 17, 1793 to April 3, 1794, are between Wayne and Henry Knox, Secretary of War. This correspondence gives a firsthand, blow-by-blow account of the Wayne Expedition from 1793 to 1794 from the moment Wayne left his camp until he reported victory at the Maumee

1116 *(continued)*

Rapids. He describes the plans, counterplans, hardships, and episodes of the campaign. The letters reveal the international implications of the British role in inspiring the Indians to oppose immigration from the eastern states and the Spanish role in influencing the Americans. Footnotes. [*Continued* in *Pennsylvania Magazine of History and Biography*, vol. 78, no. 4 (October 1954): 424–455. The letters are dated from May 7, 1794 to August 28, 1794.]

1117. Wehanownowit, *et al.* "Indian Deeds to Wheelwright and Others, 1638." *New Hampshire Historical Society Collections*, vol. 1 (Concord, 1824): 147–149.

The texts of three deeds are given. In the first, dated April 3, 1638, Wehanownowit deeds land to Wheelwright and others in exchange for presents. His mark is reproduced. In the second deed, dated April 3, 1638, Wehanownowit's mark as well as his son's is reproduced. The third deed is by Watchanowet and grants land on April 10, 1639. His mark is reproduced.

1118. Weiser, Conrad. "Notes on the Iroquois and Delaware Indians. Communications from Conrad Weiser to Christopher Sauer, Which Appeared in the Years 1746–1749 in his Newspaper Printed at Germantown, entitled 'The High German Pennsylvania Historical Writer, or a Collection of Important Events from the Kingdom of Nature and the Church.' " Compiled by Abraham H. Cassell. *Pennsylvania Magazine of History and Biography*, vol. 1, no. 2 (1877): 163–167.

Writing in December, 1746, Weiser discusses the religious beliefs of the Iroquois Indians and their neighbors based on his experiences among them from 1714 to 1746. He cites four instances in which he witnessed Indians "invoke God, trust in God, thank and honor God . . ." He concludes that although Indians have a religion, they still need true conversion.

1119. Weiser, Conrad. "Notes on the Iroquois and Delaware Indians. Communications from Conrad Weiser to Christopher Sauer, 1746–1749." Compiled by Abraham H. Cassell. *Pennsylvania Magazine of History and Biography*, vol. 1, no. 3 (1877): 319–323.

Weiser observes that Indians have no "outward forms" of religion, judging by Christian standards, but that they do, on some occasions, confess and worship "the Creator of all Things." He describes their sorcerers and their superstitions, citing incidents that illustrate the Indians' faith in "spirits in everything." He examines the great care the Iroquois take in dealing with one another at a political level as well as Iroquois justice, intemperance, and hospitality. Weiser estimates the number of warriors and the location of each Iroquois nation.

1120. Weiser, Conrad. "Notes on the Iroquois and Delaware Indians. Communications from Conrad Weiser to Christopher Sauer, 1746–1749." Compiled by Abraham H. Cassell. *Pennsylvania Magazine of History and Biography,* vol. 2, no. 4 (1878): 407–410.

Weiser lists eleven Iroquois allies, estimating that their warriors total 9,300. He briefly comments on the Indian art of war and on other manners and customs, particularly those pertaining to burials. He concludes that Indians and Christians are not unlike in their "delight" in going to war.

1121. Weitenkampf, Frank. "How Indians Were Pictured in Earlier Days." *New York Historical Society Quarterly Bulletin,* vol. 33, no. 4 (October 1949): 213–221. Illustrated.

Weitenkampf focuses on the evolution of European and American artists' portrayals of Indian racial traits in the faces of their models during three and a half centuries, 1500–1850. Changes advanced from the purely fictitious through the dubious to the realistic. He discusses such artists as John White, 1585–1586, who put European traits into the faces of Indians and placed them in conventional artistic poses. He describes the works done in the nineteenth century when Indians were more realistically portrayed and tells of those artists who began to go West to see Indians at home, away from formalities or poses caused by the official meetings with white people. Six illustrations show how Indians were pictured, circa 1505 to 1844.

1122. Welles, Thomas, Winthrop, J., and Talcott, J. [Letter to John Endicott] *Massachusetts Historical Society Collections,* ser. 5, vol. 8 (Boston, 1882): 54–55.

Writing on March 27, 1659, the three men tell the governor of Massachusetts about an Indian killed by the Narragansetts at Brewster's farm. They also describe the killing of friendly Indians by some Pocumtuck Indians.

1123. Wells, Lester Grosvenor. "Stockbridge Indians in New York State." *New York History,* vol. 27, no. 4 (October 1946): 476–491.

Wells discusses the tribal history of the Stockbridge Indians in relation to three general geographical sections: western Massachusetts, central New York, and Wisconsin. He reviews their history in New York State from 1734 until they left, tells of their move from Massachusetts to New York, and the departure of the Stockbridge Indians from New York to the West during the first quarter of the nineteenth century. He describes the missionary work, particularly by Reverend Samuel Occum, a Mohegan, among them.

1124. Weninock. "Worth While Speech of an Indian Chief." *New Jersey Historical Society Proceedings,* n.s., vol. 13, no. 4 (October 1928): 477–479.

The text of a speech by Chief Weninock made in approximately 1915 was given as testimony at a treaty conference to allow Indians to fish unmolested in their accustomed fishing places in the state of Washington.

1125. Wentworth, John. "Instructions of Governor John Wentworth to Theodore Atkinson, Commissioner to Canada, in 1724." *New Hampshire Historical Society Collections,* vol. 6 (Concord, 1851): 211.

Wentworth instructs Atkinson, along with other commissioners, to inform the Canadian governor that his assisting enemy Indians against the English must cease as it is a breach of the Treaty of Utrecht and contrary to the alliance between the kings of France and Britain. Wentworth also instructs Atkinson to insist that Canada release British subjects captured by Indians who are now prisoners of Canada. Atkinson is not permitted to make peace with the Indians in Canada.

1126. Weslager, C. A. "Indian Stone Piles in Maryland." *Maryland Historical Magazine,* vol. 42, no. 1 (March 1947): 46–49.

Weslager discusses the distribution of stone heaps in the West, describing their general use to serve as common shrines, protection for fields, household goods, dedications to deities, etc. He tells of a reference to similar stone piles found in Maryland and of depositions supplied by Marye which locate the sites of three stone heaps.

1127. Weslager, C. A. "The Nanticoke Indians in Early Pennsylvania." *Pennsylvania Magazine of History and Biography,* vol. 67, no. 1 (October 1943): 345–355.

Weslager discusses the Nanticokes from other areas who moved into the Susquehanna Valley, Pennsylvania, a haven for Indians during the colonial period. He explains why the land originally inhabited by Susquehannocks, beginning in 1698, became a temporary home for many expatriated tribes, including the Nanticokes, Choptanks, Conoys, and other Eastern Shore Indians, all of whom became known as Nanticokes. He tells of Shawnee and Conoy migrations to the Susquehanna Valley at the end of the seventeenth century and comments on the Nanticokes under Iroquois influence prior to their appearance in Pennsylvania and in New York. He reviews the way that "Nanticokes" became a generic term for other tribal groups. Weslager examines historical references to the Nanticokes and traces their descendants to the Iroquois in Canada and to a community in Delaware.

1128. West, Margery. "Deposition of Margery West Concerning Her Captivity by the Indians." *New York Historical Society Collections For The Year 1921, Cadwallader Colden Papers,* vol. 5 (New York, 1923): 94–97.

Writing on September 25, 1756, West tells of her capture on February 26th by eleven Indians, among them Fishkill, Delaware, and Hackensack Indians. She reviews her journey from Minisink to Athens, Pennsylvania, where she saw a number of Indians she knew. She mentions that she was moved to an area where corn was being planted and where she was made a mother-replacement in a Mingoe family. She describes Indians with smallpox, others with white scalps, and some with no provisions. West reveals that some Indians wanted peace with the English while others wanted to fight. She suspects that the Indians got no reward for the scalps from the French. She explains how she was freed with the help of a young Indian man, one of those who called her "mother."

1129. "An Indian Raid in West Milford." *New Jersey History*, vol. 85, no. 2 (Summer 1967): 136–137.

This is a poem that recounts the essentials of "the last Indian raid in the West Milford area," probably in the late 1700's, as tape-recorded in about 1950 by members of the West Milford Township Historical Society.

1130. Westervelt, Francis A. "The Final Century of the Wampum Industry in Bergen County, New Jersey." *New Jersey Historical Society Proceedings*, n.s., vol. 10, no. 3 (July 1925): 283–290.

This article reviews the history of the Bergen County factory which manufactured wampum, a medium of exchange used among the Indian tribes in the period from before the Revolutionary War until after 1830 when the use of wampum declined. Westervelt discusses John Campbell and four generations of his family who manufactured wampum as well as the methods they used to make it, procuring hard shell clams and conch shells. The author also describes hair pipes and other ornaments worn by Indians.

1131. Wharton, Thomas. "Selections from the Letter-Books of Thomas Wharton, of Philadelphia, 1773–1783." *Pennsylvania Magazine of History and Biography*, vol. 33, no. 4 (1909): 432–453.

In selections written from June 10, 1774 to January 18, 1775, Wharton discusses Cresap and Baker's murder of some Shawnee Indians in the Ohio country and the angry reaction by other Indians. He describes the troubles between the Indians and the Virginians and also discusses the treaties with the Indians at Fort Pitt.

1132. Wheeler, George. "Richard Penn's Manor of Andolhea." *Pennsylvania Magazine of History and Biography*, vol. 58, no. 3 (1934): 193–212. Illustrated.

Wheeler discusses the location of Andolhea, tells of the purchases of land from the Indians, and describes the hostilities in 1755 and 1763 between the Indians and the settlers in the vicinity of the Andolhea manor. There is information about a particular Indian path that provided access from northwest Pennsylvania and the Greak Lakes to the settled portions of the state, now a part of the state highway system. Included is a map of the area of Penn's Manor.

1133. Wheeler, Thomas. "Wheeler's Narrative of an Expedition into the Nipmunk Country." *New Hampshire Historical Society Collections*, vol. 2 (Concord, 1827): 2–23.

Captain Wheeler describes an expedition into Nipmuck country and

1133 *(continued)*
to Quabaug, alias Brookfield, in 1675 for the purpose of negotiating peace with the sachems. The narrative, dated July 28 to August 21, 1675, tells of the march to meet with the sachems, the attacks of the Indians, the wounding and loss of lives in his expedition, and his return to Concord.

1134. Wheelock, Eleazer. [Letter to Mr. Phillips] *New Hampshire Historical Society Collections,* vol. 9 (Concord, 1889): 69–71.
Writing on January 1, 1766, Wheelock thanks Phillips for his generous donation to the Moor's Indian Charity School. He gives an account of the plan for the English missionaries to learn Indian languages and for the Indian boys to learn to be schoolmasters. Wheelock states it was relatively inexpensive to run the school for 127 Indian children.

1135. Wheelock, Eleazer. [Letter to the Provincial Congress at Exeter] *New Hampshire Historical Society Collections,* vol. 2 (Concord, 1827): 141–143.
Writing on June 28, 1775, Wheelock comments that Canadian tribes are favorably disposed toward the colonists and their cause and suggests that frontier towns be supplied with arms and ammunition to defend themselves from hostile Indians and Canadians. He explains why no Indians accepted presents from Colonel Johnson who was trying to turn the Indians against the colonists. Wheelock describes the Mohawks and Oneidas as "firm for the colonies."

1136. White, Andrew. "Extracts from Different Letters of Missionaries, From the Year 1635. to the Year 1677." In *Narrative of a Voyage to Maryland.* ed. Reverend Edwin A. Dalrymple. *Maryland Historical Society, Fund Publication,* no. 7 (Baltimore, 1874): 62–89.
Missionaries describe conversion activities among the Potopaco, Anacostan, and Patuxent Indians between 1639 and 1642 and comment on Indian "kings" and their powers as leaders. Details are given of the conversion of Tayac, the Piscataway word for emperor, by Father Andrew White after curing the Indian from a disease. Susquehanna hostilities are also described.

1137. Whiting, William. [Letter to Fitz-John Winthrop] *Massachusetts Historical Society Collections,* ser. 6, vol. 3 (Boston, 1889): 259–261.
On August 21, 1704, Whiting reports on Colonel Schuyler's meeting with three Indians who belonged to the French army, and he explains why they wanted to meet Schuyler. Whiting adds that the colonel also met with two other French Indians whom he asked to stop fighting the governments of New England.

1138. Whittaker, Jane. "The Narrative of the Captivity of Mrs. Jane Whittaker, Daughter of Sebastian Strope, A Revolutionary Soldier." *New York State Historical Association Quarterly Journal,* vol. 11, no. 3 (July 1930): 237–251.

The narrative, dictated to Judge C. F. Avery prior to Mrs. Whittaker's death in 1852, describes the places where she was kept prisoner: Tioga Point, and Lachine, Canada. It continues with the description of her eventual return home and her reunion with her father. There are also statements by Minor Strope, a descendant of Sebastian Strope.

**1139.** Wilkes, Francis. [Letter to Governor Talcott] *Connecticut Historical Society Collections,* vol. 5 (Hartford, 1896): 14–18.

Writing on April 7, 1737, Wilkes argues against the need for a committee of review, insisting that the people of Connecticut have a valid title to the lands derived from the Indians and that the latter have more than sufficient lands for their own use. He believes that a commission investigating land titles would not only interrupt peace, but it would also be unable to resolve the question of whether Ben Uncas or Mahomet is the true sachem because the latter is dead. Wilkes declares that a commission will strengthen, not weaken, Connecticut title.

**1140.** Williams, John. "Selections from the Redeemed Captive Returning to Zion; or A Faithful History of Remarkable Occurences in the Captivity and Deliverance of Mr. John Williams, Minister of the Gospel in Deerfield." *Vermont Quarterly,* n.s., vol. 19, no. 2 (April 1951): 86–97.

This narrative, written at Deerfield by Mr. Williams after two and one-half years of Indian captivity, describes his capture on February 29, 1703 by Indians and his subsequent march to Canada, the behavior of Indians along the way, and the courteous treatment he received from the French at Chamblee.

**1141.** Williams, Roger. "Important Roger Williams Letter." *Rhode Island Historical Society Collections,* vol. 27, no. 3 (July 1934): 85–92.

Writing on June 25, 1659, Roger Williams answers "a scandalous paper" which argues against the purchase of Rhode Island. He disavows the accusation that his purchase was made from drunken Indians as well as other charges concerning the purchase.

**1142.** Williams, Roger. "A Key into the Language of America, or an Help to the Language of the Natives in That Part of America called New England." *Rhode Island Historical Society Collections,* vol. 1 (Providence, 1827): 17–163.

A sketch of the life of Roger Williams precedes his *Key* published in 1643. Williams introduces his book with general remarks about the natives and explains that the work is based chiefly on the Narragansett dialect. He provides the English equivalent of all the words. The chapters deal with words of salutation, observation, eating, entertainment, sleep, numbers, consanguinity, house, family, and parts of the body. Also included are terms for discourse and news, the time of day, the seasons of the year, travel, astronomy, weather, fowl,

1142 (continued)
plants, beasts, sea, fishing, clothing, religion, government, marriage, money, trading, debts, hunting, sports, games, wars, paintings, sickness, death, and burial.

1143. Williams, Roger. "Key into the Language of the Indians of New England, 1643." Massachusetts Historical Society Collections, ser. 1, vol. 3 (Boston, 1794): 203–238.
These pages contain extracts from Williams' Key, each of whose thirty-two chapters contain vocabulary interspersed with observations on the manners and customs of the Indians. Each chapter ends with spiritual observations and three or four verses of poetry. The bulk of the vocabulary and chapter conclusions are excluded from these extracts. A number of Indian words are retained to serve as a specimen of the language from the Narragansett dialect. [Continued as "Vocabulary of the Narragansett Language," in Massachusetts Historical Society Collections, ser. 1, vol. 5 (Boston, 1798): 80–106.]

1144. Williams, Roger. [Letters to John Winthrop] Massachusetts Historical Society Collections, ser. 4, vol. 6 (Boston, 1863): 189–311.
Written between May 1637 and January 14, 1675, Williams' letters deal with the myriad of events during and after the Pequot War of 1637 and King Philip's War of 1675. He describes the beliefs and actions of Miantonomo, Canonicus, Wequash, Uncas, and Jacquontu, a Block Island Indian, as well as their relations with the colonists in Connecticut. Williams also tells of Nipmucks, Narragansetts, Pequots, Mohawks, and other tribes.

1145. "Roger Williams and His Opposition to the King's Patent." Massachusetts Historical Society Proceedings, ser. 1, vol. 12 (1871–1873): 347–358.
A writer analyzes Williams' major theoretical objection to the patent of King James of November 3, 1620 and that of Charles I to Massachusetts. He explains that Williams felt the king had pretended to give a title to the patentees while the proprietary was actually vested in the Indians. There is a discussion of the manner in which Williams and his followers settled the colony of Rhode Island showing how Indian deeds were drawn up, how a charter of government containing no land grants was procured, and how the new government claimed exclusive right to cancel Indian title within its boundaries.

1146. Williams, Sherman. "The Iroquois Confederacy." New York State Historical Association Proceedings, Fifth Annual Meeting, vol. 4 (Lake George, 1904): 9–18.
Williams reviews the migrations and settlements of Iroquoian tribes and the growth of their confederacy. He discusses the purpose of the confederacy and the warfare of the Iroquois against their enemies. He tells of the first contact between the Mohawks and the Whites, Champlain in 1609, their conflict by firearms, and the eventual revenge by the Iroquois after 1642 in their incursions against the French in

Canada. Williams explores the elements of the power of the Iroquois, their location, character, and government. He describes the social organization, the land, and their longhouses.

1147. Williamson, Joseph. "A Memorial of Father Rale." *Maine Historical Society Collections.* Ser. 2, vol. 9 (Portland, 1898): 137–141.
Williamson discusses the discovery of a ring in 1892 on the site of the Indian village of Father Sebastian Rasles which probably belonged to the missionary.

1148. Williamson, William D. "Indian Tribes in New England." *Massachusetts Historical Society Collections,* ser. 3, vol. 9 (Boston, 1846): 92–100.
Williamson describes the Tarratines on the Penobscot River, the Openangos at Passamaquoddy, and the Maliseets on the St. John River. He discusses the leaders in each of the three tribes.

1149. Williamson, William D. "Notice of Orono, a Chief at Penobscot." *Massachusetts Historical Society Collections,* ser. 3, vol. 9. (Boston, 1846): 82–91.
Williamson discusses Joseph Orono, chief of the Tarratine Indians who were located on the Penobscot River. The author reviews the chief's ancestry, manners, influence among his people, role during the French and Indian War, treaties with Massachusetts, and his death in 1802. Williamson tells of Orono's successors.

1150. Willis, Sam. [Letter] *New York Historical Society Collections for the Year 1869, Publication Fund, vol. 2.* (New York, 1870): 374–376.
Writing on April 10, 1676, Willis and Pitkins, two agents for the Council of Connecticut, inquire about the attitudes of the Mohawks and Senecas towards the settlers in Connecticut. They ask advice on how to get the Indians to fight against the French and what kind of presents to use as bribes. The writers want permission to go to Albany and other places to stir up the Indians. There is a written answer from the governor and council of New York which says that the New York Indians have no particular knowledge which the settlers in Connecticut need to know, that the Mohawks cannot be subject to Connecticut law, and that the Connecticut people have kept New Yorkers uninformed concerning an Indian war.

1151. Willis, William. "The First Indian War." In *The History of Portland. Maine Historical Society Collections,* ser. 1, vol. 1 (Portland, 1831): 210–230.
Willis discusses the course of King Philip's War of 1675–1676 in Maine. The author describes the destructive actions of the Saco and Androscoggin Indians against a number of English families. He deals with some of the reasons for the Indians' hostility and their ability to successfully harass settlements. There are texts of letters written by Maine settlers during this period which document the depredations of Indians against settlements. One document names the inhabitants at Black Point Garrison, October 12, 1676. Willis tells of military

1151 *(continued)*
actions against the Indians and of a treaty of peace signed in 1678
which ended in war.

1152. Willis, William. "The Indians of Hudson's Bay and Their Language,
Selected from Umfreville's *Present State of Hudson's Bay.*" *Maine Historical Society
Collections*, ser. 1, vol. 6 (Portland, 1859): 265–271.

Willis provides selections from the work of Umfreville published in
1790. He reviews the lunar divisions of time used by Hudson's Bay
Indians to express some remarkable event or appearance and compares these with the names of months used by the Abenakis. He
discussed the Ne-heth-aw-a (Cree) giving the names of their thirteen
moons, the Assinee-Poetucs, and the Blackfeet. He also includes a
table of words in English and in the languages of the four tribes,
explaining that these words bear no resemblance to the language of
the Abenakis in Maine.

1153. Willis, William. "The Language of the Abnaquies or Eastern Indians."
*Maine Historical Society Collections*, ser. 1, vol. 4 (Portland, 1856): 92–117.

Willis gives a list of commonly used Indian terms, extracted from
Father Rasles' French dictionary of 1691. He includes the definitions
given by Rasles and English equivalents for the French. Willis also
provides a catalogue of Indian names for portions of Maine, with any
definitions that he has obtained. It is followed by several explanations
of Indian names for places.

1154. Willis, William. "The Second Indian War." In *The History of Portland.
Maine Historical Society Collections*, ser. 1, vol. 1 (Portland, 1831): 286–304.

Willis discusses the causes of the second Indian war, which began
around 1688, chiefly blaming the French Jesuit influence among the
Indians. He describes Indian hostilities and English military actions in
the territory of Falmouth before the 1690s.

1155. Winder, C. S. "Captain C. S. Winder's Account of a Battle with the
Indians." *Maryland Historical Magazine*, vol. 35, no. 1 (March 1940): 56–59.

In his letter dated June 2, 1858, written at Fort Walla Walla in the
Washington Territory, Captain Winder provides an account of a
battle engagement with the Indians of the Washington Territory in
1858.

1156. Winslow, Edward. [Letter to John Winthrop] *Massachusetts Historical
Society Collections*, ser. 4, vol. 6 (Boston, 1863): 174–176.

In an undated letter, Winslow reports that the Narragansetts are
preparing for war, that the Mohawks promise to aid the Narragansetts, and that the Dutch and English are pursuing the Indians.

1157. Winsor, Justin. "The Earliest Printed Books Connected With the
Aborigines of New England, 1630–1700." *Massachusetts Historical Society Proceedings*, ser. 2, vol. 10 (1895–1896): 327–359.

Winsor provides a bibliographical essay surveying the publications by English and Indian authors written between 1630 and 1700, giving the date, author and topical content. The materials concern the Pequot War, King Philip's War, and known copies of the first and second editions of the Indian Bible. Information is also given on the Indian language and on the progress made by missionaries working among the Indians. [*See also* "The Earliest Printed Sources of New England History, 1602–1629." *Massachusetts Historical Society Proceedings,* ser. 2, vol. 9 (1894): 181–192. Included in this article are ten authors who published fourteen books or tracts which are sources of Indian history for the Massachusetts region.]

1158. Winthrop, Fitz-John. "Proclamation of Fitz-John Winthrop Against the Eastern Indians." *Massachusetts Historical Society Collections,* ser. 6, vol. 3 (Boston:, 1889): 146–147.

Writing in August, 1703, Winthrop forbids English subjects to communicate with or conceal any Penacooks or other Eastern Indians since they are allied with the French and have committed atrocities against the English. He commands English subjects to "execute all acts of hostilitie upon them" and, whenever possible, to seize these Indians and bring them to the justice of the peace.

1159. Winthrop, John. "Governor John ·Winthrop's Pass to Ninigret." *Massachusetts Historical Society Collections,* ser. 5, vol. 1 (Boston, 1871): 496–497.

On March 14, 1647, Winthrop grants safe conduct to Ninigret, a Niantic, to go to Boston to meet with commissioners and to return home unmolested.

1160. Winthrop, John. [Letter to Edward Hopkins] *Massachusetts Historical Society Collections* ser. 5, vol. 8 (Boston, 1882): 38–39.

On February 10, 1647, Winthrop repeats the speech of Nenekummatt, a Naganticut.

1161. Winthrop, John. [Letter to the Governor of the Corporation for the Propagation of the Gospel in New England] *Massachusetts Historical Society Collections,* ser. 5, vol. 9 (Boston, 1885): 45–46.

In an undated letter, Winthrop makes five proposals concerning the English employing the Indians in New England, including the suggestion that Indians would wear English apparel if they knew how to purchase it.

1162. Winthrop, John. "Letter to Major Savage and Other Officers of the Army." *Massachusetts Historical Society Collections,* ser. 5, vol. 8 (Boston, 1882): 172–174.

Writing on July 12, 1675, Winthrop tells of some Narragansetts who helped the English in the war against the Pequots. He says it is necessary for the English to continue their friendship because of the size of the Narragansett Nation and its proximity.

1163. Winthrop, John, Jr. [Letter to Edward Hopkins] *Massachusetts Historical Society Collections*, ser. 5, vol. 8 (Boston, 1882): 38–39.

On February 10, 1646, Winthrop tells of "Nenekummatt," an Indian, who made a speech confessing his fear of the English and his desire to keep peace with these white men. Winthrop also mentions that some Niantics killed deer but did not know what to do with the skins.

1164. Winthrop, John, Jr. [Letter to Governor John Winthrop] *Connecticut Historical Society Collections*, vol. 21 (Hartford, 1924): 217–218.

Writing on July 26, 1675, Winthrop describes how one of Ninigret's Indians brought a head of one of King Philip's Indians and demanded a coat that was promised by a Boston man who had offered the coat as a reward for every head the Indians brought in.

1165. Winthrop, John, Jr. [Letters to Richard Nichols, Governor of New York] *Massachusetsts Historical Society Collections*, ser. 5, vol. 8 (Boston, 1882): 96–101, 107–114.

Writing in 1665 and 1667, Winthrop talks of the alliance with the Indians from the Hudson River to Canada, of their war with the Mohawks, and of the possibility of their attacking the English. He discusses how the Mohawks have come close to the Massachusetts frontier towns and killed Indians, not the English. He comments on the French involvement in the war against the Mohawks, the need for a posture of defense, and the actual French military actions. Winthrop fears that Indians in Massachusetts may confederate with the French against the English.

1166. Winthrop, Wait. [Letter to Governor John Winthrop] *Connecticut Historical Society Collections*, vol. 21 (Hartford, 1924): 209–211.

Writing on July 8, 1675, Winthrop discusses the need to prevent the Narragansetts from joining with King Philip. He explains how Ninigret, a Niantic sachem, is willing to talk at his fort but advises against bringing any Mohegans along. He says he will give his reasons at the meeting. Winthrop tells how some of Philip's men have gone for relief to one of the Narragansett sachems and how some remote Narragansetts have been hostile.

1167. Winthrop, Wait. [Letter to Sir Henry Ashurst] *Massachusetts Historical Society Collections*, ser. 6, vol. 5 (Boston, 1892): 120–121.

Writing on September 13, 1703, Winthrop reports that several bands of Eastern Indians, headed by French officers, have been stirred up by French priests and have massacred and carried away white prisoners. He describes how a French priest exhorts the Indians to destroy heretics and assists them in doing so. He explains that the French marry and mix with the Indians and, therefore, have ties with the Indians that the English do not have. Furthermore, he claims the Indians are fond of priests because they supply Indians with crosses, beads, and trinkets.

1168.  Wister, Owen. "Letters of Owen Wister, Author of *The Virginian.*" ed. Fanny Kemble. *Pennsylvania Magazine of History and Biography*, vol. 83, no. 1 (January 1959): 3–28.

Wister discusses a collection of letters between Owen Wister and Captain Frank Augustine Edwards, an experienced Indian fighter who in 1893 commanded the U.S. Army post at San Carlos in the Arizona Territory. In the letters dated from July 23, 1893 to August 25, 1894, Wister receives information from the captain about his Indian campaigns.

1169.  Witthoft, John. "An Outline of Pennsylvania Indian History." *Pennsylvania History*, vol. 16, no. 3 (July 1949): 165–176.

Witthoft discusses Pennsylvania Indian sites and their general characteristics. He reviews the Historic Period, from about 1600 until the Indians are driven away. He describes the tools found in this period. He then deals with the Late Woodland Period, approximately 1200 A.D. to 1600 A.D.; the Middle Woodland Period, approximately 900 A.D. to 1200 A.D.; the Early Woodland Period, approximately 600 A.D. to 900 A.D.; a transitional period in Pennsylvania and Maryland, the Late Archaic Period, approximately 500 B.C. to 500 A.D.; the Early Archaic Period; and the Paleo-Indian Period. Using an outline, he interprets Pennsylvania archaeology according to the characteristics of the eight stages. There is a tabulation of the catalogue, numbers, and location of specimens, Pennsylvania projectile points, all illustrated in a photograph.

1170.  Wolcott, Roger. "The Wolcott Papers: The Correspondence and Documents of the Colony of Connecticut, 1750–1754 with Some of Earlier Date." *Connecticut Historical Society Collections*, vol. 16 (Hartford, 1916).

There are brief references to Indians throughout this volume.

1171.  Wolfe, Theodore F. "Origin of the Name Succasunna." *New Jersey Historical Society Proceedings*, n.s., vol. 9, no. 4 (October 1924): 334–338.

Wolfe traces the origin of Succasunna, one of the oldest towns in Morris County. He employs Lenape words from the Unami-Lenape dialect for his analysis. Citing suffixes *ung, ong,* and *ing* which terminate many Algonquian geographical names, he accounts for the origins of the name Suckasunning which he argues means "place of the black stones."

1172.  Wroth, Lawrence C. "The Story of Thomas Cresap, a Maryland Pioneer." *Maryland Historical Magazine*, vol. 9, no. 1 (March 1914): 1–37.

A portion of this biography deals with Cresap's life during the eighteenth century and his relationship with Indians who frequented his house on the Potomac. The text of a letter dated around 1751 from a group of Six Nations Indians to Governor Ogle explains why they killed some of Cresap's animals. Wroth discusses the Indians with

1172 *(continued)*
whom Cresap came in contact and tells of his life in 1756, one of
waging defensive and offensive war against Indians.

1173. Wroth, Lawrence C. "Variations in Five Copies of Roger Williams' *Key
into the Language of America.*" *Rhode Island Historical Society Collections*, vol. 29, no.
4 (October 1936): 120–212.
 Wroth discusses a list of five typographical variations which are without significance but are worth recording because of the importance of
the Williams' treatise.

1174. Wyllys, George. "The Wyllys Papers: Correspondence and Documents
Chiefly of Descendants of Governor George Wyllys of Connecticut, 1590–
1796." *Connecticut Historical Society Collections*, vol. 21 (Hartford, 1924).
 Indian names are mentioned throughout the volume and indexed.

1175. Wynne, John J. "Mohawk Martyr Missionaries." *New York History*, vol. 13,
no. 1 (January 1932): 59–74. Illustrated.
 Wynne tells of French missionaries who first appeared in the Mohawk
Valley in the early seventeenth century, describes their work with
Indians, and explains how the "Black Robes" became objects of
hatred. He discusses the murder of Isaac Jogues by the Iroquois in
1646 and the martyrdom of other missionaries. He also mentions
subsequent baptisms of hundreds of Indians. A painting of Jogues
and copies of pages from his manuscript are provided.

1176. Yeates, Jasper. "The Indian Treaty at Fort Pitt in 1776." *Pennsylvania
Magazine of History and Biography*, vol. 5, no. 4 (1881): 484–485.
 Writing on November 6, 1776, Yeates, one of the commissioners of
the United States chosen to deal with Indians at Fort Pitt, keeps notes
in his account and memorandum book. He includes lists of the chiefs
at the signing of the treaty in October 1776, notes on Indian names
given the commissioners by the Indians, translations of Indian names
into English, and items about the tribes which compose the Delawares,
Six Nations, and the Shawnees.

1177. Yeates, Jasper. "Letters of Honorable Jasper Yeates to Honorable James
Wilson." *Pennsylvania Magazine of History and Biography*, vol. 29, no. 3 (1905):
359–361.
 Writing from July 30 to August 31, 1776, Yeates discusses his fear of a
general Indian war, suggests that garrisons at several places be rein-
forced and supplied, and adds that it was a big error to have a treaty
conference deferred until September.

1178. Young, Henry J. "A Note on Scalp Bounties in Pennsylvania." *Pennsylvania History*, vol. 24, no. 3 (July 1957): 207–218. Illustrated.

Young argues that the Pennsylvania government bears a degree of historical responsibility in the spread of scalping. He explains why the government proclaimed general bounties for Indian scalps on three occasions, 1756, 1764, and 1780. He offers reasons to explain why most Americans accepted the ethics of scalp-buying by the 1750's. Young tells how these bounties encouraged frontier people to carry on a private war against Indians and endangered friendly Indians. The bounty proclamations of 1764 and 1780 are reproduced.

1179. Zane, Isaac. "Journal of Isaac Zane to Wyoming, 1758." ed. Joseph H. Coates. *Pennsylvania Magazine of History and Biography*, vol. 30, no. 4 (1906): 417–426.

There is a brief description of Isaac Zane who was paid by the Friendly Society to go to Wyoming to assist Delaware Indians in building Teedyuscung's town, making a settlement there, and opening a road to it. Writing between May 21 and June 1, 1758, Zane tells of his journey to the Indian town and the deliberations of Teedyuscung concerning whether or not to remain at Wyoming because of the recent attacks by hostile Indians. Zane also mentions his efforts to persuade the Indians to stay and build houses.

1180. Zeisberger, David. "Essay of an Onondaga Grammar, or a Short Introduction to Learn the Onondaga Maqua Tongue." *Pennsylvania Magazine of History and Biography*, vol. 11, no. 4 (1887): 442–453.

Zeisberger, a German, thought it convenient to spell the Onondaga words in the German or the Latin way. He discusses the pronunciation of letters, accents, simple or compound words, parts of speech, gender, numbers, declensions of Onondaga nouns and adjectives, indeclinables and declinables, cardinal numbers, temporals, and coalescing words. [*Continued* in *Pennsylvania Magazine of History and Biography*, vol. 12, no. 1 (1888): 65–75. In this part, he discusses comparatives, superlatives, pronouns, verbs, verb tense, and verb conjugation. *Continued* in *Pennsylvania Magazine of History and Biography*, vol. 12, no. 2 (1888): 233–239. In this part he discusses verb conjugations. *Continued* in *Pennsylvania Magazine of History and Biography*, vol. 12, no. 3 (1888): 325–340. He discusses verb conjugations, participles, adverbs, prepositions, interjections, and conjunctions.]

1181. Zeisberger, David. "Some Remarks and Annotations Concerning the Traditions, Customs, Languages of the Indians in North America." *Historical Society of Pennsylvania Proceedings*, vol. 1, no. 4 (December 1845): 30–44.

1181 *(continued)*
Zeisberger tells of the Delaware, Mohawk, and Mahican Indians' traditions, political constitutions, customs, and languages. He gives a collection of words in the three languages.

1182. Zeisberger, David, and Mack, John Martin. "An Account of the Famine Among the Indians of the North and West Branch of the Susquehanna, in the Summer of 1748." *Pennsylvania Magazine of History and Biography*, vol. 16, no. 4 (1892): 430–432.

Writing from July 9 to July 28, 1748, the two Moravian missionaries record the presence of famine and disease, especially smallpox, among the Susquehannock Indians.

# INDEXES

Mary [Oneida]    *Courtesy of the New York Historical Society, New York City*
Watercolor and pencil drawing of an Oneida woman done by the Baroness Hyde de
Neuville in 1807

# INDEX OF SUBJECTS

*See also* English-Indian policy; English trade with Indians; French

English-Indian policy, administration of, at local levels, 187, 212–13, 741; administration of, North American, 77, 358, 805; development of, 243; Indian medals of, 363; influence of intercolonial politics on, 916; intrigue among Indians, American Revolution, 461, 471, 944, 947, 979, 1049, 1060, 1135; intrigue among Indians, post-Revolution, 18, 34, 421, 471, 1116; intrigue among Indians (War of 1812), 922; land policy, 72, 106, 167, 188, 196, 205, 237, 551, 741, 767, 784, 805, 835, 907, 1145; Proclamation (of 1763), 72, 784, 987; Quebec Act, 784; treatment of Indians, 565; turn Indians against Indians, 184–85; Yorke-Camden opinion circumvents Proclamation (of 1763), 987

English trade with Indians, abuses of, 39, 173, 210, 212, 532, 535; C. Colden's suggestions for, 183; Croghan's fur trade activities, 1083, 1089, 1091; descriptions of, 556, 559, 908, 969, 1036; during American Revolution, 1082; Franklin's opinion of, 351; Gage's opinion of, 358; goods too expensive, 157, 343, 759; W. Johnson's suggestions for, 206, 527, 532–35; license required, 204; liquor branch of, 192, 507, 535, 854; map of, 305; policy of, 77, 173, 191–92, 197, 702, 741, 756, 784; rivalry among colonies, 592; rivalry with Americans, 18; rivalry with France, 17, 173–74, 186, 467, 525, 720, 738, 751, 985; traders reimbursed with land, 1041

**《 F 》** Finnish, treatment of Delawares, 94

Firearms, illustration of Indians with, 803; types of, used in U.S. trade with Indians, 803

Forbes Expedition (1758), Colonel Burd's role in, 773; English destroy Fort Duquesne, 87, 280, 773, 810; Grant's Hill battle during, 810

Forts, daily life in, during Indian war, 673; English, on U.S. soil, 8, 1032; French, in Canada, 900, in Indian territory, 13, 17, 128, 176, 183, 276, 304, 523, 751–52, 758; in Maine, 635; in New Jersey, 430; in New York, 248; in Ohio country, 879; in Pennsylvania, 252, 280, 465, 567–68, 768, 817

French, contempt for Treaty of Utrecht, 17, 165, 183, 758; during American Revolution, 307, 570, 938, 943, 1031; during King George's War, 12, 144, 218–19; during King William's War, 67, 233, 931; during Queen Anne's War, 13, 500; during Seven Years' War, 78, 87–88, 97, 138, 154–55, 181, 183, 186, 190, 204, 231, 276, 347–48, 405, 417, 557, 646, 773, 976, 1083; forts in Indian territory, 13, 17, 128, 164, 176, 183, 276, 304, 523, 751–52, 758; Indian allies of, 1, 138, 146–48, 164, 405, 557, 646, 703; place priests among Iroquois, 173, 282, 698, 700, 1034, 1175; responsible for Indian wars against New England colonists, 58, 146, 216, 573, 770, 899, 924, 927, 1167; rivalry with English for Indian allies, 1, 17, 138, 145–48, 157–58, 164–65, 307, 405, 514, 523, 555–56, 659, 896, 985; rivalry with English for North America, 138, 231, 233, 304, 467, 514, 1034, 1083–84; schemes to break up Indian-English alliance, 637, 899; schemes to break up Iroquois-English alliance, 17, 40, 140, 142, 145, 147, 157, 172–73, 175, 181, 183, 191, 213–14, 219–20, 223, 297, 523, 525, 711, 713, 715, 720–21, 724, 729, 732, 738, 743, 765, 1097; supply Indians with ammunition, 180, 186, 190, 227

French and Indian War. *See* Seven Years' War

French trade with Indians, abuses of, 559; description of, 1036; fur trade system of, 680; in Canada, 900; in Illinois, 186; on the Missis-

Indian deeds *(continued)*
930, 1094; New York, 418, 480, 549, 662, 891, 956; Pennsylvania, 110, 137, 478; Rhode Island, 121, 626, 684, 952, 998; English and Maine Indians differ over meaning of, 894; should be fully explained to Indians, 171

Indian disease, blindness, 159; epidemic, Long Island, 360; inflammation of eyes, 159; lung problems, 949; sickness among Indians, 112, 232, 246, 254, 413, 425, 547, 575, 1128, 1136, 1182; scrofula, 53
*See also* Indian medicine

Indian education, by Jesuits, 250; by Moravians, 396; by Society for the Propagation of the Gospel, 568; in Connecticut, 310, 695; Lee's opinion on, 580; Michaelius' opinion on, 655; state of Penobscot, 368; teachers of Indians, 431, 893, 963–64; teachers' salaries, 964; teaching English to Indians, 312, 959; White Eyes at Princeton, 472
*See also* Indian schools

Indian food and cookery, general discussion of, 19, 246; in California, 406, 1112; in Delaware, 424; in New Jersey, 247, 413, 837, 847–48, 908, 957; in New York, 606; in Northwest Coast, 406; in Oregon, 406; in Pennsylvania, 413, 440; in Vermont, 547; in Virginia, 440; in Washington, 406

Indian forts, Annacostin, 620; in Champlain's 1619 narrative, 968; Queen's, 131; Rondout-Neversink Valley, 65

Indian games and amusements (colonies and states), California, Northwest Coast, Oregon, Washington, 406

Indian games and amusements (tribes), Delawares, 847, 1094; Iroquois, 329; western tribes, 329

Indian graves, in Rhode Island, 133, 483, 485; openings of, 133; robbings of, 133

Indian hemp, 410

Indian hospitality, 19, 413

Indian housing and villages, general discussion of, 19; in California, 406; in Maine, 515; in New England, 425; in New Jersey, 247, 847–48; in New York, 606, 769; in Oregon, 406; in Northwest Coast, 406, 1013; in Pennsylvania, 440; in Virginia, 440; in Washington, 406

Indian hunting and fishing, fish weir, 482, 974; speech about fishing rights, 1124; Stockbridge hunting described, 1003

Indian implements, agricultural, in Rhode Island, 130, in Vermont, 52; carved representations on, 134; classified, 35; in Maine, 57; in Maryland, 619; in Massachusetts, 486; in New Jersey, 838; in New York, 35, 901; in Rhode Island, 130, 134, 484, 898; in Vermont, 44, 62, 827
*See also* Bone implements; Stone implements, Wood implements

Indian-Indian conflicts, Delaware-Iroquois, 136, 179, 185, 191, 199, 209, 395, 531; intertribal fighting, 254, 556, 685; Mohawk-New England Indians, 30, 437, 442, 1069, 1165; Mohegan-Narragansett, 916; Montauk-Niantic, 91; Montauk-Block Island, 360; Pequot-Narragansett, 374; Susquehannock-Piscataway, 139, 1136; in Vermont, 787

Indian intemperance, abuses by settlers, 166, 212, 524, 536; Colden's opinion on, 267; Cornplanter's opinion on, 234; evil effects of, 21, 234, 493, 854, 862, 1029; in deeds, 38, 368, 478, 652; in land agreements, 241, 519, 1141; in trade, 192, 507, 656, 815, 937; Indian statements against, 819, 883, 949, 1058; missionary Ranney's opinion on, 886; of Delawares, 22, 1094; of Eastern Abenakis, 499; of Iroquois, 51, 234, 949, 1119; of Logan, 649; of Mahicans, 949; of Massachusetts Indians, 408, 431; of Mohegans, 629, 1058; of Nova Scotia, 958; of Ohio Indians, 583; of Penacooks, 815; of Penobscots, 63, 1015; of Pennsylvania In-

Indian physical characteristics *(continued)*
988; in New England, 425; in New York, 769; in Northwest Coast, 406; in Nova Scotia, 958; in Oregon, 406; in Pennsylvania, 440; in Virginia, 440; in Washington, 406; traits of, 1121
Indian pictographs, Abenaki method of, 1077; founding of Iroquois in symbols, 592; Handsome Lake story in, 333; Indian personal name marks reproduced, 121, 241, 494, 610, 663, 826, 888, 891, 956, 998, 1057–58, 1117; inscribed rocks, 268–73, 281, 518, 574; Maine, 586; Mayan calendar hieroglyphics, 1037; Pennsylvania Indian marks explained, 819
Indian pipes, in Maryland, 619; in Massachusetts, 486; in New Jersey, 848; in Rhode Island, 130, 134, 898; tomahawk pipe invented for Indian trade, 910
Indian place names, Algonquian, 914, 1048; discussions of, 108, 111, 324, 386, 420, 449, 458, 687, 914, 967, 1033, 1048, 1074, 1077; from Icelandic, 881; in Delaware deeds, 301; in Maine, 866, 1153; Maryland, 108, 353, 414; in Massachusetts, 15, 52, 386; in New Jersey, 247, 414, 420, 593, 835–36, 841–43, 846, 848, 914, 919, 1074, 1076; in New York, 914, 1070; in Pennsylvania, 300, 305, 328, 413–14; in Rhode Island, 52, 111, 324, 868, 1033; in Vermont, 449, 452, 458; in Virginia, 414; Dutch and English-Indian compounds, 1074; into Dutch, 32, 438, 1076; Iroquois, 458, 914; maps of, 459–60
Indian political institutions. *See* Indian social and political institutions
Indian population, aboriginal, 284; census (1920), 284; decline of, 42–43, 100, 584–85, 625; during American Revolution, 253
Indian population (colonies and states), of California, 406; of Connecticut, 782, 1001, 1022; of Maine, 391; of Maryland, 954–55; of Massachusetts, 408, 893; of New Hampshire, 298; of Northwest Coast, 406; of Oregon, 406; of Pennsylvania, 284; of Plymouth, 431; of Rhode Island, 783; of Washington, 406
Indian population (tribes), of Abenakis (Eastern), 1001; Apache, 932; Caddo, 932; Cherokee, 932; Cheyenne, 932; Chickasaw, 932; Chippewa, 932; Choctaw, 932; Creek, 932; Crow, 932; Eel River, 932; Iroquois, 297, 336, 949, 1119–20; Kansas, 932; Kickapoo, 932; Kiowa, 932; Mahican, 949; Mandan, 932; Mashpee, 1001; Menominee, 932; Miami, 932; Missourias, 932; Mohegan, 664, 1022; Montauk, 786; Mountaineer, 932; Narragansett, 868, 1022; Nausets, 1001; Niantics, 1001; Osage, 932; Pawnee, 932; Penobscot, 391; Pequot, 1000, 1022; Ponca, 932; Potawatomi, 932; "Praying" Indians, 318–19; Saconnets, 1001; St. John's River, 391; Sauk, 932; Shawnee, 932; Sioux, 932; southern tribes, 882; Susquehannock, 23; Wea, 932; western tribes, 932; Winnebago, 932; Wyandot, 932
Indian pottery, Abenaki, 57; adornment of, by Narragansets, 487; in New Jersey, 835, 838; in Rhode Island, 130, 487, 898; in Vermont, 44, 827; stylistic methods of decorating, 1037
Indian property concepts, of Algonquians, 76; Iroquoian, 188, 193, 949; Maine tribes, 241, 894; Narragansetts, 683; Sascoes, 503; Vermont groups, 260; white theories about, 106, 580, 584
Indian religion (colonies and states), California, 406; Delaware, 424; Maine, 515; New England, 375, 425; New York, 908; Northwest Coast, 406; Oregon, 406; Pennsylvania, 440, 921; Plymouth, 431; Virginia, 440; Washington, 406
Indian religion (tribes), Abenaki, 33, 57, 575; Delawares, 247, 556, 847–48, 932, 1094, 1118–19; general, 19, 100; Iroquois, 51, 505, 949, 1104, 1118–19; Narragansetts exhorting, 600; western tribes, 246, 932

**《 M 》** Maps, Abenakis, old French, 451; Achter Col Colony, 605; Adlum's (1790), of northwestern Pennsylvania and western New York, 8; Algonquians in Vermont, 452; Brodhead Expedition, 1006; Champlain's (1616 and 1632), 558; Chickasaw Removal, overland route of, 804; Croghan's trading activities, 1085; Crown Point Road, 135; Delaware River Valley settlements, 94; Delisle map (1729), 517; Fort Piscataway, 337; Fort Pitt, 243; Franklin's scene of frontier service, 568; Groveland, 287; Hubbard's, 264; Hudson River Valley, 914; Hutchin's, 879; Indian place names in Vermont, 459–60; Indian trader's, 305; Iroquois, 383, 458, 1101; Johnson, Guy (1768), 72; Lake Ontario, 514; Maryland Indian trails, 624; Minisink country, 934; Mohawk sites in Canada, New Hampshire, and Vermont, 452; Narragansett Bay inscribed rocks, 272–73; New England (1677), 572; New Jersey (early Dutch), 438; Niantic Territory, 953; Ohio country, 467; Onondaga Trail, 1097; Pattin, possible author of, 305; Pennsylvania Indian trails, 1102, 1132; Presque Isle, 243; Smith's, 350; Stockwell route on Vermont trails to Canada, 367; Sullivan Expedition, 287, 344, 599, 1021, 1067; Susquehanna Valley, early, 592; Vermont, Algonquians in, 452; Vermont Indian place names in, 459–60; Virginia, western, 624; Wallum Pond, 52

Mayan civilization, calendar hieroglyphics, 1037; historical development of, 1037

Missionaries, salaries of, 352; should be recruited from converted Indians, 913, 961; unsuccessful work among Indians, 42, 64, 440, 854; work with Indian languages, 251, 282, 316, 388, 490, 603, 853, 1130

Missions and missionaries (Catholic) discussions about work of, 58, 114, 117, 173, 250, 266, 282, 587, 660, 677, 698, 700, 776, 785, 888–89, 973, 1147, 1167, 1175; writings by, 250, 292, 401, 514, 785, 890, 1136

Missions and missionaries (Protestant) discussions about work of, 266, 315, 320, 388, 390, 396, 470–71, 473, 505, 544, 566, 602–603, 712, 776, 841, 855, 913, 1012; writings by, 43, 49, 51, 64, 73, 112–13, 236, 312, 314, 316–19, 327–28, 330, 338, 341, 389, 408, 413–17, 424, 445, 447, 563–64, 590, 645, 655, 660, 672, 786, 853–55, 857, 886–87, 893, 921, 932, 949, 986, 991, 1004, 1038, 1040, 1087, 1095, 1142–44, 1180–82
  *See also* Moravians; Quakers

Moravians, contributions of, 396, 602; diaries of, 417, 672; missions to Indians, 112, 388, 396, 416, 602; move Indian converts to Canada, Indiana, Michigan, Ohio, 381; philosophy of, 602; treaty with Iroquois, 991, 1107; treatment of Indians just, 1071; want land, 112

**《 N 》** Neutrality policy of Indians, French allied and English allied, during King George's War, 146–47, 164, 214; of Consora, 156

Northmen, inhabited New England, 881

**《 O 》** Onondaga Council, during King George's War, 219; missionaries' proposal, to learn Iroquois dialects, 603; proposal to remove Moravian Indians of Shecomeco, 991; proceedings of described, 603; Weiser underpins authority of, 1098

Origins of American Indians, 7, 57, 151, 375, 1015; of Mongolian descent, 151; of Celt, Jewish, Norman, South Sea descent, 362

by whites, 26, 379, 589, 1115; during American Revolution, 945; during Sullivan Expedition, 26; Governor Morris reward for Indian, 339; Pennsylvania bounty proclamation, facsimile, 1178; Sewall papers discuss, 965

Scots-Irish, dispute with sects over Indian treatment, Pennsylvania, 566; settlement in Raritan Valley, 1075

*See also* Paxton Boys

Scrofula, 53

Sermons, in Indian languages, 236

Seven Years' War (1754–1763), Benjamin Franklin's role, 568; Braddock Expedition during, 78, 88, 97, 508, 672, 773, 1085; Croghan's role during, 242–43, 245, 1085; Eastern Indians, impact of, on, 1015; English-French rivalry for Indian allies, 158, 514, 555–56, 659, 896; English-French rivalry for North America, 138, 233, 339, 467, 514, 1034, 1083–84, 1095; expedition against Crown Point, 276, 405, 1008; expedition against Fort William Henry, 104, 154–55, 651; expedition against Kittanning, 280, 339, 469; Indian attacks during, 63, 136, 154, 160, 181, 338, 347, 417, 432, 469, 559, 773, 793, 969, 1105; Iroquois during, 2, 104, 115, 183, 191, 231, 276, 343, 405, 430, 524, 646, 670, 976; letters about, 969, 972, 1114; lists of settlers taken prisoner or murdered during, 581, 820; military service during, 54; Orono's role during, 1149

Stone implements of Indians, in Maryland, 619; in Massachusetts, 486; in New Jersey, 838; in New York, 35; in Rhode Island, 130, 134, 484, 898; in Vermont, 44, 827; ornamentation of, 130, 838

Sullivan Expedition (1779); bibliographical note about, 1067; bibliography of, 1020; celebration, 1020; criticisms of, 344; destructiveness of, 26, 59, 118, 412, 591, 599, 647, 1018, 1035, 1067, 1082; early discussion of, 942; Indian resistance during, 591, 1035; Iroquois opinion about, 977; James Sullivan to join, 149; journals of, 55, 118, 287, 322, 448, 591, 604, 801, 1035, 1067; letters from Tory-Indian side, 344; lists of journals of, 238, 257; maps of, 287, 344, 599, 1021, 1067; new sources of information on, 344; numbers of forces in, 344; purposes and results of, 26, 344, 412, 599, 1006, 1019–20, 1067, 1082; should be renamed Sullivan-Clinton Campaign, 344; sketches of troop movements during, 1020, 1067; Sullivan markers, pictures of, 344, 1020

Swedish, interest in Burlington Island, 688; missionary work of Hesselius, 424; purchase Indian lands, 299–300; Sandel's observations of Pennsylvania Indians, 921; travels of Kalm, 547; treatment of Delawares, 94

**≪ T ≫** Tayacs, Piscataway leaders, 625, 1136

Tomahawks, uses of, 410

Tools of Indians. *See* Bone implements; Indian antiquities; Indian implements; Stone implements; Wood implements

Tories, activities in Indian country, American Revolution, 149, 215, 344, 434, 1049, 1060; Colonel McKee's activities in Ohio country, 434; disguised as Indians, American Revolution, 1049, 1060; Robert Land's activities, Indian country, 215

Trade articles, beads, 332; brass tubes, 332; dentalium shells, 332; hair pipes, 332

Trade with Indians. *See under* Dutch. *See* English trade with Indians; French trade with Indians

Treaties, of 1638 (English-Narragansetts, Mohegans), 868; of 1643 (Dutch-Delawares), 605; of 1644 (English-Narragansetts), 380,

# INDEX OF
# PERSONS, PLACES AND TITLES

**P**

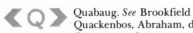

notes about Delawares and Iroquois, 1118–20; Pennsylvania governor's agent to Indians, 400; policy of, to keep Delawares in fear of Iroquois, 1098; rivalry with Johnson over control of Iroquois, 1097; Thomas' letter to, 1029

Weitenkampf, Frank, artistic renderings of racial traits of Indians, 1121

Welles, Thomas, letter about Indians killed, 1122

Wells, Lester Grosvenor, history of Stockbridge Indians, 1123

Wells (Maine), agreement with Indians of, 610; Indian attack on, 233; needs protection from Indians, 500

Wells River (Vermont), 367

*Welsh Collection,* correspondence of Indian Rights Association, 443

Wenemovet (*Penobscot*), peace made with Massachusetts Bay, New Hampshire, and Nova Scotia, 216

Weninock, speech about Indian fishing rights, 1124

Wentworth, Benning (Governor, New Hampshire), letters to, about Indian depredations, 371, 432; letter about redeeming Indian captives, 446; message about keeping Iroquois allied to English, 493

Wentworth, John (Governor, New Hampshire), instructions of, about negotiating with Canada, 1125

Wequalia (Captain Charles), death by hanging, 441, 841; of Middlesex, New Jersey, 841

Wequash (*Pequot*), advises Pequots to flee their country, 823, 1144

Wequashcooke, captured, 631

Weslager, C. A., Indian land purchases, Delaware, 301; Indian stone piles in Maryland, 1126; Nanticokes in Pennsylvania, 1127; Swedish Indian land purchases, 300

Wessagusset. *See* Squantum Island

Wessells, Major, tries to prevent Iroquois from making peace with French, 713

West, Benjamin, accuracy sacrificed in "Picture of the Treaty of the Indians," 53; legends connected with painting of Penn's Treaty, 982

West, Margery, Indian captivity of, 1128

West Creek (New Jersey), Indian origin of, 919

West Jersey, Indian lands deeded to, 1094

West Medford (Massachusetts), Indian antiquities found in, 486

West Milford (New Jersey), poem about Indian raid in, 1129

Westerly (Rhode Island), Narragansetts in, 116; Niantics in, 116

Westervelt, Francis A., wampum industry in Bergen County, 1130

Westmoreland County (Pennsylvania), Delaware Indian place names in, 414

Wetumpka, 29

Weymouth, Captain George, involved in Plymouth settlement, 562; kidnaps Maine Indians, 263

Wharton, Richard, title to land at Pejepscot, 826

Wharton, Thomas, letter books about Lord Dunmore's War, 1131

Wheeler, Captain Thomas, narrative of expedition to Nipmuck country, 1133

Wheeler, George, Indian-white conflicts near Penn's manor, 1132

Wheelock, Eleazer, letter about Moor's Indian Charity School, 1134; letter about pro-American Indians, American Revolution, 1135; painting of, 390; rivalry with William Johnson for Oneida alliance, 390

Wheelwright, John, authenticity of deed of, 861; Indian deeds to, 1117

Wheelwright, John, letter about Indian dangers, 500

White, Andrew, attempts to convert Piscataways, 114, 1136; Indians of Chesapeake, 401

White, John, observed and painted Indians, 331, 1121

White Eyes, George W., attends Princeton University, 472

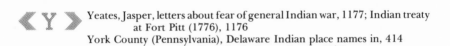
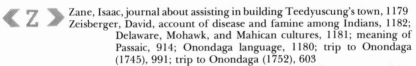

# INDEX OF INDIAN NATIONS

Crees, moons of, 1152; place names of, 1048
Crows, report on location, territory, numbers, language, and religion
among, 932

**《 D 》** Dartmouth Indians (Wampanoag descent), pro-English, 256
Delawares (Lenapes), affiliate with Stockbridge and Munsees in Wisconsin
and Kansas, 981; alliance with French, diplomacy to end, 468,
557; art of, 838; captives of, surrendered, 122, 356–57, 428;
characteristics of, representative of Algonquians along Atlantic,
994; charges against Pennsylvania whites, 280; chiefs discussed,
247; culture of, 34, 247, 362, 569, 606, 847; during Seven Years'
War, 16, 84, 86, 115, 179, 252, 395, 468–69; expedition against
Kittanning (1756), 280, 339, 469; expedition against (1764), 6,
356; factions, 357; food of, 837; Heckewelder's account of, 413,
1104; history of, 34, 94, 247, 413, 811, 994, 1104; hostility to
United States, 98, 909; influence western nomenclature, especially Ohio, 911; interval without leadership, 508; kinship relationship with other tribes, 992, 994; knowledge of whales, 327;
land transactions of, 362, 835; language of, 96, 279, 311, 413,
687, 847–48, 932, 1181; legends of, 848; of Hunterdon County,
836; of Middlesex County, 841; of Monmouth County, 834; of
Morris County, 842; of Somerset County, 843; of South Jersey,
848; of Union County, 835; origins of, 1094; place names, 247,
300, 414, 420, 835–36, 841–43, 846, 848, 1048; population of,
94, 932; reaction to eclipse, 466; relations with Dutch and English, 94, 362, 467, 1094; relations with Iroquois, conflictual,
136, 179, 185, 191, 199, 200, 209, 531; political, 467, 508, 992,
1098–99, 1101; relations with New Jersey, 20, 247, 362; relations
with Swedish and Finnish, 94; religion of, 247, 556, 932, 1118–
19; St. Memin sketches of, 594; speeches of, 34, 413, 557, 873;
treaties with, Easton (1758), 20, 280, 511, 842, 1098; Bradstreet
(1764), 83, 186, 206, 372, 436, 533, 670, 1031; (1765), 541, 1041;
(1785), 279; (1785), 279; (1795), 278; Weiser's account of,
1118–20; Weiser's relations with, 1098
*See also* Munsees; Unalachtigos; Unamis (subtribes)
Doags (Conoy subtribe), location in Maryland, 955

**《 E 》** Eel River (Miami), report on location, territory, language, and religion
among, 932
Eries, extracts from *Jesuit Relations* about, 309
Eskimos, influence in Vermont, 326; origins of, 151; relationship to
Canada and upper half, New York, 35; semilunar knives of, 326;
similar tools to, found in New York, 35
Esopus Indians (Munsee), boundaries with other Munsee groups, 294, 296;
captives of, 294–95; clans of, 404; in New Jersey, 247, land
purchased from, 81; treaty with English (1665), 951; renewals of,
951; Wars, First (1660), 404, 951, Second (1663), 65, 404, 951
Etchemins (Maliseet-Passamaquoddy), domestic life of, 1078

**《 F 》** Farmington Indians, grievance regarding land, 335
Flatheads (in Southeast), allied with English in Carolina and Virginia, 745;
Iroquois refuse not to war against, 745; war with Tuscaroras, 744

**《 G 》** Gay Head Indians (Wampanoag), customs and traditions of, 232; no plot
against English, 650

*See also* Cayugas; Mohawks; Oneidas; Onondagas; Senecas; Tuscaroras

**« K »** Kansas, report on location, territory, numbers, language, and religion among, 932

Kennebecs (Eastern Abenakis), Sewall's opinion on friendship with, 963; treaty conference with (1717), 498

Kickapoos, dread Shawnees and Iroquois, 542–43; repentent about attacking Croghan, 542; report on location, territory, numbers, language, and religion among, 932

Kiowas, report on location, territory, numbers, language, and religion among, 932

Kitchawanks (Wappinger Confederacy), 76

Kwakiutls, descriptions of, 406

**« L »** Lenapes. *See* Delawares (Lenapes)

**« M »** Mahicans, Heckewelders' experience among, 1103; language of, 311, 1181; move to Stockbridge, Massachusetts, 449; New Hampshire asks for help of, 692; of New York, 470, 1003; of Vermont, 260, 449, 452, 459, 1003; religion among, 949
*See also* River Indians (New York)

Maine Indians, articles of peace with English (1685), 30; damage to English property by, 1043; deed coastal Maine to English, 895; in documents, 610; kidnapping of, 263; land tenure concepts of, 241, 894; myths and legends of, 894; usufruct policy of, 894
*See also* Abenakis (Eastern)

Maliseets (Eastern Abenaki), location in Maine, 560, 1148; principle men of, 1148
*See also* Etchemins

Mamekoting (Munsee), Esopus clan, 404

Manamoyik (Nausets), 1762 population of, 1001

Mandans, report on location, territory, numbers, language, and religion among, 932; St. Memim sketch of, 594

Marumscos, location in Maryland, 954

Maryland Indians, locations of, 954; notes on, 23; population of, 954; reservations for, 419, 864, 955, 1002; treatment of, 1002
*See also* Acquaskacks; Annacostins; Assateagues; Choptanks; Chopticons; Doags; Marumscos; Matapeakes; Mattanpanients; Mattwas; Nanticokes; Ozinies; Patuxents; Piscataways; Potopacos; Secowocomocos; Susquehannocks; Tockwoghes; Wicocomicos

Mascoutins, attack Croghan, 542; dread Shawnees and Iroquois, 542–43

Mashpees, 1762 population of, 1001

Massachusetts, language of, 236, 316, 853, 1048; place names, 1048; relations with Narragansetts, 380; relations with Plymouth, 317, 380

Matapeakes, location in Maryland, 954

Mattanpanients, location in Maryland, 955

Mattwas, location in Maryland, 954

Menominees, report on location, territory, numbers, language, and religion among, 932

Miami Confederacy, battles with U.S., 98, 278; report on location, territory, language, and religion among, 932
*See also* Piankashaws; Weas

Micmacs (Eastern Abenakis), chiefs of, list, 1001; description of (1755),

Nottoways (Iroquois), present-giving to, 85, 874
Nova Scotia Indians, 1782 description of, 958

**《 O 》** Ohio Indians, resist English settlements, 6, 54, 83, 86, 200, 235, 356, 434,
649, 873, 1116, 1131; resist U.S. settlements, 98–99, 125, 415,
434, 648, 995; U.S. treats unsuccessfully with (1793), 583
*See also* Western Indians
Oneidas, ask Sullivan not to destroy Cayuga crops, 790, 1017; Brothertons
go to live with, 362; Champlain and Hurons attack, 79; daily life
of, 64, 769; factions, 336, 390; famine and lack of ammunition of,
750; flee when Canada invades country of, 727; fraudulent grant
obtained from, 540; history of reservation of, 429; hostile to
missionaries, 603, 711; missions to, 64, 564, 949, 1012; murders
white, 423; New York purchases land from, 564; pro-American,
American Revolution, 390, 941–42, 944, 979, 1049, 1135; pro-
English, American Revolution, 265; state of religion among, 949;
stockaded village of, 79; Sullivan's speeches to, 1016–18
*See also* Iroquois
Onondagas, deed of, 956; during King George's War, 219; during King
William's War, 706, 727; French manipulate, 732, 735, 743;
history of reservation of, 429; language of, 1180; missionaries
visit, 603; names of months, 794; pro-American, American Revo-
lution, 941, 979; pro-English, American Revolution, 942
*See also* Iroquois
Openangos (Western Abenakis), principal men of, 1148
Oregon Indians, descriptions of, 406
Osages, Great and Little, history of, 594; report on location, territory,
numbers, language, and religion among, 932; reports of visit to
Washington, D.C., and other cities, 594; St. Memin sketch of, 594
Ottawas, during American Revolution, 942; speech of, 242; speech to, 242;
trade with, 67
Ozinies, location in Maryland, 954

**《 P 》** Pamunkeys, Bacon leads people against, 1080
Passamaquoddies, location of, in Maine, 560; numbers of, 391; treaty with
Massachusetts (1794), 1045; vocabulary of, 552
Patuxents, conversion activities among, 1136; location in Maryland, 955
Pawnees, Ranneys, missionaries to, 886; report on location, territory, num-
bers, language, and religion among, 932; sketch of buffalo hunt
of, 1063
Pawtuckets (Western Abenakis), Penacooks belong to, 334
*See also* Penacooks (Western Abenakis)
Penacooks (Western Abenakis), documents pertaining to Indian murder
and intemperance, 815; fear Mohawks, 437, 442; of New Hampshire, 560; of Vermont, 452, 459; peaceful disposition of, 442;
relations with English, 334, 1158; resettle in Canada among St.
Francis Indians, 47, 334
Penobscots (Eastern Abenakis), Bashaba, meaning of, 369; French influence among, 1015; history of, 1015; kill cattle, 63; land settlements of, 368; location of, in Maine, 560; Maine gives bond for
townships to, 608; numbers of, 391; on Oldtown Island, 368;
Shirley's letter to, 970, plans for building fort with approval of,
378; state of education of, 368; trading with, unlawful, 31; traditions of, 46; treaties (1726), 494, 496; (1727), 496; (1749), 497,
1015; (1786), 641; (1818), 1045; (1821), 1046; refuse to sign
(1857), 590
*See also* Abenakis (Eastern)

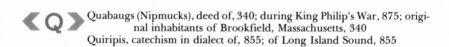

should avenge injuries of, 502; Massachusetts frontier towns should not be visited by, 723; messages about allying with Iroquois against French, King George's War, 148, 905, and Queen Anne's War, 741; Minisink country, want to settle in, 710
See also Mahicans

**‹ S ›**

Sacos, conflicts with English, 988, 1151; descriptions of, 988
Saconnets, Awasuncks, woman sachem of, 36–37; population of, 1001
St. Francis Indians (Western Abenakis), border raids against English, 33, 56, 216; destitution of, 33; espionage and scouting of, 33, 456; factionalism during American Revolution, 33, 456; families of, wish to settle on Connecticut River during American Revolution, 940; Joseph-Louis Gill adopted by, 460; life of, in nineteenth century, 33; Mississquoi River settlement of, 450; Odanak, headquarters of, 451; Penacooks settle among, 47; raid against (1759), 33, 56, 261, 373, 460; religious life of, 33; treaty conference with Massachusetts (1735), 494
   See also Abenakis (Eastern)
St. John's River (Maliseets), location of, in Maine, 560; numbers of, 391
Sascoes, deed of, to Fairfield, 925; fight with Pequots against English, 491, 788; title to land, 503
Sauks, report on location, territory, numbers, language, and religion among, 932
Scatacooks, treaty conference with (1728), 349; (1735), 494
Schagticoke Indians, will maintain friendship with English, 928
Secowocomocos (Conoy subtribe), location in Maryland, 955
Senecas, deed of, 956; descriptions of, 8; during American Revolution, need punishment, 55, 939, 944, 1006, 1035; during Pontiac's War, 104; during Seven Years' War, 182–84, 204, 395, 530, 957; economic conditions of, 407; factionalism of, 73, 613; French fort in country of, 751; French intrigue among, 182–83, 191, 297, 523; history of embitterment with English, 1006; history of reservation of, 429; intemperance among, 234; lands sold to New York, 1010; life of, on upper Allegheny River, 8, 505; mercenaries selling ammunition to, 527; message to Governor Gordon, 467; missions to, 73, 505; Ogden Land Company acquires reservation of, 612; Schuyler to live among to promote trade, 756; Arts Project of, 407; spiritual renaissance among, 505; treaty conference (1664), 1044; (1764, Bradstreet), 83, 186, 206, 372, 436, 533, 670, 1031; War of 1812, loyal to U.S. in, 797
   See also Iroquois
Shawnees, attack frontiers, western Pennsylvania, 136, 252; Baltimore County settlements of, 624; battle with U.S., 909; captives of, surrendered, 122, 356–57; during Lord Dunmore's War, 649, 873; during Seven Years' War, 115; expedition against (1764), 6, 356; hostility to U.S., 98; Kinnan captured by, 1086; Lord's Prayer in, 966; Minisink country, wish to settle in, 710; movements of, before and after Pennsylvania domicile of, 350, 592; Old Towns of, on Potomac River, 624; relations with Iroquois, 136, 179, 199, 209, 471, 649; removed from Lancaster County, 350; report on location, territory, language, numbers, and religion among, 932; speeches of, 34; steal horses, boats, 84; Susquehanna Valley settlement of, 649, 1127; treaty of 1764 (Bradstreet), 83, 186, 206, 372, 436, 533, 670, 1031; (1765), 541, 1041; treaty making with U.S., 278; Virginians attack, American Revolution, 977; vocabulary of, 279; western nomenclature influenced by, 911